Gender is a fascinating category, central and pervasive in some
languages and totally absent in others. In this new,
comprehensive account of gender systems, over 200 languages
are discussed, from English and Russian to Archi and
Chichewa. Detailed analysis of individual languages provides
clear illustrations of specific types of system. The basis of gender
distinction, its reflection in syntax, and areas of special interest
such as 'hybrid' nouns are all presented in a lively way. *Gender*
will be invaluable both for class use and as a reference resource
for students and researchers in linguistics.

CAMBRIDGE TEXTBOOKS IN LINGUISTICS

General Editors: B. COMRIE, C. J. FILLMORE, R. LASS, D. LIGHTFOOT, J. LYONS, P. H. MATTHEWS, R. POSNER, S. ROMAINE, N. V. SMITH, N. VINCENT.

GENDER

In this series:

P. H. MATTHEWS *Morphology*
B. COMRIE *Aspect*
R. M. KEMPSON *Semantic Theory*
T. BYNON *Historical Linguistics*
J. ALLWOOD, L.-G. ANDERSON, Ö. DAHL *Logic in Linguistics*
D. B. FRY *The Physics of Speech*
R. A. HUDSON *Sociolinguistics*
J. K. CHAMBERS and P. TRUDGILL *Dialectology*
A. J. ELLIOT *Child Language*
P. H. MATTHEWS *Syntax*
A. RADFORD *Transformational Syntax*
L. BAUER *English Word-formation*
S. C. LEVINSON *Pragmatics*
G. BROWN and G. YULE *Discourse Analysis*
R. HUDDLESTON *Introduction to the Grammar of English*
R. LASS *Phonology*
B. COMRIE *Tense*
W. KLEIN *Second Language Acquisition*
A. CRUTTENDEN *Intonation*
A. J. WOODS, P. FLETCHER and A. HUGHES *Statistics in Language Studies*
D. A. CRUSE *Lexical Semantics*
F. R. PALMER *Mood and Modality*
A. RADFORD *Transformational Grammar*
M. GARMAN *Psycholinguistics*
W. CROFT *Typology and Universals*
G. G. CORBETT *Gender*

GENDER

GREVILLE G. CORBETT

PROFESSOR OF LINGUISTICS
UNIVERSITY OF SURREY

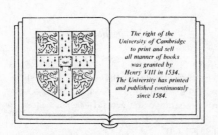

The right of the
University of Cambridge
to print and sell
all manner of books
was granted by
Henry VIII in 1534.
The University has printed
and published continuously
since 1584.

CAMBRIDGE UNIVERSITY PRESS

CAMBRIDGE

NEW YORK   PORT CHESTER

MELBOURNE   SYDNEY

Published by the Press Syndicate of the University of Cambridge
The Pitt Building, Trumpington Street, Cambridge CB2 1RP
40 West 20th Street, New York, NY 10011, USA
10 Stamford Road, Oakleigh, Melbourne 3166, Australia

First published 1991

Printed in Great Britain by the University Press, Cambridge

British Library cataloguing in publication data
Corbett, Greville G.
    Gender. – (Cambridge textbooks in linguistics).
      1. Languages. Grammar. Gender
I. Title
      415

Library of Congress cataloguing in publication data
Corbett, Greville G.
    Gender / Greville G. Corbett.
          p.   cm. – (Cambridge textbooks in linguistics)
      ISBN 0-521-32939-6. – ISBN 0-521-33845-X (pbk.)
      1. Grammar, Comparative and general – Gender.   I. Series.
    P240.7.C67   1991
    415 – dc20   90-33171 CIP

ISBN 0 521 32939 6 hardback
ISBN 0 521 33845 X paperback

UP

For Judith, David, Ian and Peter

CONTENTS

List of figures   *page* xiii
List of tables   xv
Preface   xvii
List of abbreviations   xix

1 INTRODUCTION   1
1.1 Gender in the languages of the world   1
1.2 General approach and outline of the book   2
1.3 Presentation of data   6

2 GENDER ASSIGNMENT I: SEMANTIC SYSTEMS   7
2.1 Strict semantic systems   8
2.1.1 Tamil and other Dravidian languages   8
2.1.2 Other strict semantic systems   11
2.2 Predominantly semantic systems   13
2.2.1 Zande   14
2.2.2 Dyirbal   15
2.2.3 Ket   19
2.2.4 Ojibwa and other Algonquian languages   20
2.2.5 Lak and other Caucasian languages   24
2.2.6 Other partially semantic systems   29
2.3 The criteria on which semantic systems are based   30
2.4 Conclusion   32

3 GENDER ASSIGNMENT II: FORMAL SYSTEMS   33
3.1 Morphological systems   34
3.1.1 Russian   34
3.1.2 Swahili and other Bantu languages   43
3.1.3 The features on which morphological systems are based   49
3.2 Phonological systems   51

ix

Contents

3.2.1 Qafar   51
3.2.2 Hausa   52
3.2.3 Godie and other Kru languages   53
3.2.4 Yimas   55
3.2.5 French   57
3.2.6 The features on which phonological systems are based   62
  3.3 General characteristics of assignment systems   62
3.3.1 Overt and covert gender   62
3.3.2 Overlapping of assignment criteria   63
3.3.3 Problematic nouns   66
  3.4 Conclusion   68

  4 THE PSYCHOLINGUISTIC STATUS OF GENDER ASSIGNMENT   70
  4.1 Borrowings   70
4.1.1 Assignment of borrowings by normal rules   71
4.1.2 Claims for special assignment rules   75
  4.2 Child language acquisition   82
  4.3 Experimental evidence   89
  4.4 Residual meaning of gender   92
  4.5 Diachronic evidence   97
  4.6 Conclusion   104

  5 GENDER AGREEMENT   105
  5.1 Elements showing gender agreement   106
  5.2 The form of gender agreement   115
5.2.1 The morphology of gender agreement   115
5.2.2 Alliterative concord   117
5.2.3 A complex example: Khinalug   119
  5.3 Limits on gender agreement   123
5.3.1 Syntactic restrictions   124
5.3.2 Interaction with tense   125
5.3.3 Interaction with person   126
5.3.4 Interaction with number   132
5.3.5 Interaction with case   132
5.3.6 Morphological class   133
5.3.7 Phonological constraints   134
5.3.8 Lexical restrictions   134
  5.4 Lack of agreement: classifiers   136
  5.5 The gaining and losing of gender agreement   137
  5.6 Conclusion   143

6 ESTABLISHING THE NUMBER OF GENDERS   145
6.1 Terms   146
6.2 Agreement classes   147
6.3 Controller genders and target genders   150
6.3.1 The relation of gender and number   154
6.3.2 Relation to semantics   158
6.3.3 The relation of controller genders to target genders   159
6.4 The maximalist problem   161
6.4.1 Subgenders   161
6.4.2 Overdifferentiated targets and pronominal gender
      systems   168
6.4.3 Inquorate genders   170
6.4.4 Defective nouns   175
6.4.5 Consistent agreement patterns   176
6.4.6 Combined gender systems   184
6.5 Conclusion   188

7 TARGET GENDERS: SYNCRETISM AND ENFORCED GENDER
   FORMS   189
7.1 Gender and number   189
7.1.1 Syncretism: further examples of convergent and crossed
      systems   190
7.1.2 Types of syncretism   194
7.1.3 Diachronic implications   198
7.2 Neutral agreement   203
7.2.1 The problem   204
7.2.2 Strategy 1: the use of a regular gender/number form   205
7.2.3 Strategy 2: the use of a unique neutral agreement form 214
7.2.4 Extension of use of neutral agreement forms   216
7.2.5 Neutral agreement: summing up   217
7.3 Gender agreement with noun phrases involving
    reference problems   218
7.3.1 Use of one possible form by convention   219
7.3.2 Use of an 'evasive' form   221
7.3.3 Use of a special form   223
7.3.4 No strategy   223
7.4 Conclusion   223

8 HYBRID NOUNS AND THE AGREEMENT HIERARCHY   225
8.1 The Agreement Hierarchy   225

Contents

8.1.1 Data   226
8.1.2 Wider considerations   236
8.2 Personal pronouns   241
8.3 Diachrony   248
8.4 Conclusion   259

9 GENDER RESOLUTION RULES   261
9.1 Features requiring resolution   262
9.1.1 Person resolution   262
9.1.2 Number resolution   263
9.1.3 Gender resolution   264
9.2 The application of resolution rules   264
9.2.1 Agreement with one conjunct   265
9.2.2 Factors favouring resolution   267
9.3 Semantic gender resolution   269
9.4 Syntactic gender resolution   279
9.5 Mixed semantic and syntactic gender resolution   284
9.6 Strategies for gender resolution   290
9.6.1 Markedness: an inadequate motivation   290
9.6.2 Semantic justification and clear marking of plurality   293
9.7 Diachrony   299
9.8 Conclusion   306

10 GENERALIZATIONS AND PROSPECTS   307
10.1 Meaning and form   307
10.1.1 A perspective on gender systems   307
10.1.2 Earlier research on gender   308
10.2 Diachrony   310
10.2.1 The rise of gender systems   310
10.2.2 The development of gender systems   312
10.2.3 The decline of gender systems   315
10.3 Prospects   318
10.3.1 Descriptive studies   319
10.3.2 The function of gender   320
10.3.3 Collaborative work   323

References   324
Author index   352
Language index   357
Subject index   361

FIGURES

3.1   Russian declensional types   *page* 37
3.2   Sex-differentiable nouns in Russian   38
3.3   The gender pattern of Russian   39
3.4   Gender assignment in Russian   41
6.1   The gender system of Rumanian   152
6.2   The gender system of French   152
6.3   Verbal agreement forms in Telugu   153
6.4   Telugu personal pronouns   153
6.5   The gender system of Lak   154
6.6   Target genders in French   155
6.7   Target genders in German   155
6.8   Target genders in Tamil   155
6.9   Target genders in Chibemba   156
6.10 The gender system of Lak   157
6.11 The gender system of Slovene   157
6.12 The gender system of Archi   158
6.13 The gender system of Serbo-Croat   165
6.14 Genders and subgenders in Russian   167
6.15 The gender system of Russian   167
6.16 Agreement classes in Tsova-Tush   171
6.17 Gender in Tsova-Tush (excluding inquorate genders)   172
6.18 Agreement classes in Lelemi   174
7.1   Gender in Hausa   190
7.2   Target genders in Chamalal   191
7.3   Target genders in Fula   191
7.4   The gender system of Seneca   192
7.5   The gender system of Upper Sorbian   193
7.6   Gender syncretism   194
7.7   Target genders in Zande   194
7.8A Gender in Andi: conservative dialects (type A)   198

List of figures

7.8B Gender in Andi: dialect type B   199
7.8C Gender in Andi: Rikvani dialect (type C)   199
7.8D Gender in Andi: dialect type D   200
7.9   Development of gender in Grebo   200
7.10 Loss of class ten agreement in the Ngemba group   201
7.11 Gender in Tamil   202
7.12 Gender in Telugu   202
7.13 Gender in Kolami   203
8.1   Evidence for the Agreement Hierarchy   237
8.2   Agreement with Russian hybrid nouns (by age of speaker)   251

TABLES

2.1	Assignment in Tamil	*page* 9
2.2	Assignment in Zande	14
2.3	Genders in Dyirbal	15
2.4	Assignment in Dyirbal	16
2.5	Genders in Ket	19
2.6	Assignment in Lak	25
2.7	Genders III and IV in Archi	27
2.8	Contrasts between genders III and IV in Archi	28
3.1	Assignment in Russian (semantic criteria only)	35
3.2	Examples from the semantic residue in Russian	35
3.3	Noun paradigms in Russian	36
3.4	Outline of Swahili gender forms	47
3.5	Personal pronouns in Godie	53
3.6	Assignment of inanimates in Godie	53
3.7	Semantic assignment in Yimas	56
3.8	Phonological assignment in Yimas	56
3.9	Gender assignment in French	59
3.10	Non-attested system of conflicting assignment rules	63
4.1	The distribution of nouns in Russian by gender	78
4.2	Loans entering the masculine gender in Russian	78
4.3	Assignment of invented nouns to gender in French	91
4.4	Gender, perception of attributes and personification in German and English	96
4.5	Kikuyu nouns used in the triad test	97
5.1	First type of gender/number markers in Khinalug	120
5.2	The verb *k'i* 'die' in Khinalug	120
5.3	Second type of gender/number markers in Khinalug	121
5.4	Third type of gender/number markers in Khinalug	121
5.5	Imperative of 'be' in Khinalug	121
5.6	Pronominal gender/number markers in Khinalug	122
5.7	'Cause to forget' in Khinalug (past concrete)	123

5.8	Personal pronouns in Shilha	130
5.9	Second person pronouns in Diuxi Mixtec	130
5.10	Third person pronouns in Diuxi Mixtec	130
5.11	Some singular forms of Russian *ètot* 'this'	132
5.12	Gender agreement of Latin adjectives	133
5.13	Noun prefixes and gender agreement markers in Ngangikurrunggurr	140
6.1	Attributive agreement in Serbo-Croat	162
6.2	Predicate agreement in Serbo-Croat	163
6.3	Attributive agreement in Russian	166
6.4	Inquorate genders in Serbo-Croat	173
6.5	Main agreement classes in Lelemi	174
6.6	Agreement forms in Yimas	176
6.7	Agreement patterns in Russian	178
6.8	Consistent agreement patterns in English	180
6.9	Agreement with *vrač* and similar nouns in Russian	184
6.10	Personal pronouns in Mba	185
6.11	Consistent agreement patterns in Mba	187
7.1	Target gender forms in Upper Sorbian	193
7.2	Verb agreement markers in Qafar	195
7.3	The associative particle in Bayso	195
7.4	The definite article in Somali	196
7.5	Agreement markers in the Rendille possessive construction	197
7.6	Predicate agreement markers in Serbo-Croat	197
7.7	Agreement markers in Khinalug (type 2)	198
7.8	Loss of class ten agreement in the Ngemba group	201
7.9	Gender agreement in Lak	208
7.10	Personal pronouns in Godie	210
7.11	Patterns of syncretism in Bayso and Qafar	211
8.1	Evidence for the Agreement Hierarchy	235
9.1	Agreement with conjoined noun phrases (controller factors)	267
9.2	Agreement with conjoined noun phrases (target factors)	268
9.3	Predicate agreement forms in Slovene	280
9.4	Predicate agreement forms in Polish	284
9.5	Agreement markers in Slovene	295
9.6	Agreement markers in Polish	296
9.7	Agreement markers in Latin	298
9.8	Agreement markers in Icelandic	298
9.9	Predicate agreement forms in Serbo-Croat	299
10.1	Target gender forms in Chamalal (Gigatl′ dialect)	315

PREFACE

This book has required a great deal of informant work and many hours of consultation with experts on particular languages and language groups. It is a pleasure to record my gratitude to all those who have been generous with their time and expertise, in providing examples or references, discussing data, or commenting on parts of the book: Jean Aitchison, Keith Allan, Gunilla Anderman, R. E. Asher, Stephen Barbour, Michael Barlow, Ruth Berman, Catherine Chvany, Ulrike Claudi, Joseph Clements, Richard Coates, N. E. Collinge, Francis Cornish, Merton Dagut, Anna Morpurgo Davies, Margaret Deuchar, R. M. W. Dixon, Donka Farkas, William Foley, Ives Goddard, Nigel Gotteri, Joseph Greenberg, Dick Hayward, Bernd Heine, Eugénie Henderson, Richard Hogg, Dee Ann Holisky, Dick Hudson, Jim Hurford, Larry Hyman, Ewa Jaworska, A. A. Kibrik, Ewan Klein, A. I. Koval', Graham Mallinson, Naomi Martin, Igor Mel'čuk, Anne Mills, Ngessimo Mutaka, Yoni Neeman, Almerindo Ojeda, John Payne, David Perlmutter, Rebecca Posner, Malathi Rao, Bob Rothstein, Linda Schwartz, Roland Sussex, Karen Taylor-Browne, and W. A. A. Wilson. F. R. Palmer, who has read and commented on each draft chapter, deserves special thanks. Naturally, those listed do not necessarily agree with my analyses. Graphic representations are a great help in giving a clear account of some parts of the topic, and I am grateful to Ian Clark, Annie Read and Kevin Shaughnessy for artwork. Some examples with numerous diacritics almost required artwork too, so the word-processing skills of Carole D'Arcy, Pauline Rayner and Philippa Galloway were appreciated. Finally I would like to thank the team at Cambridge University Press, especially Penny Carter, Marion Smith, Judith Ayling and Jenny Potts for their helpfulness and expertise.

The book is based in part on research funded by the Economic and Social Research Council (ESRC), reference number C00232218. This support is gratefully acknowledged. Chapter 6 includes a considerably reworked version of Corbett (1989). Oxford University Press have kindly given permission for the use of artwork from that paper, as have Routledge to reproduce figure 8.2, taken from Corbett (1983a). Section 7.2 is appearing separately as Corbett (forthcoming a), and Chapter 9 takes some of its material from Corbett (1983b). The version here supersedes previous ones, and the integration of the material into a general account of gender is new.

ABBREVIATIONS

ACC	accusative	NEG	negative
AG	agreement marker	NEUT	neuter
ANIM	animate	NOM	nominative
AUX	auxiliary	NP	noun phrase
DAT	dative	OBJ	object
DEF	definite	PL	plural
ERG	ergative	POSS	possessive
FEM	feminine	PRES	present
FUT	future	REFL	reflexive
GEN	genitive	SG	singular
INAN	inanimate	SUBJ	subject
INS	instrumental	1ST	first person
LOC	locative	2ND	second person
MASC	masculine	3RD	third person
MASC_PERS	masculine personal		

1
Introduction

Gender is the most puzzling of the grammatical categories. It is a topic which interests non-linguists as well as linguists and it becomes more fascinating the more it is investigated. In some languages gender is central and pervasive, while in others it is totally absent. One of its attractions for linguists is that there are interesting aspects of the study of gender in each of the core areas of linguistics. And work on it promises practical benefits, even in the short term, in meeting the problems which gender causes in second-language learning. In the longer term, research into gender will be important for at least two other areas: first, it can shed light on the way in which linguistic information is stored in the brain; and second, it has implications for natural language processing, notably for the elimination of local ambiguities in parsing. To understand what linguists mean by 'gender', a good starting point is Hockett's definition: 'Genders are classes of nouns reflected in the behavior of associated words' (1958: 231). A language may have two or more such classes or genders. The classification frequently corresponds to a real-world distinction of sex, at least in part, but often too it does not ('gender' derives etymologically from Latin *genus*, via Old French *gendre*, and originally meant 'kind' or 'sort'). The word 'gender' is used not just for a group of nouns but also for the whole category; thus we may say that a particular language has, say, three genders, masculine, feminine and neuter, and that the language has the category of gender.

1.1 Gender in the languages of the world

Discussions of gender as a category have tended to centre on relatively small numbers of languages, and often on selections which are not typical of the systems found in the world's languages. In contrast, we shall look at over 200 languages. Some will appear only briefly, because of some special point of interest, others will run like threads through the book showing how the different aspects of gender systems relate to each other. Grammatical gender is certainly widespread, and so a brief account of its distribution may

1

prove helpful. Europe is dominated by the Indo-European language family, which also extends well into Asia. Many Indo-European languages show gender (some with three genders, others having reduced the number to two); a few have lost gender, while others, notably the Slavonic group, are introducing new subgenders. Uralic has some members in Europe (like Hungarian), and others in the northern area where Europe and Asia meet, and is devoid of grammatical gender. Joining Europe and Asia in the south we find the Caucasus, where the languages of the northern Caucasus, some thirty-five in number, show particularly interesting gender systems, which contrast markedly with those of Indo-European. Several of the major families of Asia provide no material for our investigation, but in south India we find the Dravidian family, which includes languages like Tamil and Telugu, which are of great importance for the typology of gender. Bridging Asia and Africa, the Afro-Asiatic family offers numerous two-gender systems, some of which are of special importance. The other three families of Africa, namely Nilo-Saharan, Niger-Kordofanian and Khoisan, all have languages with gender systems. Niger-Kordofanian provides some of the most extensive examples, in terms of the numbers of genders and the degree to which gender is reflected in syntax. Heine (1982: 190) estimates that 600 African languages (some two-thirds of all African languages) are gender languages. New Guinea has around 1,000 languages, a substantial proportion of the world's languages, and gender is widespread here too. In Australia gender is found in various languages, mainly in those of Arnhem Land and the North Kimberleys. Finally, in the Americas, the examples of gender languages are few and are generally isolated. The most important exception is the Algonquian family, whose two-gender systems will figure prominently in our study. In comparing data from languages of such variety we must be careful to ensure that we are comparing like with like. To do this we shall be explicit about the techniques used, the sources of data and, of course, the definitions of the terms we use.

1.2 General approach and outline of the book

The book is designed for various types of readers. First, for the student of linguistics, it is an introduction to an area of obvious interest, one which is poorly represented in the standard texts. And through this topic the book attempts to give an insight into the richness and variety of the world's languages. Second, it is intended to help those doing research on specific languages or groups of languages, whether for an undergraduate dissertation or a major research project. Seeing a familiar language analysed in the broader context of languages with comparable but different systems can give a new perspective on familiar material. For some languages, the accounts of gender set in their particular grammatical tradition obscure similarities to other genetically distant or unrelated languages. An overview of this type seeks to highlight such similarities and to suggest new ways of approaching old problems. References to work on specific languages can be found by checking relevant sections identified using the language index. Of those researching individual languages, field-workers are a special category. It is hoped that the definitions provided will help to ensure that the invaluable work done in the field – particularly on languages with uncertain futures – will not be undermined through the contradictory use of terms (which has hampered this topic in the past) or the failure to obtain data which are of special value for understanding gender more generally. There will also be readers, from various disciplines, concerned with sexism in language. This is a topic on which several interesting studies have appeared recently, but not one which is central to this book. However, it is hoped that material presented here will contribute to that debate in two ways. First, the systematic presentation of linguistic data from many different languages may help to broaden a discussion which has tended to centre on English. It will also show how divisions into animate and inanimate, or human and non-human, function in language exactly as does the division into female and male. Second, by drawing attention to languages where the feminine rather than the masculine is in some sense favoured, it may suggest possible comparative approaches. The book is therefore planned to be a source book as well as a textbook, with extensive references for those who wish to go further, whether into particular topics or into particular languages.

Different readers will have different requirements, so it will be useful to outline the structure of the book, to make clear which parts will be most relevant to particular needs. Chapters 2–5 are all concerned with gender assignment, that is, the way in which native speakers allocate nouns to genders. The type of question at issue is how speakers know that, for example, the word for 'house' is masculine in Russian, feminine in French and neuter in Tamil. In chapter 2 we analyse languages where the meaning of a noun is sufficient to determine its gender: thus 'house' in Tamil is neuter because it does not denote a human. Then in chapter 3 we move to languages where meaning is not adequate to determine gender on its own, but has to be supplemented by formal criteria. These additional criteria may be morphological, that is, relating to word-structure: 'house' can be assigned to the masculine gender in Russian, given the declensional type to which it belongs. Or the criteria may be phonological, relating to sound-structure: hence 'house' is feminine in French because of the phonological shape of the word. In these two chapters we look at the straightforward linguistic evidence, and we find that the regularities which justify the analyses offered are striking. In

3

chapter 4 we go on to examine other types of evidence which support the rules proposed, suggesting that they do indeed form part of the native speaker's competence. The evidence comes from the way in which nouns borrowed from one language into another gain a gender, children's acquisition of gender, psycholinguistic experiments, the curious effects of the residual meaning of gender, and from the investigation of the way in which gender systems change over time. This fourth chapter will be of central interest to some readers but can safely be skipped by those wishing to gain an initial outline of the subject. In chapters 2–4 we assume that we can determine analytically the number of genders in a given language and the gender of a particular noun; our task is to determine how the native speaker assigns nouns to genders (and so can produce the examples which form our data).

In many languages there is no dispute as to the number of genders, but there are other languages where the question is far from straightforward; consequently it is important to investigate how we solve such cases. While nouns may be classified in various ways, only one type of classification counts as a gender system; it is one which is reflected beyond the nouns themselves in modifications required of 'associated words'. For example, in Russian we find: *novyj dom* 'new house', *novaja gazeta* 'new newspaper' and *novoe taksi* 'new taxi'. These examples demonstrate the existence of three genders, because the adjective *nov-* 'new' has to change in form acording to the gender of the noun. There are many other nouns like *dom* 'house', making up the masculine gender, many too like *gazeta* 'newspaper' (the feminines) and numerous nouns like *taksi* 'taxi' (the neuters), each requiring the appropriate ending on the adjective. There are various other ways in which nouns could be grouped: those denoting animals, those which are derived from verbs, those whose stem has three syllables or more, those whose stress changes from singular to plural. These groupings are not genders in Russian because they do not determine other forms beyond the noun; they are classifications internal to the class of nouns.

All this means that the determining criterion of gender is agreement; this is the way in which the genders are 'reflected in the behavior of associated words' in Hockett's definition given earlier. Saying that a language has three genders implies that there are three classes of nouns which can be distinguished syntactically by the agreements they take. This is the generally accepted approach to gender (other suggestions prove unsatisfactory, as we shall see). Given its importance for the analysis, agreement in gender is considered in detail in chapter 5, and it turns out to be varied and complex. It is not only adjectives and verbs which can show agreement in gender, but in some languages adverbs agree, in others numerals and sometimes even conjunctions agree in gender. Since agreement is taken as the criterion for gender, there are no grounds for drawing a distinction between languages in which nouns are divided into groups according to sex, and those where human/non-human or animate/inanimate are the criteria. Thus many languages described as having 'noun classes' fall within our study. The number of genders is not limited to three: four is common and twenty is possible. On the other hand, classifiers fall outside our study because they do not show agreement; but they are discussed in chapter 5, because they are a source for gender systems. A further consequence of having agreement as the criterion is that the definition of agreement itself becomes important. Most scholars working on agreement include the control of anaphoric pronouns by their antecedent (*the girl ... she*) as part of agreement. If this is accepted, then languages in which pronouns present the only evidence for gender should be recognized as having a gender system. This is the approach we shall adopt but, because it is not universally accepted, we shall call such systems 'pronominal gender systems'. Since it raises these problems and illustrates the possible divergence in gender agreement, chapter 5 is particularly important for those whose knowledge of languages is predominantly in the field of 'standard average European'.

Chapter 5 also serves as an introduction to chapter 6, where the major definitions and procedures are given and illustrated, allowing us to determine the number of genders in a given language and giving terms to describe the complex gender systems which occur surprisingly frequently in the languages of the world. Chapter 6 is central, forming the basis for the analysis of gender systems which underpins the entire study. Though we find gender systems which appear to differ radically, we see how they can be analysed within a common framework. The next two chapters are devoted to topics highlighted by chapter 6. In chapter 7 we examine problems concerned with the 'agreement target', the item which shows agreement in gender. There is the question of syncretism, where particular agreeing items have 'too few' forms in that they do not distinguish as many gender forms as might be expected. There is also the situation in which the target has 'too many' forms; the existence of gender agreement can impose a problematic choice if, for example, the speaker has to choose between masculine and feminine even though the sex of the referent is not known. Chapter 8 is devoted to 'hybrid' nouns; these are nouns which are not assigned to a single gender by the assignment rules. They therefore take different gender agreement according to what is agreeing with them (an example is German *Mädchen* 'girl'). The different patterns of agreement with hybrid nouns seem confusing at first sight, but we discover that their distribution is predictable to a large degree and that they offer a route for change in gender systems. Chapter 9 examines the rules which determine agreement in gender when there is more than one noun phrase; for example, if the subject consists of two noun phrases, one headed by a feminine noun and the other by a neuter noun, there must be a rule to determine which gender the verb or predicative adjective will stand in. The data here are varied and unexpected. Finally, chapter 10 attempts to draw together various threads. In particular, the question of change in gender systems, which is dealt with at appropriate points throughout the book, is surveyed more generally. We concentrate on the analysis and description of changes for which firm data can be found, since much of the earlier work on the origin of gender in particular was largely speculative. In the final chapter we also look forward to how the study of gender may progress, looking at possibilities for further work, both elementary and advanced.

In broad outline, the first part of the book, chapters 2–4, is concerned with the genders into which nouns can be divided, and the middle, chapters 5–7, is more concerned with elements which agree in gender. The two sides of the analysis come together in chapters 8 and 9, while chapter 10 looks back over the topics covered and forward to possible advances.

1.3 **Presentation of data**

The orthography used in examples normally follows that of the original sources, so that the interested reader can refer back to them easily. However, if they are in a non-Roman script, a standard transliteration is used. The languages of the Caucasus pose special problems and, where possible, minor amendments have been made in transliteration in order to be consistent with Kibrik, Kodzasov, Olovjannikova & Samedov (1977: 41). Descriptions of Algonquian languages indicate length in a variety of ways: to avoid confusion we shall use a colon to mark length of the preceding vowel for all Algonquian examples. Occasionally italics are used to draw attention to part of an example for discussion in the text. Examples are followed by morpheme glosses, which are intended solely to help with understanding the point at issue; they are not full glosses. When words are segmented in the example, the same segmentation is used in the gloss, for example *laugh-s* laugh-3RD.SG, in which the *s* is glossed as '3RD.SG'. Since the *s* cannot be segmented into constituent morphs representing third person and singular number separately, the glosses for these morphemes, abbreviations in this case, are joined by a stop. Abbreviations are listed on page xix. A translation is also given, unless the meaning of the example is fully clear from the gloss.

2
Gender assignment I: semantic systems

An intriguing question, which interests non-linguists as well as linguists, is the way in which nouns are allotted to different genders. The linguist who wishes to establish the gender of a given noun can use agreement as a test (for details see chapter 6). However, the native speaker of the language must know the gender of a noun in order to produce the correct agreements (the evidence which the linguist uses). The amount of information is substantial, since native speakers know the gender of many thousands of nouns. For foreign learners of the same language, in contrast, this knowledge often proves elusive in the extreme. How then does a native speaker know the gender of a particular noun? One possible answer would be that the speaker simply has to remember the gender of each noun. This suggestion would involve a considerable feat of memory. It seems an unlikely answer, though many linguists have been ready to accept it. For example, in an often quoted remark, Bloomfield (1933: 280) claimed that:

> There seems to be no practical criterion by which the gender of
> a noun in German, French, or Latin could be determined.

This pessimism now appears misplaced in view of the following evidence. First, native speakers typically make few or no mistakes in the use of gender; if the gender of every noun were remembered individually, we would expect more errors. Second, words borrowed from other languages acquire a gender, which shows that there is a mechanism for assigning and not just remembering gender. And third, when presented with invented words, speakers give them a gender and they do so with a high degree of consistency. Thus native speakers have the ability to 'work out' the gender of a noun; models of this ability are called 'assignment systems'. Convincing accounts of gender assignment in French have in fact been offered and, while German gender appears more complex than French gender, recent analyses have gone a long way towards establishing practical criteria for gender assignment in German too.

Assignment may depend on two basic types of information about the noun:

its meaning (semantics) and its form. Information about form may in turn be of two types: word-structure, comprising derivation and inflection (morphology), and sound-structure (phonology). In this chapter we concentrate on semantic factors, and in chapter 3 we turn to morphological and phonological factors. Languages may use different combinations of these factors and may also permit varying numbers of exceptions. Mel'čuk (1958 [1974: 33]) makes the point that rules are valuable even if there are exceptions; a rule which assigns a large proportion of the nouns correctly is of theoretical interest and practical use. From the theoretical point of view, assignment systems have important implications for attempts to determine the structure of the lexicon. And given the ease with which native speakers assign nouns to genders, and the difficulty experienced by foreign learners of many gender languages, an understanding of gender assignment systems is of considerable practical importance.

In a sense all gender systems are semantic in that there is always a semantic core to the assignment system (Aksenov 1984: 17–18). However, we shall consider here those languages where semantic factors are sufficient on their own to account for assignment. We shall first examine strict semantic systems, then move to those which are primarily semantic but which allow varying numbers of exceptions.

2.1 Strict semantic systems

These are systems in which the meaning of a noun determines its gender and in which, equally, given the gender of a noun we can infer something about its meaning. This is the sort of system we might have expected to find as the normal case. While there are several examples in the Dravidian family (section 2.1.1) and various others scattered around the world (section 2.1.2), overall this type of system is not particularly common.

2.1.1 *Tamil and other Dravidian languages*

Gender is found in most Dravidian languages and nouns are assigned to gender according to their meaning. We take as our first example Tamil, one of the major Dravidian languages. It has some 50 million speakers, mainly in Tamil Nadu in south-east India, but also in Sri Lanka and various other parts of the world. The data on colloquial Tamil are from Asher (1985: 136–7), supplemented by Arden (1942: 74) and Andronov (1966: 54–5), who describe written Tamil; their examples have been retransliterated according to Asher's system (1985). Nouns may be divided into rational and non-rational (neuter). The rationals may in turn be divided into two groups, masculine and feminine. Nouns are assigned to these three genders as shown in table 2.1.

Table 2.1 *Assignment in Tamil*

Criterion	Gender	Examples	Gloss
god or male human	masculine (= male rational)	aaṇ	man
		civaN	Shiva
goddess or female human	feminine (= female rational)	peṇ	woman
		kaaḷi	Kali
other	neuter (= non-rational)	maram	tree
		viiṭu	house

This assignment system operates with a high degree of consistency. Given the meaning of a noun, its gender can be predicted without reference to its form. Thus, for example, one can be confident that a noun denoting a female will be feminine, and that a noun which is feminine will denote a female, Such systems are sometimes called 'natural gender systems'. There are a very few apparent exceptions to the rules given above. The words *cuuriyaN* 'sun' and *cantiraN* 'moon' are both treated as masculine, as are other heavenly bodies; this is explained by the fact that they are also the names of gods. Words for child, such as *makavu*, are usually neuter but may also be masculine or feminine. There is some scope for metaphoric use of gender; *yaaNai* 'elephant' with masculine or feminine gender would refer to a man or woman with some elephant-like qualities. Animals may be treated as persons in fables; normally, however, even when there are distinct words for the male and female of animals, all nouns referring to animals are neuter. In some instances there is also a morphological clue as to gender, but this is an additional regularity since the meaning of a noun is sufficient in itself.

At this stage, it is worth pointing out that the names used for different genders are not significant. The traditional Tamil terms for the two main classes of nouns are 'high-caste' and 'no-caste' (rational and non-rational in more modern terms). This primary division is reflected in morphology (see figure 6.8) and will be of importance too when we analyse gender resolution (section 9.3). As far as assignment is concerned, however, nouns must be divided into three classes and nothing rests on the actual labels used. Equally, different languages may have similar systems but linguists working on them may use different labels. For instance, several North-East Caucasian languages have three genders and assign nouns to them using the same semantic factors as does Tamil. They include Akhvakh, Bagval, Godoberi and Karata (all Andi languages of the Avar-Andi-Dido group of North-East Caucasian). Linguists working on these languages normally use the labels I, II and III. While names for genders are helpful, there is much to be said for the numbering system, since it prompts us to spell out exactly which types of nouns are included. For languages where the use of names like 'masculine' and 'feminine' is normal, it is important to remember that, say, the feminine gender in one language may contain a rather different set of nouns from the feminine gender in another: the feminine gender in Tamil does not include inanimates, but there are large numbers of them in the feminine gender of French. It should also be said that, while in Dravidian linguistics it is normal to talk of 'genders', those working on Caucasian languages usually talk of 'noun classes' rather than 'genders'. The use of 'gender' or 'noun class' is also more a matter of tradition than of substance, as we shall see in section 6.1. The choice is not important; for consistency, we shall normally use the term 'gender'.

Turning now to other members of the Dravidian family, we find that in Kannada the situation is similar to that in Tamil. There is a very small number of exceptions to the semantic principle: *basava* 'bull' and *koona* 'buffalo' are masculine (Andronov 1969: 29). These are not arbitrary exceptions; rather, their gender reflects the special status of these higher animals. However, though the nouns given are masculine in the singular, they are neuter, as expected, in the plural; these nouns therefore form an 'inquorate' gender (see section 6.4.3). Like Kannada, other Dravidian languages such as Telugu have the same semantic assignment rules as Tamil (Arden 1873: 46) although, as we shall see in section 6.3, the morphological structure of gender in Telugu is rather different. Once again male humans are masculine, female humans feminine and others neuter. The gender of divine beings depends on their role in mythology (Malathi Rao, personal communication): thus *ganga* (the river Ganges) is feminine, *hanumantuDu* (Hanuman, a monkey) is masculine and *kaamadheenuvu* (divine cow) is neuter, and so on, because of the parts these divine beings play in myths. Gender according to role in mythology is something we shall find in languages from all over the world.

Some Dravidian languages have two genders rather than three. The languages involved include Kolami (Emeneau 1955: 73), Ollari (Bhattacharya 1957: 19) and Parji (Burrow & Bhattacharya 1953: 9), all members of the Kolami-Parji subgroup. These languages show what is probably a development of the situation found in Telugu; the feminine and neuter genders have coalesced (but see section 6.4.2) so that masculine is now opposed to non-masculine (more details in section 7.1.3). Thus the masculine gender includes nouns denoting male humans and the non-masculine gender includes all others. The situation of gods is not clear, but in Parji, according to Burrow & Bhattacharya (1953: 9), all supernatural beings, including gods and goddesses, are treated as neuter. These languages all have semantic assignment systems but divide the nouns into different semantic groups. The criteria we have observed are widespread: human is distinguished from non-human (gods and spirits being treated sometimes as human and sometimes not). The nouns denoting humans are in turn divided into those denoting males and those denoting females.

2.1.2 *Other strict semantic systems*

While the Dravidian family shows a particularly high concentration of strict semantic systems, similar gender systems can be found in various languages around the world. We have noted examples in some North-East Caucasian languages and we will now review a selection of instances in other language families.

A noteworthy two-gender system is found in Diyari, an Australian Aboriginal language spoken by about a dozen people near Lake Eyre, which is in the north of the state of South Australia. The first gender is for 'all animates whose reference is distinctly female, for example, women, girls, bitches, doe kangaroos, etc.'; the second is for 'all others, that is, male animates, non-female animates, non-sexed animates and all inanimates' (Austin 1981: 60). Here then the semantic dividing line is not human/non-human but comes lower to include cases where sex is differentiated within the non-human animates. The genders of Diyari are reflected in the third-person singular pronouns, which can also occur within noun phrases in the role of a definite article. The converse system, in which nouns denoting males are singled out as a masculine and all others are feminine, occurs in Kala Lagaw Ya, the language of the western Torres Straits Islands. However, the moon is also masculine (Bani 1987), as is generally the case in the languages of Australia.

The Omotic language Dizi (Maji) is spoken by about 7,000 people in the Kefa province in the south-west of Ethiopia. It has two genders, as shown by adjectival and verbal agreement and by pronoun selection (Allan 1976). The feminine gender consists primarily of two groups of nouns. First, nouns denoting females are feminine: *dade* 'girl', *kuocin* 'woman', *wete* 'cow'. And second, diminutives are also feminine: *kieme* 'small pot', *orce* 'small broom'. Other nouns are masculine: *dad* 'boy', *yaaba* 'man', *kiemu* 'pot', *orca* 'broom'. Thus most nouns are masculine. It is worth noting that feminine nouns can also be identified formally, since they have the suffix *-e* or *-in*. A very similar pattern is reported in Halkomelem, a Salish language, which is spoken in British Columbia by fewer than a thousand speakers. Like Dizi, it has two genders. The first comprises nouns denoting female persons and all diminutives; the latter shows a distinctive reduplication pattern. The

11

remaining nouns belong to the other gender (Anderson 1985: 177–8).

Defaka (Afakani) is a recently discovered South Central Niger-Congo language, spoken in the Niger Delta (data from Jenewari 1983: 103–6). Its gender system, unusual in South Central Niger-Congo, is based on exactly the same semantic distinctions as that of Tamil: one gender consists of all nouns denoting male humans, a second is for those denoting female humans and the third is for remaining nouns. It differs from Tamil in that it has a 'pronominal gender system': gender is marked solely on personal pronouns (see section 6.4.2).

English too has a gender system based on semantic criteria. It is again a pronominal gender system, since gender is reflected only in personal, possessive and reflexive pronouns. The use of *he, she* and *it* is determined by principles similar to those of Tamil: male humans are masculine (*he*), female humans are feminine (*she*) and anything else is neuter (*it*). There is, however, a high degree of variability with animals. Domestic animals, particularly if they are named, are masculine or feminine according to sex; and, especially in children's stories, many animals have a particular gender by convention. In addition, there are some well-known exceptions, such as *ship* often taking the pronoun *she*. As we shall see in the further discussion in chapters 6 and 8, such exceptions are in fact 'hybrid' nouns (see also section 7.3.1 for the generic use of pronouns in English, and see Cooper (1983: 175–94) for an account of the formal semantics of gender agreement in English).

The principles given operate in standard English. There are cases where the straightforward semantic rules are overridden by emotive and affective factors (Vachek 1964). And for some groups, in colloquial usage, considerable variation is possible. Mathiot & Roberts (1979) give examples from American English: humans may be downgraded, by the use of *it*, but upgrading – the use of *he* or *she* for inanimates – is more common. Thus a female customer at a store, referring to a bedspread, asked:

    (1) Is *he* washable?

And a teenage boy, advising on surfing, uttered the following in reference to a wave:

    (2) Catch *her* at *her* height!

See Mathiot & Roberts (1979) for more examples and for a discussion of the motivations behind such use; there is also a wealth of data from written sources in Svartengren (1927). While such examples seem far-fetched for some native speakers, careful observation in the right type of setting will reveal that the gender system of English, though certainly based on semantics, is not totally dependent on the straightforward criteria of humanness and biological sex, but may be affected by pragmatic factors.

2.2 **Predominantly semantic systems**

In the languages we have considered so far, it is sufficient to know the meaning of a noun in order to determine its gender. There may be occasional exceptions, but the basic principle is quite clear. We now move on to languages which have semantic assignment rules which appear to allow sets of exceptions. These may not be particularly significant as a proportion of the nouns in the languages, but they cannot be dismissed as mere sporadic exceptions. To analyse such languages, the notion of 'semantic residue' will prove helpful. The semantic residue comprises nouns whose gender is not assigned according to a positive semantic criterion (compare Dixon 1972:311). This concept can be illustrated from the languages just discussed. In the Dravidian language Kolami, for example, there is a semantic assignment rule stating that nouns denoting male humans belong to the masculine gender. Remaining nouns, the semantic residue, make up the other gender. This second rule is analogous to an 'elsewhere condition'. Similarly in Diyari, nouns denoting females are feminine, nouns in the semantic residue are masculine. And in Dizi, females and diminutives are feminine, almost all the rest are masculine.

In these cases it would be possible to write the rules differently: for Kolami we could have a rule stating that all nouns *not* denoting male humans are feminine, and the rest are masculine. Though this approach appears counter-intuitive, it would work. However, in languages where the semantic assignment rules do not apply so consistently, the counter-intuitive solution proves more obviously unsatisfactory. The reason is that the exceptional nouns are almost always exceptional in a particular way: nouns which do not meet the relevant semantic criterion are treated as though they did, rather than vice versa. We therefore exclude rules based on negatives; semantic assignment rules refer to positive criteria and semantic residues are, as previously defined, nouns where gender is not assigned according to a positive semantic criterion. We can see that, in these terms, even a language with very consistent semantic assignment like Tamil has a semantic residue. Nouns denoting male rationals or female rationals are assigned by this positive criterion to masculine or feminine gender; the remaining nouns, the semantic residue, are neuter. We now turn to languages which have semantic assignment systems in which the nouns in the semantic residue are not all assigned to a single gender; these are still semantic systems but they have 'leaks'.

2.2.1 *Zande*

The affiliation of Zande is complicated; it is a member of the Zande subgroup of the Ubangian branch of Adamawa-Ubangian. Adamawa-Ubangian is in turn a branch of Niger-Congo, which is the major part of the Niger-Kordofanian family. According to the data available, Zande has something over 700,000 speakers; the majority (about half a million) live in Zaire, most of the rest in the Sudan and 25–30,000 in the Central African Republic (data in this section are from Claudi (1985); details of original sources are given there).

Table 2.2 *Assignment in Zande*

Criterion	Gender	Example	Gloss
male human	masculine	kumba	man
female human	feminine	dia	wife
other animate	animal	nya	beast
residue	neuter	bambu	house

Gender is reflected primarily in the personal pronoun, but agreement in gender is spreading to other sentence elements. There are four genders, assigned as in table 2.2. The first two genders are straightforward: nouns denoting male humans are of masculine gender and, equally, nouns of masculine gender denote male humans. Feminines are similar. The one minor complication is that for small children the pronoun for animals is used. (In various languages small children are treated grammatically as not being quite human.) But Zande uses the animate/inanimate distinction as well as human/non-human, and the other two genders are more interesting. In the majority of cases, nouns are assigned to them according to the rule given, but there are about eighty exceptions. Significantly, these are all inanimates (which we would expect to be neuter) which are in the animal gender. Thus the 'leaks' are from the residue into one of the semantically defined genders. The exceptions include:

1. nouns denoting heavenly objects: *diwi* 'moon', *wangu* 'rainbow';
2. metal objects (many of which are round): *bande* 'hammer', *tongo* 'ring (for finger)';
3. edible plants (including round ones): *abangbe* 'sweet potato', *baundu* 'pea';
4. non-metallic objects (mainly round): *mbasa* 'whistle', *badupo* 'ball';
5. other: *ze* 'scar'.

In a small number of cases the exceptions might be explained by appealing to the mythology of the Zande but in most cases we can at present say no more than that they are exceptions.

The basic semantic assignment is based on the criteria male human/female human/animal/residue. In the closely related Nzakara, the first two go together; thus the system is human/animal/residue (Tucker & Bryan 1966: 146–7; Claudi 1985: 136).

2.2.2 *Dyirbal*

Dyirbal is an Australian language spoken in north-east Queensland; few speakers remain. Dyirbal has been of major importance in linguistic research as a result of Dixon's work, which shows it to be a remarkably consistent example of an ergative language. Its gender system is also of considerable interest (data from Dixon 1972: 44–7, 60–2, 306–12;

Table 2.3 *Genders in Dyirbal*

I (*bayi*)	II (*balan*)	III (*balam*)	IV (*bala*)
men	women		parts of the body
kangaroos	bandicoots		meat
possums	dog		
bats	platypus, echidna		
most snakes	some snakes		
most fishes	some fishes		
some birds	most birds		
most insects	firefly, scorpion	honey	bees
	crickets		
	hairy mary grub		
	anything connected		
	with fire or water		
moon	sun and stars		
storms, rainbow			wind
boomerangs	shields		yamsticks
some spears	some spears		some spears
etc.	some trees	all edible fruit	most trees
	etc.	and vegetables	and vines
		and plants that	
		bear them	
			grass, mud,
			stones
			noises and
			language
			etc.

1982; 178–83). Nouns are divided into four genders or noun classes as shown in table 2.3. (Dixon 1982: 178; reproduced with the consent of Mouton de Gruyter; the label given to each gender (*bayi*, for example) is the appropriate form of the 'noun marker', for which see section 5.1).

It might appear that the assignment of nouns to genders is somewhat random. However, Dixon points out that children learning the language appeared not to have to learn the gender of nouns individually and that loanwords were assigned immediately to the same gender by different speakers. He demonstrates that there are indeed semantic grounds for assignment (1972: 308–12; see also Schmidt (1985: 151–3) for a clear summary of the principles involved). The semantic basis for each gender is as shown in table 2.4.

Table 2.4 *Assignment in Dyirbal*

gender I (*bayi*)	male humans, non-human animates
gender II (*balan*)	female humans, water, fire, fighting
gender III (*balam*)	non-flesh food
gender IV (*bala*)	residue

Several large groups of nouns can be assigned by these criteria; but there are numerous exceptions. Most of these can be covered by three principles:

1. Mythological association

Nouns whose referents play important roles in beliefs and myths will generally take their gender from their mythological role. Thus birds (which are animate and so would be expected to be in gender I) are believed to be the spirits of dead human females: they are therefore in gender II. But some individual birds have mythological associations which put them in gender I.

2. Concept association

If a noun is strongly linked conceptually with a noun in a different gender, it may be assigned to that gender. Thus, 'fishing line' and 'fish spear', which we would expect to find in gender IV, are in gender I, because of their association with fish (gender I because animate).

3. Marking of important property

If nouns forming a subset in a particular category are distinguished by an important property, they may be assigned to a different gender. Usually the property is 'harmfulness'. Fish, as we have just seen, are in gender I. Two harmful species of fish, the stone fish and the gar fish, are set apart in gender II. Harmful subsets are frequently assigned to gender II; perhaps the association is with fire and fighting. Another example would be two stinging trees and a stinging nettle vine, which are in II rather than the expected gender IV.

These three principles interact with the main assignment rules in interesting ways. Light is associated with fire, hence is in gender II, as are the stars. One might expect the sun and moon to be in this gender too; but in mythology the moon is the husband (hence gender I) of the sun (gender II). This brief account cannot do justice to Dixon's analysis, which accounts for most of the nouns of Dyirbal. Nevertheless, a few remain as exceptions. It is not known, for example, why the nouns denoting dog, bandicoots, platypus and echidna are in gender II. Perhaps they were assigned on the basis of mythological associations since lost.

It is particularly fortunate that besides Dixon's account of Traditional Dyirbal, we also have a description of the Dyirbal of some of the remaining speakers, the children and grandchildren of Dixon's informants. The traditional way of life has been radically changed and English is replacing Dyirbal. In the last phase of its existence Dyirbal has altered dramatically. These changes have included the gender system, as documented by Schmidt (1985: 151–68); we will consider those speakers for whom the development has gone furthest. The changes are as follows:

1. Loss of gender III

The noun marker for gender III is not used and nouns denoting edible substances are assigned to the residue gender (IV).

2. Reduction of range of gender II

Only females are assigned to gender II. Nouns associated with water, fire and fighting (like 'shield') are reassigned, mainly to gender IV (residue).

3. Loss of assignment by association

Mythological association is lost: birds, the spirits of dead human females, which were in gender II, are now reassigned to gender I (animate). Similarly, concept association disappears: 'fishing line' and 'fish spear', previously gender I by association with fish, are reallocated to gender IV. And the marking principle for distinguishing subsets (usually harmful) ceases to

17

operate: 'gar fish' and 'stone fish' move from II to I, since they are animate, while 'stinging nettle' moves to IV.

4. Regularization of exceptions

Unexplained exceptions are reassigned: 'dog' and 'platypus' were in gender II but move to gender I (animates).

The resulting system is simple; Young People's Dyirbal has the following assignment rules:

1. female humans are assigned to gender II;
2. other animates are in gender I;
3. the residue is in gender IV.

Thus from a semantic system with considerable complications a strict semantic system has developed. Note that for non-human animates gender I is unmarked; gender II is used for specifying female sex of an animal when required. The changes may result from the loss of traditional beliefs and myths. The influence of English is probably partly responsible; however, the system has not simply followed English, in that non-human animates remain in gender I while English groups them with inanimates. And simplification during language death plays a role: the central members of the genders (like 'man' and 'woman') are retained while more peripheral members are assigned by more general rules (see Lakoff 1986). Another account of a gender system in a dying language is provided by Dorian (1976, 1981: 124–9), who gives data on gender in the terminal stages of East Sutherland Gaelic.

When we compare Dyirbal with other languages already analysed we see that Young People's Dyirbal has a strict semantic system, like those discussed first. This has developed from the more complex system of Traditional Dyirbal. There we found leaks from the residue gender (gender IV); in Dyirbal the leaks are into both genders I and II. Moreover, there are leaks both ways between genders I and II. The situation is thus considerably more complex than in a language like Zande. The additional difficulty in analysis comes from the association principles: though the association in examples such as 'fishing line' and 'fish' is fully plausible, it is impossible to predict in which cases gender assignment will be affected by such associations. For further discussion of the Dyirbal data, in which the central members of the first three non-residual genders (human males, human females and edible plants) are opposed to the peripheral members, linked to them by 'chaining principles', see Lakoff (1986, 1987: 91–104). Perhaps the most significant point about genders in Traditional Dyirbal is that there is a semantic assignment system, but one which can be understood only by reference to the world view of the speakers.

2.2.3 *Ket*

Ket is spoken by 800 or so ethnic Kets living in Siberia by the River Yenisey and some of its tributaries well to the north of Krasnoyarsk. Ket is a notable language isolate (though related Yeniseyan languages are known to have existed, the last of which, Kott, died in the nineteenth century). But Ket is not only an isolate; from a typological point of view, it is radically different from all the other languages of Siberia. And one of its distinguishing features is its gender system. Ket has three genders, as shown by various types of agreement including that of the verbal predicate; the distribution of nouns over these three genders is given in table 2.5 (Krejnovič 1961: 114–16; 1968a: 456; 1968b: 154–5, 185–92).

Table 2.5 *Genders in Ket*

Masculine	Feminine	Neuter
male humans	female humans	
male animals	female animals	
some other living things	other living things	part (of whole)
fishes (three exceptions)	three fishes: burbot, ruff, perch	
all growing trees	some plants	
large wooden objects (stakes, poles, hoops, large sheets of birch-bark)		the residue (the majority of nouns)
the moon	the sun (and some other heavenly bodies), fire	
some religious items	some religious items, soul some body parts, and some skin diseases	

The major system of classification is clear enough: it is male animate, female animate and residue. All nouns denoting living things, from animals down as far as insects, are of masculine or feminine gender, but the division between these two genders is sometimes hard to understand for non-sex-differentiable animates. (Non-sex-differentiables are cases where a single noun is used for both sexes, like *mouse* in English.) Krejnovič suggests that those which show a higher degree of activity are masculine, but this hardly accounts for the fact that nouns denoting the following non-sex-differentiables are feminine: hare, squirrel, chipmunk, rat, mouse and mole. These he believes are feminine because they are of no importance to the Kets (1968c: 28). In the light of the gender systems already examined, it is not surprising to find fishes and trees being singled out, in this case being assigned to the masculine gender. Possible explanations offered by Krejnovič for two of three exceptional types of fish are that the ruff is a not particularly active fish, and the perch is not favoured as food by the Kets. Wood plays a major role in Ket culture, hence its special place in the gender system. Size is also significant: certain large wooden objects are masculine (from the association with trees), but similar small objects are neuter. The neuter is also used for parts of wholes; thus 'fish' is masculine, but the same noun treated as a neuter noun means 'a piece of fish'. Mythology too is an important factor; it accounts for the gender of 'sun' (feminine), 'moon' (masculine) and 'fox' (feminine), all determined by their role in myths. Note that 'fire' is feminine, because the spirit of fire is believed to be a woman. While the neuter, which is the largest gender, contains almost all inanimates (including original animates made inanimate, as in 'piece of fish'), there are a few inanimates in both the other genders, such as some body parts (for example, 'heart' and 'tongue'), which are feminine, and other isolated exceptions, masculine and feminine, which are not included in the table. Mythology accounts for the gender of religious items, and may well offer an explanation for some of these other exceptional inanimates.

2.2.4 *Ojibwa and other Algonquian languages*

Ojibwa is an Algonquian language with around 30,000 speakers in the United States, in Minnesota, Wisconsin, North Dakota and Montana, and around 20,000 speakers in the Canadian provinces of Ontario, Manitoba and Saskatchewan (Hallowell 1955 [1967: 116]). As with the other Algonquian languages, which are distributed widely across North America, its nouns can be divided into two genders. These are established on the basis of the agreement of verbs and demonstratives and are usually called animate and inanimate. In Ojibwa, nouns denoting persons, animals, spirits or trees are animate, for example: *enini* 'man', *enim* 'dog', *menito:* 'manitou', *mettikumi:šš* 'oak'. (Note that ':' indicates a long vowel.) Most other nouns are inanimate: *essin* 'stone', *peka:n* 'nut', *pekkwe:šekan* 'bread', *wa:wan* 'egg'. Different genders may correspond to different meanings: *mettik* can mean 'tree' and is animate, or it can mean 'piece of wood' and is then inanimate (Bloomfield [1957]: 31–2).

It appears that we have a straightforward semantic system. There are various exceptions, however. Some cause little surprise: *ukima:* 'chief' is, of course, animate; when used in the meaning 'king' (in cards) it remains animate. But others are more difficult; all the following are grammatically animate: *a:kim* 'snowshoe', *a:sso:kka:n* 'sacred story', *eko:n* 'snow', *enank* 'star', *epateniss* 'button', *esse:ma:* 'tobacco', *menta:min* 'maize', *meskomin* 'raspberry', *po:kketo:ns* 'pear', *uppwa:kan* 'pipe' (for smoking). Diminutives of animates remain animate. *Ekkikk* 'kettle, pot' is, surprisingly, animate; its diminutive *ekkikko:ns* 'small kettle' is also animate. The apparent exceptions given so far are nouns which are animate when they might be expected to be inanimate rather than vice versa; members of the semantic residue are again 'promoted'. This is the predominant pattern of exceptions in Algonquian; it has led Hockett (1966: 62) to call the animate gender 'absorptive', by which he means that 'there are routes for a shift of gender from inanimate to animate, but not the opposite'.

We might conclude simply that gender in Ojibwa is assigned by a semantic principle, according to animacy: animates include trees, and there is some indeterminacy over other plants. In addition there is a sizable list of exceptions. However, Black-Rogers has taken the investigation further. Following earlier work by Hallowell (1955, 1960), she made a detailed study of the world view of the Ojibwa in the community of Ponemah (Northern Minnesota). Her informants spoke the Minnesota-Chippewa dialect, so forms are not identical to those quoted from Bloomfield (the latter being from the Ottowa dialect). The relevance of her study to the problem of gender is demonstrated in Black (1969) and Black-Rogers (1982).

The dominant element in the world view of the Ojibwa is 'power', which will be described following closely Black-Rogers (1982: 63). Power is essential for life, and all 'living' (or powerful) things have some. There is no clear division between natural and supernatural power. However, the source of power may differ; human beings must derive it from inherently powerful non-humans. Power is unevenly distributed, in terms of amount and type. Furthermore, this distribution can be worked out only by the observation of specific events – it is not dealt with in the abstract. The relevance of these beliefs to gender assignment is the hypothesis that it is precisely things which have power which are grammatically animate. An immediate problem is raised by the point that there is no definitive 'agreed list' of what has power. There are some indisputable cases, including all living things, and religious objects. But in other cases, whether something possesses power can be established only after it has demonstrated it in some way. However, Ojibwa rules of conduct, especially those specifically relating to conversation, militate against this.

Given that one cannot know how much of what kind of power other participants (including non-humans) in an event may have, the sensible strategy is caution: more powerful entities must not be provoked. In terms of language behaviour, disrespectful talk is to be avoided. 'The most respectful kind of talk is *no talk*' (Black-Rogers 1982: 64). This means that the relative

21

power of factors which contributed to an event will certainly not be argued out. Different views will be held privately, and indeterminacy is inherent in the belief system:

> the loci of power vary for different individuals and also over time, with a stockmarket type of fluctuation that must be constantly monitored and one's own input taken into consideration. At the same time, behavior rules indicate that power is a private matter which is not alluded to directly, by speech or other overt action, nor is it to be advertised of oneself but rather kept as hidden as possible. (Black-Rogers 1982: 64)

Thus there can be no definitive list of the entities which have power since different speakers have different perceptions of what is a fluid situation. There is also the practical problem that speakers may be reluctant to talk about powerful entities. Nevertheless, Black-Rogers maintains that the Ojibwa power belief system is the most likely source for the problematic cases of gender assignment. Suppose that at a particular time a given entity was associated with power. The noun denoting it would be made animate. It appears that once grammatically animate, nouns are unlikely to be demoted to the inanimate category. Not surprisingly, there are discrepancies between the nouns of this type which are animate in Ojibwa and those which are animate in related Algonquian languages, spoken by different cultural groups. There are even differences between dialects: 'stone' is inanimate in some Ojibwa dialects like Ottowa, and animate in others (Ives Goddard, personal communication).

The basic situation, however, in which there are two genders, one comprising nouns denoting animates, the other consisting of nouns denoting inanimates, with various apparent exceptions (nouns unexpectedly in the animate gender), appears to be general in Algonquian (Bloomfield 1946: 94). For example, considerable similarities to the situation in Ojibwa are found in Menominee (Bloomfield 1962: 26–36) and in Cree (see Darnell & Vanek 1976, best read in the light of Black-Rogers 1982; Joseph 1979; and Craik 1982).

Another Algonquian language whose gender system has been systematically studied is Northern Cheyenne. The relevant paper (Straus & Brightman 1982) has the intriguing title 'The implacable raspberry'. To understand this title one needs to know that, in his brief description of gender in Algonquian, Bloomfield (1946: 94) listed various exceptional animates including 'raspberry' but not 'strawberry'. This contrast might suggest considerable arbitrariness in the system. These same examples were used by Greenberg (1954: 15–16) in a discussion of the relation between linguistic and nonlinguistic data. His point was that 'animate' (or, say, 'gender I') is a purely linguistic characterization, unless it can be shown that speakers behave differently towards the referents of nouns in the two genders: if, for example, speakers have a shrine to the raspberry but not to the strawberry then the nouns of this type could be defined according to non-linguistic behaviour. Greenberg was arguing against the simplistic approach which draws conclusions of an anthropological kind directly from linguistic data (for example: 'raspberry' is grammatically animate therefore speakers conceive of raspberries as animate).

Although Greenberg's argument is clearly correct, his example may not have been well chosen since research has suggested that many of the apparent anomalies in Algonquian gender have a semantic basis. (Indo-European languages would have provided clear cases: *table* is feminine in French but it does not follow that French speakers conceive of tables as female.) Indeed, the anthropologist Hallowell (1960: 24) took up Greenberg's challenge and showed how, in the case of Ojibwa, the category of animacy can be better understood, once the beliefs, attitudes and conduct of the Ojibwa are considered. And this is precisely the point made by Black-Rogers and by Straus & Brightman: gender is semantically motivated to a great extent in Algonquian, provided one adopts an Algonquian perspective. Straus & Brightman show how animates in Northern Cheyenne are essentially things which are 'powerful', including living things, sacred things and various others. Things which grow from the earth form an intermediate category – some powerful, some not (hence the apparent anomalies of similar objects belonging to different genders). More generally, they claim that 'gender is overwhelmingly definable. We have not found shrines to the raspberry, but we have found a cultural explanation for this and other instances of apparently indefinable gender' (Straus and Brightman 1982: 99). Their analysis is similar to that of Black-Rogers and indeed draws on her earlier work. We shall not therefore review it in detail. A particularly valuable feature of their paper is that they provide a wealth of data, in the form of long word-lists of animates in various semantic categories, together with examples from narratives (from Cree). They give plausible explanations for the gender of several items whose gender was previously thought to be arbitrary. There are several other points of interest. The evidence from borrowings provides further support for semantic assignment. Not only can speakers assign gender to English words, but they can do so without problem if an item for which they cannot recall the Cheyenne word is merely pointed out (the informants were bilingual). Thus the referent is sufficient to enable gender to be assigned – the linguistic form is not required. Note too that dangerous things are grammatically animate,

23

which shows a similarity to the situation in Dyirbal (section 2.2.2). Finally, they quantify the claim that gender in Northern Cheyenne is semantically based; the unproblematic cases account for more than 85 per cent of the animate nouns listed in the dictionary. This figure is more impressive than it at first appears, since the inanimate gender is simply the remainder category and contains no further exceptions.

Our main conclusion, then, is that gender in Algonquian is semantically based, but that the semantics are rooted in a culture which is difficult for the outsider to grasp. Fluidity is an essential part of the world view, with the result that gender assignment too can vary. There is, however, a tendency for nouns to remain animate, even if the motivation for this gender is lost for particular nouns, so that sporadic exceptions occur, which are no longer motivated for present speakers. Thus there will be synchronic exceptions to the semantic assignment rules. These are considered further in section 3.3.2.

2.2.5 *Lak and other Caucasian languages*

Most of the thirty-five languages of the northern Caucasus have gender systems. (For a general overview of Caucasian languages see the chapter by Hewitt in Comrie 1981: 196–237.) The number of genders ranges from two in Tabasaran up to eight in Tsova-Tush (but see section 6.4.3). Tabasaran has one gender for humans, with all other nouns assigned to the second gender (a strict semantic system). The languages with a larger number of genders all have a gender for male humans and another for female humans. To this extent the systems are semantic; the degree to which the assignment of the remaining nouns (not denoting rational beings) depends on semantic criteria varies from language to language. (As mentioned earlier, these genders are traditionally referred to as 'noun classes' in the literature on Caucasian linguistics, even though male human and female human are normally two of the classes. The reason why some have not used the term 'gender' seems to have been the fact that nouns are assigned to the human classes on a strictly semantic basis, which is different from the situation in Indo-European gender systems. However, there is no fundamental difference between these noun classes and the genders we find elsewhere and so we shall refer to them as genders.)

Of all these languages, Lak is a particularly good case to consider here. First, it is fairly typical of the Caucasian gender systems in having four genders; several others either have four genders or can generally be shown to have developed from a four-gender system. And second, a considerable amount of work has been done on its genders; we shall draw on Žirkov's grammar (1955), Murkelinskij's overview (1967) and work by Khaidakov

(1963, 1966, 1980:204–13; the last reference revises Khaidakov's earlier work). Lak is spoken in the central zone of the Dagestan highlands around Kumukh, by something over 80,000 speakers. It belongs to the North-East Caucasian family, sometimes called Dagestanian, and forms a subgroup of this family together with Dargva.

Table 2.6 *Assignment in Lak*

Criterion	Gender	Example	Gloss
male rational	I	las	husband
female rational	II	ninu	mother
other animate (but: some female humans and many inanimates)	III	nic	bull
residue	IV	nex	river

Gender assignment in Lak may be summarized as in table 2.6. The first two genders include only humans (and spiritual beings); there are no 'leaks' into them from other genders. The third gender comprises most non-rational animates (animals, birds, fish, insects) and the majority of inanimate objects (for example, the heavenly bodies: sun, moon, star). We will return to the female humans shortly. Gender IV includes a very few animates (spider, earwig, dragonfly, also butterfly and cat in some dialects), some concrete objects (though fewer than in III), most liquids (water, rain, milk, wine) and almost all abstract nouns. On the other hand, it is difficult to see any semantic motivation in the modern language for the distribution of some types of noun between genders III and IV: plants are found in both categories; the months belong in gender III while the days of the week and the seasons are gender IV. Some nouns have slightly different meaning according to whether they are gender III or IV: *čan* means 'human leg' (gender III) or 'hind leg of animal' or 'leg of table' (gender IV). There is one noun which does not fit into the four genders described, namely *q̄aīa* 'house'. This noun behaves like a gender III noun in the singular but a gender IV in the plural (we return to its status in section 6.4.3).

Apart from this exception, we have a four-gender system. Nouns appear to be assigned to the four genders as follows: male rational, female rational, animate (and many inanimates) and residue (a few animates, some inanimates including most abstracts). This may well be a reasonable account of an earlier stage of the language, but it does not accurately represent the modern situation, because it ignores the group of nouns denoting female humans found in the animate gender. At the earlier stage there was a significant

25

exceptional noun: the word *duš* 'girl, daughter', which was gender III instead of the expected gender II. Gender III agreements then became a sign of politeness when addressing young women (Khaidakov 1963: 49–50), particularly those earning their own living, and words referring to them have been transferred to gender III. The convention has been extended so that now any woman outside the immediate family will be addressed using gender III agreements. Within the family older women such as *ninu* 'mother' and *amu* 'grandmother' are still addressed using gender II forms, for younger ones such as *šu* 'sister' gender III is used; disregarding this rule is insulting. For referring to rather than addressing older women, gender II is still used; nevertheless, the number of nouns in this gender has been significantly reduced. In one dialect, the Arakul' dialect, all nouns denoting female rationals are in gender III; gender II has been completely lost according to Khaidakov (1966: 131).

This is an interesting example of change in a gender system. An exception in gender III provided the stimulus for a subset of the nouns in gender II, defined by a semantic criterion, to be transferred to gender III (for a similar phenomenon in Konkani see section 4.5). The motivation involved politeness and, as frequently occurs similarly in address systems, the use of the polite form has steadily extended. In the three-gender system of the Arakul' dialect, one gender is restricted to male rationals; the second includes female rationals, almost all other animates and most inanimates; and the third is for the semantic residue.

Returning to the assignment system of the main variant of Lak, we saw that semantic rules work for the first two genders (male rational, female rational); for the other two, there is some correlation with semantics (animates belong mainly in gender III), but there are exceptions. Similar systems, with varying degrees of mixing between genders III and IV, are found in several other North-East Caucasian languages, such as Bezhti, Archi, Khinalug, Kryz, Rutul and Tsakhur. Dido shows a different type of mixing: gender I is for male rationals only, but gender II includes some inanimates ('shirt', 'dress', 'mouth', 'back', 'pine', 'snow' and others) as well as female rationals. Gender III comprises non-rational animates and many inanimates, while gender IV includes only inanimates (Bokarev 1967a: 407). Dido therefore allows leaks from the inanimate gender IV into both gender II (female rational) and gender III (non-rational animate), but not from gender III into gender IV. Other languages have maintained the two human genders but have splits within genders III and IV. Some dialects of Andi have five genders, while the Rikvani dialect has added a sixth, mainly for nouns denoting insects (see section 7.1.3).

We shall look at one more Caucasian language, namely Archi, a member of the Lezgian subgroup of North-East Caucasian, which has about 900 speakers, mainly in the inaccessible settlement Archi, high in the mountains of central Dagestan. Archi has been chosen because of the fine description in Kibrik, Kodzasov, Olovjannikova & Samedov (1977: 55–66). It has four basic genders, marked by pervasive agreement. The first two genders are straight-

Table 2.7 *Genders III and IV in Archi*

Gender III	Gender IV
domestic animals and birds	young animals and birds (wild and domestic)
xIon 'cow', x̃iIili 'bull', dogi 'donkey', qaz 'goose'	biš 'calf', k'eIrt 'foal (of donkey)'
larger wild animals and birds pil 'elephant', jam 'wolf', liqI' 'eagle', isu 'owl'	smaller wild animals and birds ojomči 'hare', mejmanak 'monkey', hud-hud 'hoopoe', žibela 'swallow'
all insects hilku 'fly', nibsu 'moth'	
mythical beings žin 'genie', ilbis 'devil'	
musical instruments	most tools and cutting instruments
parx 'drum', moxol 'tambourine'	bel 'spade', dab 'awl', k'os 'knife'
cereals qoqol 'wheat', maxa 'barley'	cloth, most clothing at'ras 'satin', palatnoj 'linen', k'az 'shawl', xalac'i 'sleeve'
trees had 'lime', kal 'fir'	metals lacut 'iron', qalaj 'tin'
water phenomena x̃at 'sea', baIri 'lake', bix̃ 'whirlpool', qol 'ice'	liquids x̃an 'water', čixir 'wine', nabq 'tears', x̄Iel 'rain'
astronomical and meteorological phenomena bac 'moon', barq 'sun', marx̄əla 'snow', x̄umuš 'snowstorm'	abstracts (including some temporal concepts) qIiīaqI 'summer', soīaq 'autumn', iq 'day', šan 'year', mukul 'beauty', eImt'i 'cry'

forward. Male rationals are in gender I: *dija* 'father', *dozja* 'grandfather', *allah* 'God'. Female rationals constitute gender II: *dozba* 'grandmother', *baba* 'aunt', *qart* 'witch'. There are no non-rationals in these genders. When we turn to III and IV we find a more complex situation, which is summarized in table 2.7.

There is a certain degree of overlap with morphological and phonological criteria. Nouns formed with the suffixes *kul*, *mul* and *t'i* (as in the last two examples in table 2.7) generally denote abstracts and so are found in gender IV. Similarly masdar forms (a type of verbal noun) take gender IV agreements; these too may be seen as abstracts. And nouns beginning in *b* or *m*, or ending in *n* or *u* are usually in gender III: e.g. *bat* 'horn', *mat'i* 'bough', *xam* 'wax', *gidu* 'circle'. In some cases these markers are petrified gender markers (preserved from a period when Archi nouns were marked for gender – that is, it had overt gender).

The major interest in this system is, however, the overlapping semantic criteria. Note that for animals sex is of no importance: the words for 'cow' and 'bull' are both in gender III. There is a division between domestic animals and birds (all III) and wild animals and birds. The latter divide into larger (III) and smaller (IV), though exceptionally *noqI'on* 'mouse' is in III. The young of animals and birds are in IV. There is thus a correlation between large (III) and small (IV), which is confirmed by examples of nouns denoting concrete objects (many of which are otherwise problematic). We find pairs like those in table 2.8. While in some cases different words are involved, in others, as in the last two examples in table 2.8, there are doublets differing in the size of the object denoted and in gender. Given the correlation between larger size and gender III, it is remarkable that insects are in that gender.

Table 2.8 *Contrasts between genders III and IV in Archi*

Gender III	Gender IV
sahru 'town'	xIor 'village'
xIit 'scoop'	xIit 'spoon'
k'unk'um 'large pan'	k'unk'um 'small pan'

A second correlation is that concrete objects tend to be in III and abstracts in IV, as seen from the last categories in table 2.7. Further connections could be made: there are some similarities between cloth and liquids (both IV), both being non-count and non-rigid (though the same could be said of cereals, which belong to gender III). And the items listed in table 2.7 under 'water phenomena' (III) are typically larger, more specific instances of liquids than the general terms in IV. But the argument is becoming tenuous. We may say that prototypical members (that is, best or most central instances) of gender III are concrete and large (*pil* 'elephant', *kal* 'fir', *bac* 'moon'). The typical member of IV is neither of these (*nabq* 'tears', *mukul* 'beauty'). In other instances the reason for assignment to gender III or IV is not straightforward; this is particularly true for nouns denoting inanimates not covered by the criteria given.

2.2.6 *Other partially semantic systems*

The pattern of two genders with a clear semantic basis and others for which the assignment rules are problematic is common in the Caucasus. Similar patterns (in which the semantic basis for some genders is clear but not for others) are found in Australian languages of the Northern Kimberleys. In some there are two genders for male and female humans, as in Ungarinjin; in others, like Forrest River, there is one gender for humans and another for other animates. (Other nouns are found in these genders by the principle of concept association, as in Dyirbal.) But there are also up to three additional singular genders for inanimates. Some regularities can be found: nouns denoting items connected with the earth ('ground', 'river', 'camp', 'cave', 'valley') are generally found in one gender, and in Forrest River manufactured articles ('canoe', 'string', clothing) belong to one gender. Nevertheless it is difficult to account for assignment within these non-human genders (Capell & Coate 1984: 58–90). Similar patterns, with relatively clear assignment rules for humans but less so for others, are found in neighbouring Australian languages of Arnhem Land, such as Ngandi (Heath 1978: 35–6, 171–4) and Nunggubuyu (Heath 1984: 177–93). In such cases we should keep an open mind; Anindilyakwa, spoken on Groote Eylandt, Northern Territory, was once believed to have a gender system with a considerable degree of arbitrariness. Worsley (1953–4) suggested that there was much more regularity than had previously been believed, and this has proved correct. After a careful study of the lexis, Leeding (1989: 221–87) has shown that gender in Anindilyakwa is semantically based. An important part of coming to understand the system was an approach which attempted to understand the world view of the Aboriginals; concept association (as in Dyirbal) is also an important component of the system.

The balance may appear to be tipped even further against semantic assignment, as in !Xũ, which is a Northern Khoisan (click) language, spoken in Botswana, Namibia and Angola. !Xũ has four genders (Köhler 1971). The basis of the first is quite clear; it contains only nouns denoting humans, spirits,

God and animals (with a very few exceptions). From the data available, the basis for assignment to the other three genders is not clear, though it appears that liquids and abstracts belong to the same gender (as we noted in Archi); they are found in gender IV, which also contain most body parts, most trees and plants, together with a variety of other nouns.

2.3 The criteria on which semantic systems are based

In our consideration of semantic assignment systems, certain common patterns have emerged. Animate is often distinguished from inanimate, human from non-human, male from female and so on. And similar distinctions are found in languages of totally unrelated families, such as Dravidian and North-East Caucasian. Gender systems may be classified according to the patterns of distinctions involved. Such a scheme was proposed by de la Grasserie (1898: 614–15), in an essay based on an impressively wide range of languages. De la Grasserie proposed eight main types, which distinguish in turn animate/inanimate, rational/non-rational, human/non-human, male human/other, strong/weak, augmentative/diminutive, male/other, masculine/feminine/non-sexed. While we have already observed most of de la Grasserie's patterns, we can go beyond his scheme in certain respects.

First, some of his patterns can be seen as being based on combinations of criteria. Given that in some languages the distinction human versus non-human is of relevance and in others the division between male and other has a role, then the scheme male human/other can be analysed as a combination of these two systems, with nouns referring to male humans in one gender, and nouns of all other types in the other. A second point is that there are systems as well as particular criteria of which de la Grasserie was unaware. Besides languages in which males are assigned to a separate gender, there are languages where nouns denoting females occupy a favoured position, as in Diyari, and in most of the Omotic languages, such as Dizi (already discussed), Koyra and Wolaitta (Hayward 1989). As far as criteria missing from de la Grasserie's list are concerned, we saw that the Rikvani dialect of Andi has a gender for insects, while Dyirbal has one for non-flesh food. Ngangi-kurrunggurr (a member of the Daly group of northern Australia) has eight genders, including ones for canines and one for hunting weapons (see section 5.5); and Anindilyakwa draws a distinction between items whose lustrous surfaces reflect light and others (Leeding 1989: 248). (De la Grasserie considered similar examples of which he was aware to constitute a different type of classification, concrete rather than abstract, but in linguistic terms there seems no justification for treating the genders just listed as different from the more familiar ones.) Thus the list of criteria on which gender systems are based must include not only the frequently occurring ones like rational, human, male, female, animate but also insect, large/small, edible (non-flesh edible in the case of Dyirbal) and others too. A criterion which is the main defining factor for a complete gender in one language may be one contributory factor in another. Thus Chichewa and several other Bantu languages have a gender for diminutives; diminutive is one of the criteria for a gender in Dizi, Halkomelem and Archi, but not the only one. Fula has a gender for liquids, also some collectives and abstracts (Arnott 1967: 66), while these form a small part of gender IV in Archi. And some criteria appear never to define a gender completely; thus the names of languages are all in class 7 in the Bantu language Kirundi (Mel'čuk & Bakiza 1987: 330), but class 7 includes nouns of other types too. A similar situation obtains in many central Bantu languages (Larry Hyman, personal communication). I have not found a language of any family in which there is a gender exclusively for the names of languages. An eventual aim should be to draw up a definitive list of criteria underlying gender assignment systems. A potential pitfall here is that some of the cases quoted in the literature do not in fact come from true gender systems. Sometimes it is claimed, for example, that a language has a particular gender on the basis of a set of nouns with similar morphological behaviour. On this basis, it could be claimed that English has an 'abstract' gender, comprising nouns ending in *-tion*. Clearly, this is unsatisfactory and we shall limit ourselves to true gender systems which can be demonstrated on the basis of agreement evidence (see section 6.1 for further discussion).

It is nevertheless interesting to note that several of the criteria which underlie gender systems also turn up regularly in other aspects of morphology and syntax. The features diminutive and augmentative are often marked morphologically on nouns, even when the distinction is not reflected in the gender system. The feature animate is particularly pervasive. In Tlapanec (an Oto-Manguean language), basic word-order is determined by animacy. Transitive verbs always have animate subjects in Tlapanec; if the object is inanimate the order is VOS, but if it is animate the order is VSO or SVO (Suárez 1983: 97–8). Animacy also has a considerable influence on the relative frequency of agreement options, as will be shown in section 9.2.2. Another interesting effect is seen in Mundari, a Munda language spoken in the east of India. In Mundari, verbs and demonstratives distinguish three numbers (singular, dual and plural) but only for animate nouns. For inanimates they have no ending (Bhattacharya 1976: 191–2). We would not want to claim that Mundari has gender, rather that agreement in number occurs only with animate nouns. Thus the criteria on which gender systems are based are not restricted to gender systems but are found in other parts of linguistic structure too. The presence of such a feature does not in itself demonstrate the existence of a gender system.

In true gender systems there are instances where two different criteria may assign nouns to the same gender. Thus nouns denoting females and those denoting diminutives may belong to the same gender, as in some Cushitic languages (Castellino 1975: 353). In instances like these the links between the criteria are clear. Similarly, in Alamblak (a Sepik Hill language of Papua New Guinea) there are two genders, masculine and feminine. Besides males, the masculine includes nouns whose referents are tall, or long and slender, or narrow, such as fish, crocodile, long snakes, arrows, spears and tall, slender trees. The feminine comprises, besides females, nouns denoting short, squat or wide entities: turtle, frog, house, fighting shield and trees which are typically more round and squat than others (Bruce 1984: 96–8; Foley 1986: 80–1). In other languages the links between the criteria are not so clear. We saw how in Archi insects belong in gender III. This criterion does not fit in any obvious way with the other criteria by which nouns are assigned to gender III; we might rather have expected insects to be assigned to gender IV, along with the smaller wild animals and birds. Given that apparently unrelated criteria may assign nouns to the same gender (nouns denoting insects and those denoting musical instruments in Archi), it is tempting, when nouns do not fit into a semantic assignment system, to look for more and more semantic criteria which would account for them. In some languages, however, it soon becomes evident that this approach fails, and that there is instead a formal, rather than semantic criterion which will account for some or all of the nouns in the semantic residue.

2.4 Conclusion

We have seen how in some languages the meaning of a noun always or virtually always determines its gender (as in Dravidian languages). In other languages the role of semantics is more restricted. In both cases it is important to bear in mind that the world view of the speakers determines the categories involved, and that the criteria may not be immediately obvious to an outside observer; thus the part played in mythology may well determine the gender of a noun (as in Telugu, in Dyirbal, and in the Bantu language Kikuyu (Leakey 1959: 6–7)). In yet other languages, semantic criteria fail to account for the gender of a high proportion of the nouns, and formal criteria must be sought. Such formal criteria are the subject of the next chapter.

3

Gender assignment II: formal systems

In the last chapter we examined languages in which gender is assigned solely by semantic criteria. We also noted languages in which semantic criteria allowed various numbers of exceptions. We now come to languages in which large numbers of nouns fall outside the semantic assignment rules. These nouns may be handled instead by formal assignment rules, that is, rules which depend on the form of the nouns involved rather than on their meaning. These rules are of two types, morphological and phonological, which we will consider in turn (sections 3.1 and 3.2). Whereas the distinction between semantic and formal assignment rules is clear (though their effects may overlap), the distinction between morphological and phonological rules is not always clear-cut. As a rule of thumb, we may say that phonological rules refer just to a single form of a noun, for example, 'nouns ending in a vowel in the singular are feminine'. Typically, the most basic form of the noun is involved, though this is not always spelled out. Morphological rules, on the other hand, require more information; they need to refer to more than one form. This is not always obvious. A typical assignment rule of the morphological type might be: 'nouns of declension II are feminine'; establishing that a noun is of declension II might require information about, say, the nominative singular and the genitive singular. Note that there are no syntactic systems; the obvious syntactic system would be one in which gender was assigned to nouns according to agreement. This is indeed the definitive method by which gender can be established; however, if there were no other assignment rule, this would be equivalent to the null hypothesis, that the gender of each noun had to be remembered individually. (Noun x is feminine because it takes agreement y; in order to produce agreement y correctly the native speaker must simply remember that noun x is feminine.) Other types of syntactic assignment rule could be imagined, for example, 'nouns which take prepositional complements are neuter', but no such cases have been found. This is probably because syntactic specifications on nouns are very limited; nouns do not normally require specifications to indicate which syntactic rules they are subject to.

33

3.1 **Morphological systems**

Morphological systems are connected to the semantic systems of the previous chapter in two ways. First, they always have a semantic core. There is no purely morphological system; the morphological rules assign the nouns in the semantic residue to genders, that is, they are required where semantic rules fail. And second, they may also overlap with the semantic rules. This happens regularly in derivational morphology. Take the Russian word *šotlandec* 'Scotsman'. Nouns formed with suffix *-ec* are masculine; but more importantly, *šotlandec* is masculine because it denotes a male. Nouns formed with *-ka* are feminine; *šotlandka* 'Scotswoman' is therefore feminine, but primarily because it denotes a female. On the other hand, there are instances where morphology and semantics do not necessarily overlap; an example is declensional type, which we shall consider shortly. Declensional type may in turn overlap with phonology; it may be possible to predict the declensional type from the phonological shape of the stem. Where this is systematically the case, we shall consider it to be phonological assignment; this is the simpler claim, since phonological information must in any case be stored in the lexicon. In this section we shall look at languages where phonological assignment is insufficient and reference to morphology is required.

3.1.1 *Russian*

Russian, an East Slavonic language, has three genders, as can be demonstrated by the agreements shown by adjectives, verbs (in the past tense) and relative and personal pronouns. In addition, each of the three genders has two subgenders, which we shall consider later. The masculine and feminine genders have a semantic core, as can be seen from the semantic assignment rules.

Semantic assignment rules

1. Sex-differentiable nouns denoting males (humans and higher animals) are masculine: *otec* 'father', *djadja* 'uncle', *lev* 'lion';
2. Sex-differentiable nouns denoting females are feminine: *mat'* 'mother', *tetja* 'aunt', *l'vica* 'lioness'.

Nouns which are sex-differentiable are those where the language distinguishes a form for males and another for females. In Russian these are instances where the sex matters to humans (as in the case of humans and domesticated animals) and where the difference is striking (as in the case of lions).

While these rules operate with very few exceptions, they do not cover a large proportion of nouns, those in the semantic residue. It is certainly not the case that all the nouns in the semantic residue are neuter. Rather they are distributed over the three genders. This situation, a common one in Indo-European languages, is shown schematically in table 3.1.

Table 3.1 *Assignment in Russian (semantic criteria only)*

Gender	Criterion
masculine	male + residue
feminine	female + residue
neuter	residue

To confirm that the nouns of the semantic residue are indeed found in all three genders, consider those in table 3.2.

Table 3.2 *Examples from the semantic residue in Russian*

Masculine	Feminine	Neuter
žurnal 'magazine'	gazeta 'newspaper'	pis′mo 'letter'
dom 'house'	škola 'school'	zdanie 'building'
čaj 'tea'	voda 'water'	vino 'wine'
avtomobil′ 'car'	mašina 'car'	taksi 'taxi'
večer 'evening'	noč′ 'night'	utro 'morning'
flag 'flag'	èmblema 'emblem'	znamja 'banner'
zakon 'law'	glasnost′ 'openness'	doverie 'trust'

It does not seem possible to establish semantic factors to account for the gender of these nouns. Nevertheless, gender in Russian is highly predictable; for many nouns it is determined not by semantic but by formal factors, namely by the declensional type of the noun, as we shall see. From some of the examples given already, it might appear that simple phonological rules would be sufficient: for example, nouns ending in -*o* are neuter. Unfortunately, there are examples for which no such rule works, pairs such as *portfel′* (masculine) 'briefcase' and *pyl′* (feminine) 'dust'. (Note that ′ transliterates the Russian soft sign, which normally indicates palatalization of the preceding consonant.) The forms discussed so far are those of the nominative singular. Attempts using any other case form, which would in any case be harder to justify since the nominative is clearly the basic case, are less successful than those using the nominative, so we shall not pursue them. It could be argued, however, that since Russian has at least six cases (there are grounds for postulating more), a phonological rule should be based not upon a particular case form but upon the stem; this more consistent approach actually fares rather worse, since the two nouns above have stems identical to the nominative singular, while other nouns such as *nedelja* 'week' (feminine) also have palatalized stems (/nedel'/) which cannot be distinguished from those above.

The assignment rules then require access to more than one case form of the noun, in other words, to its declensional type; they are therefore morphological assignment rules. Russian has four main noun paradigms, which account for all but about twenty of the declinable nouns (this analysis is justified in detail in Corbett 1982: 202–11). Examples are given in table 3.3.

Table 3.3 *Noun paradigms in Russian*

	I	II	III	IV
Singular				
Nominative	zakon	škola	kost'	vino
Accusative	zakon	školu	kost'	vino
Genitive	zakona	školy	kosti	vina
Dative	zakonu	škole	kosti	vinu
Instrumental	zakonom	školoj	kost'ju	vinom
Locative	zakone	škole	kosti	vine
Plural				
Nominative	zakony	školy	kosti	vina
Accusative	zakony	školy	kosti	vina
Genitive	zakonov	škol	kostej	vin
Dative	zakonam	školam	kostjam	vinam
Instrumental	zakonami	školami	kostjami	vinami
Locative	zakonax	školax	kostjax	vinax
	'law'	'school'	'bone'	'wine'

Note: Forms are transliterated from the standard orthography, which is largely morphophonemic. Palatalization is indicated by both ' and j.

There is some correlation between phonology and declensional type; nouns in declension III all have palatalized stems, while the other three declensions all have palatalized variants (with certain automatic alternations of forms), in addition to the non-palatalized variants given. Thus *portfel'* 'briefcase' belongs to the palatalized variant of declensional type I.

Given these declensional types, it is relatively simple to predict the gender of a noun.

> *Morphological assignment rules*
> 1. nouns of declensional type I are masculine;
> 2. nouns of declensional types II and III are feminine;
> 3. others are neuter.

In these rules the neuter acts as a morphological residue. There are two reasons for this analysis. Besides the declension IV nouns which are neuter, the main group of exceptions, the dozen or so nouns declining like *znamja* 'banner' and *vremja* 'time' are also neuter. And second, items other than nouns and pronouns with which agreement may be required (such as infinitives and interjections) are treated as neuter (though in this use some neuter forms in Russian have characteristics of special neutral forms, see section 7.2.3).

It might be imagined that, given these morphological rules, the semantic rules are superfluous. *Otec* 'father' would be assigned to the masculine gender because it is in declension I, and *mat'* 'mother' to the feminine because it belongs to declension III. But this approach would not account for nouns like *djadja* 'uncle' and *deduška* 'grandfather'. They denote males and so should be masculine by the semantic assignment rules; at the same time, they belong to declension II, and so would be expected to be feminine. In fact they are masculine (just as in Latin nouns like *agricola* 'farmer' are masculine). There are also numerous hypocoristics, or familiar names, like *Saša* 'Sasha' (for *Aleksandr* 'Alexander'), which behave in the same way. Nouns like *djadja*

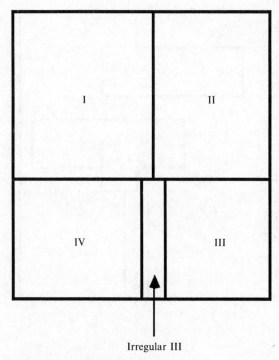

Irregular III

Figure 3.1 *Russian declensional types*

37

demonstrate that the semantic assignment rules take precedence; where there is a conflict, gender is assigned according to semantics. The morphological rules operate to assign the nouns in the semantic residue to a gender. There is an interesting case where the two types of assignment rules clash and where there is not such a clear outcome. Nouns like *vrač* 'doctor' belong to declension I. When denoting a male, such nouns are masculine. When denoting a female, they take a mixture of masculine and feminine agreements; for discussion of such 'hybrid' nouns see sections 6.4.5.2, 8.1 and 8.3. Nevertheless, taking the noun stock as a whole, there is a considerable overlap between gender and declensional type. This overlap is represented graphically. Figure 3.1 gives a rough idea of the relative importance of the different declensions (the area representing the smaller groups, particularly the irregulars, has been expanded somewhat in the interests of clarity; for statistical data see table 4.1 and Ilola & Mustajoki 1989: 9). Figure 3.2 shows the distribution of sex-differentiable nouns over these declensions; it can be seen that nouns denoting males belong primarily to declension I, though a large group is found in declension II (the *djadja* type). Nouns denoting females

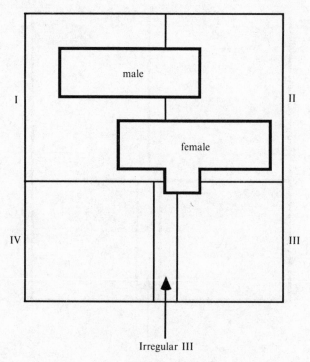

Figure 3.2 *Sex-differentiable nouns in Russian*

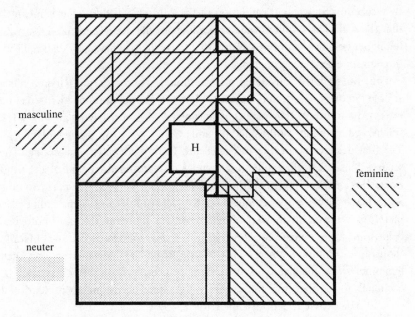

Figure 3.3 *The gender pattern of Russian*

are found primarily in declension II, though there are several in declension I; in addition there are a very few such nouns in declension III and in its irregular variant. Let us now see how these groups correlate with gender (figure 3.3).

Figure 3.3 indicates the extent to which gender and declension match. The masculine gender comprises nouns which are of declension I, except when they denote females, together with nouns of declension II when they denote males, and a single noun of irregular declension III (*put'* 'way'). The feminine gender includes all remaining nouns in declension II and those in (regular) III, together with a couple of nouns which denote females in the irregular III declension. Note that nouns denoting females which are of the first declension do not fall completely into either gender, so are labelled 'H' for 'hybrids'. The neuter gender takes in declensional type IV and almost all nouns of the irregular III declension.

This type of pattern is not unusual in Indo-European. Unfortunately, the considerable correlation between declensional type and gender frequently leads to misleading use of terms. One may read statements like 'masculine nouns take -*a* in the genitive singular' when a more accurate formulation would be: 'Nouns belonging to declension I, which contains most of the masculines, take -*a* in the genitive singular.' Or in work on child language acquisition it may be stated, for example, that the feminine gender is acquired by a certain age, when examination of the data reveals that what is meant is that the child has acquired the case endings of the declension to which most feminines belong and not necessarily that the child systematically distinguishes the feminine gender.

Thus far we have considered only declinable nouns; in fact Russian has a sizable minority of indeclinable nouns. First we should examine an interesting intermediate group, the numerous acronyms of modern Russian like *VUZ* 'higher educational establishment' and *MGU* 'Moscow State University'. The first declines according to declension I and is therefore masculine. The second does not decline and so its gender is determined by that of the head noun. It is an abbreviation of *Moskovskij gosudarstvennyj universitet* 'Moscow State University'; *universitet* belongs to declension I and is masculine; so, therefore, is the acronym *MGU*. Some acronyms show variable morphological behaviour, as in the case of *ŽÈK* (*žiliščno-èkspluatacionnaja kontora*) literally 'housing exploitation office'. This can be treated as indeclinable, and then feminine, since the head noun *kontora* 'office' is feminine. Or it can be declined, and is then masculine, since it declines according to declension I (Graudina, Ickovič & Katlinskaja 1976: 83–5).

There is also a large number of straightforward indeclinable nouns. A few of these are sex-differentiable and so have their gender determined by the semantic rules: *attaše* 'attaché' is masculine, while *ledi* 'lady' is feminine. For the rest the deciding criterion is animacy. Indeclinable nouns which are animate are masculine, while inanimates are neuter. This can be illustrated by the following contrast: *boa* 'boa' can be neuter, and means something to put round one's neck; it can also be masculine, in which case it is animate and definitely not to be put around one's neck. Less critical examples are the following: *taksi* 'taxi', *kino* 'cinema' and *pal′to* 'coat' are all neuter, while *gnu* 'gnu', *kenguru* 'kangaroo' and *marabu* 'marabou' are masculine.

We now review the rules we have identified.

Semantic assignment
For sex-differentiable nouns:

1. nouns denoting males are masculine;
2. nouns denoting females are feminine.

Morphological assignment
For declinable nouns:

1. nouns of declensional type I are masculine;
2. nouns of declensional types II and III are feminine;
3. nouns of declensional type IV are neuter.

For indeclinable nouns:

1. for acronyms, take the head noun; the gender is then determined according to the morphological rules just given (that is, go back to 'morphological assignment for declinable nouns').
2. nouns denoting animates are masculine;
3. others are neuter.

Note that these rules are ordered; semantic rules take precedence over morphological rules. There is no need to spell out, for example, that declinable acronyms take gender from their declensional type as this will be covered automatically by the morphological assignment rules for declinable nouns (which do not distinguish declined acronyms from other declinable nouns).

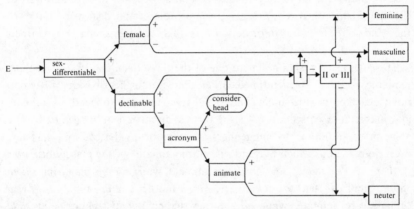

Figure 3.4 *Gender assignment in Russian*

An alternative way of presenting the same information is in the form of a flow chart, as in figure 3.4. The flow chart is entered at E, and the boxes represent decisions, with + for yes and − for no. The oval represents a procedure (assignment according to the head noun of an acronym). The outputs are the genders to which the nouns are assigned. The masculine noun *put'* 'way' is left out as an isolated exception, which needs an irregular marker in its lexical entry; in some dialects its declension has been regularized and it has been made feminine.

We have seen various rules which depend on morphological information. Sometimes this morphological information can in turn be predicted from phonological information but in other cases it cannot. Another instance where the role of morphology is evident is in the case of affective suffixes. Affective suffixes signal the speaker's attitude to the denotatum, rather than giving

41

further information on objective reality. The most common is the diminutive suffix *-išk-*. The addition of this suffix may change the declensional type of the noun, while not changing its gender, as in the following example:

> (1) èt-ogo   gorod-išk-i
> this-GEN.SG.MASC town-DIMINUTIVE-GEN.SG
> 'of this little town'

Gorod 'town' follows declensional type I and is masculine. The addition of *-išk-* in example (1) has led to its being declined according to declension II. Nevertheless, the noun does not become feminine, but remains masculine, as the agreeing determiner *ètogo* suggests (and other case forms prove). Thus the assignment rules must be able to disregard affective suffixes. When, however, a suffix changes the meaning of an item, and so becomes an essential part of the lexical entry, then gender is assigned according to the declensional type of the suffix. (For more information on this complex area see Corbett 1982: 221–3.)

The rules given assign nouns to one of the three main genders: masculine, feminine or neuter. As mentioned earlier, there is a further division of Russian nouns; each of the three main genders is divided into two subgenders: animate and inanimate (see section 6.4.1 for further discussion of subgenders). The assignment of nouns to subgenders is semantically based, and has few exceptions. Beings which live and move are animate. Of the masculines, *otec* 'father', *djadja* 'uncle', *lev* 'lion', are animate, while *žurnal* 'magazine', *dom* 'house' and *čaj* 'tea' are inanimate. *Mat'* 'mother', *tetja* 'aunt' and *l'vica* 'lioness' are animate, while *gazeta* 'newspaper', *škola* 'school' and *voda* 'water' are inanimate. Most neuters are inanimate, like *pis'mo* 'letter' and *zdanie* 'building', but a few are animate, such as *čudovišče* 'monster', *životnoe* 'animal' and *nasekomoe* 'insect'. There are a few types of problematic nouns, The noun *mikrob* 'microbe' is on the borderline but is usually animate (it is masculine in any case); plants are definitely inanimate. Then *pokojnik* 'the deceased' is grammatically animate. Where nouns which denote animates have their meaning extended to non-animates, they normally remain grammatically animate. For example, *korol'* 'king' remains animate even when it denotes a playing card or a chess piece. (This aspect of animacy in Russian recalls the situation in Ojibwa described in section 2.2.4.) On the other hand, nouns originally denoting inanimates become animate when denoting animates, for example, *tip* 'type', when used of a person.

The assignment of nouns to the animate or inanimate subgender is therefore normally based on a straightforward semantic criterion. These subgenders are a more recent development than the three main genders, where semantic assignment accounts for only some of the nouns. There is already evidence that the semantic criterion of animacy is being weakened, in that there is a small number of nouns which are of animate gender even though they do not fulfil the semantic criterion. It should also be pointed out that the hierarchical arrangement of the genders does not match that of the semantic criteria. In semantic terms, nouns can be divided into those denoting animates and those denoting inanimates; the animates can be subdivided into those which are sex-differentiable and those which are not, the former in turn being subdivided into male and female. Grammatically, however, the first division is into three main genders: masculine, feminine and neuter, as the evidence of agreement shows. Each gender is then subdivided into animate and inanimate, on the evidence of the accusative case only (see section 6.4.1). For masculines, both singular and plural are involved; feminines show animacy by agreement only when plural; neuters occupy an intermediate position in that formerly, like the feminines, they distinguished animacy only in the plural but now examples have begun to appear in which the singular is affected (Ickovič 1980: 88).

Though we say that Russian has a morphological assignment system, semantic factors still take precedence. Thus *djadja* (masculine) 'uncle' and *tetja* (feminine) 'aunt' are equivalent morphologically, but since they are sex-differentiable, the difference in meaning leads to their being of different gender. In the case of nouns like *žurnal* (masculine) 'magazine' and *gazeta* (feminine) 'newspaper', there is no semantic difference which is of significance for gender assignment; they are different morphologically and this difference leads to their being assigned to different genders.

3.1.2 *Swahili and other Bantu languages*

The Bantu languages occupy a special place in gender studies, since many of them have extensive gender systems. They are spoken across most of the southern half of Africa; some have few speakers while the most widely used, Swahili, has several million (estimates vary dramatically), including many who use it as a second language. Bantu is a relatively homogeneous group within the large Niger-Kordofanian family. Typical Bantu languages have several genders reflected in complex agreement systems. Examples such as the following Swahili sentence are often found in introductory linguistics textbooks:

(2) *ki*kapu *ki*kubwa *ki*moja *ki*lianguka
 basket large one fell
 'One large basket fell.'

The adjective, numeral and verb all carry the prefixed agreement marker *ki*-, as do other agreement targets not illustrated in this example. Given a different type of noun, they would all have a different prefix. Note that in (2) the same prefix is carried by the noun itself (*ki-kapu*). This phenomenon is known as *overt* gender: the gender is clear from the noun itself and not only from the agreeing forms (see section 3.3.1). In the plural a similar situation is found:

(3) *vi*kapu *vi*kubwa *vi*tatu *vi*lianguka
    baskets large   three fell
    'Three large baskets fell.'

Here the prefixed *vi-* appears on the head noun as a marker of plurality, for nouns like *ki-kapu*, and it occurs as an agreement marker on other sentence elements. The noun prefixes have a further role, since the same root may occur in different lexical items, which are differentiated by the prefixes:

ki-ti '(wooden) stool'   vi-ti '(wooden) stools'
m-ti 'tree'   mi-ti 'trees'

The root *ti* is associated with wood; the prefix is required to establish the meaning of the particular lexical item as well as its number. (These are 'motion' nouns, which are referred to again in section 3.3.3.2.) The same root may also occur with different prefixes to indicate augmentative or diminutive meaning. Thus *nyoka* 'snake', *j-oka* 'giant snake', *ki-j-oka* 'tiny snake' (Wald 1975: 273).

Early Bantuists like Bleek (1862–9: 148–9) and following him Meinhof (1899; 1906) gave individual prefixes a number and talked of them as 'noun classes'. (For a brief survey of the work on noun classes of these and other pioneers see Zawawi 1979: 11–36.) Thus *ki-* is the exponent of class 7, *vi-* of 8, while *m-* and *mi-* in the example above are the exponents of classes 3 and 4 respectively. Bantu languages have varying numbers of such classes, generally between ten and twenty. Grammatical number is apparently ignored since, for example, class 7 and its plural 8 count as separate classes, though usually odd numbered classes are singular and even numbered classes are plural. This method of numbering is convenient for comparative work since related forms will be given the same label in different languages. It means that particular languages may have gaps; thus Swahili has no classes 12, 13, 14 but it has a class 15. A clear account of the traditional approach is given by Welmers (1973: 159–83), from whom the Swahili data in this section are taken, where not otherwise specified.

There are difficulties with the traditional approach, however. Prefixes on the noun do not always match the agreement forms, as is illustrated in example (4):

(4) *m*tu   *a*mepotea
    person is.missing
    'A person is missing.'

Mtu 'person' is generally analysed as being in class 1, and it has the regular prefix *m-*; the verb, however, takes *a-*. This is not a serious problem; we could simply label both as class 1. However, there are nouns with no prefix at all, and others which have the 'wrong' prefix:

(5) *ki*faru   *m*-dogo *a*-likuwa hapa
    rhinoceros 1-small 1-was   here
    'A small rhinoceros was here.'

Ki-faru has the same prefix as *ki-kapu* 'basket', that of class 7; the agreements are those of class 1 (*m-* on adjectival modifiers and *a-* on verbs). This problem is the reason why we have not glossed the prefix on the noun. The situation is similar to that of Russian nouns like *djadja* 'uncle' or Latin nouns like *agricola* 'farmer' which belong to a declensional type typical of feminines but which are of masculine gender. Examples like *kifaru* have led to confusion in Bantuist usage; it was not clear whether they should be labelled as class 7 (according to their form) or class 1 (according to the agreement taken). Of course, the confusion is more serious in the other direction, when it is said that a noun belongs to a particular class and it is uncertain whether form or agreement is meant. As will become clear shortly, the agreement evidence is what counts as far as gender is concerned. But before coming to that point we should look at a second problem with the traditional numbering of noun classes, which is that it gives insufficient weight to the link between singular and plural classes. In fact, the majority of nouns take agreement of one singular class and one plural class and the number of such combinations is limited in a given language. Details on the possible correlations of singular and plural in Bantu languages, as well as on change of class for evaluative use, can be found in Toporova (1987), following work by Kadima (1969: 86–96) and Oxotina (1985). The terminology in this area is confused (as demonstrated in *Classification nominale* 1967: 391–7). According to one usage, which we shall follow, the sets of nouns which take the same agreements (typically a singular–plural pair) are called 'genders' (as, for example, in Guthrie 1948 and in contributions to Hyman 1980a). This approach has the great advantage that it allows us to compare Bantu languages with languages of other types using a consistent method of analysis. The data we have examined already demonstrate the need to distinguish the sets into which nouns are divided (controller genders) from the agreement forms found (target genders), a distinction we return to in section 6.3. The target genders in Bantu languages are relatively straightforward and the traditional numbers for these will serve well. Controller genders are established on the basis of all the agreement forms taken by particular nouns, both singular and plural. Thus nouns which take a verb in *ki-* when singular and *vi-* when plural belong to the same set as *ki-kapu* 'basket' (see example (2)). We wish to give this set of nouns, or controller gender, a label. We could use names (like 'neuter'), or single numbers (as in Watkins 1937 and Gregersen 1967), but we shall follow the convention of most modern Bantu scholars in calling it '7/8'. It should be stressed that '7/8' is a label just like 'IV' or 'neuter' for a controller gender. This solution has two advantages: first, it maintains continuity with traditional work in Bantu studies; and second, within that tradition, it serves as a mnemonic for the agreements taken (7 in the singular and 8 in the plural). *Kifaru* 'rhinoceros' will then be assigned to the 1/2 gender, according to the agreements it takes (and in spite of its prefix).

There remains the morphological problem: how is the morphology of *kifaru* recorded in the speaker's internal lexicon? One hypothesis would be that it is stored in this form (i.e. *kifaru*) and that there is an inflectional rule stating that nouns with the singular in *ki-* take the plural in *vi-*. Alternatively, the stem *-faru* could be stored, along with a marker indicating the prefixes taken, in this case perhaps [morphological class 7/8]. Note that the problem is fully analogous to Russian *djadja* 'uncle'; this must be labelled as belonging to declension II: most declension II nouns are feminine, but *djadja*, which is masculine, demonstrates that declensional type and gender can be out of step. Similarly *kifaru* belongs to morphological class 7/8 but its gender is 1/2. In Swahili as in Russian (and, more generally, in Bantu languages as in Indo-European) the morphological class of large numbers of nouns is not predictable from their meaning. On the other hand, given the morphological class, the gender normally follows, apparent exceptions being predictable on semantic grounds. Thus *djadja* 'ought' to be feminine but is not because it is semantically male; *kifaru* ought to belong to the 7/8 gender but does not because it is animate. Thus for Swahili we require semantic and morphological assignment rules.

Before setting out the assignment rules it will be helpful to consider table 3.4, which shows morphological forms and target gender forms in Swahili. As mentioned earlier, we retain the traditional noun-class numbers, using a pair to designate controller genders. The exception is class 15, which is used for infinitives and has no plural. In addition, there are examples of both *singularia tantum* and *pluralia tantum*. The target-gender forms labelled 10 (for 9/10 and 11/10) are identical for all agreement forms (not just verbs). There are three more classes (16, 17 and 18); these are locatives and differ in important ways from lexical genders, and so will not be discussed here;

Table 3.4 *Outline of Swahili gender forms*

Controller gender	Typical morphological form (prefixes on noun)	Target gender form (verbal agreements)
1/2	m-/wa-	a-/wa-
3/4	m-/mi-	u-/i-
5/6	Ø ~ ji-/ma-	li-/ya-
7/8	ki-/vi-	ki-/vi-
9/10	N-/N-	i-/zi-
11/10	u-/N-	u-/zi-
15	ku-	ku-

Note: Not all allomorphs are included here: there are relatively straightforward variants for vowel-initial stems. *N-* represents various morphophonemic alternations which affect the beginning of stems.
Source: based on Welmers (1973).

locative genders in Chichewa are discussed in section 6.3.3. Table 3.4 makes the system appear more consistent than it actually is. The main additional complication is that there are numerous nouns with no prefix; these must still be labelled for gender. In addition there are various exceptions which must be lexically marked.

Let us now consider the assignment rules (based on data in Gregersen 1967: 12–13, 17–19 and Wald 1975: 272–3).

Semantic assignment
1. augmentatives belong to gender 5/6, e.g. *j-oka* 'giant snake';
2. diminutives belong to gender 7/8, e.g. *ki-toto* 'baby', *ki-j-oka* 'tiny snake';
3. remaining animates belong to gender 1/2, e.g. *mw-alimu* 'teacher', *m-jusi* 'lizard', *jogoo* 'rooster', *ki-pofu* 'blind person', *ki-faru* 'rhinoceros', *tembo* 'elephant', *nyoka* 'snake'.

Morphological assignment
1. morphological class 3/4 (*m-/mi-*) → gender 3/4
2. morphological class 5/6 (Ø ~ *ji-/ma-*) → gender 5/6
3. morphological class 7/8 (*ki-/vi-*) → gender 7/8
4. morphological class 9/10 (N-/N-) → gender 9/10
5. morphological class 11/10 (*u-*/N-) → gender 11/10
6. infinitives (morphological class 15, *ku-*) → gender 15

These rules require a few words of comment. The semantic rules must be ordered as they are, otherwise nouns like the augmentative *j-oka* 'giant snake'

47

and the diminutive *ki-toto* 'baby' would be assigned to gender 1/2 by the third rule (there may be some dialectal variation here, see Gregersen 1967: 18–19). This third rule applies not only to nouns whose morphology suggests the 1/2 gender like *mw-alimu* 'teacher', but also to those which are morphologically 3/4 (*m-jusi* 'lizard'), 5/6 (*jogoo* 'rooster'), 7/8 (*ki-pofu* 'blind person', *ki-faru* 'rhinoceros') or 9/10 (*tembo* 'elephant', *nyoka* 'snake'). The priority of this semantic rule over the morphological ones deserves further illustration. *Kiboko* 'hippopotamus' is morphologically 7/8, but since it denotes an animate, 1/2 concords are used:

(6) kiboko   m-kubwa a-meanguka
     hippopotamus 1-big   1-has.fallen
     'The big hippopotamus has fallen.'

The forms expected from the morphology are as follows:

(7) *kiboko   ki-kubwa ki-meanguka
     hippopotamus 1-big   1-has.fallen
     'The big hippopotamus has fallen.'

Example (7) is unacceptable, unless the hippopotamus is a toy, that is to say, is not animate (Bokamba 1985: 16–17); this point emphasizes the semantic nature of the assignment rule in question. In Swahili the rule applies to all animates: in many other Bantu languages the rule is restricted to humans. Note that sex plays no role in gender assignment here.

The morphological rules apply to the remaining nouns. It might appear that they are of little interest – the point is that they apply only when not preempted by a semantic rule and almost all of them can be. Thus we have semantic rules (which in some cases assign nouns to a different gender from that which their morphology suggests) and morphological rules for the residue. Note that gender 1/2 is a purely semantic gender, containing only animates (the extension of animate concord is discussed in section 8.3). This is reflected in the fact that there is no morphological rule assigning nouns to this gender – they are all assigned by the third semantic rule.

We should also ask whether there are any further correlations between gender and semantics. It is often stated that the distribution of nouns over genders is largely arbitrary (apart from the cases covered by the semantic rules above). Certainly, it is not possible to make further consistent assignment rules. Yet there are some interesting subregularities. In Bantu languages in general, plants are often found in gender 3/4, fruits in 5/6, animals in 9/10, elongated objects in 11/10 and small objects in 12/13 (this gender has fused with 7/8 in Swahili). It should, however, be stressed that there are numerous exceptions; thus not all the nouns in 3/4 denote plants nor are all the nouns denoting plants in 3/4 (Givón 1971; Welmers 1973: 166–7). Given this confused situation, it has been suggested that earlier in the history of Bantu there was a clear semantic basis for gender (Givón 1971; Denny & Creider 1976; Herbert 1985). The subregularities found in Swahili and other modern Bantu languages would thus represent vestiges of an earlier semantic system, possibly as regular as those described in section 2.1. Both Stroganova (1952) and Givón (1971) highlight the growing importance of gender 1/2 as a major factor in the decline of the old semantic system. In modern Swahili the major division is now animate versus inanimate. As Stroganova (1952: 206–7) points out, the fact that the genders are now largely formal is shown by the assignment of loanwords, which are allocated according to their form rather than their meaning (see section 4.1).

3.1.3 *The features on which morphological systems are based*

The typical morphological feature involved in assignment systems is the feature determining the **inflectional** morphology of a noun. This was illustrated both in Russian, where a whole set of case and number forms are involved (and we used the term 'declensional type'), and in Bantu, where it is only a question of singular and plural (and so we used the more general term 'morphological class'). However, morphological features of other types may play a subsidiary part in assigning gender, in systems where morphological rules have a less central role than in the languages discussed so far. For example, in Iraqw (a South Cushitic language of Tanzania) various factors contribute to gender assignment. The fact of particular interest to us is that Iraqw verbs are divided into two classes, in order, among things, to account for the forms of the imperative. Nouns can be formed from verbs of both classes, but their gender depends on the verb class; nouns formed from verbs in the first class are masculine (even though they do not denote males), while those formed from the second class of verbs are feminine (Tucker & Bryan 1966: 573, 576, 584). Thus the **derivational** history of the noun provides the information necessary to determine its gender.

A more complex situation is found in German. The assignment rules are very involved, and there has been some particularly interesting work in recent years (for references see the discussion of the acquisition of gender in German in section 4.2). Unfortunately, most investigators assume that the inflectional morphology of German nouns should be derived from their gender, whereas the alternative approach, as adopted for languages like Russian above, appears promising. What is quite clear, is that gender can be predicted for a large proportion of German nouns, and that there is a complex interplay of overlapping semantic, morphological and phonological factors. The point of

49

interest here is the rules concerned with derivational morphology (Mills 1986: 30–1). Abstract nouns formed with the suffixes *-ung, -heit, -erei, -schaft* and *-keit* are feminine. Diminutives in *-lein* and *-chen* are normally neuter. For example, *Mann* 'man' is masculine, *Männchen* 'little man' is neuter. On the basis of these data we might reasonably conclude that the suffix determines gender. German is renowned for complex compounding, and it is regularly stated that in compounds it is the last element which determines gender. A male mouse is *Mausmännchen*; *Maus* is feminine and *Männchen*, as we have just seen, is neuter. Though the compound includes elements which would individually lead us to expect in turn feminine, masculine and neuter, it appears to be the last element, the suffix *-chen*, which determines the gender. But, as Mills points out, things are a little more complex. While most affixes which determine gender are suffixes, there is also a prefix which has this property: *Ge-*, with collective meaning, makes the resulting noun neuter. Thus we have *Strauch* (masculine) 'bush', but *Gesträuch* (neuter) 'shrubbery'. Consider now the compound noun *Muttergestein* 'parent rock'. *Mutter* 'mother' is feminine, *Stein* 'stone' is masculine and *Gestein* 'rock' is neuter. In fact, the compound *Muttergestein* is also neuter. It is not, therefore, the last element which determines the gender, but the last noun, including its affixes. (Plank (1986) argues that derived nouns in *Ge-* have a suffix *-e*, which is not always realized, though it may alter the quality of the stem vowel. This analysis would make the 'last element' rule work, provided it had access to an underlying form with the suffix present. However, there are other interesting exceptions to the 'Last Member Principle', discussed in Zubin & Köpcke 1984: 44–6.) The situation can be reversed: in the Mon-Khmer language Khasi it is the first element of compounds which determines gender. Thus *maaw* 'stone' is masculine, *dur* 'picture' is feminine, and so *maaw-dur* 'statue' is masculine (Rabel-Heymann 1977: 269–70). Here again derivational morphology determines the gender of some nouns; when we consider French in section 3.2.5 below, we shall see another instance of this type.

It is not difficult to see why information about the inflection of nouns may be a major factor in gender assignment (as in Russian and Swahili) while derivational information cannot. The difference is that in the first case every noun has a declensional type/morphological class; even nouns which are indeclinable form a distinctive group. But typically, large numbers of nouns are not morphologically derived, and so an assignment system based on derivation would leave a large proportion of the nouns unassigned.

3.2 **Phonological systems**

As stressed earlier, the primary division of assignment criteria is that between semantic and formal. A secondary division subdivides the formal type into morphological and phonological. Often these two types are closely connected. It was suggested at the beginning of the chapter that if in order to establish the gender of a noun we need to refer to more than one form, whether to different inflectional forms as in the case of Russian, or to the noun and the elements from which it is derived in the German examples just discussed, then we are dealing with a morphological assignment rule. If, on the other hand, gender can be established by reference to a single form, then we are dealing with a phonological rule. We now turn to examples of phonological systems of gender assignment.

3.2.1 *Qafar*

Qafar (Afar) is an East Cushitic language (Cushitic forming part of Afro-Asiatic), and is used by approximately 250,000 speakers in northeastern Ethiopia and in Djibouti. It shows a remarkable phonological assignment system; the data are from Parker & Hayward (1985, especially p. 225). There are two genders. Male humans and the males of sexually differentiable animals are masculine, for example *bàqla* 'husband'. Females (human and animal) are feminine: *barrà* 'woman, wife'. Note that ` is the accent position, which marks potential high tone. There are numerous pairs like the following:

Masculine		Feminine	
bàxa	'son'	baxà	'daughter'
toobokòyta	'brother'	toobokoytà	'sister'
barisèyna	'male teacher'	bariseynà	'female teacher'
kùta	'dog'	kutà	'bitch'

The semantic assignment rules are familiar enough. Consider now the phonological rules:

Phonological assignment
1. Nouns whose citation form ends in an accented vowel are feminine: *catò* 'help', *karmà* 'autumn'.
2. Others are masculine. There are two logical possibilities:
   (a) those ending in a consonant: *cedèr* 'supper time', *gilàl* 'winter';
   (b) those with a citation form ending in a vowel but with non-final accent: *tàmu* 'taste', *baànta* 'trumpet'.

There are few exceptions to these phonological rules; an example is *doònik* 'sail-boat', which 'ought' to be masculine but is feminine. When the two sets of rules are in conflict, then, as we have seen elsewhere, the semantic takes precedence. Thus *abbà* 'father' is masculine because of its meaning, even though it ends in an accented vowel, which normally indicates feminine gender. Conversely, *gabbixeèra* 'slender-waisted female' is feminine, though the accent is not on the final vowel, which is a masculine pattern.

This system is of interest for several reasons. First, the position of the accent is an indicator of gender. Second, there is an enormous overlap between the semantic and the phonological rules. When we look back to the nouns denoting males and females we see that (apart from the two exceptions, where the semantic rule takes precedence) all of the examples quoted would be assigned to the correct gender by the phonological rules. Indeed, if just the phonological rules are applied, they yield the correct result in at least 95 per cent of the cases (R. J. Hayward, personal communication). There is a further regularity that nouns ending in *-e* and *-o* are always accented on this vowel and so always feminine; this regularity reinforces the general pattern, even though it is not required for the statement of the assignment rules. Unusually, then, almost all the nouns of Qafar can be assigned to the correct gender by phonological assignment rules; many nouns are assigned by complementary semantic and phonological rules; however, in the few instances where these clash, it is the semantic rules which take precedence. Similar, though not generally quite such consistent, systems can be found elsewhere in Cushitic, for example in Rendille (discussed in a diachronic context in section 4.5).

Recent work on Qafar (Hayward, forthcoming) suggests that words with an accent on the final syllable need not be specified as such; they can be treated as unaccented, and a very general rule will assign high tone, when appropriate. (The first word in a phrase receives high tone, on its accented syllable if it has one, and on its final syllable if not.) If we follow this analysis, then our first assignment rule should be reformulated as: 'Nouns whose citation form ends in a vowel and which are unaccented are feminine.'

3.2.2 *Hausa*

Hausa belongs to the Chadic branch of Afro-Asiatic; it has around 20 million speakers in northern Nigeria and in the Niger Republic. There are two genders, masculine and feminine: nouns denoting male humans and males of sex-differentiable animals are masculine: *yáaròo* 'boy', *záakìi* 'lion'. Similarly nouns denoting females are feminine: *yáarínyàa* 'girl', *záakányàa* 'lioness'. Non-sex-differentiable nouns may be masculine or feminine: *ráamìi* 'hole' and *géefèe* 'edge' are masculine, while *rìigáa* 'gown' and *sáafíyáa* 'morning' are feminine. There is a phonological assignment rule according to which nouns ending in *-aa* are feminine; others are masculine. As in Qafar, the phonological and semantic rules overlap, as the examples above suggest. While there are exceptions to the phonological rule, there is nevertheless a strong correlation between the *-aa* ending and the feminine gender. This correlation is a relatively recent innovation in Hausa, whose origin is considered in section 4.5; see Newman (1979) for data and references to other work on gender in Hausa.

3.2.3 *Godie and other Kru languages*

The Kru languages, a group within Niger-Kordofanian whose status is still under debate, are spoken in southern Liberia and the Ivory Coast. Several have been shown to have phonological assignment systems; we shall consider Godie, which has around 20,000 speakers, as described by Marchese (1986; and especially 1988). There are two series of vowels, retracted and unretracted, and three tones: high (´) mid (not marked) and low (`).

Table 3.5 *Personal pronouns in Godie*

	Singular	Plural
Human	ɔ	wa
Non-human	ε	
	a	ι
	ʊ	

Table 3.6 *Assignment of inanimates in Godie*

Gender	Criterion	Example	Gloss
ε	large animal	lʊε	elephant
		gwε	chimpanzee
a	small animal	kɔmɔ	crab
		nʉ́	louse
ʊ	liquid	nyú	water
		mιɔ	tear
		zo	soup
	non-solid mass	gbaylʊ	smoke
		zuzu	spirit
	natural element	lagɔ	sky, God
		ylʊ	sun
		kòsu	fire

The gender distinctions of Godie can be illustrated by the forms of the personal pronoun (as in table 3.5); the forms for agreement within the noun phrase are almost identical to the pronoun. The major semantic criterion is human versus non-human. Nouns denoting humans, like *nyɐkpɔ* 'man' take *ɔ* as their anaphoric pronoun, and *ɔ* equally as their agreement marker; when plural (*nyɐkpa* 'men') they take *wa*. For nouns denoting non-humans there are also some semantic indicators (see table 3.6).

While the generalizations indicated in table 3.6 are not insignificant, they cover only part of the inventory of nouns, and there are various exceptions. There is a more straightforward set of criteria for a gender assignment:

> *Phonological assignment*
> 1. nouns whose stem ends in a front vowel (*i, ɪ, e* or *ɛ*) belong to gender *ɛ;*
> 2. nouns whose stem ends in a central vowel (*i, ɐ, ə* or *a*) belong to gender *a;*
> 3. nouns whose stem ends in a back vowel (*u, ʊ, o* or *ɔ*) belong to gender *ʊ*.

It can be easily established that these phonological criteria cover all the examples in table 3.6. They also cover cases not covered by the semantic criteria, thus *li* 'spear' ends in a front vowel and so is in the *ɛ* gender, while *sɐka* 'rice' is in the *a* gender. There are still a number of exceptions (Marchese 1988: 337) but the predictive power of the phonological assignment rules is great. What is particularly interesting about the Godie data is the close relationship between the final vowel, which permits gender assignment, and the form of the agreement marker and pronoun: nouns ending in a front vowel take a front vowel for agreement and as their anaphoric pronoun, and it may be exactly the same vowel. Moreover, the pronoun consists only of this vowel and so appears to have a null stem. This correspondence can be seen as a particular type of alliterative concord (see section 5.2.2): the agreement form and the pronoun are identical to – or at least closely related phonologically to – the end of the noun stem.

Similar situations have been reported in other Kru languages: namely, in Vata, in Tepo (Kaye 1981) and in the Gbobo dialect of Krahn (Bing 1987). These writers suggest that the distribution of nouns denoting non-humans in Vata and Gbobo is arbitrary as far as semantic criteria are concerned (whereas in Godie some semantic clusters are found). However, negative claims of this type are always open to challenge from a more detailed analysis. The significance of the Vata and Gbobo data is discussed in Zwicky (1987).

How do such systems arise? Marchese (1988: 339) gives convincing evidence to support the view that the Godie system came about through a topicalized construction, which would have looked something like the following (using modern forms):

(8) li   ɛ kò mɔ́
      spear it is over.there
      'The spear, it's over there.'

This construction was reanalysed to give:

(9) li-ɛ   kò mɔ́
      spear-DEF is over.there
      'The spear is over there.'

Such an account explains why the ending of the noun stem should resemble the pronoun; the lack of complete identity in some nouns is the result of vowel harmony and other morphophonological processes. There is considerable evidence from various languages for markers of definiteness losing their original function to become mere gender markers (Greenberg 1978). Example (9) is actually an acceptable Godie sentence. The suggestion is that (8) and (9) illustrate the mechanism by which nouns come to end in a vowel which allows their gender to be predicted. Modern examples like (9), in which the noun has what looks like the pronoun attached and which has a definite reading, illustrate the process occurring for a second time; if the definite marker again loses its specific function then Godie nouns could be doubly marked for gender.

3.2.4 *Yimas*

Phonological assignment rules are also found in languages of the Papuan families Torricelli and Lower Sepik. We have data on Yimas, a Lower Sepik language with 250 speakers in the Sepik Basin (Foley 1986: 78, 86–9 and personal communication). Yimas has eleven noun classes or genders, determined by agreement of adjectives and verbs (see section 6.4.5). The first four have semantic assignment rules (see table 3.7). The first two genders are clear. Gender III includes the higher animals but not, say, *krayŋ* 'frog', which is in gender VI. Gender IV includes those plants, and products from them, which have an important function in the culture. It should be noted that many nouns in these genders can be identified by other means: some gender II nouns end in -*maŋ*; gender III nouns can be identified by their number morphology (dual and plural forms); and gender IV nouns end in -*um*. This latter phonological criterion is a more consistent indicator of the membership of this

Table 3.7 *Semantic assignment in Yimas*

Criterion	Gender	Examples	Gloss
male human	I	namarawt	man
		macawk	father-in-law
female human	II	narmaŋ	woman
		ŋayuk	mother
higher animal	III	yuva	dog
		manpa	crocodile
plant (important)	IV	tinum	sago palm
		iripum	coconut palm

gender than is the semantic criterion, as shown by the fact that *awtmayŋi* 'sugar cane' is not in this gender.

We now turn to the genders for which there is, according to Foley, only a phonological motivation (see table 3.8). Genders VI–XI are relatively straightforward, containing nouns which meet a strict phonological criterion. Gender V includes all others (apart from those assigned by a semantic criterion, of course). It is the largest gender and contains nouns whose singular ends in *k, l, m, n, ŋ, p, r* or *t*. It is not surprising that *awak* 'star' belongs here, since it does not meet the criterion for gender X or XI. But *numpuk*

Table 3.8 *Phonological assignment in Yimas*

Singular ending in	Gender	Examples	Gloss
-ŋk	VI	kaŋk	shell
		krayŋk	frog
-mp	VII	impramp	basket
		tampaymp	hanger
-i	VIII	awi	axe
		awtmayŋi	sugar cane
-aw	IX	trukaw	knee
		yaw	road
-uk	X	antuk	mouth
		awruk	bandicoot
-uŋk	XI	awŋk	egg
		kawŋk	wall
residue	V	yan	tree
		awak	star

'mountain' is exceptional; we would expect to find it in gender X. However, the dual and plural endings of nouns in the two genders differ: gender V nouns have the dual in *-rim* while gender X nouns have the dual in *-ul*. Given the evidence available, this suggests that while the phonological rules are adequate to establish gender in almost all cases, this correspondence is in fact more complex. The phonological form of a noun is normally sufficient to predict its morphology (its dual and plural forms), and from these the gender (or class) can be predicted. In the few cases where the morphology is not predictable from the phonology, it is the morphology which determines gender. Thus gender can generally be assigned from phonological evidence, but it may be more accurate to say that these phonological rules in fact hide morphological assignment rules.

3.2.5 *French*

French is often regarded as having one of the most opaque gender systems, a belief reflected in the quotation from Bloomfield at the beginning of chapter 2. Yet rules for predicting gender in French have been established, and this helps to confirm the general validity of the notion of assignment rules. In fact, the predictability of the gender of French nouns appears to have been demonstrated in detail on three separate occasions. Bidot (1925) gave a wealth of information, with rules based on semantics and orthography, and detailed counts of the numbers of nouns covered by his rules. This work went unnoticed. Then Mel'čuk (1958) challenged the still prevalent view that French gender was arbitrary. He gave a relatively simple set of rules, based on the phonological form of the end of the noun. He then tested his rules against various samples, concentrating on the most commonly used words in the language (making use of frequency dictionaries). The rules worked for not less than 85 per cent of the frequently occurring nouns. He stressed that such rules are of both practical and theoretical value, and that wherever possible the validity of theoretical constructs should be tested by quantitative methods; he also gave an analysis of the much more straightforward system of Spanish. Some years later, and apparently without any knowledge of Bidot's or Mel'čuk's work, Tucker, Lambert & Rigault (1977) undertook a more detailed study of French and it is their account which we shall follow here.

French has two genders, masculine and feminine. Each has a semantic core, which can be captured by two relatively straightforward rules:

Semantic assignment rules
1. Sex-differentiable nouns denoting males are masculine.
2. Sex-differentiable nouns denoting females are feminine.

These rules apply to a large number of nouns: *père* 'father', *oncle* 'uncle' are masculine while *mère* 'mother' and *tante* 'aunt' are feminine. There are also some hybrid nouns like *sentinelle* 'sentry', noted in section 8.1.1.

In addition to the semantic rules, there is an interesting morphological rule (Tucker, Lambert & Rigault 1977: 19):

> *Morphological assignment*
> 1. Compound nouns formed from a verb plus some other element are masculine.

An example is *un porte-monnaie* 'a purse' (literally 'a carry-money'). *Monnaie* 'money' on its own is feminine. Thus the derivational structure of such lexical items is required to establish their gender. There are other candidates for morphological assignment rules in French. Nouns formed from verbs by means of the suffix *-ation* (/asjɔ̃/) are feminine, for example *inondation* 'flood' from *inonder* 'to flood'. However, such rules can be seen as more general phonological regularities. There are nouns in *-ation* with no motivating verb in modern French (for example *nation* 'nation'), which are also feminine. In fact, as we shall see, the majority of nouns with final /ɔ̃/ are feminine and for nouns with final /sjɔ̃/ the figure is 99.8 per cent. Thus, while again morphology and phonology overlap, and morphology is of considerable importance, in French the major generalizations can be stated in terms of phonology, as Tucker, Lambert & Rigault (1977) show. They claim that their predictions cover 84.5 per cent of the 31,619 nouns in the *Petit Larousse*. This figure is more remarkable than it at first seems, because nouns which are accounted for by the semantic and morphological rules given above are counted as exceptions by Tucker, Lambert and Rigault if their gender is not predictable by the phonological rules. Thus the proportion of nouns covered by assignment rules is actually considerably higher than 84.5 per cent.

Before we look at examples, it should be said that French orthography diverges considerably from phonetic reality, as a result of a series of sound changes. Some of these changes led to the gender system becoming less transparent, as can be seen by comparison with Spanish, where the rules allow fewer exceptions. French orthography preserves clues about gender which are lost in the spoken language (such as final consonants which are no longer pronounced). We shall concentrate on the more difficult problem, that of gender assignment based on phonological rather than orthographical information. Data on the distribution of the nouns according to the final phone are given in table 3.9. The data are from Tucker, Lambert & Rigault

Table 3.9 *Gender assignment in French*

| Nouns ending in a consonant | | | Nouns ending in a vowel | | |
Final consonant	Number of nouns	% MASC	Final vowel	Number of nouns	% MASC
/ʒ/	1453	94.2	/œ̃/	17	100
/m/	1406	91.9	/ã/	1963	99.3
/f/	301	89.0	/ɛ̃/	938	99.0
/r/	5175	76.8	/ø/	189	97.4
/g/	235	73.2	/o/	865	97.2
/k/	833	66.6	/ɛ/	625	90.2
/b/	129	65.1	/u/	171	87.7
/l/	1581	58.4	/a/	970	82.6
/t/	2269	51.2	/y/	201	71.6
/p/	214	48.6	/e/	2791	50.1
/ŋ/	69	39.0	/ɔ̃/	2665	29.8
/s/	1380	38.5	/i/	2336	24.6
/d/	714	38.1			
/ʃ/	290	34.0			
/j/	352	32.4			
/v/	143	31.5			
/n/	1135	31.5			
/z/	612	10.0			

(1977: 68–125); there are minor inconsistencies in their data, which appear to result from arithmetical and copying errors; these have been corrected here and in what follows.

In each case we have the final phone, the number of such nouns found, and the percentage of them which are masculine. Thus 94.2 per cent of nouns ending in /ʒ/ are masculine, for example *ménage* (/menaːʒ/) 'housekeeping'. At the bottom of the list, 90 per cent of the nouns ending in /z/ are feminine, for example *église* (/egliːz/) 'church'.

The extent to which prediction is possible is surprising, given that French gender has been described as largely random in the past. Nevertheless, if the assignment rules were based just on the data in table 3.9 there would be a large number of exceptions. Furthermore, there are cases where no single prediction as to gender can be made since, for example, nouns ending in /e/ are almost equally likely to be masculine or feminine. Therefore, Tucker, Lambert and Rigault took the analysis further. While sometimes the final phone is an adequate predictor of gender (as in the case of /œ̃/), in others the penultimate and even the antepenultimate must be considered. While nouns ending in /e/ may be masculine or feminine, the majority of those ending in /te/, in fact 924 out of 997, or 92.6 per cent, are feminine. Once these are separated out, the prediction about remaining nouns in /e/ improves considerably: 1,325 out of 1,794, or 73.9 per cent, are masculine.

Nouns in /ɔ̃/ provide a useful illustration of the type of regularity involved. There are actually 2,665 such nouns in the sample, of which 1,871 or 70.2 per cent are feminine. This is an interesting regularity, but a rule based on it would have a large number of exceptions. If we consider the penultimate phone and remove nouns ending in /zɔ̃/ and /jɔ̃/, the majority in fact, then the remainder show a clear picture: 97.1 per cent of the remaining nouns (629 in total) are masculine. Of the 89 nouns in /zɔ̃/, 72 are feminine (80.9 per cent); but we can do even better if the preceding phone is considered: nouns in /ɛzɔ̃/ are feminine (64 out of 65) while others in /zɔ̃/ are masculine (16 out of 24). When we look at nouns in /jɔ̃/, it is again necessary to consider the final three phones. Nouns in /sjɔ̃/ are predominantly feminine (1,689 out of 1,693) as are nouns in /zjɔ̃/ (62 out of 63), in /ʒjɔ̃/ (5 out of 5) and in /tjɔ̃/ (13 out of 17). Of the 169 remaining nouns in /jɔ̃/, 157 are masculine. Thus the majority of nouns in /ɔ̃/ is feminine, though these nouns belong to quite small subsets of the phonological possibilities. This can be seen clearly if the phonological rules for nouns in /ɔ̃/ are set out in order.

Phonological assignment (sample)
1. Nouns ending in /ɔ̃/ are masculine, unless /ɔ̃/ is preceded by /z/ or /j/ (rule covers 97.1 per cent of the 629 cases).
2a. Nouns in /ɛzɔ̃/ are feminine (98.5 per cent of 65);
  b. other nouns in /zɔ̃/ are masculine (66.7 per cent of 24).
3a. Nouns in /sjɔ̃/ are feminine (99.8 per cent of 1,693);
  b. nouns in /zjɔ̃/ are feminine (98.4 per cent of 63);
  c. nouns in /ʒjɔ̃/ are feminine (100 per cent of 5);
  d. nouns in /tjɔ̃/ are feminine (76.5 per cent of 17);
  e. other nouns in /jɔ̃/ are masculine (92.3 per cent of 169).

These rules can be written more economically as follows:

Phonological assignment (summary of sample)
1. Nouns in /ɛzɔ̃/, /sjɔ̃/, /zjɔ̃/, /ʒjɔ̃/ and /tjɔ̃/ are feminine;
2. remaining nouns in /ɔ̃/ are masculine.

Examples covered by rule 1 include *maison* /mɛzɔ̃/ 'house', *action* /aksjɔ̃/ 'action', *persuasion* /pɛrsɥazjɔ̃/ 'persuasion', *contagion* /kɔ̃taʒjɔ̃/ 'contagion' and *question* /kɛstjɔ̃/ 'question'. The predominance of sibilants in the rule is apparent. Rule 2 accounts for nouns such as *jambon* /ʒɑ̃bɔ̃/ 'ham', *rayon* /rɛjɔ̃/ 'shelf', *carillon* /karijɔ̃/ 'chime', *camion* /kamjɔ̃/ 'lorry' and *bâton* /batɔ̃/ 'stick'. The rules as they stand cover 2,617 of the 2,665 nouns, that is 98.2 per cent. When it is recalled that nouns covered by the semantic and morphological rules may be treated as exceptions in this count, then it can be seen that the phonological rules are powerful predictors of gender.

Giving a full set of assignment rules for French would take too much space; the interested reader is referred to the wealth of data in Tucker, Lambert and Rigault. The important principle established is that the final phone may provide adequate predictions, but in other cases it may be necessary to refer to the one preceding it, and so on.

> In order to decide on gender, the native speaker has merely to process a noun back from its terminal phone... The implications of this 'backward processing' are tremendously exciting for they suggest that gender classification is an active process which requires a well developed skill dependent upon the speakers' linguistic experience. (Tucker, Lambert & Rigault 1977: 62)

Our main conclusion here is that French, often quoted as a case for proving that gender is irrational, has a system of gender assignment rules. They allow more exceptions than do other systems described earlier but they nevertheless form a clear system. Once again the semantic rules take precedence. Thus nouns ending in /m/ are predominantly masculine but *femme* (/fam/) 'woman' is feminine. They also take precedence over the morphological rule: *garde-malade* 'nurse' (literally 'tend patient') ought to be masculine by the morphological rule but is in fact masculine or feminine depending on the sex of the referent (Spence 1980: 78; see this source for further information on compounds). There are overlaps, of course. Thus many nouns in /sjɔ̃/ are formed from verbs by the same suffix and have abstract meaning (an overlap of morphology and semantics with phonology). However, the major rules are phonological. This conclusion is suggested by the data we have examined already, by experimental data (section 4.3) and confirmed by another piece of evidence. Deaf children who learn to speak French do not learn to assign nouns to gender (Tucker, Lambert & Rigault 1977: 59); the reason is that they cannot hear the language and so cannot discover the assignment rules. Finally, the coverage of the rules should be emphasized. Though not without exceptions, they cover the vast majority of nouns.

3.2.6 *The features on which phonological systems are based*

The French data demonstrate that assignment rules may need to refer to the whole range of phonemes in a language, and indeed to segments of varying length of a lexical entry. In Godie the situation was simpler in that the place of articulation of the final vowel (in terms of frontness/backness) was sufficient, while the Qafar data show how the accent position may be a factor which determines gender. In German, syllabicity has an effect (see section 4.3). It would therefore appear that any phonological information in lexical entries has the potential to help determine gender; it will be interesting to see whether any constraints can be established which would preclude certain types of phonological information from being used in gender assignment.

3.3 General characteristics of assignment systems

Having looked at different types of assignment system in some detail it is worth taking a more distant perspective to consider gender assignment systems as a whole.

3.3.1 *Overt and covert gender*

Languages in which the gender of a noun is evident from its form are often described as having 'overt' gender; those where gender is not shown by the form of the noun have 'covert' gender. Clearly, then, languages with formal assignment systems are those with overt gender. However, the distinction is much less rigid than is often implied. There are many possibilities between the poles of absolutely overt and absolutely covert. A language with an ideal overt system would have a marker for gender on every noun, with only one marker per gender (for example, all masculine nouns end in -*o*, all feminine in -*a*). This would be true whether or not gender could be predicted from semantics.

Of the languages we have examined, Russian has moderately overt gender. If a noun ends in -*o* it is normally neuter, if it ends in -*a* it is usually feminine (but there are exceptions, like *djadja* 'uncle'). However, if a noun ends in a consonant it may be masculine or feminine. Yet this holds only for the nominative case; in the oblique cases it is more difficult to tell the gender from a single form, as table 3.3 shows. In fact the paradigm is required, hence we are dealing with a morphological system. Swahili has a more overt system than Russian. The form of a noun generally indicates its gender; there are numerous exceptions, but there is no complication of oblique cases.

When we turn to languages with phonological systems, we see that Godie has a remarkably overt system, the final vowel almost always indicating gender. There are, however, several possible vowels for each gender, though they are related in terms of place of articulation. Qafar stands out in terms of consistency. Certainly the gender of nouns whose gender is semantically determined can almost always be deduced just from their shape, just like those outside the range of the semantic rules. In comparison, however, French gender is much less overt. There are rules by which gender can be deduced from form, as we saw, but these are so numerous and complicated that French ranks low on the overt scale. At the bottom of the scale, with covert gender, are languages like English, with semantic assignment and with almost no formal clues. Even here gender is not absolutely covert (thus nouns ending in -*woman* are feminine), but the proportion of cases is small, so that English may be justifiably said to have covert gender. The question of overt and covert gender is taken further in section 5.2.2.

3.3.2 *Overlapping of assignment criteria*

Given that we have seen purely semantic assignment systems (as in Tamil), it is natural to ask whether purely formal gender assignment systems exist. Such a system would be one, say, in which all nouns which were vowel-initial took one type of agreement, while all consonant-initial nouns took another. For a system to be exclusively formal, there would also be no correlation between the genders established in this way and semantics: the distribution of the nouns across the genders would be completely random as far as their meaning was concerned. Such a system is not found in any natural language: gender always has a basis in semantics. Furthermore, when semantic and formal criteria are both involved in gender assignment, they always overlap to some extent. To envisage a system in which this was not the case, imagine a language in which the initial phoneme of the noun is significant. Suppose that in one gender we find nouns denoting male humans, together with members of the semantic residue (non-human in this language) which are vowel-initial. In the second gender are nouns denoting females and those in the semantic residue which are consonant-initial. If the two criteria

Table 3.10 *Non-attested system of conflicting assignment rules*

Gender	Criterion
masculine	1. male human (all consonant-initial)
	2. non-human, vowel-initial
feminine	1. female human (all vowel-initial)
	2. non-human, consonant-initial

were completely out of step, we would find that nouns denoting male humans were consonant-initial, and those denoting females were vowel-initial, as summarized in table 3.10. Systems like that presented in table 3.10 are not found. Though different assignment rules (semantic and formal) may conflict for many nouns, they nevertheless always show considerable overlap. In our fictitious language, if nouns denoting male humans and vowel-initial nouns were in the same gender, then we would expect a substantial proportion of the nouns denoting male humans to be vowel-initial.

The way in which different assignment criteria overlap has in fact been a recurring theme of this chapter. Even in a language like Tamil, where semantic criteria are sufficient for gender assignment, there are overlapping mor- phological factors: certain suffixes correlate with particular genders. In Halkomelem, diminutives have distinctive morphology as well as distinctive meaning and are all feminine. Russian has many nouns whose meaning, morphology and phonology all point to the same gender, while in Qafar, meaning, accent and final vowel (-*o* and -*e*) can all assign the same gender. It is worth asking how such cases of overlapping arise. Certainly a major route is derivational morphology. If a single suffix which has a fairly general meaning (such as 'agent', 'diminutive') becomes widely productive and imposes its gender on derived forms, this will lead to a situation in which many nouns have similar meaning, morphology, phonology and the same gender. For example, the Russian suffix -*ost'* forms abstract nouns from adjectives, thus *starost'* 'old age' from *staryj* 'old'. There are over 4,000 such forms; they all belong to declension III and are of feminine gender. Overlapping means that it is sometimes difficult to say which type of assignment system we are dealing with (as in the case of Yimas, section 3.2.4). While it may be possible to show that for nouns of a particular type one type of assignment rule takes precedence, and so is generally of greater importance than the others, it does not follow that the less important predictors of gender have no role. They no doubt have the effect of reinforcing the main rules and so of contributing to the stability of the particular system.

With the problem of overlapping in mind, it is worth comparing some of the languages covered in chapter 2 with those dealt with in this. Consider again Ojibwa (section 2.2.4). In Ojibwa and in other Algonquian languages we find animate and inanimate genders, with semantic assignment covering a large proportion of the nouns. The number of nouns not accounted for by the semantic rule is open to question but it seems clear that in synchronic terms there is at least a small group of nouns which are of animate gender though this is not motivated by their semantics. For this reason these languages were included in the 'predominantly semantic' section. Now animacy also has morphological repercussions. In Ojibwa, and in most other Algonquian languages, the plural form of a noun depends on animacy. In Algonquian languages, given the full morphology of a noun, one can predict whether it belongs to the animate or inanimate gender without exception and therefore with a higher degree of success than is possible given the meaning (Ives Goddard, personal communication). This being so, why were Ojibwa and the other Algonquian languages not treated as having morphological assignment systems? (I believe that the situation is somewhat similar in Ket, and that the same argument as that to be given for Algonquian would apply.) It is clear that lexical entries must include information as to meaning and phonological form; claims that they include other elements require justification (see Lyons (1977: 512–20) for discussion of the form of lexical entries). For nouns in Ojibwa, the meaning is sufficient to predict the grammatical gender and the morphology. Some nouns require an exceptional feature indicating that they are animate in terms of their gender and morphology, even though this would not be predicted from their meaning. Thus we have semantic assignment rules, and some nouns marked as exceptional. If we were to treat Ojibwa as having morphological assignment, then the declensional type of each noun would have to be indicated in the lexicon (by a morphological feature). The assignment rule would apply without exception, but the morphological feature would be redundant for almost every noun. Furthermore, we would fail to capture the obvious generalization that it is typically nouns of a particular semantic class (the animates) which belong to the animate gender and have the corresponding morphology. The crucial difference between Algonquian languages (and Ket) and languages like Russian is that in the former the number of paradigms matches the number of genders. Given the gender of an Algonquian noun, its morphology is also known. But this is not the case in Russian. Even if we know the gender of a Russian noun, we cannot predict its declension with certainty. Declensional type must be included in the lexical entries of Russian nouns and it therefore makes sense to claim that gender specification can be derived from it (similar arguments apply to other Indo-European languages and to Bantu languages like Swahili). It does not follow that sets of nouns assigned to gender by morphological rules are totally arbitrary in terms of semantics. Even here semantic clusters can be found – another example of the overlapping of criteria. (Rumanian is an interesting example; gender can generally be predicted from morphology, from the singular and plural form of the noun (Luxt 1970: 90–6); however, there are also semantic groups within the inanimates (Perkowski & Vrabie 1986).)

3.3.3 *Problematic nouns*

We have taken the view that the gender of nouns is normally predictable, on the basis of information which the speaker must in any case store in the lexicon. In some languages it is possible to derive the gender of a noun just from semantics, or just from semantic and phonological information. Some other languages require morphological information to be stored in the lexicon, and this information may help to assign gender. In this way we do not need to claim that gender languages are radically different from non-gender languages; they do not require an extra feature in the entry of every noun.

While we concentrated on rules which cover large numbers of nouns, we also came across various nouns whose gender is not that predicted by the regular assignment rules. While there may be interesting historical explanations for such exceptions, in synchronic terms they must simply be labelled as exceptions. As already discussed, provided they are relatively few in number, they do not vitiate the analysis. Thus Qafar has the noun *doònik* 'sailboat', which 'ought' to be masculine yet is feminine, and must be labelled as an isolated exception. Then there are cases where small numbers of nouns are exceptional in that they appear to change their gender when they change number (for example, they are masculine in the singular but feminine in the plural). Such cases are considered in section 6.4.3.

There are, however, nouns which do not fit into gender systems in a straightforward way, which are relevant to assignment systems and which are not isolated exceptions. These are of greater interest, and two different types will be considered in turn.

3.3.3.1 Hybrids

When different assignment rules conflict, normally the semantic rule takes precedence. Russian *djadja* 'uncle' is masculine according to the semantic rule but feminine according to the morphological rule. In fact it is fully masculine: all agreements are unambiguously masculine. But we also noted nouns like *vrač* 'doctor', which can denote a man or a woman. When denoting a woman, the assignment rules again conflict (the semantic rule would assign feminine gender, and the morphological, masculine), but with these nouns there is not a clear-cut result. Both masculine and feminine agreements are found. Another example is German *Mädchen* 'girl', feminine according to meaning but neuter because of the diminutive suffix *-chen*. Again this noun does not belong to a single gender since it takes the pronouns *sie* 'she' and *es* 'it'. Such examples will be discussed further in section 6.4.5.2.

They prove extremely valuable for investigating agreement systems, as shown in chapter 8.

3.3.3.2 Double- and multiple-gender nouns

We move to nouns which appear to belong fully to two separate genders. First we must exclude homonyms, like Italian *porta* (masculine) 'harbour' and *porta* (feminine) 'door'. Here we merely have two lexical items, which share the same phonological form. We must also exclude 'motion' nouns like Spanish *hijo* 'son' and *hija* 'daughter'. Here, quite clearly, we have two separate nouns, sharing a similar stem but with different inflections. These would be assigned to different genders by their semantics (and redundantly by their morphology). Then there are nouns of unstable gender. The same noun may take agreements of more than one gender, with no difference in meaning. Variation is more likely to be between speakers than within individual idiolects. Such instability is particularly common in recent borrowings where certain borrowed words are not unambiguously covered by the assignment rules (borrowing will be covered in section 4.1). Examples also arise during changes in gender systems.

There are, however, nouns which belong to two (or more) genders, which are fully stable, and for which the different genders are directly attributable to the difference in meaning. Thus the Archi word *lo* can be in gender I meaning 'boy', in gender II meaning 'girl' or in gender IV meaning 'young (of animal)' (a further complication is considered in section 7.3.2). Such nouns (usually when the choice is only masculine or feminine) are often said to be of 'common gender'. However these are to be handled in the lexicon, the important point for our present purposes is that the difference in gender results from different semantic assignments. These nouns are considered further in section 6.4.5.1.

3.3.3.3 Epicenes

Epicene nouns are not problematic as far as assignment systems are concerned. But they are sufficiently close to our topic to merit brief discussion. Epicene is sometimes used loosely as a synonym for nouns of common gender, which we have just discussed. But traditional usage distinguished common and epicene. Common nouns take two different sets of agreement forms, epicene nouns take only one, though they denote beings of either sex. In standard Russian, *kit* 'whale' may denote a male or a female whale, but it takes masculine agreement in either case; *akula* 'shark' is similarly feminine. Male and female individuals can be specified by circumlocution. Epicenes normally denote non-humans, though a few denote

67

humans, like Russian *osoba* 'person', which is feminine. Epicene nouns are therefore those which denote sexed beings but which do not differentiate them according to sex, in a given language. They are below the threshold of sex-differentiability. This threshold varies from language to language. In many languages, for example in Archi, only nouns denoting humans take their gender according to sex. But in others, notably in Indo-European languages, many nouns denoting animals distinguish sex. There may be two unrelated nouns, as in Russian *byk* 'bull' and *korova* 'cow', or they may be morphologically related, for example, *lev* 'lion', *l'vica* 'lioness'. As stated in section 3.1.1, the existence of two forms, whether related or not, may result either from their importance to man (in the case of domesticated animals), or from obvious physical differences (as with lions). When neither factor obtains, a single noun may be used, as with *kit* 'whale'. The existence of two separate nouns or of just one is a matter of lexis and morphology, not a matter of gender. In both cases – where two nouns are found and when there is a single epicene noun – the normal assignment rules are adequate. The epicene nouns *kit* 'whale' and *akula* 'shark' belong to declensions I and II and so are masculine and feminine respectively. For *lev* 'lion' and *byk* 'bull' sex is a relevant factor; they denote males and are therefore masculine (in addition they both belong to declension I and so would be expected to be masculine). *L'vica* 'lioness' and *korova* 'cow' both denote females, hence they are feminine by the semantic assignment rule (they also belong to declension II, and so they would be feminine by the morphological assignment rule).

3.4 Conclusion

We have seen that nouns may be assigned to genders according to semantic factors or according to a combination of semantic and formal (morphological and phonological) factors. While in some languages the rules are straightforward, in others they appear much less so. Nevertheless, in those languages which have been studied in depth, the gender of at least 85 per cent of the nouns can be predicted from information required independently in the lexicon. There may be considerable overlapping of factors, which makes it difficult to establish whether all or only some of the observed regularities are part of native speakers' assignment systems. Elucidating this problem will require careful research by linguists and psycholinguists. But it will have important consequences both for linguistic theory, in deepening our understanding of the structure of the lexicon, and for the practical business of teaching and learning foreign languages.

The type of assignment system found in a particular language naturally has consequences for the other components of the gender system. If there are conflicting factors at work, semantic factors usually take precedence. But the conflict may produce 'hybrid' nouns, whose interesting agreement patterns will be discussed in chapter 8. And the type of assignment system determines to some extent the gender resolution system (chapter 9). First, however, let us consider the evidence as to the psychological validity of the assignment systems we have analysed.

4

The psycholinguistic status of gender assignment

In chapters 2 and 3 we examined data from a wide range of languages and established a typology of gender systems, based on the type of criteria by which nouns are allotted to genders. We also saw that there can be considerable overlaps; a noun may be, say, feminine because of its meaning, morphology and phonology. The question then arises as to which factors are actually used by native speakers. We must therefore ask what is the evidence for the psychological reality of the gender assignment systems discussed. The major evidence is, of course, the data already presented. Given the massive regularities established, and the ease with which native speakers use gender, the most plausible explanation is that speakers assign nouns to genders without difficulty simply by taking advantage of these regularities. We now turn to other facts which help confirm that assignment rules are indeed part of the native speaker's competence and not just regularities observed by linguists. The first type of evidence is provided by borrowings (section 4.1); as new nouns are borrowed into a language they must be given a gender and this allows us to see the assignment rules operating on material which is sometimes unlike that of the native vocabulary. Then we should consider how children acquire gender (section 4.2), as they may learn parts of the system before others and so confirm that there are separate factors at work. We can also obtain data from psycholinguistic experiments, the most obvious of which involve the use of artificial nouns (section 4.3). The area links to the investigation of the 'residual meaning' of gender for nouns whose gender appears not to be semantically motivated (section 4.4). And finally, in section 4.5, we consider change in assignment systems as a source of insight into their structure.

4.1 Borrowings

The processes by which words are borrowed into a language and integrated into the word-stock are complex, as an impressive case study by Poplack, Sankoff & Miller (1988) shows. Our particular interest is in the borrowings of nouns into languages with gender systems. Such instances are like a continuously running experiment, which allows us to verify the assignment system in the languages in question. There is a vast literature on the gender of borrowings; unfortunately part of it is of little value, since some writers try to explain the gender of individual words, using a wide variety of possible causes, without relating them to an overall system. The simplest hypothesis would be that borrowings (or 'loanwords') will be assigned to a gender by the normal assignment rules and that they are therefore like any other nouns. It is certainly true that borrowings provide a great deal of confirming evidence for the assignment systems we have described, and we shall review this evidence next (section 4.1.1). Then we shall consider whether there are solid grounds for postulating any additional mechanisms which apply only to the assignment of borrowings and not to that of native words (section 4.1.2).

4.1.1 *Assignment of borrowings by normal rules*

If we look first at strict semantic systems, we find a straightforward picture. Given the meaning of a loanword in Tamil for example, its gender can always be predicted, according to the rules for native words (Asher 1985: 137); *daakṭar* 'doctor' denotes a human and so is masculine or feminine according to the sex of the referent, while *kaaru* 'car' is neuter, since it does not denote a human (A. Pavanantham, personal communication). Similarly in Telugu *maeSTaaru* 'male teacher' is masculine, *Tiicaru* 'female teacher' is feminine, while *bulDaag* 'bulldog', *bassu* 'bus' and *skuulu* 'school' are neuter (Malathi Rao, personal communication). Thus in these languages loanwords are treated just like native words. In languages with predominantly semantic systems, too, the semantic rules operate as expected. Loans into Dyirbal almost all take the gender which would be predicted: 'white man' – gender I, 'white woman' – gender II, 'flour', 'cake' – gender III (the gender for non-flesh food). A nice example is provided by the word *babuligan*; in the meaning 'publican' it is gender I, but in the meaning 'pub' it is gender IV, (R. M. W. Dixon, personal communication). Most other loans are in gender IV but *mani* 'money', a completely new concept, was unpredictably assigned to gender I. There are also cases illustrating the principle of concept association: matches and pipe are associated with fire and so are assigned to gender II. In semantic systems the form of the loan is irrelevant, as illustrated by the fact that speakers of Northern Cheyenne can assign gender simply on the basis of the referent (Straus & Brightman 1982: 100).

In the case of formal systems, semantic assignment still applies for nouns

71

which are covered by the semantic rules. Thus in Russian, *ledi* 'lady' is feminine, even though it does not follow either of the typical feminine declensions (in fact it is indeclinable) and similarly *attaše* 'attaché' is masculine. It is the nouns not covered by the semantic rules which are of particular interest. In morphological systems, like that of Russian, the loanword must be accommodated within the morphological pattern of the language. Its gender then follows from its morphology. In some instances the noun fits easily into one of the declensional types: *komp'juter* 'computer' can readily be declined as type I and so is masculine; *Panama* 'Panama (hat)' declines as type II and so is feminine. In some cases there is an established pattern of adjustment: borrowings in *-ation* take *-acija* in its place, for example, *racionalizacija* 'rationalization'. Nouns in *-acija* follow declensional type II and are feminine. Yet others do not fit into any of the declensional types and so remain indeclinable, for example, *taksi* 'taxi' (which is neuter, as it is indeclinable and denotes an inanimate). The data from borrowings confirm the previous picture: for sex-differentiable nouns, semantic considerations determine gender; otherwise morphological information is required for assignment of nouns to a gender. Some loanwords may be assigned to one of the regular declensional types and their gender then follows automatically. However, the phonological form of some borrowings means that they do not fit into any declensional type and so remain indeclinable. In such instances (non-human) animates are masculine and inanimates are neuter. (See Wissemann (1966) for helpful discussion of some apparent exceptions.)

The other morphological assignment system which we analysed in some detail was that of Swahili. Swahili does not show the many-membered nominal paradigms of Russian, but nouns show different prefixal elements for singular and plural. In a study of loanwords in Swahili, Whiteley (1967) found that the majority of nouns not denoting animates are assigned to genders 9/10 and 5/6. The reason for these choices is that morphological classes 9/10 and 5/6 are precisely the ones which include nouns with no prefix in the singular. Thus foreign words can be fitted into particular morphological classes and as a consequence they are assigned to genders 9/10 and 5/6. In some cases the initial segment of the borrowed word matches a prefix and the noun may enter the appropriate morphological class. Thus *kiplefiti* 'roundabout' (English *keep left*) may be taken to have the prefix *ki-*; the plural is then *viplefiti*, as is normal for morphological class 7/8, and it takes gender 7/8 (Whiteley 1967: 170). This confirms the view adopted earlier that Swahili, and indeed other Bantu languages, have an assignment system based on morphological criteria. While the system may have been a purely semantic one at some earlier time, this is no longer the case. It should be noted that there are considerable numbers of loans entering Swahili and the fact that certain genders, for morphological reasons, attract more than their share of loanwords may lead to imbalances in the system if those genders reach a position of numerical dominance over the others. Further examples of borrowings, including those from earlier periods, can be found in Hinnebusch (1979: 274–7) and Zawawi (1979).

The situation is simpler in Nkore-Kiga (a Bantu language with a million speakers in south-west Uganda). Since borrowed words do not have the required prefixes to fit directly into the morphological system, they are treated morphologically like non-prefixed native words made into nouns. As a result, those denoting humans (such as *gavana* 'governor') are assigned to gender 1/2, while others like *baasi* 'bus' enter gender 9/10 (Taylor 1985: 122–5). Haya also takes borrowings primarily into gender 9/10; but when nouns are borrowed from Swahili, they retain their prefixes and so go into the corresponding morphological class and take the appropriate gender (Byarushengo 1976: 80–2). In a study of over 300 English loans into Kikuyu, a Bantu language of Kenya, Kutik (1983) found that 80 per cent of the nouns were assigned to gender 9/10 (whose nouns have no prefix). Nouns denoting humans are assigned to gender 1/2 (though not all are in morphological class 1/2). But there are also instances of borrowings gaining the same prefixes as nouns of similar meaning, and hence the same gender. In others the initial sequence (sometimes modified to meet the constraints of Kikuyu syllable structure) is interpreted as a prefix and assignment follows the usual morphological rule. (This is more likely to occur if the noun would thereby enter a morphological class which would also be semantically appropriate.) The favoured status of gender 9/10 in Kikuyu is confirmed by Žurinskij (1987: 181): of 343 loans, not just from English, 73 per cent entered gender 9/10, which had only 30 per cent of the native nouns. He found a comparable imbalance in Zulu; of 575 recent loans, 63 per cent were taken into gender 5/6, which had only 20 per cent of the native nouns. As in Swahili, there is a strong possibility that borrowings will change the gender system dramatically in these languages. For further discussion of the assignment of loanwords more widely in Bantu see Richardson (1967), Luckov (1987) and the references in Whiteley (1967).

While there has been a considerable amount of work on borrowings into the languages of the Niger-Congo branch of Niger-Kordofanian, there has been little on borrowings in the Kordofanian languages; however, Faris reports on the Southeastern Nuba language (Koalib-Moro group within Kordofanian). This language is spoken by something under 2,500 people in the south-eastern corner of Kordofan in the Sudan. According to Faris (1978), it has thirteen main genders and both semantic and morphological factors are involved in the assignment of loanwords to them.

Having considered semantic and morphological systems, we naturally move on to phonological systems. The phonological system whose gender assignment of borrowings has been most extensively studied is French (for a survey of work see Desrochers 1986: 244–6). Semantic factors take precedence: nouns denoting humans take gender according to sex: *speaker* 'announcer' is masculine (it has a derived form *speakerine* for female referents). For non-humans, there is clear evidence for the operation of phonological assignment rules; for example, the English loan *budget* [bydʒɛ] ends in ɛ and so is masculine (see section 3.2.5), while *fission* [fisjɔ̃] is feminine since it ends in -*sjɔ̃*. For data on the assignment of Flemish loans into Brussels French see Beardsmore (1971). There is also some information on loanwords in Vata (Kaye 1981: 128–9); in this simple phonological system, similar to that of Godie (section 3.2.3), it is quite clear that the gender of loanwords is determined in a relatively straightforward way by their phonological shape. Thus *dùté* 'tea', from French *du thé*, takes the pronoun which is closest phonologically, namely, ɛ, as does *klè* 'hat', a word borrowed from Baule. Similarly the Baule borrowings *sĭkà* 'gold' and *jià* 'lion' take *a*. An interesting situation is found in Qafar (section 3.2.1). In this language, nouns which end in an accented vowel (which may be analysed as having no accent but gaining final high tone by a general rule) are feminine, while others are masculine. A secondary regularity is that nouns ending in -*e* and -*o* are feminine; nouns in -*a* are more often feminine than masculine. If we examine borrowings, we find that when accepting nouns from languages which have different accent systems from its own tonal accent system, Qafar cannot utilize the stress placement in the donor languages. It nevertheless retains phonological assignment. First, nouns ending in a consonant are masculine, according to its normal rule, for example, *tamaàtim* 'tomato' (from one of the Semitic languages of Ethiopia which have the form *timatim*). With other types of noun, the secondary regularity just mentioned comes into play: thus nouns in -*e*, -*o* and -*a* are made feminine: *kamadoorò* (from Italian *pomodóro*) 'tomato' and *gommà* (from Italian *gómma*) 'rubber tyre' (R. J. Hayward, personal communication).

So far we have seen that the behaviour of loanwords confirms the typology of assignment systems we have already established. Loanwords are assigned to a gender according to meaning or form, depending on the assignment system of the borrowing language. This suggests that the gender of loanwords is determined exactly like that of other nouns. In the overwhelming majority of cases this is certainly so, and much more confirming evidence is available.

However, in the literature several other factors are proposed which, it is claimed, relate specifically to loanwords.

4.1.2 *Claims for special assignment rules*

Several claims that borrowings gain their gender in a special way are at best not proven, since the investigators fail to demonstrate that the ordinary assignment rules would not give the correct result. But some of the factors proposed deserve serious attention. A review of factors claimed to influence gender assignment and relevant references is given in Poplack, Pousada & Sankoff (1982: 5–6). They too are critical of much of the earlier work. For their own study they examined *all* the English loanwords found in two corpora of spontaneous speech, one of Puerto Rican Spanish and the other of Montreal French. They found, as we would expect, that nouns with animate referents took gender according to sex, and that for others, phonological rules had a role. The interesting additional factor is the assignment of gender by *semantic analogy*, according to which the loanword takes the gender of a noun of similar meaning already in the language. As an example of the operation of this factor, they suggest that the borrowed noun *butterfly* is feminine in Puerto Rican Spanish at least in part because *la mariposa* 'butterfly' is feminine. They claim that phonological rules and semantic analogy have an independent effect (1982: 20) and that the competition between them means that the outcome in particular cases cannot be predicted; hence there is a degree of indeterminacy in the assignment of loanwords. There may be a period during which the gender of a loanword is unstable. A dramatic example is provided by Wełna (1978), who considers the conflicting factors involved in the assignment of some fifty loanwords from Latin and Old Icelandic into Old English; these loanwords had at least two genders, while some had three. And in a study of American Norwegian, Haugen (1969: 442) found that of 317 borrowed nouns 59 (18.7 per cent) showed more than one gender. According to Poplack & Sankoff (1984: 124), instability is a transitory stage. As the frequency of a loanword and its degree of phonological integration increase, so its gender tends to stabilize (see also Barkin 1980; and Poplack, Sankoff & Miller 1988: 65–7).

The factor under discussion, semantic analogy, has been put forward by various researchers (for example Wełna 1976: 97–101, 1980: 401–11; Bynon 1977: 230–1). Kibrik, Kodzasov, Olovjannikova & Samedov (1977: 62) claim that it operates in Archi, which is a language with a predominantly semantic system but with various unclear cases of assignment in genders III and IV (section 2.2.5). For example, *t'eǩ'on* 'needle' is in gender III, which is surprising since most tools are in gender IV. It is suggested that *išpric* 'syringe' (from Russian *špric*) is in gender III by semantic analogy with *t'ek'on*. Semantic analogy is also claimed to operate in languages with morphological assignment systems. English *mud* has become Polish *mada* 'mud, silt' (feminine). There is no obvious reason why it should not have been *mad* (masculine); indeed, 88 per cent of the 681 English loans investigated became masculine. Fisiak (1975: 62) claims that the form *mada* is due to Polish *gleba* 'soil'. *Gleba* belongs to a declensional type whose members are predominantly feminine; *mada* is given the same declension and so acquires the same gender as *gleba*. In a study of foreign words in Russian, another language with morphological assignment, Gimpelevič (1982) examines the difference between borrowings which occupy a previously vacant semantic slot and exotic words, used to denote foreign *realia*. The former type, which are more fully integrated, have gender assigned according to the rules given earlier, with extremely few exceptions. Exotic words, on the other hand, may have variable gender, often taking gender by semantic analogy; for example, *avenju* 'avenue' can be feminine, by semantic analogy with *ulica* 'street', which is feminine, or it can be neuter, following the general rule for indeclinables which denote inanimates. A further claim that semantic analogy is a factor in the assignment of loanwords, in this case of English loans into German, is made by Gregor (1983: 59).

We have already discussed semantic analogy in a language with a phonological assignment system, namely Spanish. In addition, Surridge (1982; 1984) presents evidence suggesting semantic analogy affects the assignment of English loanwords in the French of France and in Canadian French. Convincing examples of semantic analogy are contained in Gouffé's investigation of nearly 500 borrowings from French into Hausa as spoken in Niger (Gouffé 1971). Hausa, it will be recalled from section 3.2.2, has two genders: apart from sex-differentiable nouns, it is generally the case that those ending in *-aa* are feminine and others are masculine. It is a particularly good case to study since the phonological rule is so straightforward; this means that the predictions as to the gender of loans are clear-cut. Given the varied possibilities for final phonemes in French, we would expect that the overwhelming majority of loans (apart from those denoting humans) would be masculine. This is indeed the case; there are numerous examples like *bùroò* 'office' (< *bureau*), *kàsàroolì* 'saucepan' (< *casserole*), *làakìleè* 'key' (< *la clé*), all masculine. There are many fewer examples of feminines: *càakòolaà* 'chocolate' (< *chocolat*), *màtàlaà* 'mattress' (< *matelas*). There are also some borrowings which are assigned to the feminine gender, even though they do not end in *-aa*. For a substantial proportion of these, Gouffé suggests semantic analogies, which appear well justified. For example, we find *kaṙ* 'coach' (<

car), *tàkàsìì* 'taxi' (< *taxi*) and similar nouns are in the feminine gender in spite of the phonological rule. It is claimed that these are feminine by analogy with *mootàa* 'car'. (This is itself a borrowing from English and is feminine by the regular phonological rule.) The semantic analogy argument is strengthened by the following doublet: *pèežoò* 'Peugeot' is masculine (as expected) in the meaning 'Peugeot bicycle'. It can also mean 'Peugeot car', in which case it is feminine, because of the analogy of *mootàa* 'car'.

The semantic analogy factor should be treated carefully; as Wissemann (1966) points out, it may prevent the investigator discovering more general principles which cover larger numbers of nouns. Nevertheless, there is some evidence in favour of semantic analogy as a factor in the gender assignment of loanwords. Its effect will be to make the gender system 'more semantic' than it was before the period of borrowing. It can be argued, however, that this is not after all a factor specific to borrowings but is equivalent to 'concept association'. We met concept association, which operates for native words as well as borrowings, in our discussion of Dyirbal (section 2.2.2). We saw how, for example, 'fishing spear' could take the same gender as 'fish' because of the close association of the two concepts. There are great similarities between concept association and semantic analogy, but there is the problem that semantic analogy has been suggested as a factor which operates for loanwords in languages in which the assignment of native words can be accounted for without appealing to concept association. We have seen, however, that in languages where formal rules cover a large proportion of the nouns, there may still be secondary semantic groupings, that is, clusters of nouns of related meaning and with the same gender (see the end of section 3.3.2, where Rumanian was mentioned, and the account of German in section 4.2 below: this general point is also supported by the data presented in section 4.4). This phenomenon may also be seen as concept association. I suggest therefore that semantic analogy/concept association is always potentially available, for native and borrowed nouns. In some languages it is not powerful enough to produce any assignments out of line with the normal rules and so gives no direct evidence for its presence. In certain other languages it may be observed only in the case of borrowings, particularly when the assignment rules give unclear predictions. Examples of its diachronic effect in various Indo-European languages can be found in Shields (1979: 32–3), who draws particularly on earlier work by Malkiel. Thus semantic analogy is identical to concept association.

Poplack, Pousada & Sankoff (1982: 21–3) consider a further factor which, if accepted, would apply to the assignment of borrowings only, namely the idea that loans may be assigned to the unmarked gender, which in this context

Table 4.1 *The distribution of nouns in Russian by gender*

	Masculine (%)	Feminine (%)	Neuter (%)	Total
Overall share	46	41	13	33,952
Soviet neologisms (Mučnik)	57	33	10	869
Loans (Superanskaja)	58	37	5	4,750
Loans from German (Martysiuk)	78.5	21.3	0.2	497

is generally taken to be the one with the largest number of nouns in it. They are rightly sceptical. If one gender has more members than the other(s), this suggests that the assignment rules are slanted in its favour. It would not be surprising, therefore, to find that it acquired the lion's share of loanwords by the normal operation of these assignment rules. This point can be illustrated from statistical data on the gender system of Russian, presented in table 4.1. The first set of figures shows the share each gender has of the nouns of Modern Russian, as derived from dictionaries; the second shows the relative shares of words which have appeared since the Revolution (both from Mučnik 1971: 196–7). The masculine and feminine genders have substantially more nouns than the neuter. Data on neologisms show that the tide is running in favour of the masculine gender and against the neuter; indeed, it appears that in the long term the neuter gender is likely to be lost (Schupbach 1984: 31–2, 82–3; see also this volume, section 10.2.3). Superanskaja (1965: 47) examines a large corpus of loanwords and again the masculine is favoured. When we then look at data on 497 borrowings just from German (calculated from figures in Martysiuk 1970), we might be tempted to suggest that these borrowings tend to go into the unmarked gender. The explanation is simpler, however. A large proportion of German nouns end in a consonant; they are assigned to declensional type I, and hence to the masculine gender. Examples are given in table 4.2. This pattern of borrowing can be explained in terms of the normal assignment rules of Russian, without appeal to the extra criterion of assignment to the unmarked gender. And the difference in the assignment

Table 4.2 *Loans entering the masculine gender in Russian*

German noun	Gender	Russian noun	Gender	Gloss
Kran	masculine	kran	masculine	tap, crane
Fackel	feminine	fakel	masculine	torch
Butterbrot	neuter	buterbrod	masculine	sandwich

of German loans and others results from differences in the typical phonological structures of nouns in the source languages.

In an interesting study of loanword assignment in some of the Togo Remnant languages Heine (1968a) proposes another factor: 'automatic' assignment. There are fourteen Togo Remnant languages spoken in Eastern Ghana, Togoland and Dahomey; they belong to the Niger-Congo family, though their precise place within it is not clear. They have taken large numbers of loans from Ewe and Twi and, through them, from West European languages. Most of the Togo Remnant languages have several morphological classes of nouns. In five of the languages examined, all spoken in Ghana, Heine found different strategies for dealing with loanwords. Lelemi, spoken in the Volta Region, has been analysed as having eleven genders (but see section 6.4.3). Loans are assigned according to the semantic principle: animates are assigned to gender I and inanimates to II. The present tendency is for loans not to take prefixes: they remain uninflected. For example, *téla* 'tailor' (plural also *téla*) is in gender I, while *wáci* 'watch(es)' is in gender II. In both Bowili (Volta Region) and Likpe (Togolese border area) loans denoting animates are assigned to gender I. As in Lelemi, inanimates are generally assigned to gender II. However, if their initial segment resembles one of the nominal prefixes, the loanword may be analysed as morphologically complex and may accordingly be assigned to a morphological class and hence to the appropriate gender. Thus Ewe *afɔkpa* 'shoe' becomes Likpe *a-fokpá* 'shoes', in which *a-* is the plural prefix of morphological class III. The singular in Likpe is *le-fokpá* and the noun belongs to gender III. So far, the Togo Remnant languages provide interesting confirmation of the claim made earlier, that loanwords are assigned according to regular criteria (semantic and morphological in these cases). However, in two more of them, Nyangbo (eastern Ghana) and Santrokofi (Volta Region), Heine claims that there is a different factor at work, namely 'automatic' assignment. By this he means that loanwords are allocated to a particular gender simply by virtue of their being loanwords. On general theoretical grounds we should be unwilling to accept this factor, since it involves unnecessary duplication. In order for automatic assignment to operate, loanwords would have to be identified as loanwords. Whatever it was that identified them (their morphology or phonology), this information, which is necessary in any case, could equally well provide the means for allocating them to a gender. And this certainly appears to be the case here. In both languages, borrowings are assigned primarily to gender I, and in both languages gender I includes nouns with no nominal prefix. Thus borrowings are interpreted as having no prefix (even if their initial segment resembles a native prefix) and are thus assigned (by what is in our terms a morphological principle) to the morphological class with no prefix in the singular. Being in morphological class I they are therefore in gender I. In both languages these borrowings have had a considerable effect on the semantics of the gender system, since gender I previously had in it only nouns denoting animates but now it includes inanimates. The interesting differences in the allocation of loanwords in these related languages can therefore be seen mainly as a consequence of the way in which loans are treated in terms of morphology: initial segments may or may not be reinterpreted as native prefixes; native prefixes may or may not be added. We are not, on the evidence given, forced to accept the notion of automatic assignment and so, of course, we should not do so.

A final factor we should consider is the gender of the noun in the donor language, which is sometimes proposed as a factor in the assignment of loanwords. At first sight we might dismiss it as unlikely except perhaps in the case of learned borrowings, where the small number of people using them is able to impose an externally valid gender (as in the case of Latin loans into Old English, Wełna 1980: 400–1). In nineteenth-century Russian we find nouns maintaining their original gender; *kašne* 'scarf, muffler', which was indeclinable and so would be expected to be neuter, was in fact masculine, since *cache-nez* is masculine in French (Mučnik 1971: 282). In contemporary Russian it is neuter, as the rules given earlier would predict (section 3.1.1). According to Thomas (1983: 196), the use of borrowings with the gender of the donor language in the nineteenth century by bilingual intellectuals represented 'deliberate codeswitching'. We should remember, however, that there are many speech communities in which a high proportion is bilingual, and it is here, if anywhere, that convincing cases are likely to be found. A promising situation in this regard is provided by Upper Sorbian, a West Slavonic language spoken in Lusatia, which is to the south-east of Berlin. Taken together with the related Lower Sorbian, the total number of speakers is around 60,000. There are no monolingual adult speakers: all are bilingual with German, though some speak Sorbian better than German. German is, not surprisingly, the main source of loanwords (in some cases it serves as an intermediary, passing on words which it has borrowed itself). Both languages have the three traditional Indo-European genders; Upper Sorbian has four main declensional types, in broad outline similar to those of Russian given in section 3.1.1 above. Thus we have speakers bilingual in languages with similar gender systems. If the gender of the noun in the donor language is to have an effect anywhere, it should do so under these ideal conditions.

At first glance it appears that the original gender does have an effect, since nouns which are masculine in German are always masculine when borrowed into Upper Sorbian (data from Fasske 1981: 402–3, 492–3). In many cases, however, this is what would in any case be expected from the normal assignment rules, either because the noun denotes a male, or because it ends in a consonant and so fits easily into the normal masculine declensional type. But this is not true of the noun *puma* 'puma', which is masculine in German and remains masculine in Upper Sorbian. This appears surprising, since it ends in -*a* and might therefore have been expected to go into the predominantly feminine declension and so be feminine (this is possible but less usual). The fact that *puma* is masculine suggests that the gender of the donor language has an effect. However, German *Zebra* 'zebra', which is neuter, is also masculine (*cebra*) in Upper Sorbian. It turns out that the gender of both *puma* and *cebra* is determined by their morphology (indeclinable in the singular) and their meaning, since both denote non-human animates. The rule is similar to that of Russian (section 3.3.1). There is no need to appeal to the noun's gender in German, and in some cases that approach gives the wrong result. Indeed, German neuters rarely preserve their gender in Upper Sorbian. German feminines, on the other hand at first do seem to support the theory of the influence of the gender in the donor language; borrowed feminines may be modified morphologically so as to follow the typical feminine declensional type and so be feminine according to the normal assignment rules. For example, *Portion* 'portion' becomes *porcija* (feminine). However, this is in the literary language. In the dialects the form is *porcijón*, which is masculine, exactly as the normal assignment rules would indicate. It appears, therefore, that even in these ideal conditions, the influence of the gender of nouns in the donor language is hard to substantiate, except when it results from a conscious effort of educated speakers (as in the literary language).

We have seen that the assignment of loanwords depends on the same types of factor as the assignment of native words, which therefore confirms our account of these factors. We considered the evidence for semantic analogy as an additional factor and concluded that it is equivalent to concept association, but that it may be more evident in loanwords than in native words, since the former may fit less readily with the main assignment rules. To substantiate a claim for the effect of any other factor believed to operate exclusively in the assignment of loanwords requires first an account of gender assignment of native words in a given language, and then the analysis of all borrowings in a set period. Only if the rules for native words do not cover all the cases is there any justification for postulating additional factors. The normal situation is one in which borrowings are assigned in essentially the same way as are native words.

Borrowings may quite rapidly be assimilated to such an extent that speakers cannot distinguish them, consciously or unconsciously, from native words. Their accumulated effect may, however, lead to considerable changes in the gender system. In Nyangbo and Santrokofi a semantically homogeneous gender (restricted to animates) has been opened up to inanimates because of its morphological properties. In Russian the expansion of the masculine and the contraction of the neuter (in terms of number of nouns) are being accelerated by the assignment of loanwords. In French in the seventeenth century the genders were evenly balanced (51 per cent of nouns were masculine). By this century, the percentage for the masculine gender has risen to 61 per cent. A major contributory factor (according to Surridge 1984) has been English loans. Of 1,432 nouns borrowed from English since the seventeenth century, 86 per cent became masculine. Thus, while borrowings are treated as far as is possible as native words, from which they may quickly become indistinguishable, they can have considerable effects on the gender system of the language which receives them.

4.2 **Child language acquisition**

Work on children's acquisition of language can be expected eventually to provide a clearer picture of how assignment systems work. However, such work depends on a basic linguistic description of the phenomena to be investigated in the speech of children, and such descriptions are often lacking. As a result, some of the work done on the acquisition of gender is disappointing; those working on Indo-European languages, for example, sometimes fail to distinguish gender from declensional type, which makes it almost impossible to interpret their results. They also tend to take a simplistic view of gender, underestimating the extent of the regularities found in gender systems. In acquiring a gender system, the child must first recognize the patterns – the fact that the occurrence of certain agreeing forms (of verbs, adjectives and so on) depends on the presence of nouns of a certain gender. The way in which such distributional patterns are learned is far from clear; it is discussed by Maratsos & Chalkley (1980) and Braine (1987). Gender is, of course, only one of these patterns. We shall concentrate here on the problem which is more specific to gender: once the patterns have been recognized and the existence of a gender system established, how does the child acquire the knowledge equivalent to that which we have modelled as assignment systems?

We would expect semantic assignment systems to be acquired relatively easily. There is unfortunately a dearth of information here. But in English, where the rule is straightforward, acquisition of gender can be late. The author has data on a boy (with two brothers and no sisters) who at age 4;2, that is four years two months, did not use *he* and *she* as in adult speech. He could distinguish males and females without difficulty, and used *he* consistently for males but sometimes also for females as well as *she*. By age 4;9 he was correcting his younger brother. More serious studies also show frequent errors in four-year-old children (Mills 1986: 100–1). Though *he* and *she* are common forms, the fact that gender is restricted to pronouns helps to explain the surprisingly late acquisition in this case. Very interestingly too, a bilingual Dutch–English child acquired those Dutch pronouns which are semantically determined before the English ones (which are not embedded in such a complex system); the acquisition of the two systems seems to be largely independent (De Houwer 1987).

Most of the work on the acquisition of gender has been on languages with morphological assignment systems. Levy's (1983) assessment of Hebrew and other data suggests that children use formal indicators for assigning gender from an early age. Berman reports that children learning Hebrew make errors with nouns whose gender is not that which would be predicted from the morphology (1985: 299–301). This could be interpreted as indicating that children have acquired the morphological assignment rules but have not learned the individual exceptions to them. She also reports (1985: 273) that gender concord appears after number concord. This order also occurs in French (Clark 1985: 699); but in Portuguese, and in Latvian, it is reported that gender distinctions are learned before number distinctions (Hooper 1980: 176–7). In work on Polish, Smoczyńska (1985: 625–6) found that feminine nouns with zero ending in the nominative singular (like *kost'* in Russian, table 3.3) cause problems. Children sometimes used a diminutive form; alternatively they declined these nouns according to the pattern found with masculines (and used masculine agreements) or made them regular feminines. Again the children had acquired the basic morphological assignment rules (as they apply for the main declensional types). What they had not acquired was the anomalous declension of one type of noun. A surprising finding is that most Polish children have acquired gender distinctions by the age of two (Smoczyńska 1985: 644–8). This is considerably earlier than Russian children, who are faced by an apparently similar system (Gvozdev 1949; Popova 1958: 106–9; Zaxarova 1958: 83). Two reasons are suggested for this later acquisition. The first is the fact that in Russian unstressed *o* and *a* are pronounced identically. This means that the child has a more difficult problem in determining the declensional type of a given noun, and of establishing its gender from agreement evidence. The second is that Russian has numerous hypocoristics like *Kolja*, which is a boy's or man's name but has the declension typical of feminines. The Polish child has clearer data as regards declension and agreement and many fewer confusing masculine nouns ending in -*a*. Work on Russian shows that, as in Polish, children have problems with the anomalous feminines. Furthermore, the formal rule may be applied to those nouns where in adult speech it is overridden by a semantic rule: thus *djadja* 'uncle', which follows the typically feminine declension but is masculine, may take feminine agreement in children's speech: *djadja sidela* (feminine) 'uncle was sitting' (Popova 1958: 109). This latter phenomenon was also found in two Czech children aged 1; 9 and 2; 10 (Henzl 1975: 193–4). Mulford (1985) investigated eighty Icelandic children aged four to eight using both ordinary and nonsense nouns. Formal information on its own in nonsense words was little help to children before the age of seven. Not surprisingly, children did best when faced with familiar words denoting humans, which also had a formal indication of gender.

Probably the fullest account of child acquisition of gender to date is Mills' study of German and English (1986). Such an investigation requires first an account of the complex gender system of German, and there has been some fine recent work in this area, notably by Kőpcke and Zubin (Zubin & Kőpcke 1981, 1984, 1986; Kőpcke 1982; Kőpcke & Zubin 1984). This work deserves study in the original since a brief account cannot do it justice. In addition to the references given, there is an extensive literature, for which see Corbett (1986). In outline (and a good summary can be found in Mills 1986: 16–35), we may say that German has semantic, morphological and phonological assignment rules. As expected, nouns denoting males and females are generally masculine and feminine respectively. But there are much smaller clusters of nouns whose meaning and gender correspond. For example, nouns denoting superordinate categories are usually neuter: *Instrument* 'instrument' (compare *Guitarre* 'guitar', feminine), *Obst* 'fruit' (compare *Apfel* 'apple', masculine), *Gemüse* 'vegetable' (compare *Erbse* 'pea', feminine); see Zubin & Kőpcke (1986: 146–9). Colour terms are normally neuter: *das Pink* 'pink', *das Orange* 'orange'. Then there are the morphological rules. As pointed out in section 3.1.3, various affixes determine the gender of a noun, and in compounds the derivational history is important. Furthermore, though this is often ignored, inflectional morphology has a considerable role. As an example, Zubin & Kőpcke (1981: 443) point out that nouns which form the plural in -(*e*)*n* are almost all feminine. Finally, there are several phonological rules. A relationship between syllabicity and gender was suggested by Arndt (1970) and this has been confirmed by Kőpcke (1982: 45). Of the 1,466 monosyllabic nouns in his corpus, 940 (64 per cent) are masculine. Evidence from loanwords confirms the link between monosyllables and masculine gender (Carstensen 1980: 21–2). Then the end of the stem may be indicative (though this could be interpreted as predicting the set of inflectional endings, which in turn would predict gender). Thus nouns ending in /ur/ and /ür/ are predominantly feminine (131 out of 141); for example, *Tür* 'door' is feminine, despite being monosyllabic. There is also, as in French, evidence that the beginning of the noun has an effect; given that monosyllables are more likely to be masculine than not, the likelihood of masculine gender is increased if the monosyllabic noun begins in /kn/, for example *Knopf* 'button' (Köpcke & Zubin 1984: 29). Normally semantic rules take precedence followed by morphological ones. It is clear that there is massive overlapping of rules: a given noun may have several factors, each of which would account for its gender. A good deal remains to be done in establishing the relative importance of different factors and the ways in which they interact; see Steinmetz (1986) for an unusual approach to the problem and Steinmetz (1985) for comparative data from Icelandic.

Let us now turn to Mills' investigation of the acquisition of German. One problem soon becomes apparent. Even though there were previous observational studies of various children, it is extremely difficult to acquire sufficient data in this way. Therefore Mills conducted several experiments to supplement the observational data. A less obvious, and perhaps more significant difficulty concerns the child's vocabulary. We may have a rule which applies to a substantial number of nouns in the language of adults, but it is implausible to suggest that the child has acquired the rule, unless several of the nouns involved have been learned. After the first few hundred words are learned it becomes difficult to maintain an accurate record of a child's vocabulary.

Consider first the main semantic rule, which is based on the sex of the referent. In spontaneous utterances German children make few errors, using appropriate gender forms of the article for human referents when as young as two. English children, as noted anecdotally earlier, may make numerous errors in production of pronouns at age four, though comprehension causes few problems (see also Chiat 1986: 390–2). Experimental work showed that German children do better at pronoun selection than English children of the same age (Mills 1986: 98–109); recall too the earlier acquisition in Dutch mentioned above. It is surprising that German children acquire this rule earlier, since it is but one of many in a complex system, while the child learning English would appear to have a simpler task in this respect. Mills suggests two reasons: first, since gender is marked on many parts of speech the German child has more opportunities to learn it; and second, there is a clear phonetic contrast between the masculine forms *er* and *der* on the one hand, and the feminine forms *sie* and *die* on the other, while *he/she/her* are less clearly differentiated. As far as non-human animates are concerned, the distinction between animate and inanimate is acquired early in both languages. However, children aged five to six still showed errors when investigated experimentally. German children sometimes avoided the neuter for nouns denoting animals, even though they were grammatically neuter. Older children had little problem. English children, however, continued to use *he* and *she* in instances when adult language requires *it*, though they consistently used *it* less frequently with animates than with inanimates. Their use of pronouns increasingly approximates to that of adults. When the basic rule is established, around age ten, children have something yet to learn, since they are still less likely to use *he* and *she* for personification in appropriate contexts than are adults (Mills 1986: 86–98).

We now turn to the formal assignment rules of German. An investigation of data from children aged 3;2–6;3 suggested that some phonological rules were being applied. More convincing evidence comes from an experiment using nonsense words with children aged seven to eight; statistically significant results were obtained for several rules. For example, the nonsense word *Knich* was made masculine in 77 per cent of the cases (most monosyllables in /kn/- are masculine). However, the first such rule to be learned is that nouns in *-e* are usually feminine; this rule affects the largest number of nouns (of which a sufficient number is found in the child's vocabulary) and it has the fewest exceptions. While several phonological rules are in place at age eight, others are still being acquired (Mills 1986: 62–85).

Perhaps the most interesting part of Mills' discussion concerns the relation between semantic and formal rules in acquisition. She claims that her German data provide no evidence to suggest that one type is acquired before the other but that they seem to run in tandem. The order of acquisition of rules will depend, according to Mills, on their relative 'clarity'; a clear rule being one with few or no exceptions, covering a large number of items (available to the child), with other functions related to it (Mills 1986: 109–16). There will therefore be differences in the order in which assignment rules are acquired in different languages (and also, perhaps, in different learners of the same language). Given the complexity of gender assignment in German, it is not surprising that our understanding of acquisition is far from complete. An interesting recent development is the attempt to model the acquisition of the gender clues discussed above using connectionist networks, presented in Taraban, McDonald & MacWhinney (1989). (The acquisition of German gender by those learning it as a second rather than as a first language also causes problems (Rogers 1987).) And indeed, the acquisition of English gender is less straightforward than might have been expected. We must hope that work will be done on languages with simpler assignment systems (such as

Tamil or Qafar) so that the number of factors to be taken into account will be made more manageable. We have now seen evidence for the acquisition of both semantic and formal rules of gender assignment. The order of acquisition is not fixed, either relative to each other or to other rules. The time at which they are acquired depends on their complexity and on the ways in which gender is reflected in the language in question.

Studies of the acquisition of morphological assignment systems outside Indo-European are just beginning: there is some work on Bantu, but researchers have worked more on the acquisition of class prefixes than on gender agreement (Demuth, Faraclas & Marchese 1986: 463–7; see also Kunene 1986 on Siswati; and Orr 1987 on Chichewa). Demuth (1988) gives useful references; her own investigation involves ninety-three hours of recordings of four children acquiring Sesotho. Despite this considerable corpus, the acquisition process is far from clear; it seems that semantic indicators have no special role, and that agreement forms are found prior to overt markers on the noun, though both appear by age three. A major difficulty is that elements which are missing in comparison with adult speech may not appear because of regular phonological rules. Thus to obtain a clear picture of the acquisition of gender, one would need an analysis of the child's phonology at each stage.

For data on the acquisition of a largely phonological system we turn to French, for which, as part of a large-scale investigation of determiners, Karmiloff-Smith included experiments involving gender (1979: 148–69). By using invented words with different phonological shapes (typically masculine, typically feminine and ambiguous), she claims to show that even the youngest children studied (aged three) took advantage of phonological clues. Most relevant for our purposes is her experiment 10, in which children were shown pictures of imaginary Martian-like persons, which they could recognize as male or female. These were referred to by the experimenter using invented words; in some cases the phonological clue provided by the form of the word clashed with the semantic clue of the picture (for example, the picture showed two female figures, which were described as *deux bicrons*, where *bicron* is an invented word with a typically masculine form). Up to the age of nine, the phonological clue provided by the last syllable of the word tended to outweigh the semantic clue in the picture. This strategy, applied to adult French, gives the right answer most of the time since, though semantic rules take precedence, there are relatively few words where the semantic rule overrides a conflicting phonological one.

Karmiloff-Smith was primarily interested in the gender of the article and the statistics she gives relate to this. However, other data provided reveal that children under six tended to treat nouns with conflicting clues as 'hybrids' (see section 6.4.5.2): agreement within the noun phrase was based on the phonological criterion, while that outside it was semantic. The following example is taken from a child aged 5;7 (Karmiloff-Smith 1979: 164):

(1) Bon, y   avait une fois un   bicron vert   et
Well, there was once   a.MASC bicron green.MASC and
un   bicron brun.   Elles   étaient très amies...
a.MASC bicron brown.MASC They.FEM were   very friends...
'Well, there was once a green bicron and a brown bicron. They were close friends...'

It is too simplistic, therefore, to say that children used the phonological clue: rather, faced with an unusual situation, they used both criteria, in a way which occurs frequently in a several other languages (see section 8.1.1). Children over eight, however, did in some instances continue with pronouns based on the phonologically predicted gender (*il* 'he' in the case of *bicron*). Alternatively, they used the semantic form *elle* 'she', and then modified the noun (to *bicronne*) to give it a phonological shape consistent with it being of feminine gender. Karmiloff-Smith's data are of interest, even though she was not primarily concerned with gender and does not provide all the information which we would like. Her work would suggest that French-speaking children adopt a strategy (using the phonological rule) which will work most of the time, though in the mature system it is the semantic rule which takes precedence. The question of the acquisition of French gender by second-language learners was investigated by Stevens (1984) and by Taylor-Browne (1984), both using procedures as similar as possible to those of Karmiloff-Smith; learners had considerable difficulties. An interesting line of enquiry was pursued by Magnan (1983), who investigated the reactions of native French speakers to various non-native errors in spoken French. The youngest informants (schoolchildren) were most sensitive to errors in gender, those at high school were slightly less sensitive, while adults were least troubled by errors in gender. She reports somewhat similar findings by other researchers working on German. Data on Spanish-speaking children, monolingual and bilingual, are provided by Sadek, Kiraithe & Villarreal (1975). They tested only nonsense words, whose pictorial representations showed that they denoted inanimate objects, and found evidence that the children used phonological indicators, even though the full assignment system was not in place (the eldest children were in the third year of school).

A problem already mentioned in relation to work on Bantu languages is that progress on understanding the acquisition of gender depended in part of an understanding of the child's phonology. Similarly, where semantic factors are involved, it is important to have an account of the child's knowledge of the world, particularly of the hierarchical structuring of this knowledge. But these are in themselves major research projects. Thus, while results from child language acquisition will continue to be of interest, it is unreasonable to expect unambiguous evidence bearing on gender assignment in the near future.

4.3 Experimental evidence

There have been various attempts to confirm hypotheses about gender systems by direct experiment. Thus Deutsch & Wijnen (1985) present psycholinguistic evidence that gender in Dutch is represented as an abstract binary feature. Champagnol (1982, 1984), using recall experiments in French, claims to show that the processing and encoding of gender (and number) morphemes – as opposed to that of lexemes – is partly autonomous. The most obvious type of experiment to elucidate gender assignment is to present the native speaker with unfamiliar nouns (unfamiliar either because they are rare or because they are artificial nouns invented by the linguist) and to give a test, typically a phrase involving agreement, to see which gender they are assigned to. We have already seen this approach in the previous section, since various investigators have used it in their investigations of children's acquisition of gender; it is, of course, equally possible to investigate the adult system in a similar way.

Experiments involving invented nouns have obvious advantages, since the factors one wishes to investigate can be juggled at will. Consonant combinations, position of stress, meaning and so on can be exactly as the investigator chooses. The problem comes in presenting the information to the subject. If semantic information is presented directly ('This word means...') then the subject has a strong indication of what the investigator wants. If, on the other hand, the information is presented pictorially, there is the question of knowing whether the subject is using this information when responding (particularly in the case of children). But with ingenuity, tests can be devised. In investigating a previously proposed connection between diminutives and the feminine gender in French, Chastaing (1973) asked subjects about the relative size of the objects denoted by various terms (some existing in French and some invented). He was able to show that the simple link proposed does not hold: while the feminine can signal smaller diminutives than the masculine, it can also signal larger augmentatives. Braine (1987: 77–80) reports an experiment in which subjects had to learn two small artificial languages, consisting of nouns and number words. Each language had two genders, indicated by agreement on the number words. In one language there was a semantic assignment rule based on sex, which covered half of the nouns. There was no such rule in the other. Not surprisingly, subjects had a greater success in learning the first 'language'.

For investigating morphological systems the problems involved in using invented forms are much worse; it is difficult to give the necessary information on the paradigm of an invented noun in a natural way. A variant of this approach was suggested by Greenberg (1962: 173), namely to ask Bantu speakers who know European languages to assign genders to nouns from these languages, even though they have not been borrowed – an artificial borrowing experiment; results obtained by Richardson (1967: 378–80) proved 'tantalizingly enigmatic'.

The systems for which the methodology works best are phonological assignment systems. We have already discussed work by Karmiloff-Smith on French (section 4.2) and in section 3.2.5 we looked at the analysis of French nouns by Tucker, Lambert & Rigault (1977). Having established the regularities found in the nouns in a dictionary of reasonable size, they went on to test their predictions on large numbers of speakers, over 1,000 in all. Speakers were asked to give the gender of nouns, some of which were genuine French nouns in common use, some were rare, others were invented nouns designed to test the validity of the predictions made. In some tests there was a visual stimulus; we shall be concerned with tests where the subjects heard the nouns on a tape. The nouns in common use were regularly assigned to the correct gender and can tell us rather little, so in what follows we will concentrate on the other types of prompt. Let us again consider nouns in /ɔ̃/. As we saw in section 3.2.5, the vast majority of nouns in /sjɔ̃/ are feminine. In the tests 402 informants, aged eight to thirteen, were asked to assign nouns to gender, including two rare nouns in /sjɔ̃/. In 89 per cent of the cases, averaged for the two nouns, the feminine gender was chosen. With rare nouns in /ijɔ̃/, which is normally an indication of the masculine gender, the masculine was chosen in 84 per cent of the cases.

The invented nouns gave particularly interesting results. Three different initial syllables were chosen: *déb-*, which is found in sixty-three masculine and seventeen feminine nouns, and so is predominantly masculine; *flor-*, found in seven feminine and three masculine, counted as predominantly feminine; and *feuill-*, the 'ambiguous' root since it occurs in six feminines and nine masculines. The results are presented in table 4.3 (from Tucker, Lambert & Rigault 1977: 26). The table shows that in the overwhelming majority of cases, nouns ending in /ijɔ̃/ were believed to be masculine and those in /sjɔ̃/ feminine (since only a maximum of 21 per cent chose the masculine). The raw

Table 4.3 *Assignment of invented nouns to gender in French (assignments to the masculine gender)*

	Ambiguous initial syllable /fœ:j/ (%)	Masculine initial syllable /deb/ (%)	Feminine initial syllable /flɔr/ (%)
Masculine ending /ijɔ̃/	91	99	82
Feminine ending /sjɔ̃/	17	11	21

figures are not available; nevertheless, it is claimed that the results would arise by chance less frequently than once in a hundred tries. The important point is that, when faced with a new word (either because it was rare or because it had been invented), speakers behaved as would be predicted if the assignment rules are indeed part of their linguistic competence. Another study showed that children's ability to assign nouns to gender following the majority pattern improves with age. The data amply confirm the validity of the assignment rules:

> The results of these studies substantiate the observations made earlier that native speakers, even the very young, experience no difficulty in making consistent gender choices. The findings also suggest that they somehow make these choices through a process of inference based on experience with the language that has led to an accumulated storehouse of information about regularities that are associated with gender. (Tucker, Lambert & Rigault 1977: 46)

There is a secondary point of interest in the data in table 4.3, namely that the initial syllable also appears to have a small effect on gender assignment: /debijɔ̃/ was considered masculine by more speakers than was /flɔrijɔ̃/, because /deb/ occurs mainly in masculines and /flɔr/ is found mainly in feminines. This is an unexpected result. Though the phonology of the end of French nouns is the major factor determining gender assignment, it seems that the initial syllable also has a role. In a later experimental study using written prompts, Desrochers, Paivio & Desrochers (1986) established that the predictors for gender which appear strongest from the sort of linguistic evidence we have been discussing prove under experimental conditions to allow subjects to assign nouns to gender faster than other predictors. This sort of tie-up between linguistic and psycholinguistic work appears particularly promising.

Continuing with phonological systems, let us consider again Qafar, which has straightforward phonological assignment rules. R. J. Hayward (personal communication) constructed the following phonotactically possible nouns: (1) *Dùrra*; (2) *Kaabìs*; (3) *Buulà*; (4) *Tattibè*; (5) *Gòxa*; (6) *Gooxò*; (7) *Fuùn*; (8) *Sorokòyta*; (9) *Cindì*; (10) *Xinintà*. According to the rules given in section 3.2.1, we would expect 1, 2, 5, 7 and 8 to be masculine and the remainder feminine. The informant was told that they were the names of men or women. They were presented orally in the frame: *X taaxige?* 'Do you know X?' And the response requested was to be *Yey, kàa/tet aaxige* 'Yes, I know him/her.' The point of giving them in object position is that some masculine nouns have nominative marking; by using a construction which requires the nouns to appear in the absolute form, which has no morphological marker, this complication was eliminated. The informant was able to produce the answer rapidly and in every case the gender assigned was that which is predicted by the assignment rules. Interestingly, he was very puzzled as to how he had done it, though he was well educated. This suggests that even simple assignment rules do not operate at a conscious level. The phonological assignment rules of German are more complex. Kőpcke & Zubin (1984: 31–2) nevertheless achieved interesting results; Mills (1986: 45–50) extended their experiment and obtained statistically significant results, showing that postulated assignment rules do indeed account for the gender assigned to nonsense words.

Even when the results are clear-cut, the question remains as to how they relate to natural behaviour. The conclusive evidence as to a noun's gender comes from agreement. But having learned the gender in this way, it may be that the learner does not store it as additional information but, for many nouns at least, applies a rule which allows the gender to be derived from other information (meaning or form). Suppose, then, that a speaker hears a new noun (whether under natural or experimental conditions) without agreement evidence as to its gender. In normal acquisition the noun might be provisionally assigned to a gender, subject to confirming data being heard. And what the speaker does in experimental conditions may not match the natural situation in a straightforward way. There is a great deal to be done in this area.

4.4 Residual meaning of gender

In languages in which gender is determined by semantic rule for only a proportion of the nouns, gender may nevertheless appear meaningful in the residue under special circumstances. Jakobson (1966: 236–7) talks of 'everyday verbal mythology and poetry' as potential circumstances and gives examples like the following. There is a Russian superstition that if a knife is dropped a male guest will come, and if a fork a female guest can be expected. *Nož* 'knife' is masculine, while *vilka* 'fork' is feminine. In Russian too, Death is depicted as a woman (*smert'* 'death' is feminine), but as a man in German (*Tod* 'death' is masculine). As curiosities, we may note that according to Superanskaja (1965: 58), before the Revolution the Russian names of towns on the left bank of the Volga were feminine, and those of towns on the right bank were masculine. And Spitz (1965: 38) states that the names of the rivers of central Europe are feminine in German, while other rivers are masculine.

If a language has grammatical gender it is not surprising that personification is in accord with gender. But the personification may seem fully natural to the native speaker, who is not aware of the grammatical gender. The question is then whether this association of grammatical gender with meaning is potentially available for any noun. The problem of the connotations of gender was taken up by Ervin (1962). She concocted nonsense words which, given the regular assignment system of Italian (nouns in -*o* are normally masculine and those in -*a* feminine), could easily be assigned to a gender. She presented them to informants and asked them to rate the nouns according to whether the items denoted were good, pretty, strong and large. Then the informants were asked to assess men and women according to the same criteria and they rated women as prettier, weaker, smaller and, though less consistently, better than men. What then of the nonsense words? Those which appeared to be grammatically feminine were rated as prettier, weaker, smaller and better than the apparent masculines. These results suggest that the 'connotations' of gender can be brought to the surface (in unusual circumstances, as also in Jakobson's examples). The factors which help determine the semantic rule, that is, the things which help us establish a person's sex, can be extended beyond their obvious domain and be applied to nouns which would normally belong in the semantic residue. Results pointing in a similar direction were obtained in a comparative study of speakers of Arabic and English by Clarke, Losoff, McCracken & Still (1981), though other factors may have contributed to their results. Speakers were asked to evaluate objects along a masculine–feminine scale; comparison of the responses of the two groups suggests that the gender of the nouns in Arabic affected the response of the Arabic speakers. Thus nouns like 'necklace' and 'perfume', whose equivalents are masculine in Arabic, received a higher masculine rating from Arabic than from English speakers. A further type of link between grammatical gender and perception was explored by Guiora, Beit-Hallahmi, Fried & Yoder (1982), who suggest that children learning Hebrew, which has grammatical gender, come to recognize their own gender identity earlier than those learning English (in which gender has a minor role) or Finnish (which has no gender category).

Impressive and somewhat surprising evidence is presented by Zubin & Kőpcke (1984). They examine German compounds in *-mut*, which express moods and personality characteristics. Though the last element normally determines gender in German (section 3.1.3), some of these compounds are masculine and others feminine; speakers show much greater variation than is recorded in dictionaries. Zubin and Kőpcke asked forty speakers to rate such nouns using the semantic differential technique. They used pairs such as 'active–passive', 'loud–soft', which were chosen as facets of the general notions of 'extroversion–introversion'. There is a clear correlation. Nouns which were rated high in terms of 'extroversion', like *Hochmut* 'arrogance' and *Übermut* 'bravado', are masculine. Those rated as showing 'introversion' like *Anmut* 'gracefulness' and *Wehmut* 'sadness', are feminine. They also present diachronic evidence to back their claim. In the eighteenth and nineteenth centuries, new compounds were formed with *-mut* and, following the Last Member Principle (section 3.1.3), they were masculine. Since *-mut* has ceased being a productive formative, the Last Member Principle no longer applies absolutely and those nouns which had 'introverted' affect (like *Zagemut* 'timidity') have switched to feminine gender. Moreover, nouns in the same general semantic area, but formed differently, show similar effects. Nouns in *-nis* may be feminine or neuter: those which show 'introverted' feelings or mental states are feminine (though this does not account for all the feminines). Thus we find *Besorgnis* (feminine) 'fear' but *Wagnis* (neuter) 'risky undertaking'. 'Introversion–extroversion' may not be ideal terms for the distinctions involved here. Some would be tempted to see the distinction as basically male–female. However, Zubin and Kőpcke contend that 'there could be a deep-rooted polarity in our understanding of personality and affect which influences the assignment of a gender on the one hand, and influences our stereotypic attitudes about maleness and femaleness on the other' (Zubin & Kőpcke 1984: 94). What is particularly noteworthy in this research is the establishment of meaning distinctions which correlate with gender in the least likely part of the lexicon, the abstract nouns.

Mills (1986: 117–41) also investigated meaning distinctions which correlate with gender, and obtained interesting results, which show that the area is much more complex than might be imagined. In her comparative German–English investigation, she considered nouns denoting ten animals and objects (bear, elephant, ball, cat, mouse, clock, pig, horse, car, book). The gender of the German nouns is known. For the English nouns, Mills wanted to establish the gender used in 'lively style', which she did by means of a story with gaps (a cloze test). The subjects were asked to complete gaps such as the following (a game of hide-and-seek is in progress): 'The mouse's whiskers were tickled..........a draught. "Atishoo"..........sneezed violently and so the ball found..........straight away' (Mills 1986: 150). There is a correlation between the pronoun used in such examples (in the second and third gaps) and that used in actual children's literature. Similarly there was a correlation between the sex assigned in personification in German children's literature and the grammatical gender of the items involved.

Mills showed toys representing the ten animals and objects to German and English children, and asked them to give each a name. Adults were simply given a list. Usually the name indicated a sex; if not, the subject was asked which sex was intended. An interesting result was that of the younger children: girls tended to favour female names and boys male names. This tendency decreases with age. Not surprisingly, there is a high correlation between gender and the sex assigned for personification. But the question remains as to whether subjects perceived sex-related attributes in the objects. To establish this a semantic differential test was used, in which subjects were asked to rank the objects on scales such as large–small, strong–weak, tense–relaxed, which were shown to correlate with man–woman. Most interestingly, the ten animals and objects were rated similarly by German and English speakers. The profiles for *bear*, *elephant*, *pig*, *horse* and *car* were found to correlate positively with the profile for *man*; those for *cat*, *mouse* and *clock* correlated with the profile for *woman*; those for *ball* and *book* correlated with neither. How, then, do these profiles correlate with grammatical gender and with the sex accorded in personification? The results are given in table 4.4, where M, F, N represent the predominant use of masculine/male, feminine/female and neuter as appropriate. The degree of similarity between German and English speakers is striking. It suggests that the differences in the gender systems of the two languages do not affect speakers' perceptions of reality. The sex assigned to animals and objects correlates highly with grammatical gender in German and pronoun use (in lively style) in English. But what of those which do not fit, particularly the German neuters? It might be said that German speakers treat them as male because of their perceived attributes; but equally it could be said that anything which is not of feminine gender will be personified as male in German, since *Ball* and *Buch*, which did not correlate either with *Mann* or *Frau*, were both personified as male.

An intriguing case is the *Uhr/clock* pair. Though perceived as having female attributes, *clock* took masculine pronouns in lively speech and was personified as male. Mills takes this as evidence that grammatical gender is the dominant influence on the choice of sex. An alternative hypothesis would be that English

Table 4.4 *Gender, perception of attributes and personification in German and English*

| Noun | Gender | | Attributes (semantic differential test) | Sex assigned | |
	German	English (lively speech)		German	English
Bär/bear	M	M	M	M	M
Elefant/elephant	M	M	M	M	M
Ball/ball	M	M	neither	M	M
Katze/cat	F	F	F	F	F
Maus/mouse	F	F	F	F	F
Uhr/clock	F	M	F	F	M
Schwein/pig	N	M	M	M	M
Pferd/horse	N	M	M	M	M
Auto/car	N	M	M	M	M
Buch/book	N	M	neither	M	M

and German differ, as a result of English having only pronominal gender, which is heavily dependent upon animacy. In English, only animate nouns perceived as having female attributes were personified as female and took feminine pronouns in lively style; all others were male/masculine. (This usage clearly differs from the use of *he/she* for inanimates mentioned in section 2.1.2.) In German, which has a much more extensive gender system, personification was female for nouns which are grammatically feminine and male for all others. This analysis fits the data. However, the important evidence consists of only a single pair of nouns, *clock* and *Uhr*. Several more cases like these would have to be identified before convincing claims could be made. Despite Mills' painstaking work, we still have insufficient evidence to select between alternative hypotheses. We can certainly conclude that the relations between gender, sex and perception of attributes are much more complex than is usually assumed.

Burton & Kirk (1976) had the interesting idea of using triad tests to investigate gender in the Bantu language Kikuyu. They used the nouns given in table 4.5, all concerned with flight, and investigated semantic clusters within some of the different genders (undulation, animals and ritual), following suggestions by Leakey (1959). Subjects were asked in Kikuyu to 'sort words by the images which the words brought to mind' (Burton & Kirk 1976: 163). When they were presented with three nouns from the list they had to select 'the one most different in meaning from the other two'. Forty-six such triads

Table 4.5 *Kikuyu nouns used in the triad test*

	Kikuyu	English gloss	Gender
1.	ruhuhu	bat	11/10 (undulation)
2.	ruigi	hawk	11/10 (undulation)
3.	ruoya	feather	11/10 (undulation)
4.	ruagi	mosquito	11/10 (undulation)
5.	ruruto	preying mantis	11/10 (undulation)
6.	nderi	vulture	9/10 (animals)
7.	ngi	housefly	9/10 (animals)
8.	ndahi	grasshopper	9/10 (animals)
9.	ithagu	wing	5/6 (ritual)

were investigated. The results showed a clear division between small things (mosquito, house-fly, preying mantis, grasshopper) and the rest. Phylogeny was also important. Both these classifications cut across the gender groupings. But when these two classifications were held constant, shared gender was found to have an effect. Unfortunately, despite the instruction to the subjects, the results must be taken as provisional, since the phonological similarity of the items in the various genders could account for the result rather than semantic similarity. But the experiment is worth quoting since it uses a method well established elsewhere in the social sciences which could prove valuable in studies of gender.

Before leaving the residual meaning of gender, consider the translation problem faced by a missionary working on the Peve language in south-west Chad (Venberg 1971). He discovered that *Ifray* 'God' took the pronoun *Ta* 'she'. Converts claimed not to think of God as having a sex and suggested the use of *Mum* 'he' for the Christian God, because of phrases like *God the Father*. But to outsiders, this sounded strange grammatically and was inconsistent with their idea of creation (it is women who give birth/create). And so *Ta* 'she' was reinstated.

4.5 Diachronic evidence

Change over time gives insights into the way in which a system works. Having already noted some changes in assignment systems, we now look at such changes together, starting with those which affect larger or smaller numbers of nouns (including cases where as a result a particular assignment rule changes) and moving to those which change the whole principle on which assignment operates in a given language.

Let us consider first the less radical changes. The minimal change is one in which a noun (or group of nouns) is involved in a change which affects its input to the assignment rules in a relevant way. We would predict that its gender will change as a result. Thus Standard Russian has fourteen nouns, like *imja* 'name', which belong to an irregular declensional type and, according to the algorithm in figure 3.4, are neuter. In certain Russian dialects some members of this small class have been absorbed by the regular declensional type II. As a result, they are feminine in gender. Such a change may affect a small number of nouns and leave the assignment system exactly as it was before. Yet such evidence strongly supports the claim that assignment systems are part of the native speaker's competence; if they were not, we would have no reason to believe that a change in declensional type would affect gender. (For many more examples from various Indo-European languages see Fisher 1973.)

Let us now consider examples in which the assignment system itself undergoes change. We noted earlier various cases of positively specified genders with numbers of 'leaks'. In Dyirbal, for example, the gender for male humans and animates includes 'fishing line' by concept association with 'fish'. It is a reasonable hypothesis, though there is no documentary evidence in this case, that apparent exceptions of this type represent a later development to a system which originally had simpler semantic rules. Fortunately, there are cases where comparative or documentary evidence makes the development clear. In the Bantu languages, gender 1/2 is typically for nouns denoting humans. Swahili, however, is just completing a change which makes gender 1/2 the gender for all animates. Some other languages are at various stages in this development (considered in more detail in section 8.3). We should examine how changes of this type are set off. Lunda, a Bantu language of Angola, assigns all animates to gender 1/2, while the closely related language Luvale has only a few non-human animates in this gender (data from Greenberg, reported in Childs 1983: 28). They include *muumbe* 'jackal'. Greenberg suggests that jackal is treated in this way because a personified jackal often appears in folk tales. Once there are exceptions to the requirement that nouns must denote humans to be in gender 1/2, the rule is weakened over time to include all animates (as has happened in Lunda). The development depends on nouns like 'jackal', which we shall term 'Trojan horses', since they get into the closed gender for special reasons, but then open the door for many more nouns of the same type (animate in this case) which are not special cases.

A somewhat similar development is found in the Slavonic family. Having inherited the three Indo-European genders, Slavonic innovated with a new subgender. Originally the nouns involved were singular nouns denoting specific male humans (Huntley 1980: 205–6). There is evidence that even within the male human category the rule applied primarily to free adult males in Old Russian (Dietze 1973: 264–6), not to serfs and children. Over the centuries, other nouns followed these Trojan horses and in the different Slavonic languages, all masculine nouns denoting humans were included, followed by all other animates (within the masculine singular). Some Slavonic languages have gone even further than this; Russian, described in section 3.1.1, distinguishes animates for all genders in the plural. It is generally, though not universally, accepted that a major factor in this development was the requirement to distinguish subject from object in languages with word-order determined by information structure, rather than by grammatical relations (Comrie 1978; Klenin 1983 gives a different view). For most masculine nouns, the morphological distinction between nominative and accusative was lost in the singular. The use of genitive for accusative allowed the distinction to be made; this is clearly most necessary when human referents are involved (since here confusion of subject and object is most likely). But in time all animates were included. As we saw in section 3.1.1, there are nouns which may denote animates or inanimates, and these tend to be treated as grammatically animate. These serve as Trojan horses for a further weakening of the semantic condition on the subgender. In Polish we find various inanimates being treated as grammatically animate (for example, *banan* 'banana', *mat* 'checkmate', *pech* 'bad luck'), though not necessarily by all speakers or in all syntactic environments (Wertz 1977: 57–9). These nouns may in turn serve as Trojan horses for the final loss of the animacy distinction (all masculine nouns would be allowed into the animate category). Note that in these Slavonic examples the original motivation lay outside the gender system. Since adjectives and other targets must show agreement, these reflect the case distinction and hence there are grounds for postulating a subgender. In most cases the noun's inflectional morphology is changed, and as a result it moves into the animate subgender. (In contrast, the morphology may not be affected by gender change, as we shall see in some Bantu examples in section 8.3.)

Potential Trojan horses may arise from conflicts within the assignment system itself. In German, nouns denoting females are normally feminine, and diminutives are neuter. In a small number of cases the two factors conflict, as in *Mädchen* 'girl'. The result here is that most agreements are neuter but the personal pronoun is usually feminine; in other words, *Mädchen* and similar nouns are 'hybrids' (see section 6.4.5.2). At present there is no sign of a flow of other nouns into the neuter gender in German. The conflict between human and diminutive is, however, a common source of Trojan horses with dramatic effects. We saw how in Lak, *duš* 'girl' was in gender III with non-human animates and how, in a relatively short time, all nouns denoting female humans have been transferred into that gender, except those denoting older females within the family. There has therefore been a major redistribution of nouns between the genders and the core meaning of genders II and III has changed (section 2.2.5). An equally radical change has occurred in some dialects of Konkani, an Indo-European language (Indic branch), spoken on the west coast of India (Miranda 1975: 208–13). Konkani inherited the traditional Indo-European three-gender system. The item of particular interest is the neuter noun *čeḍū*, which meant 'child' but has come to mean 'girl'. It retains consistent neuter agreements. And the meaning of the neuter gender has changed as a result: the neuter pronoun *tẽ* in isolation normally means 'she', referring to a young female, or one relatively younger from the speaker's standpoint. The feminine pronoun *ti* 'she' is used only for an old, or relatively older female. Some nouns, like *bayl* 'woman' have acquired double gender, being feminine, as before, when an older woman is involved, and neuter when it is a younger woman. Other nouns, like *awoy* 'mother' have not gone so far; when denoting relatively younger females they take some feminine and some neuter agreements. In Konkani, then, because of a small number of items, possibly a single one originally, the neuter has gained some frequently occurring nouns and has changed its core meaning, as shown by the interpretation of the neuter pronoun when used in isolation.

A similar change in the core meaning of genders has occurred in some southern Polish dialects and those transitional to Czech and Slovak (Zaręba 1984–5). In several of these dialects, nouns denoting girls and unmarried women (irrespective of age), and including hypocoristics, are of neuter gender: *Zuzię poszło* (neuter) 'Zuzia has gone.' Neuter agreements are employed when unmarried women are addressed, and they use them for self-reference: *jo było* (neuter) *na grziby* 'I was mushrooming.' In a smaller area, near the Czechoslovak border to the south-west of Krakow, instead of the neuter the masculine is used: *Hanik przyszoł* (masculine) 'Hania came', *jo szół* (masculine) 'I was going.' In both types of dialect, the feminine is used for married women. The difference between the two dialects helps confirm the origins of this interesting development. Hypocoristics and patronymics, which are used for girls and unmarried women, are formed in two different ways. In the first type, we find forms like *Heczę* 'daughter of Heczko', which follows a declension whose nouns are normally neuter. In the second, there are forms like *Hanik* 'Hania (familiar)', which follow a typically masculine declension. What appears to have happened is that such forms took neuter and masculine agreements respectively (as would be predicted from the morphology) and that then all nouns and pronouns denoting unmarried females began to take neuter or masculine agreement (depending on the dialect). The change from neuter or masculine to feminine for a particular woman occurs immediately after the church wedding ceremony; the communities involved are small, and so there is no difficulty about knowing who is married and who is not (A. Zaręba, personal communication). In this case the Trojan horse was a particular type of morphological formation; instead of the semantic assignment rule (nouns denoting females are feminine) overriding the morphological rule, as is normally the case, the gender consistent with the morphology was retained. Then other nouns were drawn in to the same gender, resulting in a change in the meaning of the genders. In most of the dialects, the neuter is used to refer to unmarried women; in a minority of the dialects the masculine is used in this case, as well as for males. As a result, the meaning of the feminine has changed in both cases, being restricted now to denote married women. (Feminine nouns in the residue, which are not semantically motivated, also remain feminine.) In section 8.3 we discuss this change briefly from the point of view of the agreements involved. Borrowings, which were discussed in section 4.1, may also act as Trojan horses. Suppose we have a language in which formal and semantic factors overlap to a large extent: borrowings are unlikely to share this overlapping and so will lead to a weakening of the link between semantic and formal assignment, no matter which gender they join. We saw how in Nyangbo and Santrokofi gender I comprised nouns which were semantically animate and formally lacking prefixes. Borrowings may lack prefixes yet denote inanimates. They are assigned to gender I, whose semantic homogeneity is thereby undermined.

Some of the changes we have observed have been in the direction of weakening the semantic boundaries of a particular gender or genders. Others have involved a realignment of genders, leaving the semantic boundaries no stronger or weaker than before. There are also examples of change towards a clearer semantic system. For example, in Young People's Dyirbal, the unexplained irregularities of Traditional Dyirbal have been eliminated (section 2.2.2), and a gender has been completely lost. This considerable change leads us to the even more radical type of change, that in which the very type of assignment system changes. Probably the best-known example here is English. English formerly had a morphological assignment system. However, even Old English shows examples of the gender of personal pronouns being determined by semantic criteria (irrespective of grammatical gender); most significantly, inanimates could take a neuter pronoun, even though they were grammatically masculine or feminine (Baron 1971: 121–3). Of course, the fact that English lost almost all declensional distinctions meant that the system of gender assignment would in any case be changed. But the change is not as straightforward as is often believed; indeed it has been called 'one of the most difficult problems of English philology' (Ross 1936: 321). What is commonly misunderstood is that the change to a semantic assignment system during Middle English had already begun before the loss of the declensional distinctions (Baron 1971). While the stages of the change involve considerable complexity (Jones 1967a, b, 1988; Mitchell 1985: 29–37), the nature of the change is clear: English moved from having a morphological assignment system to a semantic one. Dutch is at an earlier stage in a similar development (Dekeyser 1980). Elsewhere in Germanic too, loss of morphological distinctions leads to gender change (Beito 1976). It is interesting to note that as morphological assignment weakens, so new semantic assignment rules are arising. In several Germanic languages and dialects, the count–mass distinction is taking a role as a criterion for semantic assignment. For example, Danish *øl* 'beer' is normally neuter, but is of common gender when used as a count noun: *en øl* 'one beer' (Haugen 1976: 371). Another change from morphological to semantic assignment gives a rather different result in the East Iranian (Pamir) language Yazgulyam (which has 1,500–2,000 speakers in Tadzhikistan, USSR). Two of the Indo-European genders survive; the feminine is used for nouns denoting female humans, and also animals; while the masculine is used for nouns denoting males and inanimates (Efimov 1975: 44, 87–8; Payne 1989: 429). As in English, gender is found only in pronouns, which favours a shift to semantically based assignment (compare section 8.2).

Change can occur in a different direction, from a morphological to a phonological system. It has been argued that such a change can be demonstrated in Rendille, an East Cushitic language, spoken by some 15,000 nomadic people in northern Kenya (Oomen 1981). Rendille has a phonological assignment system, similar to that of Qafar in that the position of the accent is a determining factor. Simplifying somewhat, we may say that masculine nouns typically have penultimate accent (counting in moras, not syllables; a long vowel is two moras), while feminines have final accent. Oomen claims that at an earlier stage all nouns had penultimate accent. A suffix *-(e)t*, for which there is independent evidence, was added to many nouns, which had the effect of making them feminine, for example, **méel + et* 'place'. Since penultimate accent was still the rule, the accent shifted to give **meél-et*. The final *t* was subsequently lost: the *e* is retained in the nominative, but not in the absolute form of the noun, which is *meél*. This hypothesis, supported by evidence within Rendille and comparative data from other Cushitic languages, suggests that at an earlier stage gender could be predicted from the presence or absence of a particular suffix, and that the loss of the suffix has left its mark on nouns by the position of the accent. Rendille no longer has fixed accent position, and so the stress of the feminines remains where it was before the loss of the suffix, which means that there is now a contrast with the masculines. Thus a morphological assignment system has become a phonological one. Recent work on Rendille suggests that syllable-final consonants also count as moras, which leads to a generalization which allows fewer exceptions: masculine nouns are those with antepenultimate accent, counting in moras, and feminines are those with penultimate accent (Pillinger 1989). Another example of a phonological system with a morphological origin is found in the Chadic language Hausa. The present rule is that nouns ending in -*aa* are feminine (section 3.2.2). This results first from a derivational process (nouns denoting females were derived with the suffix -*nyàa*), and then from overt characterization, that is, the addition of the feminine suffix -*aa* to nouns of feminine gender (Newman 1979). In the modern language the simple phonological rule 'nouns in -*aa* are feminine' is the result of processes which were originally morphological.

We saw earlier how semantic systems can be weakened by the effects of Trojan horses. If sufficient weakening occurs, so that a large proportion of the nouns are not covered by a semantic rule, then another type of assignment rule will cover the semantic residue and so we shall have a change of assignment system (the semantic rules will not be totally replaced, since gender systems always have a semantic core). This may have occurred during the history of Bantu languages. It is widely believed that the genders or noun classes of Bantu were once consistently motivated in semantic terms. The meaning of a noun determined both its gender and its morphology. In the modern Bantu languages, as we saw in section 3.1.2, this is no longer the case. The gender of many nouns cannot be predicted from their meaning, but can be predicted from their morphology. If the opinion about the earlier state is correct, we have an example of a change from a semantic to a morphological system.

It appears likely, then, that a semantic system can change to a morphological one. We have also seen evidence that a morphological system can change to a semantic one or to a phonological one. Further research is needed to establish whether a semantic system can develop into a phonological one, or vice versa, and whether a phonological system can move to a morphological one. Perhaps surprisingly, a complete assignment system can be taken from another language, replacing the original one. In the Indian village of Kupwar in Sangli district, Maharashtra, near the Mysore border, there are speakers of Kannada, Urdu and Marathi. As we noted in section 2.1.1, Kannada has a semantic system (male rational, female rational and non-rational). Marathi (which has masculine, feminine and neuter genders) and Urdu (masculine and feminine) have systems typical of Indo-European, with the semantic residue distributed over all genders. In the varieties spoken in this village, both systems have been reshaped along the lines of Kannada. In the local variety of Marathi we find semantic assignment using the criteria male human, female human and other, while in local Urdu, nouns denoting female rationals are feminine and all others masculine (Gumperz & Wilson 1971: 155–6).

As a postscript, let us consider a fascinating example of conflicting changes, provided by Wolof (Irvine 1978). Wolof belongs to the West Atlantic branch of Niger-Congo; it has over 600,000 speakers in Senegal and Gambia. (A survey of gender in West Atlantic is provided by Sapir 1971.) Wolof has eight genders, with assignment depending partly on semantic factors (kinship terms, trees versus fruits, large versus small) and partly on phonological factors (the initial consonant). Working in Senegal, in a village near Tivaouane, Irvine found that speakers of higher rank, especially upwardly mobile, middle-aged men, are changing the gender of some nouns. They tend to assign to the most common of the genders nouns which previously belonged to other genders, and indeed are retained in those genders by other speakers. Such usage represents at least partially conscious error. To understand this it is necessary to know that society is stratified, and that nobility is shown by restraint. A noble does not distinguish himself by fluent speaking; quite the contrary, if he needs to make a speech he hires a lowly speech specialist. Certain speech errors thus signal rank. The practice of making errors in gender assignment, by moving nouns into the most common gender, would lead to a reduction of the gender system, as more and more nouns joined the residue gender. But other speakers tend to move nouns out of the most common gender, sometimes to a gender which contains semantically similar nouns, or to the gender indicated by the initial consonant. We thus find conflicting trends operating at the same time.

4.6 Conclusion

The evidence of borrowings, child language acquisition, experiments, residual meaning of gender and of diachronic developments provide confirming evidence for our analysis of assignment systems. Often the data are less clear-cut than we would like. Sometimes this is because investigations are based on inadequate descriptions of the primary linguistic data. In other cases it is because the complexity of the gender system introduces large numbers of variables, whose effects cannot yet be disentangled. There is certainly a good deal of interesting work to be done, even on the simplest of gender systems, in all these areas.

5
Gender agreement

Up to this point we have assumed that nouns can be divided into genders and we have analysed the composition of these genders, considering whether they are based solely on semantic criteria, or whether formal factors also have a role. We now turn to gender agreement. This is important for two reasons: first, it is the way in which gender is realized in language use; and second, as a consequence, gender agreement provides the basis for defining gender and for establishing the number of genders in a given language. In this chapter we concentrate on the variety of ways in which gender is exemplified in the languages of the world, leaving to chapter 6 the procedures for determining the number of genders in a given language. While there is a broad consensus on the core cases of agreement, there is no generally accepted definition; there is a problem as to the outer limit of phenomena properly described as agreement, as we shall see when the personal pronoun is discussed in section 5.1. A working definition is provided by Steele (1978: 610):

> The term *agreement* commonly refers to some systematic covariance between a semantic or formal property of one element and a formal property of another. For example, adjectives may take some formal indication of the number and gender of the noun they modify.

For other attempts to define agreement see Keenan (1978: 167) and Lehmann (1982: 203). *Concord* is generally treated as synonymous with *agreement* and we shall use it in this way; some authors distinguish the two, but often in idiosyncratic ways.

We first consider where agreement in gender can be found (section 5.1). Then we investigate the form of gender agreement (section 5.2) and limits upon it (section 5.3). The subject of classifiers is raised in section 5.4; though outside the scope of agreement and not coming within what we understand by gender, they are important in terms of the development of gender agreement markers, which is discussed in section 5.5.

5.1 **Elements showing gender agreement**

Agreement in gender may occur in a wide range of agreeing elements. It is particularly common in **adjectives**. In Russian, for example, we find:

(1) nov-yj   žurnal   nov-aja kniga   nov-oe   pis′mo
    new-MASC magazine   new-FEM book   new-NEUT   letter

The adjectival stem is *nov-* and the endings *-yj*, *-aja* and *-oe* show masculine, feminine and neuter agreements respectively; thus the attributive adjective agrees in gender. Adjectives may occur in other syntactic positions, notably the predicate, and show gender agreement there. There are various other types of attributive modifier which may be involved; for example, **demonstratives** frequently show gender agreement. In Russian we have *tot žurnal* 'that magazine', *ta kniga* 'that book' and *to pis′mo* 'that letter'. And in Archi we find *jow bošor* 'this man' as opposed to *jar x̌onnol* 'this woman', and so on (Kibrik, Kodzasov, Olovjannikova & Samedov 1977: 25). In Dyirbal gender is marked on what Dixon calls 'noun markers', which are analogous to demonstratives. Nouns are usually accompanied by a noun marker, which agrees with the noun in case, and gives information about location (here/there, visible/not visible):

(2) balan   ḍugumbil   yaŋgul
    there.visible.NOM.II   woman.NOM   here.visible.ERG.I
    yaṟaŋgu   bayan
    man.ERG   sing
    'The man here is singing to the woman there.'

Since Dyirbal is an ergative language, it is the man in (2) which is the 'subject'. Noun markers may also occur without a noun, in which case they function syntactically more like pronouns. What is important for our purposes is that the distinction between *balan* and *yaŋgul* in (2) is not explicable solely in terms of case and location. If the woman was singing to the man, who was there and visible, the appropriate form for a gender I noun in the nominative would be not *balan* but *bayi*. Thus these noun markers agree in noun class or gender (Dixon 1972: 44–7). There are four such genders (see section 2.2.2).

Definite and indefinite **articles**, in languages which have them, may also show gender agreement. French has *le jour* (masculine) 'the day' and *un jour* '*a day*' *contrasting with la nuit* (feminine) 'the night' and *une nuit* 'a night'. In French, and many other languages, the indefinite article also functions as the numeral 'one' and agrees in gender in this function too. In French this is the only example, but in other languages **numerals** more generally agree in gender. We can see this in Chichewa, which is a Bantu language spoken in Malawi; it is a variety of the language which is called Chinyanja in neighbouring Zambia, Zimbabwe and Mozambique. In Chichewa the numerals from one to five all agree in gender (data from Sam Mchombo, personal communication):

(3) phiri   li-modzi
    mountain 5-one
    'one mountain'

(4) mapiri   a-wiri
    mountains 6-two
    'two mountains'

Phiri 'mountain' is a gender 5/6 noun; when singular, as in (3), it takes class 5 agreements, and when plural, as in (4), class 6 (see discussion of Bantu class markers in section 3.1.2). *Chipewa* 'hat' belongs to gender 7/8:

(5) chipewa chi-modzi
    hat   7-one
    'one hat'

(6) zipewa   zi-wiri
    hats   8-two
    'two hats'

While the numerals up to five agree in this way, six to nine are compound numerals:

(7) zipewa zi-sanu ndi chi-modzi
    hats   8-five and 7-one
    'six hats'

Zisanu 'five' agrees directly with *zipewa* 'hats'; *chimodzi* 'one' agrees with the understood noun *chipewa* 'hat'.

Staying within Bantu, we may note the 'associative' morpheme. This is one of a range of constructions which are used in different languages for the possession relation, in its broadest sense. Such **possessives** often mark gender agreement, as this Swahili example of the associative morpheme shows (Welmers 1973: 175):

(8) kisu ch-a   Hamisi
    knife 7-ASSOCIATIVE Hamisi
    'Hamisi's knife'

Here the associative morpheme *a* takes agreement in gender with the possessed noun phrase (*kisu* 'knife' is in gender 7/8). The associative morpheme may be combined into a more complex structure; the following examples are from Shona (Welmers 1973: 178; for Luganda examples see Givón 1972: 27, 92):

(9) imbwa na-vana   v-a-dz-o
   dogs   and-young 2-ASSOCIATIVE-10-their
   'the dogs and their pups'

The last item shows agreement with both nouns. The head noun *imbwa* 'dogs' belongs to gender 9/10, and the agreement marker is *-dz-*; the associated noun *vana* 'children, young' is gender 1/2 and takes the agreement marker *v-*. Of course, both nouns may happen to be of the same gender:

(10) buve   na-dandadzi r-a-r-o
    spider and-web   5-ASSOCIATIVE-5-its
    'the spider and its web'

In (10) both nouns are in gender 5/6 and take the agreement marker *r-*.

Archi also has some interesting possessives (Kibrik 1977a: 128–30, 320):

(11) d-ašá-r-ej-r-u-t̄u-r
    II-of.myself-II-SUFFIX-II-SUFFIX-SUFFIX-II
    'my own'

(12) w-ašá-w-ej-w-u-t̄u-∅
    I-of.myself-I-SUFFIX-I-SUFFIX-SUFFIX-I
    'my own'

The root is *aša* 'of myself', *ej* and *u* are suffixes, as is *t̄u*, which forms adjectives. It is the remaining elements which are of special interest here. In (11) the initial *d* and the three occurrences of *r* all mark gender II agreement; the form would be used for agreement with a gender II noun, in a phrase like 'my wife'. In (12), the three occurrences of the *w* marker all show gender I agreement (in final position *w* is not realized, hence the ∅); this form would be appropriate in phrases like 'my husband'. Thus this one word has no less than four agreement slots. In one way this is more complex than the Shona construction, since there are four agreement markers instead of two; but conversely, all four show agreement with the same item, while in Shona there are two different agreement controllers. Lehmann (1982: 209–11) illustrates how in possessive constructions agreement can go in either direction. It is common for the possessed noun to show agreement with the possessor, as in the North-West Caucasian language Abkhaz (Hewitt 1979: 116).

(13) à-č'k°'ən yə-y°nə̀
    the-boy OBLIQUE.3RD.SG.HUMAN.MALE-house
    'the boy's house'

Here the possessed noun phrase bears a marker agreeing with the possessor in gender (among other categories). Less commonly, we find the possessor agreeing with the possessed noun phrase, as in the North-East Caucasian language Chamalal (Magomedbekova 1967b: 388). There are five genders (or noun classes); in our examples, the noun *hek'wa* 'man' is in the genitive case and agrees in gender with the following noun phrase (which denotes what is possessed):

(14) hek'wa-šu-∅ wac
     man-GEN-I brother
     'the man's brother'
(15) hek'wa-šw-i jac
     man-GEN-II sister
     'the man's sister'
(16) hek'wa-šu-b č'atw
     man-GEN-III horse
     'the man's horse'
(17) hek'wa-šu-l īsa
     man-GEN-IV cheese
     'the man's cheese'
(18) hek'wa-šw-i anna
     man-GEN-V ear
     'the man's ear'

(The forms for genders II and V, though identical in the singular, are distinguished in the plural, where there are two forms, human and non-human.) This interesting pattern, in which the possessor agrees in gender with the possessed, may well have arisen from a construction like that in Swahili (example (8)), with a morpheme similar to the Bantu associative morpheme having become permanently attached to the noun as a case marker.

A further type of agreeing modifier within the noun phrase is the **participle**. Some languages have sets of participles which are formed from verbs, but which are morphologically similar to adjectives and show agreement in gender. In Russian we find:

(19) žurnal, ležašč-ij na stole
     magazine lying-MASC on table
     'the magazine lying on the table'
(20) kniga, ležašč-aja na stole
     book lying-FEM on table
     'the book lying on the table'

(21) pis′mo, ležašč-ee   na stole
    letter   lying-NEUT on table
    'the letter lying on the table'

We have seen that various attributive modifiers, particularly those discussed at the beginning of the section, often show gender agreement. It is also common to find **verbs** showing agreement in gender. Again in Russian we find:

(22) žurnal   ležal-∅   na stole
    magazine lay-MASC on table
    'the magazine lay on the table'

(23) kniga ležal-a na stole
    book lay-FEM on table
    'the book lay on the table'

(24) pis′mo ležal-o   na stole
    letter   lay-NEUT on table
    'the letter lay on the table'

The agreement markers are -∅ (masculine), -*a* (feminine) and -*o* (neuter). Now compare Swahili examples (Welmers 1973: 171-2):

(25) mtu   a-li-kuja
    person 1-PAST-come
    'A person came.'

The *a*- shows class 1 agreement; the verb agrees with the subject, which is a singular noun of the 1/2 gender. The form changes if we have a gender 3/4 noun:

(26) mshale u-li-anguka
    nail   3-PAST-fall
    'A nail fell.'

In Swahili and in Bantu languages in general, unlike Russian and other Indo-European languages, agreement markers are found before the stem. A more important feature of Swahili is illustrated in the next example:

(27) ni-na-u-taka   mshale
    1ST.SG-PRES-3.OBJ-want nail
    'I want the nail.'

In (27) we have a first person singular form *ni*-; we also see that Swahili can show agreement with the direct object as well as with the subject. Note that subject agreement comes before the tense marker, while object agreement is found between the tense marker and the verb root. Unless emphasized, personal pronouns are usually omitted, the same information being recoverable from the agreement markers:

(28) ni-li-m-tafuta
1ST.SG-PAST-1.OBJ-seek
'I looked for him/her.'

Here the *ni-* shows that the subject is the first-person singular and the *-m-* indicates a singular direct object from gender 1/2. The question of which types of noun phrase can control agreement in Bantu is complex: for a review see Hyman & Duranti (1982). In Kirundi (Mel'čuk & Bakiza 1987: 316–17) the verb may apparently agree with the indirect object and a locative expression as well as with subject and direct object, but the fact that these agreements (apart from subject agreement) are optional, suggests that clitic pronominal forms are involved. Agreement in gender with the indirect object (as well as with subject and direct object) is also reported in the Papuan language Yimas (Foley 1986: 94).

In several of the languages discussed, in Russian and in Bantu languages like Swahili, we find both adjectival agreement and agreement of the verb. This conforms to Greenberg's Universal 31 (Greenberg 1963: 112), which we reformulate as follows: a language which has agreement of the verb in gender with subject or object will also have agreement of the adjective with its head noun. It follows that, though relatively common, verb agreement in gender will be less widespread than adjectival agreement. An idea of its frequency can be gained from Bybee's survey of fifty languages, selected so as to be free of areal and genetic bias (1985: 18); gender agreement was found in the verb in 16 per cent of the languages (no figure is given for the adjective).

Pronouns also frequently vary in form according to gender. Taking the **relative pronoun** first, we note that this occurs within the noun phrase and so it might have been dealt with earlier. But, as we shall see in section 8.1.1, in terms of agreement it comes between the verbal predicate and the personal pronoun. We return to Russian for examples:

(29) žurnal, kotor-yj ležal-∅ na stole
magazine which-MASC lay-MASC on table
'the magazine, which lay on the table'

(30) kniga, kotor-aja ležal-a na stole
book which-FEM lay-FEM on table
'the book, which lay on the table'

(31) pis'mo, kotor-oe ležal-o na stole
letter which-NEUT lay-NEUT on table
'the letter, which lay on the table'

In each example the relative pronoun *kotor-* shows agreement in gender, masculine, feminine and neuter respectively (and since it is the subject of the subordinate clause the verb agrees with it). The **personal pronoun** frequently varies according to gender. This too can be illustrated from Russian:

> (32) Ivan kupil   knig-u   i   poslal
>   Ivan bought book-ACC and sent
>   ee   Vladimir-u
>   it.FEM.SG.ACC Vladimir-DAT
>   'Ivan bought a book and sent it to Vladimir'

The pronoun *ee* in (32) is feminine and singular because its antecedent *knigu* is feminine and singular (its case is determined within its own clause). As was mentioned earlier, the extent of the phenomena covered by the term agreement is disputed. According to the definition given at the beginning of the chapter, the pronoun *ee* in (32) would be said to agree with its antecedent. And in most mainstream work (for example, Givón 1976, Moravcsik 1978, Lehmann 1982, Lapointe 1988), agreement is taken in the wide sense, and so includes the determination of the form of personal and relative pronouns, and so on. This view makes good sense: it is evident that the same categories are regularly involved in both the undisputed cases of agreement and in disputed cases like anaphoric pronouns. We need look no further than gender, which is marked by both. Moreover, the data to be examined in chapter 8 show clearly that attributive modifiers and pronouns are linked as poles of a single hierarchy, which suggests that they should be treated as parts of the same phenomenon. Recent work on the problem is reviewed by Barlow (1988: 134–52), and he concludes that there is no good basis for distinguishing between agreement and antecedent-anaphora relations, even when cross-sentential.

Some take a different view; thus Wiese (1983) argues that pronominal anaphora should be excluded from agreement. However, those who restrict the range of agreement draw the boundary in different places. And it is clear that even if 'agreement' is reserved for a narrower class of phenomena, the excluded areas such as anaphora still share a great deal with it and, for our purposes, would have to be treated with it. Thus while different theories may force people to draw a boundary line at various points, this would not be appropriate here. We shall follow the widespread usage according to which agreement covers areas such as the determination of the form of anaphoric pronouns. An important consequence is that we shall recognize languages as having a gender system even if this is reflected only in the pronoun (see section 6.4.2 for discussion).

Having examined agreement of attributive modifiers, the predicate, and relative and personal pronouns, we might expect that we had reached the end of the list. But Lak, discussed in section 2.2.5, illustrates a further possibility, namely agreement of the **adverb** (Khaidakov 1980: 206):

(33) k'i-*j*-a ars ša-*w*-a   ∅-ušar
     two.I son at.home.I I-be
     'Two sons are at home.'

In (33) the italicized forms and ∅ all mark agreement with gender I, since *ars* 'son' belongs to this gender. To show gender I agreement, numerals (which are followed by a singular noun) take the marker *j*; not all adverbs agree, but those which do take *w*, while adjectives and verbs (again not all show agreement) have the null form (∅). Kala Lagaw Ya, the language of the western Torres Straits Islands, also appears to have adverbs which show agreement in gender (Bani 1987: 189, 199), as does Italian to a limited degree (Napoli 1975).

Adpositions (prepositions and postpositions) may agree with their noun phrase. We return to Abkhaz for examples of postpositions agreeing in gender (Hewitt 1979: 113–14, further examples on pages 103, 125–37):

(34) Àxra yə-zə̀
     Axra 3RD.SG.HUMAN.MALE-for
     'for Axra'

Abkhaz has three genders, male human, female human and non-human; the postposition shows agreement with the noun phrase, which here consists of the proper name *Àxra*. With a non-human, there is a different marker:

(35) a-žaħ°à   à-la
     the-hammer 3RD.SG.NON_HUMAN-with
     'with the hammer'

Agreement of adpositions in gender, as found in Abkhaz, is rare.

There is some evidence that even **complementizers** can show agreement in gender. In West Flemish, a dialect spoken in rural West Flanders, we find these data (Bennis & Haegeman 1984: 41):

(36) ...datje (jij) komt
     that (he) comes
(37) ...dase (zie) komt
     that (she) comes
(38) ...dat (et) komt
     that (it) comes

The form of the complementizer varies according to the gender of the subject pronoun, which would normally be omitted (hence the parentheses), unless stressed. However, while agreement in number is general, agreement in gender occurs only when the subject is pronominal (whether actually present or not); it cannot occur with a noun phrase headed by a noun. An alternative analysis would treat the agreement markers on the complementizers as clitics, but there are problems with this analysis since West Flemish has clitics which have a different distribution to that of the markers on the complementizer (see the data in Bennis & Haegeman (1984: 52). While the case is not clear-cut, it is at least plausible that we have gender agreement here. Even if it can be demonstrated that clitics are involved, these are a major source of agreement markers and so full gender agreement may result in time.

To conclude this section let us examine a particularly interesting type of agreement found in Archi (Kibrik 1972: 124; Kibrik, Kodzasov, Olovjan-nikova & Samedov 1977: 25). Like Lak, Archi is an ergative language. Intransitive verbs agree with their subject:

> (39) dija   qI$_o$a
> father   came
> (40) buwa   daqIa
> mother came

Dija 'father' is a gender I noun, *buwa* 'mother' is gender II, and the verb varies accordingly. (The normal agreement marker for gender I is *w*, which we shall see below; in (39) it labializes the initial consonant. In (40) the marker is *d*.) Now consider examples with a transitive verb and with a first-person pronoun (Roman numerals again stand for gender agreement markers):

> (41) w-ez   dija   ǩ'anši w-i
> I-1ST.SG.DAT   father   like   I-is
> 'I like father.'
> (42) d-ez   buwa   ǩ'anši d-i
> II-1ST.SG.DAT   mother like   II-is
> 'I like mother.'
> (43) b-ez   dogi   ǩ'anši b-i
> III-1ST.SG.DAT donkey like   III-is
> 'I like the donkey.'
> (44) Ø-ez   motol   ǩ'anši Ø-i
> IV-1ST.SG.DAT   kid   like   IV-is
> 'I like the kid.'

In these examples the verb, or rather the part of it which conjugates, the link verb 'be', agrees with the object, by means of the agreement markers *w*- (gender I), *d*- (gender II), *b*- (gender III) and *∅*- (gender IV). But it is the personal pronoun which provides the surprise. With verbs of perception and emotion, the noun phrase denoting the experiencer stands in the dative; thus *-ez* is the dative case form of the first person singular pronoun. This pronoun agrees with the noun phrase which controls verb agreement: *w-ez* is gender I, agreeing with *dija* 'father', *d-ez* gender II, agreeing with *buwa* 'mother', *b-ez* gender III, agreeing with *dogi* 'donkey' and *∅-ez* gender IV, agreeing with *motol* 'kid'.

5.2 **The form of gender agreement**

We must now examine the means by which agreement in gender is realized. We will first consider the morphological devices available (section 5.2.1), and then move on to a particular case, the phenomenon known as alliterative concord (section 5.2.2). Then we work through a complex example of gender agreement (section 5.2.3).

5.2.1 *The morphology of gender agreement*

The more common means of marking gender agreement have already occurred in earlier examples; typically, we find inflectional affixes, which stand before or after the stem. Agreement markers occur before the stem in Bantu languages, as in the Swahili examples quoted above (for example, in (25), the form *a-likuja* 'came' has the marker *a*-, which marks gender 1/2 singular). Agreement markers typically come after the stem in Indo-European, as in the Russian examples above (for example in Russian *nov-aja* 'new', in example (1), the *-aja* indicates feminine singular nominative). While some languages treat all gender agreement in the same way, others do not. In Babanki, a language of the Ring group, part of the Western Grassfields division of Bantu, spoken in north-west Cameroon (Hyman 1980b: 237), gender agreement may occur as a prefix or as both a prefix and a suffix: thus numerals take only a prefix while adjectives take prefixes and suffixes. In Yimas, verbs take prefixed gender markers while adjectives take suffixes (as we shall see in table 6.6).

The last and least usual form of gender agreement is infixed agreement. We saw agreement markers occurring inside the word, as in the Archi example (11), which we repeat here:

(45) d-ašá-r-ej-r-u-t̄u-r
     'my own'

In this example the first occurrence of -*r*- signals gender II singular agreement. Some would treat this as an infix; others would argue that we have a compound stem here, and that the r is a prefix on *ej* and so better described as 'internal' rather than 'infixed'. This example shows all the possibilities discussed so far, namely prefixed forms (the *d*-), suffixed forms (the final -*r*) and internal forms (the other occurrences of *r*). While the Archi examples may be analysed in such a way as to avoid postulating infixes in the strict sense there seems to be no such alternative for the next set of data. Marind appears to mark gender agreement by ablaut forms. It belongs to the family of the same name and has about 7,000 speakers in southern Irian Jaya; data, originally from Drabbe, are presented in Foley (1986: 82–3). Marind has four noun classes or genders, and nouns are assigned to them according to these criteria: gender I is for male humans, gender II for female humans and animals, gender III is mainly for plants and trees, while the semantic residue makes up gender IV. This system recalls that found in Dyirbal, though there animals are found in the same gender as male humans. Our main interest, however, is the agreement forms, which can be seen in these sentences (Roman numerals denote gender agreement markers):

(46) e-pe   anem   e-pe   akek   ka
I-the   man   I-the   light.I   is
'The man is light.'

(47) u-pe   anum   u-pe   akuk   ka
II-the   woman II-the   light.II   is
'The woman is light.'

(48) e-pe   de   e-pe   akak   ka
III-the wood   III-the light.III is
'The wood is light.'

(49) i-pe   behaw i-pe   akik   ka
IV-the pole   IV-the light.IV is
'The pole is light.'

The forms of the adjective *ak-k* 'light' mark gender by the infixed vowel:-*e*- for gender I, -*u*- for II, -*a*- for III and -*i*- for IV. (It is worth noting in passing that the plural marker for genders I and II is *i*, the same as the singular for gender IV, a type of pattern we shall meet again in certain Caucasian languages. Genders III and IV have no distinct plural forms.) Thus gender can be indicated by infixed agreement markers, as well as by prefixes and suffixes. This same feature is found in various Pamir languages (Iranian languages of Tadzikistan and Afghanistan), such as Roshani, but it is restricted to certain adjectives and to some intransitive verbs in the past tenses (Payne 1989: 429, 436–8).

5.2.2 *Alliterative concord*

Alliterative concord involves a particular type of gender agreement, which can be illustrated with examples like this Swahili sentence (Welmers 1973: 171):

> (50) ki-kapu ki-kubwa ki-moja ki-lianguka
> 7-basket 7-large 7-one 7-fell
> 'One large basket fell.'

Two features of this type of gender agreement system need to be separated out:

1. the noun itself includes a form which is identical to the gender agreement marker and which clearly indicates the gender of the noun;
2. the same gender agreement marker is used for different agreement targets.

When the gender of a noun is clear from its form (in the way discussed in chapter 3), we talk of 'overt' gender; when the form does not give a clear indication of gender we are dealing with a 'covert' gender system. But as we saw in section 3.3.1, this distinction is really a question of degree. In Qafar, the form of almost every noun gives away its gender, while in French, there are more exceptions and the rules are more complex. In Russian and Swahili, the form of a noun generally indicates its gender. In example (50), the initial *ki-* shows that *kikapu* belongs to morphological class 7/8, and so is of gender 7/8. There are, however, many examples where the morphological indicator is overridden by a semantic factor. In section 3.1.2 we discussed nouns like *kifaru* 'rhinoceros', which is morphologically similar to *kikapu* 'basket' in (50) above, but which takes different gender agreement (since it denotes an animate). This shows that Swahili gender is not completely overt. And in the Marind examples in the previous section, certain nouns had an infixed vowel appropriate to their gender (*anem* 'man' with the *e* of gender I as compared to *anum* 'woman' gender II, while others did not: *behaw* 'pole', gender IV, with no *i* vowel). Thus gender in Marind is partially overt. More generally, a system may be overt to a greater or lesser degree.

If a language has overt gender it does not necessarily follow that it has alliterative concord. For a language to qualify as having an alliterative system, the formal marker on the noun must be the same as that used for agreement.

In Qafar, the accent position on the noun frequently reveals its gender, but this is not the agreement marker found on verbs, and so Qafar has not got alliterative concord. In the Swahili example (50) on the other hand, the initial *ki-* on the noun *kikapu* is identical to the marker found on various agreement targets in the sentence. But this is not invariably the case in Swahili:

> (51) m-shale u-lianguka
> 3-nail 3-fell
> 'A nail fell.'

Here the noun prefix does not match the agreement markers, and so the system is not fully alliterative.

This brings us to the second point about alliterative concord. In an ideal system of this type, all targets take the same form. If we have, say, an adjective, numeral and verb agreeing in gender with a given noun, the agreement forms will be identical, and there will be no variation in agreement within word classes (for example, all verbs will behave identically). In example (50) we found *ki-* on each target. Had we used a target with a vowel-initial stem, like *-angu* 'my' we would have found the allomorph *ch*, in *ch-angu*. More serious irregularities are found in Swahili in gender 1/2:

> (52) m-tu   m-moja a-likuja
> 1-person 1-one a-1-came
> 'One person came.'

In this gender the numeral takes an alliterative form, while the verb, with the prefixed form *a-*, does not (as we noted in section 3.1.2). Again languages vary according to this parameter. Some have identical or extremely similar agreement forms, others vary widely. In the Russian examples in section 5.1 we saw that the attributive adjective and relative pronoun have identical forms:

> (53) nov-aja kniga, kotor-aja...
> new-FEM book which-FEM
> 'the new book, which...'

On the other hand, the personal pronoun is *on-a*. Thus we find *-a* as a marker of the feminine gender, though it may be extended. Examples of such similarities, without complete matching, are widespread.

Alliterative concord is therefore not something which languages simply have or do not have; rather, it is one pole of a scale along which languages can be measured. A language with consistent alliterative concord would be one with completely overt gender, and with the formal device which distinguishes nouns being identical to the agreement marker for all possible agreement targets. It may be that no language has totally consistent alliterative concord, but many Bantu languages show such concord to a high degree, with systems considerably more consistent than that of Swahili. Particularly consistent alliterative concord systems are found elsewhere in the Niger-Congo group, for example in Amo (spoken in north-central Nigeria; see Anderson 1980) and in Uskade (a Lower Cross language; Connell 1987). Near the other end of the scale we find Indo-European languages, not often mentioned in discussions of alliterative concord, but which show the phenomenon to some degree; thus Russian has alliterative concord to a considerable degree, provided nominative case forms are considered; in the oblique cases the correspondences are less clear. In the extreme case languages always have some degree of similarity between forms for agreement with particular genders for some agreement targets and so might be said to show minimal alliterative concord. In the next section we consider a language with an extremely low rating in terms of alliterative concord: gender cannot normally be inferred from the form of a noun and furthermore the agreement markers on different targets show considerable dissimilarities.

5.2.3 *A complex example: Khinalug*

Agreement in gender is often illustrated with straightforward examples. It is worth remembering that it can be a complex phenomenon, as the present data will show. Khinalug is an unwritten North-East Caucasian language of the Lezgian subgroup, with about 1,000 speakers in Azerbaydzhan. As already mentioned (section 2.5.5), it has four classes or genders (I male rational; II female rational; III most remaining animates and some inanimates; IV residue). The data which follow are mainly from Kibrik, Kodzasov & Olovjannikova (1972: 117–28) and Kibrik (personal communication), though Magometov (1976) has also proved useful.

Agreement in gender is found on the demonstrative pronouns, on adjectives (when used without a noun) and on certain verbs. Khinalug has a wealth of verbal forms, non-finite as well as finite, and we shall concentrate on these. There are relatively few simple verbs; most verbs consist of a first element (typically nominal or adverbial) and a second, conjugated part, which can occur independently (often it is the verb 'be'). There are different types of agreement markers: the first set is shown in table 5.1. Note that in the singular the markers for genders I and IV are identical, the null form, and this form also serves as the plural for genders III and IV. The plural form for genders I and II is the same as the singular for gender III. Nouns, however, distinguish singular and plural; there are therefore both formal and semantic grounds for separating singular and plural. Since genders I and II can be distinguished in

119

Table 5.1 *First type of gender/number markers in Khinalug*

Gender	Singular	Plural
I	$\emptyset$	b
II	z	b
III	b	$\emptyset$
IV	$\emptyset$	$\emptyset$

the singular, we might have expected two separate forms in the plural. In fact the two forms are identical. This is an example of a phenomenon called 'syncretism': the identity of two or more morphosyntactic forms of the same lexeme. Thus lexemes which add agreement markers of type 1 show syncretism of the agreement forms for gender I plural, gender II plural, and indeed of gender III singular.

It is worth pausing for a moment to re-examine table 5.1. It is arranged in a way suggesting that there are four genders, but this is the result of the analysis just given. It does not follow directly from the data. Thus we need criteria for analysing such cases which will enable us to determine the number of genders in a given language. We shall not pursue the point here, but will consider it in detail in chapter 6.

Table 5.2 *The verb* k'i '*die*' *in Khinalug*

Gender	Singular	Plural
I	$\emptyset$-k'iʃæmæ	b-i-k'iʃæmæ
II	z-i-k'iʃæmæ	b-i-k'iʃæmæ
III	b-i-k'iʃæmæ	$\emptyset$-k'iʃæmæ
IV	$\emptyset$-k'iʃæmæ	$\emptyset$-k'iʃæmæ

Gender markers in Khinalug have various allomorphs, whose appearance is determined by complex phonotactic constraints. The morpheme *z* may surface as *z*, *s*, *ts^h* or *zi*, while *b* may appear as *b*, *p^h*, $\emptyset$ and *bi*, as seen, for example, in the past tense of *k'i* 'die' in table 5.2. The final *mæ* marks indicative mood, and *ʃæ* immediately preceding it indicates past tense. The example shows a simple verb; in compound verbs the first type of marker occurs before the conjugated part. There is a second type of agreement marker; its forms are shown in table 5.3. The syncretisms are as before, and

Table 5.3 *Second type of gender/number markers in Khinalug*

Gender	Singular	Plural
I	j	v
II	z	v
III	v	j
IV	j	j

again there are various allomorphs. Both types of marker may be found in the same verb, as in these two forms of the nominalization of the verb 'burn':

gender I   j-æk-∅-k^hirval   gender II   z-æk-s-k^hirval

Here the initial *j* and *z* are type 2 markers, and ∅ and *s* are type 1 (*s* being an allomorph of *z*). Thus agreement (with the object in this instance since Khinalug is an ergative language) is marked twice in the examples above. A third type of marker is found in the imperative of 'be' and its compounds and in some forms of 'go' (see table 5.4). For illustration of these markers we take the imperative of 'be' (see table 5.5).

So far we have seen that there are three types of gender marker. In order to make appropriate agreement in gender the native speaker needs information of different kinds. First, the lexical entry for the verb must include information as to whether it has an agreement slot or not; some verbs, a minority, do not take a prefixed agreement marker, and this is not predictable; thus -*k^hui* 'to do' agrees, while *kui*, which is one of the suppletive forms of the verb 'to be',

Table 5.4 *Third type of gender/number markers in Khinalug*

Gender	Singular	Plural
I	h	f
II	s	f
III	f	h
IV	h	h

Table 5.5 *Imperative of 'be' in Khinalug*

Gender	Singular	Plural
I	h-ar	f-ar
II	s-ar	f-ar
III	f-ar	h-ar
IV	h-ar	h-ar

does not. Second, the appropriate set of markers must be selected. The third type of marker is restricted to a small number of verbs in certain morphological forms (and is found only before a vowel). Apart from these exceptional cases, type one is used before a consonant and type two before a vowel. In some cases, as we have seen, the speaker may be required to mark gender more than once in the same verb. However, the three types of marker are similar in that they have the same syncretisms or identities of form. In all types the forms for I singular, IV singular and III–IV plural are identical, as are those for III singular and I–II plural. There is, however, a further type of marker, which is rather different; it has the forms shown in table 5.6. These markers are very similar to the forms of the demonstrative pronoun *du* 'this', which is clearly their origin. They differ from the markers already discussed in three important respects. First, they are regular: they can in principle be used with any verb and they are not subject to the same range of allomorphic variation as the other markers. Second, they are not purely agreement markers. They also indicate tense (past or future). And third, their pattern of syncretism differs from that of the other markers. Like them, they have only two plural forms, one for genders I and II (nouns denoting rationals) and one for genders III and IV (non-rationals). But in the singular, genders II and III have the same form, and I and IV differ. This has important consequences as we shall see.

Table 5.6 *Pronominal gender/number markers in Khinalug*

Gender	Singular	Plural
I	du	dur
II	dæ	dur
III	dæ	ʒi(tʰ)
IV	ʒi	ʒi(tʰ)

The tense-forming function of these markers does not interfere with the use of the other markers, so that a verb may show three agreement markers at the same time, as shown in table 5.7. In the forms given, the preverb *k'úr* and the root *qχin* together form a verb meaning 'forget'. It has an internal agreement slot, and the markers here, like the other two, show agreement with the direct object in gender and number, according to the indications on the left. These first markers are of type 1, with the appearance of particular allomorphs being determined by the following consonant. The second root *kʰu* 'do', makes the verb causative. This root takes a prefixed agreement marker, also of type 1, but realized by slightly different allomorphs. After the second root there is a

Table 5.7 *'Cause to forget' in Khinalug (past concrete)*

	Preverb	– AG	– Root	– AG	– Root	– AG/tense	– Indicative
Singular							
I	k'úr	– ∅	– qχin	– ∅	– kʰu	– d	– mæ
II	k'úr	– s	– qχin	– s	– kʰu	– dæ	– mæ
III	k'úr	– pʰ	– qχin	– ∅	– kʰu	– dæ	– mæ
IV	k'úr	– ∅	– qχin	– ∅	– kʰu(i)– ꙅ		– mæ
Plural							
I	k'úr	– pʰ	– qχin	– ∅	– kʰu	– dur	– mæ
II	k'úr	– pʰ	– qχin	– ∅	– kʰu	– dur	– mæ
III	k'úr	– ∅	– qχin	– ∅	– kʰu(i)– ꙅitʰ		– mæ
IV	k'úr	– ∅	– qχin	– ∅	– kʰu(i)– ꙅitʰ		– mæ

third agreement marker, of the pronominal type. Like the other markers, it agrees with the direct object, but unlike them it has a second function, to mark the tense (past definite). Finally, there is the indicative marker.

These patterns may seem slightly less surprising if we recall the more familiar examples of compound tenses in Indo-European, in which the auxiliary agrees in person and number, and the participle in gender and number (examples (70) and (71) below). In Khinalug we find gender and number repeated through the verb form. The pronominal gender/number markers are an innovation in Khinalug. This is suggested by their regularity compared to the other forms and confirmed by the fact that no similar development is found in the related languages of the Lezgian subgroup. The development represents a strengthening of the gender system. The old markers do not distinguish gender I from gender IV in the singular, and they have zero allomorphs in many instances. The form most often distinguished is that of gender II singular. The new forms mean that the genders are clearly marked in many more instances: their weak spot, the syncretism of genders II and III in the singular, is of little significance, since the old markers distinguish these genders adequately.

Khinalug shows that gender agreement can be complex, with the form to be used depending both on the verb in question and the particular tense/aspect form involved. It also illustrates the renewal of gender agreement through the use of an originally pronominal form, a point taken up in section 5.5.

5.3 **Limits on gender agreement**

In descriptions of individual languages, we may find it stated that members of a particular word-class show agreement in gender. Such statements can be misleading. It may well be that all members of the word-class in question (say adjectives) always show agreement. But it may be that all members of the word-class show agreement, but not under all circumstances. Or it may be that some but not all members of the word-class show agreement in gender. We will therefore review the different restrictions on gender agreement.

5.3.1 *Syntactic restrictions*

German adjectives show agreement with their head noun:

(54) warm-er   Tee
    warm-MASC tea
(55) warm-e   Milch
    warm-FEM milk
(56) warm-es   Wasser
    warm-NEUT water

When, however, the adjective stands in the predicate, it is invariable:

(57) der Tee ist warm
    the tea is warm
(58) die Milch ist warm
    the milk is warm
(59) das Wasser ist warm
    the water is warm

Thus German adjectives show agreement in gender only when in the right syntactic configuration.

In various Germanic languages, there are interactions between the different modifiers of a single noun, and a relevant one involving definiteness can be illustrated from Swedish. Within the noun phrase, Swedish distinguishes common gender from neuter gender. ('Common gender' when used of Scandinavian languages is simply the name of a gender which combines the earlier masculine and feminine; it does not suggest that the nouns involved are of double gender. For a note on the four gender distinctions made by the pronouns see section 8.2.) The two forms found within the noun phrase are illustrated in the following simple phrases:

(60) en   grön   färg
    a.COMMON green.COMMON colour
(61) ett   grönt   hus
    a.NEUT green.NEUT house

Here the article and the adjective both show agreement in gender. If the noun phrase is made definite the picture changes:

(62) den   grön-a   färg-en
     the.COMMON green-DEF colour-DEF.COMMON

(63) det   grön-a   hus-et
     the.NEUT green-DEF house-DEF.NEUT

When the noun phrase is definite, there is a marker of definiteness on the noun, -*en*/-*et*, which also marks gender. If there is an adjective present, as in (62) and (63) above, then a preposed definite article also appears (*den*/*det*), and this too agrees in gender. The adjective itself takes the definite ending -*a*, but, as the examples show, this does not vary for gender. Thus definite noun phrases show agreement in gender, but not on the adjective. In the case of adjectives, therefore, whether they show agreement in gender or fail to do so depends on the definiteness of the noun phrase.

In Classical Arabic, word-order is a determining factor. In verb-initial sentences, agreement in gender is optional. Examples like the following are found:

(64) ḥaḍar-a   l-qāḍiya ('i)mra'atun
     came(before)-MASC.SG the-judge woman
     'A woman came before the judge.'

Here we find the default form of the verb, the masculine singular. In sentences in which the subject precedes the verb there is agreement in gender (Russell 1984: 124–5). Returning to verb-initial sentences, we find that if the noun phrase is definite, agreement in gender is much more likely:

(65) jā-at   hindun
     came-FEM.SG Hind (female proper name)
     'Hind came.'

Thus gender agreement may depend both on word-order and on definiteness; in the case in question it appears that we can see agreement with the topic in the course of developing into subject–verb agreement.

More generally, the point of this section is to show that elements which are morphologically capable of showing gender agreement may be restricted to doing so in specific syntactic environments.

5.3.2 *Interaction with tense*

There are various grammatical categories which may restrict the possibilities of gender agreement. We begin with tense. In Russian, as we have already noted, verbs agree in gender with the subject:

125

(66) Ivan čital-∅
Ivan was.reading-MASC
'Ivan was reading.'

(67) Irina čital-a
Irene was.reading-FEM
'Irene was reading.'

However, this is true only of the past tense (and the conditional). In other tenses, verbs agree in person and number but not gender:

(68) Ivan čitaet
Ivan is.reading

(69) Irina čitaet
Irene is.reading

Gender agreement therefore depends on interaction with tense. The situation has arisen from a compound tense consisting of the verb 'be' and a past participle which, like an adjective, agreed in gender. The present tense of the verb 'be' in Modern Russian is the null form, which has left the original participle as the only verb element present. (It cannot be analysed as a participle synchronically since its syntactic and morphological behaviour differs from that of adjectives and that of other synchronically motivated participles.) The pattern like that found in earlier stages of Russian, which is widespread in Indo-European, is also of interest for the role of person, which we discuss next.

5.3.3 *Interaction with person*

Our first examples are from the South Slavonic language Serbo-Croat:

(70) Ljubomir je došao
Ljubomir is come.MASC
'Ljubomir has come.'

(71) Snežana je došla
Snežana is come.FEM
'Snežana has come.'

Here the auxiliary verb *je*, a form of *biti* 'to be', agrees in person and number with the subject. If the subject were first person singular, the form would be *sam*, and if second person, *si*. Similarly if the number of the subject were to change, so would the form of the auxiliary. For example, the third plural form is *su*. But its form is not affected by the gender of the subject; we find *je* in (70) where the subject is masculine and in (71) with a feminine subject. On the other hand, the participial part of the verb phrase agrees in gender and number: it is masculine singular in (70) and feminine singular in (71). The masculine plural form would be *došli* and the feminine plural form *došle*. The person of the subject is irrelevant. Thus in Serbo-Croat, finite verbs agree in person and number, participles (and adjectives) agree in gender and number; there is no item which agrees in person and gender. As already mentioned, this is a common situation.

A rather different relation between gender and person is found in Archi. In this language, and several related ones, there are no distinct forms for agreement in person. In other words, agreements found with first and second person pronouns can all also be found with third person pronouns. In the singular, the situation is relatively straightforward: *zon* 'I' and *un* 'you' take gender I or gender II agreements, according to whether the speaker is male or female for the first person and according to the sex of the addressee for the second person. (Agreement markers on the pronoun itself in an oblique case were illustrated in (41)–(44) above.) In the plural the situation is more interesting. There are two available agreement markers, as opposed to four in the singular. In the third person, $b(a)$- is for genders I and II plural (so for all humans):

(72) teb ba-qIa
     they I/II.PL-came
     'They came.'

Example (72) can be used provided *teb* denotes humans; the same agreement form would be used if, instead of the pronoun, we had a plural noun denoting humans. *Teb* 'they' can also be used with the other plural agreement form $\emptyset$-, used for genders III and IV:

(73) teb $\emptyset$-qIa
     they III/IV.PL-came
     'They came.'

This is appropriate when *teb* denotes non-humans; the same verb form would be found with plural nouns of genders III and IV. Now consider the following:

(74) nen $\emptyset$-qIa
     we.EXCLUSIVE 1ST.PL-came
     'We came.'

(75) $\check{z}_0$en $\emptyset$-qIa
     you.PL 2ND.PL-came
     'You came.'

Since both pronouns denote humans, we might have expected the form *ba-qIa*. In fact, we have agreement in person, the first and second persons taking the agreement marker ∅-. This happens to be the same as the plural for genders III and IV. Thus, in the plural, the marker for first and second persons is ∅-, which also serves for genders III and IV in the third person. The third person plural marker for genders I and II is *b(a)*-. There is indeed no unique form for person agreement. However, if we did not recognize person agreement in Archi, the resolution rules to be discussed in section 9.3 would become very complex. While in Archi it is necessary to know the person of the subject in order to select the appropriate agreement marker for the verb, there is no marker which is specific to person agreement; they are all used for gender agreement.

There is an obvious link between agreement in person and the personal pronouns. Many languages have different forms of pronoun, which depend on the gender of the referent. Thus, as already mentioned, Russian has *on* 'he, it' for masculines (not just males), *ona* 'she, it' for feminines and *ono* 'it' for neuters. In contrast, the first person pronoun *ja* 'I' and the second person *ty* 'you' have only one form. However, forms agreeing with them show gender agreement:

(76) ja čital-∅
    I read.PAST-MASC
    'I was reading' (male speaker)

(77) ja čital-a
    I read.PAST-FEM
    'I was reading' (female speaker)

In the second person the gender depends on the sex of the addressee:

(78) ty   čital-∅
    you read.PAST-MASC
    'You were reading' (male addressee)

(79) ty   čital-a
    you read.PAST-FEM
    'You were reading' (female addressee)

This split between the third person (with separate forms of the pronoun) and the other two (without) is relatively common.

Before going on to languages in which separate forms are found in the other persons, it is worth stopping to consider what the examples just discussed show us about the nature of agreement in gender. In transformational accounts, the gender feature is copied from the controller on to the target. In

128

such an approach, it is necessary to say that *ty* 'you' is masculine in (78), but that the identical form is feminine in (79). In more recent work, notably in Generalized Phrase Structure Grammar, features are freely instantiated on controller noun phrases and on targets; only those structures meeting certain constraints, typically identity of certain features, are grammatical. In various models where unification plays an important role (for which see Shieber 1986) feature sets need not be fully specified. Thus a reasonable analysis for (79) is that the pronoun is second person singular, but does not indicate gender; the verb shows feminine gender and singular number, but does not vary for person. Unification of the two gives the values second person, singular, feminine. There is no need to specify two separate pronouns, one masculine and one feminine (see Barlow 1988: 22–45). In such frameworks there is not necessarily any directionality or asymmetry of agreement (as is implied by the copying of features from the noun phrase on to a target, say a verb phrase). We should nevertheless reconstruct the notion of asymmetry, because it represents an important intuition. A noun typically has only one gender: its form cannot be modified to accommodate that of a verb. On the other hand, the verb has alternative forms to match that of a particular subject in a given sentence. Linked to this is the fact that in many instances the gender feature on the noun is semantically justified – it correlates with a classification of real-world objects. In comparison, the gender markers on targets such as verbs are secondary. This becomes clear if in an example like (79) we replace the pronoun by a noun phrase, say *Irina* 'Irene' (which was the case in example (67)). In such an example *Irina* is feminine because it denotes a female. But the verb *čitala* 'read' is feminine only because the subject is feminine, and not because the reading is feminine. This asymmetry is captured in Generalized Phrase Structure Grammar by the Control Agreement Principle, based on an idea of Keenan's (Gazdar, Klein, Pullum & Sag 1985: 83–94).

Let us now consider further the interaction of person and gender, looking at languages which have separate gender forms not just in the third person. Afro-Asiatic provides numerous examples; we will consider Shilha (a member of the Berber branch, described by Applegate 1958: 19); the forms are given in table 5.8: Here we find separate forms in all but the first person singular. Several other Afro-Asiatic languages such as Arabic and Hebrew are similar, except that no first person form distinguishes masculine and feminine. In Spanish, in the plural, we find separate forms for all persons including the first: *nosotros* (masculine)/*nosotras* (feminine) 'we', *vosotros* (masculine)/ *vosotras* (feminine) 'you', and *ellos* (masculine)/*ellas* (feminine) 'they'. Further cases are listed by Forchheimer (1953: 29–37). It is often assumed that, as in the examples given, gender distinctions in the first person depend

Table 5.8 *Personal pronouns in Shilha*

| | Singular | | Plural | |
	Masculine	Feminine	Masculine	Feminine
1st person	nki		nukni	nuknti
2nd person	kii	kimi	kuni	kuninti
3rd person	nta	ntat	ntni	ntnti

on the sex of the speaker and those in the second person on that of the addressee, but this is not invariably the case.

Table 5.9 *Second person pronouns in Diuxi Mixtec*

| Speaker | | Addressee | | |
| | | Adult | | Child |
	Respect	Familiar	Neutral	
Male	ndiší	ndoʔó	meén	meén
Female	ndiší	yoʔó	meén	meú

In Diuxi Mixtec, a language of Mexico belonging to the Oto-Manguean group, the form of the second person pronoun depends on, among other things, the sex of the speaker, as table 5.9 shows (based on Kuiper & Pickett 1974: 54–5). The form to be used depends on the sex of the speaker, the age of the addressee (adult or child) and the type of relationship between them. The sex of the addressee is not a factor (except in that women may use respect forms to their husbands). Sex is not a direct factor in the choice of the first person pronoun, but for the third person (given in table 5.10), the sex of both speaker and referent are relevant. Note that both types of speakers have a three-way division when referring to humans (there are other pronouns for

Table 5.10 *Third person pronouns in Diuxi Mixtec*

| Speaker | Referent | | | |
	Man	Boy	Girl	Woman
male	meés	meés	meí	meñá
female	meté	meí	meí	meñá

non-human referents): for males it is male/girl/woman, for females it is man/child/woman. The North-East Caucasian language Andi (Cercvadze 1967: 285) also has pronominal forms whose selection depends on the sex of the speaker, in this case in the first and second persons singular. But in both languages, especially in the case of second person pronouns, we are moving beyond grammatical gender into the sociolinguistic area of forms of address and into the related area of men's and women's language. Thus in several languages, including Mixtec, the selection of the appropriate term for a sibling depends in part on the sex of the speaker (Nerlove & Romney 1967: 180). So the fact that men use *ndoʔó* where women use *yoʔó*, is to be considered in the same way as, for example, the use of different intonation patterns or different interjections by men and women in English. Where the choice of pronoun depends on the sex of the speaker who is not the referent (that is, in the second and third person pronouns) we are dealing with men's/women's language. This is, of course, related to gender and is a possible source for gender distinctions (compare Royen 1929: 276–7). Other types of difference between the speech of men and women, particularly in the Muskogean language Koasati, are described by Haas (1944), and a more general account is provided by Trudgill (1974: 84–102); for further references see section 7.3.1. As a curiosity, it is worth recording that Ket uses different forms for 'say', depending on the sex of the person whose speaking is reported; *bada* means '(a man) said' and *mana* means '(a woman) said' (Dul'zon 1964: 65).

Let us return to the interaction of person and gender, which has been little studied. However, Greenberg (1963: 96) claims that: 'If a language has gender distinctions in the first person, it always has gender distinctions in the second or third person, or in both' (Universal 44). The text makes it clear that he has pronouns rather than verbal morphology in mind. This universal claims that we shall not find languages in which the pronouns distinguish gender just in the first person. It is natural to go on to ask what happens if gender occurs in just one person. An obvious suggestion for a universal here would be that if a language has a gender distinction in any pronoun it will be in third person pronouns. While this is supported by a good deal of evidence, it turns out to be a tendency rather than a universal: a counter-example is the language Angas (West Chadic, Afro-Asiatic), which has gender in the second person only, except for reported speech (Burquest 1986). There is a functional explanation for the greater likelihood of gender differentiation within the third person, namely that third person forms are the most likely to be referentially ambiguous. The first and second persons are defined in terms of speaker and addressee respectively, while the third person is neither of these. Hence it is the third person which is the one most in need of further means to ensure referential clarity, and gender can fulfil this role (a point taken up in section 10.3.2).

One further point should be noted briefly here. Sometimes it is stated that a language has no third person pronouns, but uses demonstratives or noun markers instead. This is common in Caucasian languages. The distinguishing feature is that the forms in question can occur in attributive position as well as standing as full noun phrases. But the boundary is sometimes difficult to draw (Greenberg 1978: 75).

5.3.4 *Interaction with number*

Number is the category most intimately bound up with gender; it will figure prominently in the next two chapters. Here we merely record its importance and illustrate it briefly. If we take the Russian examples in (1) and make them plural, the result is as follows:

(80) nov-ye žurnaly   nov-ye knigi nov-ye pis′ma
new-PL magazines new-PL books new-PL letters

Although the nouns are of different genders, the agreement form is the same for all. Gender agreement in Russian is restricted to the singular number. In Khinalug (section 5.2.3) the relationship is more complex; while there is agreement in gender in the plural as well as in the singular, there are fewer gender distinctions in the plural, since in the plural the forms for genders I and II are always identical, and similarly the forms for genders III and IV are identical. Other types of interaction with number are found in languages with 'augmented' as a number category, for example in the Australian language Ndjebbana (McKay 1979; see Alpher 1987: 175–7 for comparative data).

5.3.5 *Interaction with case*

Consider the partial paradigm of the Russian demonstrative *ètot* 'this' in table 5.11. Since Russian does not distinguish gender in the plural, we

Table 5.11 *Some singular forms of Russian* ètot '*this*'

	Masculine	Neuter	Feminine
Nominative	ètot	èto	èta
Genitive	ètogo	ètogo	ètoj
Dative	ètomu	ètomu	ètoj
Instrumental	ètim	ètim	ètoj
Locative	ètom	ètom	ètoj

consider only the singular forms here. The three genders are clearly distinguished in the nominative. In the other cases given, only the feminine is distinct. Observe, too, how case is not differentiated in the oblique cases of the feminine but is differentiated for the masculine and neuter. The accusative case forms are not included in table 5.11, since there are complications here; we shall discuss these in section 6.4.1 when we consider subgenders, which form another type of interaction between gender and case.

5.3.6 *Morphological class*

Agreeing elements may fall into different types, with varying agreement possibilities. Latin has three genders, as shown by many adjectives (though not in all of the cases). Thus the nominative singular forms for 'good' are *bon-us* (masculine), *bon-a* (feminine) and *bon-um* (neuter). Adjectives which belong to this morphological class distinguish the three genders. But other adjectives, those of the third declension, show various possibilities (table 5.12). *Acer* 'sharp', and other adjectives like it, also distinguish three genders; adjectives like *facilis* 'easy', on the other hand, show no distinction between masculine and feminine. *Vigil* 'alert' and similar adjectives show no evidence of gender agreement in the nominative singular (certain other forms, however, distinguish neuter from the other genders).

Table 5.12 *Gender agreement of Latin adjectives*

Masculine	Feminine	Neuter	Gloss
acer	acris	acre	sharp
facilis	facilis	facile	easy
vigil	vigil	vigil	alert

It is worth noting how this situation differs from that described in the previous section. In Russian, the syncretisms described run right through the system. Thus there is no agreeing element which can distinguish masculine from neuter in the genitive, dative, instrumental or locative. In the Latin nominative case forms given we can see that the number of distinctions made varies according to declensional type. (There are further general syncretisms similar to, but less extensive than, those of Russian.) Some see the data in table 5.12 as supporting the claim that Indo-European once had two genders (hence the *facilis* type of adjective); one of these genders later split into masculine and feminine (see section 10.1.2).

5.3.7 *Phonological constraints*

It is not unusual to find that phonological conditions produce a situation in which gender is not differentiated. In the spoken French of Paris, for example, many adjectives cannot distinguish gender:

(81) un mot   vrai-∅
    a   word true-MASC
    'a true word'

(82) une histoire vrai-e
    a   story   true-FEM
    'a true story'

Although orthographically different, the pronunciation is identical [vrɛ] (Grevisse 1964: 170, 279). Other adjectives do distinguish gender:

(83) un mot   court-∅ [ku:r]
    a   word short-MASC
    'a short word'

(84) une histoire court-e [ku:rt]
    a   story   short-FEM
    'a short story'

One analysis of this phenomenon would use underlying forms similar to the historical and orthographical forms, with feminine marked by the addition of *e*. This vowel is not realized itself, but it has the effect of preserving an underlying stem-final consonant (as in (84)); however, it has no effect after a non-nasal vowel, as in the case of *vrai* 'true'. There are lexical exceptions but in the main it is adjectives ending in a consonant or a nasal vowel which can mark gender in spoken French.

5.3.8 *Lexical restrictions*

Lexical restrictions imply a less regular situation than that covered in previous sections. We find cases where even within a lexical category, some items show gender agreement and others do not, and the distribution cannot be explained in terms of more general morphological classes or of phonological rules. It is often the case that some, but not all, numerals show agreement in gender. We noted Chichewa examples in section 5.1. And in Russian, the numeral *odin* 'one' agrees in gender and in the subgender of animacy; *dva* 'two' also agrees in gender, but it distinguishes only the feminine from the masculine and neuter – it agrees less fully than does *odin*. *Tri* 'three' and *četyre* 'four' do not distinguish the main genders, but they agree in animacy, as indeed does *dva*. Higher numerals do not agree in gender. In Ket (Krejnovič 1961: 108) there are three genders; in predicative use, the numeral 'one' distinguishes all three genders; 'two' to 'five' distinguish the neuter from the masculine and feminine, while higher numerals make no distinction. In these cases it can be seen that the distribution is not random. For the simple cardinal numerals, as their arithmetical value increases, so the possibility of agreement in gender decreases. There is a widespread tendency for lower numerals to be more like adjectives, and for higher numerals to be more like nouns, and so not to agree in gender. This morphological tendency is complementary to a syntactic generalization, namely that for the simple cardinal numerals, any difference in their syntactic behaviour will be in terms of their becoming more like nouns (Corbett 1978). But as Hurford has shown, the morphological behaviour of numerals does not always mirror this syntactic regularity (1987: 190–3; see also Corbett 1978: 363–4). A striking counter-example is found in the North-Central Caucasian or Nakh languages, Chechen, Ingush and Tsova-Tush, in all of which the numeral 'four' is the only one which agrees in gender (Dešeriev 1967: 187). In the North-East Caucasian language Kryz, on the other hand, according to Saadiev (1967: 634) it is normal for numerals to agree in gender, but the numeral for 'thousand' is a borrowing from Persian and does not do so.

More irregular is the behaviour of adjectives in Tabasaran (also North-East Caucasian), as described in Xanmagomedov (1967: 550–1). The majority show the opposite pattern to German, that is they agree only when in predicative position. But just two, *užur* 'good' and *učur* 'beautiful', also agree in gender when in attributive position. These are therefore lexical exceptions. And in the discussion of Khinalug in section 5.2.3, we noted that most verbs take agreement markers, while some do not, and that their behaviour is not predictable.

We have seen therefore that even within a lexical class it may be necessary to label certain members as exceptionally agreeing in gender or failing to agree in gender. In concluding this section we should bear in mind that the possibility of marking agreement in gender may depend on any of the grammatical categories we have discussed. When in the next chapter we come to the analysis of gender in particular languages, we shall naturally look to those agreeing elements and combinations of categories which give the greatest range of possibilities. But, as we shall see in section 5.5, some of the surprising facts noted here receive a partial explanation in diachronic terms. Before looking at gender from this perspective, however, we should consider classifiers.

5.4 **Lack of agreement: classifiers**

For reasons we will discuss, classifiers do not fall within the scope of this book, but we should consider them briefly, since they are a source for gender agreement markers. Classifiers are of different types, of which numeral classifiers are particularly well known, In a language with numeral classifiers, noun phrases including a numeral and a noun will normally include a third element, the classifier, as in English phrases like *forty head of cattle*. Thus in Burmese (a Sino-Tibetan language), 'one river' might in the appropriate circumstances (where the context involves a river on a map) be translated as *myiʔ tə tan,* literally 'river one line'. It is the last element which is the classifier. Such classifiers are free forms, often appearing also as fully fledged nouns. This is illustrated in the following example (the unmarked case for 'river'): *myiʔ tə myiʔ* 'river one river'; here the noun is repeated as a classifier. It is frequently the case in classifier systems that classifiers do not co-occur with certain nouns, and for others that clasifiers may be obligatory or their use may vary according to speech style. Often different classifiers are possible with the same noun, and the choice depends on meaning. Thus, apart from the two classifiers already given with the Burmese noun *myiʔ,* there are several other possibilities (Becker 1975: 113):

myiʔ tə yaʔ	'river one place' (e.g., destination for a picnic);
myiʔ tə hmwa	'river one section' (e.g., a fishing area);
myiʔ tə ′sin	'river one distant arc' (e.g., a path to the sea);
myiʔ tə θwɛ	'river one connection' (e.g., tying two villages);
myiʔ tə ′pa	'river one sacred object' (e.g., in mythology);
myiʔ tə khu′	'river one conceptual unit' (e.g., in a discussion of rivers in general).

Some languages have classifiers which are not restricted to numeral phrases but which occur freely in ordinary noun phrases. The Australian language Yidiny is an example. Furthermore, in Yidiny two classifiers may be found with a single noun (Dixon 1982: 192):

(85) bama   waguuja wurgun
     person man   pubescent.boy
    'teenage boy'

Here the first two elements are both classifiers. It should be clear that, since gender systems have agreement as their defining characteristic, classifiers are a different phenomenon; classifiers do not show variation of a formal property (as is the case when, say, an adjective marks agreement in gender), rather the selection of one classifier as opposed to others is involved. Classifiers are independent items, selected largely according to semantic criteria, while gender markers typically appear attached to agreement targets. Besides following from our definition of agreement, the conclusion that classifiers are outside the scope of a study of gender appears correct, since classifiers differ from gender markers in various ways. These differences between classifiers and genders (or noun classes) are drawn clearly by Dixon (1982: 212–18) and we shall not labour the point here. This is not to dismiss classifiers; they are of great interest, as shown by the considerable literature on the subject (see the references in Dixon 1982 and in the relevant papers in Craig 1986a). There are some similarities too; the selection of classifiers is based on principles which in some respects resemble the assignment rules investigated in chapter 2. However, classifiers and gender systems tend to be found in languages of different morphological types. Languages of the isolating type by definition do not have agreement systems and so do not have gender systems. But they commonly have classifiers. Such languages are widespread in East and South-East Asia, an area conspicuously absent from our survey of places where gender systems are found (section 1.1). Languages of the fusional type, like most Indo-European languages, often have gender systems. Agglutinating languages fall between these two types, and vary, of course, as to the degree to which they are agglutinating. Some have classifier systems, some have gender systems (and some have neither). Thus there is a correlation between language type and the presence of classifiers or genders, and this correlation is exactly as we would expect. It suggests that the two systems may perform similar roles in languages of different morphological types. But the correlation is far from absolute. Exceptionally, a language can have both gender and classifiers. Dongo (a member of the Mba group, which belongs to the Ubangian branch of Niger-Kordofanian) has a complex gender system (see section 6.4.6) and is in addition developing a system of possessive classifiers (Pasch 1985; 1986: 245–55).

The special relevance of classifiers here is that they are a source of gender systems, as we shall see in the latter part of the next section.

5.5 **The gaining and losing of gender agreement**

This is an appropriate point to consider how languages gain and lose agreement markers. The most influential paper on the rise of agreement is Givón (1976; see also Givón 1984: 360–85). He claims that agreement markers on verbs develop from anaphoric pronouns. This idea was not completely new but it was Givón who worked it through. The phenomenon

137

of verb agreement arises from topic–verb agreement, more specifically from topic-shifting constructions where the noun phrase which is topicalized is coreferential to one of the verb's arguments. This is shown schematically as follows; in (86) we have a shifted topic:

> (86) the man,   he   came
>   TOPIC   PRONOMINAL.SUBJ VERB

In this marked construction, the pronoun represents topic agreement. This construction may become reanalysed as a neutral sentence type, as has occurred in many non-standard dialects of American English:

> (87) the man he-came
>   SUBJ   AG-VERB

This reanalysis results from the over-use of a powerful discourse device, which is a reasonable strategy, particularly if conditions for communication are difficult. Two interesting predictions follow. First, languages which use zero-anaphora in place of anaphoric pronouns will not develop verbal agreement. And second, since the subject noun phrase typically has more features favouring topicalization than have other noun phrases, it is more frequently topicalized, and so subject agreement is a precondition for agreement with other arguments (Moravcsik 1974: 27–8). As is implicit in this account, Givón suggests that agreement and pronominalization are 'fundamentally one and the same phenomenon' (see the discussion of the personal pronoun in section 5.1 above).

Givón claims that evidence for pronouns becoming subject agreement markers can be found in English and French dialects and in related pidgins and creoles. Particularly good evidence is found in various Bantu languages, as is illustrated using Swahili data:

> (88) kikopo ki-li-vunjika
>   cup   AG-PAST-break
>   'The cup broke.'

The *ki-* agreement marker on the verb is generally believed to result from an earlier pronoun. According to Givón, the subject agreement markers retain their older anaphoric function, as can be seen when there is no subject present:

> (89) ki-li-vunjika
>   it-PAST-break
>   'It (the cup) broke.'

It is interesting to note that this sequence is repeated, so Suzman (1982) claims, in children's acquisition of such forms. In a study of the acquisition of

Zulu, she found that agreement markers were acquired first in anaphoric function.

Besides subject agreement, Swahili data can also help us to understand the rise of object agreement. Objects may be topicalized:

(90) kikopo, ni-li-ki-vunja
cup I-PAST-it-break
'The cup, I broke it.'

Here we find -*ki*- functioning as an object marker. Provided the object is definite, it may in Swahili occur in its usual place after the verb and without the disappearance of the marker -*ki*-. This means that (definite) object agreement has developed. Various Bantu languages are at different stages in the development of object agreement (see Hyman & Duranti 1982; Wald 1979 gives a detailed study of discourse data in Swahili, while Chichewa is examined by Bresnan & Mchombo 1986, 1987). Turning to the development of agreement in other languages, data on Italian discourse are given by Duranti & Ochs (1979), while Claudi (1985: 105–14) documents the early stages of the development of predicate agreement in Zande. There is good evidence for Givón's claims concerning verb agreement, though anaphoric pronouns may not be the sole source of agreement markers (see, for example, Russell 1984).

Let us now move on to the agreement of targets other than verbs. Greenberg (1978: 75–8) discusses how agreeing articles can arise from demonstratives (which may also be the source of anaphoric pronouns). Thus the definite article *le/la* in French, and similar forms elsewhere in Romance, are derived from Latin *ille* 'that'. If articles go on to attach permanently to the noun, then the form of the noun will clearly indicate its gender and we shall have a case of overt gender (see sections 3.3.1 and 5.2.2); the prefixes on Bantu nouns are believed to have arisen in this way. Greenberg also suggests (1978: 76) that phrases like *the good one* may be a source for the agreement of other noun-phrase elements. If *one* is a pronoun, marked for the category of gender, then adjectives with potential agreement forms arise. Alternatively, the adjective may stand alone and just in this role acquire a gender marker to establish its referent clearly (this stage of development is attested in Kannada, according to Miranda 1975: 200). If these gender markers are then used redundantly even when the noun is present, then gender agreement spreads to adjectives in all syntactic positions, including attributive use.

A different source is suggested by evidence from the Daly languages of north-west Australia, whose significance was noted by Greenberg (1978: 51–2, 74). Comparison of languages within the group suggests that a small number of nouns have come to be used as classifiers (Tryon 1970, superseded by Tryon 1974: 289–94). In languages of the Maranunggu subgroup, like Ami, the words for 'meat', 'vegetable food' and 'tree/stick', which occur as free forms, also occur as prefixes on nouns, and they denote in turn animals hunted for meat (*awa-wanka* 'shark', literally 'animal-shark'), vegetable food and plants (*miya-mimi* 'round yam', literally 'plant-round yam') and weapons and wooden implements (*yili-mitiwur* 'nullanulla', literally 'stick-nullanulla'). Other nouns, like *piya* 'head', have no prefix. In the Brinken subgroup, there is an additional distinction (nouns denoting trees are separated out), but here the prefix is a reduced form of the original noun in some cases, and it occurs not just on the noun but also on the adjective or possessive adjective, both of which stand after the noun: thus in Mirityabin we find *yeli-meltem yeli-yikin* 'my digging-stick' (literally 'stick + digging-stick stick + my'). Some might argue that this is already an agreement system; others would prefer to analyse it as having repeated classifiers. But repetition of the classifier is an important step (found also in the Oceanic language Kilivila; see Senft 1986: 69). A subsequent stage, which is certainly an agreement system, occurs in the Tyemeri group of the Daly languages. Here we find that the prefix differs according to whether a possessive adjective or some other adjective is involved. Nouns which themselves have no prefix, may take two different forms of the possessive adjective, as shown in table 5.13 (forms from Ngangikurrunggurr, Tryon 1974: 231–3). The origin of the agreement markers is still clear; in many cases the agreement marker is identical to the marker on

Table 5.13 *Noun prefixes and gender agreement markers in Ngangikurrunggurr*

Gender		Marker on noun	Possessive adjective marker	Adjective marker
I	most natural objects, kinship terms, some body parts	Ø-	Ø-	Ø-
II	hunting weapons	Ø-	ali-	ali-
III	most body parts	de-	yer-	Ø-
IV	trees, most wooden implements	yer-	yer-	yer-
V	most animals hunted for meat	a-	a-	a-
VI	edible plants	mi-	mi-	mi-
VII	male animates (excluding dogs)	wa-	Ø-	wa-
VIII	female animates	wur-	Ø-	wur-
IX	canines	wu-	wu-	wu-

the noun, whose origin is a separate noun. But in some instances, the agreement marker differs from the marker on the noun (gender III). And sometimes, as in genders VII and VIII, the agreement marker changes according to the target involved (possessive adjective or other adjective). Here we find agreement in gender, but with its origin still evident. These languages give a clear picture of how agreement within the noun phrase can arise from classifiers. Dixon (1982: 171–3) also considers the Daly evidence. He proposes a slightly different scenario for the development of gender agreement in Dyirbal. As we saw in section 5.1, Dyirbal has what Dixon calls 'noun markers', which are a type of demonstrative indicating location and visibility. Dixon suggests that classifiers like *mayi* 'non-flesh food', which is widely attested in the area, stood between the demonstrative-like noun markers and the noun and were subsequently reduced, producing agreement forms:

(91) bala   mayi   NOUN
     visible.there   CLASSIFIER
     → bala-m   NOUN
     NOUN.MARKER-GENDER.AG

Here again, nouns being used as classifiers would have given rise to agreement forms. Elements like *bala-* can also function rather like pronouns and it could be that the classifier was first attached in this use. These possible sources of agreement forms all deserve further investigation. None of them implies that verb agreement need exist as a prerequisite for the development of agreement within the noun phrase.

When we turn to other types of agreement the picture is even less clear. It should be said that one unusual case can be handled readily within the scheme of agreement developing from clitic pronouns: while the verb is the most likely place for permanent attachment (giving rise to agreement) there are other possible sites. Thus in West Flemish, clitics have attached to complementizers, as illustrated in examples (36)–(38) above, a situation which Bennis & Haegeman (1984) consider to be agreement of the complementizer. Another type of agreement for which a pronominal source has been suggested is the agreement of possessive heads with possessors, as in this example from the 'more literary level' of Modern Hebrew (Givón 1979: 216–17):

(92) bet-o   shel   Yoav
     house-his that.to Yoav
     'Yoav's house.'

Such constructions could plausibly arise from afterthought topics. They may in turn give rise, according to Keenan (1978: 175), to a relatively unusual type of agreement: that of prepositions and postpositions with the noun. Adpositions can arise from possessive constructions; thus a phrase like *behind it* may be expressed as *at back of it*. If the language in question also has agreement of possessive heads with possessors, then agreement of such prepositions (or postpositions) could result:

(93) at-back-his of-John → at-back-MASC of-John

A large gap in our understanding is the way in which verb systems not based on topic or subject arise. In ergative agreement systems, the verb may agree with the noun in the absolutive case (the agent of intransitives and the patient of transitives). Givón (1984: 370) suggests that such systems arise from the reanalysis of passive constructions in nominative–accusative systems. This is plausible, since it is established that ergative constructions can arise from passives; but ergative constructions can in turn develop into nominative–accusative constructions (Payne 1980: 147–8). It is therefore well worth investigating whether ergative agreement systems can have an independent source. Whatever their original source, such systems can renew themselves without any appeal to reanalysis. This can be seen from the Khinalug data analysed earlier (section 5.2.3). We saw that Khinalug has a set of old agreement markers, and a new set of agreement markers, which are clearly based on the demonstrative pronoun. The important point is that these new markers behave just like the old ones in that they mark agreement with the same noun phrase – the one in the absolutive case, according to the ergative pattern. (For an overview of the development of agreement in general see Lehmann 1982: 251–7.)

While the account so far allows for affixed gender agreement markers, we should also ask how internal agreement arises. For examples like Khinalug (as in table 5.7), the development is still evident in that the joining of more than one root into a single word leaves agreement markers 'sandwiched' in internal position. But the internal vowel alternations in languages like Marind (section 5.2.1) are more difficult. Here we can look to evidence from the Pamir languages, where we find examples like Roshani *sut-* 'went' (masculine) and *sat-* 'went' (feminine). Earlier forms are **šu-ta* (masculine) and **šu-tā* (feminine). The long *ā* of the feminine caused umlaut of *u > a* as part of a more general sound change; then after the loss of the final vowel, and other changes, the modern forms *sut-* and *sat-* resulted (Payne 1989: 437).

If we consider the loss of gender agreement, we find that there are patterns which are much more interesting and illuminating than might be suspected. Attrition may give rise to a situation in which some agreement targets of a particular type mark agreement while others do not. We noted how the loss of French 'mute *e*' means that in the spoken language some adjectives agree in gender while others do not (section 5.3.7). The position is often not so straightforward; in the Caucasus there is great diversity between related languages as to the number of adjectives which mark agreement. More significantly, different types of agreement targets lose agreement at different times. In various Cross River languages (a language group within the Niger-Congo branch of Niger-Kordofanian), numerals and adjectives lose agreement first, while it is retained in verbs and pronouns (Demuth, Faraclas & Marchese 1986: 458–9). More detailed data are available on nine Kru languages, a group of Niger-Kordofanian languages spoken in southern Libya and Ivory Coast (Marchese 1988: 332–6). Pronouns generally retain agreement, but attributive modifiers are losing gender agreement. (For example in Godie, where gender agreement is most extensive, eight out of ten adjectives agree in gender. In Wobe only one adjective still agrees in gender, while in Klao there is no gender agreement within the noun phrase.) Numerals in the nine languages do not show agreement – this probably represents loss of agreement. Within the noun phrase, adjectives lose agreement in these languages before determiners, and adjectives preserve agreement in number longer than agreement in gender. Priestly (1983: 343–6) provides an interesting comparison: he is concerned with the gender agreement in Indo-European languages and shows how it is usually preserved best in the pronoun and less well in the adjective. There is fruitful work to be done in this area, investigating other language groups to find the order in which different types of target lose agreement, and the way in which the loss of gender agreement relates to that of other categories such as number, person and case, and the factors which determine which items within a target type (which attributive adjectives, for example) will retain agreement longest. Massive loss of gender agreement can occur during pidginization, as has happened in Yimas Pidgin (Foley 1988: 170–1) and widely in Africa (Heine & Reh 1984: 42). For a more detailed account of the development and loss of agreement see Corbett (forthcoming b).

5.6 Conclusion

Agreement is the means by which gender is realized, and it shows great variety, both in the types of element which can carry a gender agreement marker and in the formal means employed. But gender agreement may have restrictions of various types: syntactic, morphological, phonological and lexical. By accepting the view that agreement is a prerequisite for a gender system, we exclude classifiers from consideration, except as a source for gender markers. We now move in the next chapter to an examination of the way in which we can take the agreement markers of a particular language and from them establish the gender system.

6
Establishing the number of genders

In the first chapters of the book it was largely taken for granted that the number of genders in a given language could be readily established, and we tackled the problem of how nouns are assigned to particular genders. Then in the preceding chapter we considered the syntactic means by which gender is manifested. And we saw that in some instances the evidence is complex. We need, therefore, to work out how we determine the number of genders in a given language. In several of the more familiar languages, the gender pattern is straightforward and the way in which the system is analysed is taken as self-evident. In other languages, linguists may present the pattern as though it were equally uncontroversial, but we find that similar situations are described differently by those working on different language families. In contrast, the number of genders in a particular language can be the subject of interminable dispute. Given this unsatisfactory situation, we must develop a consistent approach to analysing gender. For those most familiar with languages which have relatively transparent gender systems, this chapter may appear unduly detailed. But in order to make meaningful comparisons between such languages and those with more complex gender systems we need to ensure that the starting point is the same. After a brief discussion of terminology (section 6.1), we move on to the central notion of 'agreement class' (section 6.2). In section 6.3 we investigate how the nouns in an agreement class may make up a 'controller gender'. Controller genders must be distinguished from 'target genders', and this distinction allows us to solve one of the perennial problems in the study of gender, namely the number of genders in Rumanian, and to describe other complex systems in a consistent way. For all its advantages, the agreement class approach runs into what may be termed the 'maximalist problem', where more agreement classes are identified than the intuitively satisfying number of genders in a given language. Principled reasons are proposed for determining which types of agreement class should be recognized as genders (section 6.4). We shall see that in many cases, deciding the number of genders in a language is a genuinely difficult problem. In some instances we reach solutions similar to traditional ones but we are able to put these traditional solutions on a sounder theoretical base.

6.1 **Terms**

The use of terms in this area has become confused, as Harris (1986: 58–61) points out. There is little point in trying to maintain a strict distinction between 'gender' and 'noun class' since similar systems are described as genders in one language family and as noun classes in another. As mentioned in section 2.1.1, there are several points of similarity between, for example, Tamil and Karata; Tamil is said to have three genders, since it is a Dravidian language, while Karata is described as having three noun classes, because it is a North-East Caucasian language. The difference is one of grammatical tradition rather than of linguistic data. Those who do try to maintain a distinction between gender and noun class often depend largely on a contrast between Indo-European and Bantu languages (which belong to the Niger-Kordofanian family). These attempts generally prove less convincing when Dravidian languages and languages of the Caucasus are taken into account, since these languages share characteristics with Indo-European languages and with Bantu languages (and indeed with each other) and so undermine the contrasts drawn. We have used the term 'gender', which has the advantage of avoiding potential confusion with 'agreement class', an important term which we define in the next section.

As stated at the beginning of the last chapter, we shall follow the widely accepted view that the existence of gender can be demonstrated only by agreement evidence; this view is implicit in most work on gender, and it is stated explicitly in, for example, Fodor (1959: 2), Greenberg (1978: 50) and Heine (1982: 190). The point is that evidence taken only from the nouns themselves, such as the presence of markers on the nouns, as prefixes or suffixes, does not of itself indicate that a language has genders (or noun classes); if we accepted this type of evidence, then we could equally claim that English had a gender comprising all nouns ending in *-tion* (as pointed out earlier in section 2.3). Generalizations concerning English nouns in *-tion* are a matter for lexical semantics and derivational morphology; there is no case for claiming that a gender category is involved in such instances. In this respect, gender must be treated differently from number and case. This is because gender is inherent to the noun, while case and number are not. A noun has typically one value for the gender feature, which it brings with it from the lexicon (determined by the assignment rules). But a noun can normally take more than one value of the number feature (it can, say, be singular or plural) and similarly it can take more than one value of the case feature (say nominative, accusative or dative). In the latter instances, the morphological material on the noun itself may be sufficient to postulate the category in question (thus oppositions like *hat* ~ *hats* allow us to demonstrate a category of number in English). The different morphological forms of a set of nouns prove the point. But since nouns normally have a single gender, such an opposition is not available. Nevertheless, we maintain the requirement that to demonstrate the existence of a category, evidence of distinctions in form is necessary. In the case of gender, the evidence comes from agreement markers attached to other sentence elements, whose form is determined by the gender of the head noun of the controller.

6.2 Agreement classes

The approach based on agreement classes is usually associated with the name of Zaliznjak (1964); the approach is partly foreshadowed by Schenker (1955). A more formal, mathematical treatment is given by Gladkij (1969; 1973a; 1973b), who reaches results similar to those of Zaliznjak. The major alternative approach is that of Marcus (1962; 1963; 1967: 115–55; 1970), who, following ideas of Revzin, also proposed a formal definition of gender. But his notion of 'class of distribution' proves too wide, and leads to the postulation of large numbers of genders. By treating, for example, the difference between proper and common nouns as a question of gender, he moves away from the central, well-established problems of gender. Most seriously, it is not clear that there is necessarily any upper limit to the number of genders to be identified in a given language. Probably the most recent example of work in this framework is the analysis of Greek by Cosmas (1981; 1982).

Given the problems with the analyses proposed by Marcus, we will adopt the agreement class approach. An **agreement class** may be defined as follows (this definition is a reworking of the idea found in Zaliznjak 1964: 30):

> An agreement class is a set of nouns such that any two members
> of that set have the property that
> > whenever
> > > (i) they stand in the same morphosyntactic form
> > and
> > > (ii) they occur in the same agreement domain
> > and
> > > (iii) they have the same lexical item as agreement
> > > target
> > then
> > their targets have the same morphological realization.

The intuitive content of the definition is that two nouns are in the same agreement class provided that, given the same conditions, they will take the same agreement form. The three numbered clauses of the definition spell out what is involved in 'the same conditions'. Being in 'the same morphosyntactic form' (clause (i)), or the same 'grammatical' form, means that the nouns have the same specifications for all relevant syntactic features. The features most commonly involved are number and case. We rely on the notions of number and case being given; this is reasonable since they are simpler notions, which can often be justified simply on morphological evidence, without reference to agreement, as discussed in section 6.1. It must be stressed that identity of morphosyntactic form does not imply morphological identity. Two nouns may be in the same morphosyntactic form and yet differ morphologically; for example, Russian *mat'-∅* 'mother' and *sestr-u* 'sister' are both in the accusative singular, and are thus in the same morphosyntactic form. Yet their morphological realizations are different – they take different endings. Such nouns have different morphological features in their lexical entries, indicating that they belong to different declensional types. Conversely, two morphosyntactic forms may have a single morphological realization; for example, Russian *okn-o* 'window' may be the nominative singular or the accusative singular (two morphosyntactic forms for which many other nouns have distinct morphological realizations). Provided that the nouns stand in the same morphosyntactic form (meeting the requirement of clause (i)), then they start out, as it were, on level terms.

Clause (ii) requires that the nouns occur in the same agreement domain. This means that the configuration in which agreement applies must be identical in each case: it might be the agreement of modifiers with the head of a noun phrase, subject–verb agreement, and so on. Thus the two nouns must be in the same environment.

Clause (iii) requires that the lexical item which stands as the agreeing element or target must be the same. Since not all lexical items have the same agreement possibilities, as we saw in sections 5.3.6 to 5.3.8, it would not do to use, say, in one instance an adjective which distinguished gender and in the other an adjective which did not, nor adjectives which distinguished different numbers of genders. The point of clauses (ii) and (iii) is to take account of the great variety of situations described in sections 5.1 and 5.3. The possibilities for gender agreement can vary according to the syntactic construction, and so for comparison this variable must be held constant. And within the same syntactic construction, lexical items may differ as to whether or not they show agreement in gender or as to the number of gender forms they distinguish. In all instances we are interested in agreement domains and lexical items which allow the largest number of forms; by specifying that identity must be found 'whenever' the conditions listed are met, we ensure that the domain most favourable to gender agreement and the most differentiated target will be included. Clause (iii) ensures that the nouns are tested in an identical way. Then, if the same result follows with the two nouns, they must be in the same agreement class. This clause depends on the notion of agreement which was discussed at the beginning of chapter 5.

Our definition of agreement class above requires two additions. For technical reasons we should add a clause that the nouns in question must share at least one morphosyntactic form. This is to cover the limiting case in which two defective nouns could never stand in the same morphosyntactic form and so the conditions would be filled vacuously. The second addition, which is found in Zaliznjak's definition, is that the target may take not only the same morphological realization but also the same set of stylistically variant forms. This is to cover the situation in which a given combination of syntactic features may have alternative realizations (for example, Russian adjectives mark the feature set instrumental singular feminine with -*oj* or, archaically and poetically, with -*oju*).

Let us first consider French, for a straightforward illustration of the basic notion of agreement classes:

(1) un grand garçon   compare: *une grande garçon
     a   big   boy

(2) un grand jardin   compare: *une grande jardin
     a   big   garden

(3) une grande femme   compare: *un grand femme
     a   big   woman

(4) une grande fleur   compare: *un grand fleur
     a   big   flower

In these examples we have ensured that the nouns being tested occur in identical conditions: they stand in the same morphosyntactic form (the relevant feature specification is singular), in the same agreement domain (agreement of modifiers within the noun phrase), and the lexical items involved as agreement targets are the same (*un-* and *grand-*; either would be sufficient). The nouns *garçon* and *jardin* require the article and the attributive adjective to stand in the same form ((1) and (2)). If we consider other possible agreement targets, or if we change to the plural, we still find that the agreements required by *garçon* and *jardin* are identical. They therefore belong to the same agreement class. The nouns *femme* and *fleur* differ from *garçon*

149

and *jardin*, and require the same agreements as each other ((3) and (4)). They belong to the second agreement class. There are many thousands of nouns in each of these two classes, which are the traditional masculine and feminine genders.

6.3 Controller genders and target genders

Not surprisingly, the agreement class approach deals easily with a language like French. Rumanian, also a Romance language, provides a sterner test. Its gender system has been the source of continuing disagreement, and the literature on it is extensive; it includes contributions by Jakobson (1971), Rumanian linguists such as Graur (1937), Rosetti (1965: 83–92; 1983: 382–404) and notably Marcus (1967: 115–55), and many more; for further references see Hall (1965: 421–2), Marcus (1967: 153–5), Wienold (1967: 75, 170), Luxt (1970 88–9), Windisch (1973), Priestly (1983) and Mallinson (1984: 450–1). There is evidently a problem worthy of investigation. Consider the following data (from Mallinson 1984: 441): concerning the nouns *bărbat* 'man', *fată* 'girl' and *scaun* 'chair'.

(5) bărbatul e bun
man.the is good
'The man is good.'
(6) scaunul e bun
chair.the is good
'The chair is good.'
(7) fata   e bună
girl.the is good
'The girl is good.'

(Note that the definite article is postposed; in nouns like *fată* its effect is to change the quality of the final vowel (mainly by lowering) to *fata*.) The evidence so far, from the agreement of *bun-* 'good', demonstrates the existence of two agreement classes, one including nouns like *bărbat* and *scaun* and the other comprising nouns like *fată*. There is a second case (genitive–dative), but in the singular *bărbat* and *scaun* again take identical agreements while *fată* differs. But the situation is more complex, as emerges when we consider the same examples in the plural:

(8) bărbaţii sînt buni
men.the are good
'The men are good.'

(9) scaunele sînt bune
   chairs.the are good
   'The chairs are good.'

(10) fetele   sînt bune
    girls.the are good
    'The girls are good.'

If we had only the data of (8)–(10), then we would postulate two agreement classes – one for nouns like *bărbat* and one for nouns like *scaun* and *fată* (the oblique case in the plural shows the same pattern, separating *bărbat* from the other two). The argument, which has gone on for decades, is whether we have two genders or three. The problem is that nouns like *scaun* have no agreement forms which are used uniquely for them. In terms of agreement classes, however, the situation is clear: we must set up three classes as follows:

I nouns taking -$\emptyset$ in the singular and -*i* in the plural (*bărbat*);
II nouns taking -$\emptyset$ in the singular and -*e* in the plural (*scaun*);
III nouns taking -*a* in the singular and -*e* in the plural (*fată*).

Thus we have an unambiguous answer: there are three agreement classes, and there is no reason not to recognize each as a gender. However, simply to say that Rumanian has three genders suggests that it is like German, Latin or Tamil, even though in each of these languages, intuitively, the situation is rather different. All of them have some agreement forms which are unique to each gender. The point is that the agreement class approach leads us to the number of sets into which *nouns* are to be divided or, in a feature-based approach, to the number of different feature specifications which are required on nouns to enable gender agreement to operate correctly. It is certainly the case that *bărbat*, *scaun* and *fată* (and the hundreds of other nouns similar to each of them) require three different labels. Nevertheless the morphology of agreeing forms (targets) is simpler than is implied by the statement that Rumanian has three genders. We should therefore differentiate *controller genders*, the genders into which nouns are divided, from *target genders*, the genders which are marked on adjectives, verbs and so on (depending on the language, as illustrated in section 5.1).

The distinction is illustrated in figure 6.1. It can be seen that Rumanian has two target genders in both singular and plural; it has three controller genders, indicated by the lines and labelled I, II and III. I is usually called 'masculine', II is the 'feminine' and III is the disputed gender sometimes called 'neuter' and sometimes 'ambigeneric'; the latter is a useful term, provided it is used not to imply that there is no distinct gender but rather that the situation is different from the more common Indo-European three-gender system.

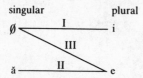

Figure 6.1 The gender system of Rumanian

Diagrams like figure 6.1 can be labelled in various ways and the alternatives deserve brief consideration. The first controller gender is designated '$\emptyset$' on the basis of adjectives like *bun* 'good'. However, not all adjectives take this form: *aspr-u* 'rough' has *-u*, as shown by comparison with *aspr-ă* (feminine) corresponding to *bun-ă*. We have chosen to give a typical allomorph for each target gender. This method avoids the danger of premature naming of genders; on the other hand, problems can arise when the typical forms chosen suggest similarities which are not general through the system. (Taking Latin adjectives, we might suppose that the feminine singular *-a* is equivalent to the neuter plural *-a*; however, not all adjectives have identical morphological realizations for these two morphosyntactic forms.) A way of avoiding the latter problem is to list all the allomorphs, but this can become unwieldy. Since it is hardly practical to keep referring to strings of allomorphs, names such as masculine, feminine and neuter tend to be preferred. Let us consider French again using this convention (figure 6.2).

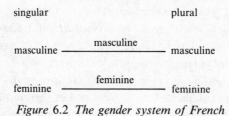

Figure 6.2 The gender system of French

As before, the labels for the sets into which nouns are divided (controller genders) are placed above the lines; for French, 'masculine' and 'feminine' are used, rather than 'I' or 'II'. But, as just discussed, the sets of agreement forms (target genders) are also generally called 'masculine' and 'feminine' (rather than '$\emptyset$' and so on), hence the use of these names in the singular and plural columns.

In a language of this type, such an overlap of labels causes little difficulty. It is when this usage is carried over into more complex systems that difficulties arise. Indeed, although the distinction between controller and target genders may seem an obvious one, there are numerous examples in the literature of the number of genders being given for a particular language, in cases where the situation is complex, without any indication as to what is meant.

While there are many languages where the number of controller and target genders are the same, mismatches of the type we have seen in Rumanian are not uncommon. Another example is found in Telugu, a Dravidian language (South Central Group). Figure 6.3 gives the verb agreement forms (I am most grateful to Malathi Rao for the data on Telugu; her Koosta dialect varies slightly from that described in Krishnamurti & Sarma 1968.) Again there are three controller genders and two target genders (in both singular and plural). However, I is masculine, II feminine and III irrational or neuter.

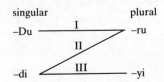

Figure 6.3 Verbal agreement forms in Telugu

Unlike Rumanian, where the personal pronouns follow the same pattern as the other agreement targets, in Telugu the pronouns are more complex. There is a set which corresponds closely to the verb agreements (figure 6.4). There are alternatives to *vaaDu* 'he', and their use depends on varying levels of formality and respect (the plural is also used to signal respect). These do not affect the analysis. But with *adi* 'it' things are somewhat different; *adi* is used for reference to animals and things and sometimes for reference to girls. For reference to a woman, there is a different form *aaviDa* 'she' (partly formal or formal) which can take singular or plural agreement. It is not used for inanimates. The existence of this pronoun means that pronoun targets distinguish feminines from neuters. This confirms the analysis which claims three controller genders (compare section 6.4.2); it also breaks the parallelism with Rumanian.

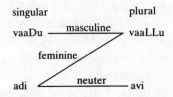

Figure 6.4 Telugu personal pronouns

153

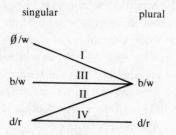

Figure 6.5 The gender system of Lak

A more complex system is found in Lak, a North-East Caucasian language (see section 2.2.5). Agreement is marked on certain attributives, verbs, adverbials and pronouns, some of which were illustrated in section 5.1. The pattern of typical verb agreement markers is given in figure 6.5 (data from Kibrik (1979: 4); since we give the typical allomorphs, the forms like -*j*- found in numerals are not included; there are also numerous alternations, but these do not provide grounds for further divisions). By convention, forms before the slash are prefixal, those after are internal or suffixal. There are four controller genders in Lak. Then there are three target genders in the singular and two in the plural. It is noteworthy that there are only three different sets of forms (∅/*w*, *b*/*w* and *d*/*r*) covering eight theoretical forms. (The interested reader can now reconsider the Khinalug data given in section 5.2.3 in a similar way.)

We have established the value of distinguishing the notions controller gender and target gender, in our analysis of complex gender systems. The distinction leads to other fruitful lines of enquiry as we shall see in the sections which follow.

6.3.1 *The relation of gender and number*

As far as controller genders are concerned, gender and number are typically independent; a noun has a particular gender, irrespective of the number it stands in. Gender is inherent to the noun and is in a sense prior to the number in which it occurs in a given sentence. (There are occasional exceptions, which must be labelled as such in the lexical entry of the nouns involved; see section 6.4.3 for some examples.) Target genders, on the other hand, may be found in combination with other categories and so they may vary according to the other categories involved. There are interesting areas to investigate in these interactions. Some were considered in sections 5.3.2–5.3.5, but the most important, the relation with number, will be examined in more detail here. Our main concern will be the patterns of matching between singular and plural.

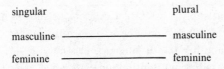

Figure 6.6 *Target genders in French*

The most straightforward system is that in which each singular target gender matches one plural gender and vice versa. Gender in one number determines gender in the other and vice versa: there is a one-to-one mapping of the target genders in one number onto the target genders in the other. We call such systems 'parallel' systems. French can serve as an example of this type (figure 6.6). Then there are 'convergent' systems, in which the target gender in one number determines gender in the other, but not vice versa: there is a many-to-one mapping of target genders in one number onto target genders in the other. (Parallel and convergent systems taken together are what Heine terms 'paired systems' 1982: 196–7). A clear example of a convergent system is found in German (figure 6.7).

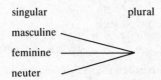

Figure 6.7 *Target genders in German*

In Tamil, a Dravidian language, three singular target genders correspond to two plural genders (figure 6.8). This too is a convergent system. An identical

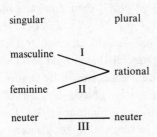

Figure 6.8 *Target genders in Tamil*

155

system is found, as mentioned earlier, in the North-East Caucasian language Karata (Magomedbekova 1967a: 324–5, 327). In Chibemba, a Bantu language, there are considerably more target genders, as shown in figure 6.9 (data from Givón 1972: 14–17). We omit here the locative genders, which are discussed in relation to another Bantu language in section 6.3.3. The labels 1–15 in figure 6.9 are the traditional Bantu noun class labels, which serve well for indicating target genders. (Controller genders are labelled according to the agreements taken, for example, 1/2 or 7/8; see section 3.1.2.) Once again, the target gender in one number (the singular) determines gender in the other, but not vice versa; we therefore have a convergent system.

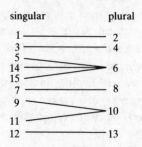

Figure 6.9 *Target genders in Chibemba*

The third possibility is what Heine calls a 'crossed' system (1982: 197). In such a system, gender in neither number determines the gender in the other; there is what some would call a many-to-many mapping between the target genders in the different numbers. Examples are Rumanian (figure 6.1), Telugu (figure 6.3) and Lak (given again for convenience as figure 6.10). Here we see a system with four agreement classes, but with three target genders in the singular and two in the plural. The fact that we find such systems, as well as convergent systems like those above, with more singular target genders than plural, but not the converse (with more plural than singular genders) is, of course, a reflection of Greenberg's Universal 37: 'A language never has more gender categories in nonsingular numbers than in the singular' (1963: 112). If we adopted just the agreement class approach, there would be no way in which to state Greenberg's universal, since differences caused by change in number lead to the setting up of additional agreement classes. In terms of agreement classes, figure 6.10 simply provides evidence for four classes. Clearly, then, Greenberg's universal must be stated in terms of target genders.

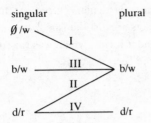

Figure 6.10 *The gender system of Lak*

For simplicity we have so far discussed languages with only singular and plural. When we turn to fuller number systems, we find that the types established – 'parallel', 'convergent' and 'crossed' – hold between each pair of numbers, rather than of the system as a whole. This can be seen from the gender system of Slovene, a South Slavonic language (see figure 6.11; we omit here two subgenders, which are just as in Slovene's closest relative Serbo-Croat, described in section 6.4.1). We can see that the feminine and neuter share forms in the dual only. Thus there is a relation of convergence between singular and dual and between plural and dual, but of parallelism between singular and plural.

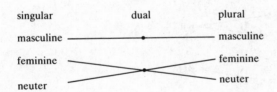

Figure 6.11 *The gender system of Slovene*

Before we leave the question of gender and number, two points should be mentioned. First, we should consider the justification for linking particular target genders in the singular with others in the plural. In languages like French, the point may seem too obvious for discussion; but there are instances where the analysis is not so clear-cut, and in any event, we must recognize that it is a matter of analysis, not a fact. To justify associating particular singular and plural target genders (and target genders in different agreement targets, such as attributive modifiers and predicate verbs), we need the notion of 'consistent agreement pattern'. This concept is discussed in section 6.4.5; it

157

gives a principled basis for associating particular agreement forms. And second, once controller and target genders are distinguished, we can approach the question of syncretism of target gender forms, which was raised in section 5.2.3; we shall return to this question in section 7.1.1.

6.3.2 *Relation to semantics*

The semantic aspect of gender is most evident in controller genders; the assignment of nouns to genders according to semantic criteria was discussed in chapter 2. It is less frequently observed that the question of semantic justification can also be pursued with regard to target genders. If the controller genders of a language are based solely on semantics, then the appearance of a particular gender agreement form will provide unambiguous information. Thus a feminine agreement form in Tamil implies that a female human is referred to at some point, while a feminine agreement form in French or German does not necessarily do so. When we turn to convergent and crossed systems, we find that the syncretic forms may have varying degrees of semantic justification. Compare Lak, as presented in figure 6.10, with Archi (Kibrik 1972), which is given in figure 6.12. The plural target

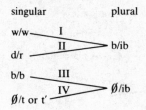

Figure 6.12 *The gender system of Archi*

gender forms of Lak have no direct semantic correspondence. In Archi, the semantics of the target genders are clear, once the controller genders are given: gender I comprises nouns denoting male humans, God and other spiritual beings considered male, II is similarly for females, III is for most animals and some inanimates and IV includes the remainder (some animals and the remaining inanimates). Thus the target gender *b/ib* in the plural implies reference to rational beings, while *∅/ib* is for non-rationals. (For other examples see Khaidakov 1980, and Drossard 1982: 159–61.)

6.3.3 *The relation of controller genders to target genders*

In many languages, as noted earlier, there is a straightforward one-to-one relation between the two types of gender. We have also seen several examples of languages in which the number of controller genders exceeds the number of target gender forms distinguished in either number. For example, Rumanian has three controller genders, but only two target gender forms in both singular and plural.

It is also possible to find languages in which the number of target genders exceeds the number of controller genders, if we include within the target genders what we shall term 'non-lexical genders'. These are of two types; the first, the neutral gender, is a target gender form which cannot normally have a prototypical noun phrase headed by a noun or pronoun as its controller. A good example is found in the Surselvan dialect of Romansh (Haiman 1974: 130–4). The agreement class approach leads us to postulate two genders; one takes the ending -*s* on predicative adjectives and participles (masculine), sometimes with a change of root vowel, while the other takes -*a* (feminine). There is, however, a third agreement marker, namely -∅; this occurs with controllers which are not specified for gender and number: sentential subjects, the demonstrative pronoun *quei* 'that' and the impersonal pronoun *igl*. For example:

(11) sgarscheivla   ei la   paupradad
    wretched.FEM is the poverty

(12) in urezi   ei sesalzaus
    a storm is arisen.MASC

(13) igl   ei sesalzau   in urezi
    there is arisen.NEUTRAL a storm

The form which is found in (13) cannot occur with a noun phrase headed by a noun as controller; we term this target gender the 'neutral' gender.

The second type of non-lexical gender (and so the second way in which target genders may exceed controller genders) involves 'minor target genders'. These differ from the neutral gender in that they can have a nominal controller. They differ from ordinary target gender forms in that there are no nouns regularly assigned to a corresponding controller gender. Examples would be the locative genders of Bantu; consider the following example from Chichewa, a Bantu language spoken in Malawi:

    (14) mu-nyumba mu-kutentha
           LOC-house   LOC-is.hot
         'It is hot in the house.'

Nyumba 'house' belongs to gender 9/10 and would normally take the prefixed agreement forms *i-* (singular) and *zi-* (plural). However, in (14) it has the prefix *mu-*, meaning 'in', and the verb takes the same prefix *mu-* as an agreement marker. No other gender has this marker, so we could treat it as a separate target gender form. But there are no nouns which must take *mu-* as their agreement form; apart from semantic restrictions, any noun could take the prefix *mu-* and become part of this locative gender. Thus the agreement form *mu-* represents a minor target gender; such genders are clearly rather different from the more familiar genders. (For numerous examples see Bresnan & Kanerva 1989.)

A word on terminology is in order here: Greenberg (1978: 53) and Heine (1982: 198) both use the term 'minor gender' for what we have called 'minor target gender' (further examples of the phenomenon are given in Greenberg 1978: 79); but the term 'minor gender' has also been used to signify simply an agreement class with few nouns in it (for example, by De Wolf 1971: 42 and Watters 1980: 135). An alternative term for an agreement class with few members is 'minority gender' (Voorhoeve 1980: 68). We shall suggest in section 6.4.3 that the status of agreement classes with few members depends on the agreements they take; the particular cases analysed by Watters and Voorhoeve are inquorate genders in our terms, while some classes with few members are recognized as genders (as we shall see in the case of Lelemi). The potential for confusion over the different uses of the term 'minor gender' is not great. To distinguish them, however, Greenberg's use can be seen as relating to target genders (minor genders are, in our approach, target gender forms with no nouns regularly assigned to a corresponding controller gender), while De Wolf's use involves controller genders (minor genders are agreement classes with relatively few members). To be unambiguous we can use the terms 'minor target gender' and 'minor controller gender'.

Thus far the agreement class approach appears to give useful results, provided it is recognized that it gives an analysis of one side of the problem – the controller genders – and that it must therefore be supplemented by the notion of target genders.

6.4 **The maximalist problem**

A problem which arises with the agreement class approach is that the number of classes may be considerably larger than the traditional (and often intuitively satisfying) number of genders generally accepted for a given language. Zaliznjak and Gladkij were both aware of the problem and addressed it directly. Some later investigators carefully establish agreement classes but take the analysis no further; in some cases the agreement classes are claimed to be genders. Thus Quirk, Greenbaum, Leech & Svartvik (1985: 314) propose nine genders for English. While it is important to identify all the classes of nouns which differ in their agreement possibilities, the raw analyses which result tend to be unsatisfactory for two reasons: first, they miss generalizations (some of which are captured in more traditional accounts); and second, they make similar systems appear more different than they really are. We shall, therefore, investigate how the number of agreement classes may be reduced, in principled ways, to give a lower number of genders. The distinction between controller and target genders will again prove helpful.

6.4.1 *Subgenders*

The notion of subgenders is useful and intuitively clear, though it proves difficult to formalize. Consider the data from Serbo-Croat given in table 6.1. Serbo-Croat has two further cases, the vocative and the locative, but these are somewhat marginal and can be left out of account here. The nouns given belong to four different agreement classes, as can be seen by looking at the italicized agreement forms, those of the accusative singular. We could simply say that there are four genders in Serbo-Croat. Given appropriate agreement rules this solution would work, but it appears unsatisfactory. The intuition we wish to capture is that the difference between the behaviour of words like *student* 'student' and *zakon* 'law', as shown in table 6.1, is less significant than that between both of them and those like *škola* 'school' or *vino* 'wine'. The agreements required for *student* and *zakon* differ in only one instance out of ten (while *zakon* and *škola* differ in seven agreement forms out of ten, *zakon* and *vino* in four out of ten, and *škola* and *vino* in eight out of ten). The discrepancy is highlighted if we look at the agreement markers, found in the predicate, for instance on the participle (see table 6.2). The agreement forms labelled 'A' are used for both *student* and *zakon*; those labelled 'B' are for *škola*, while 'C' is for the *vino* type. Thus the forms for *student* and *zakon* are identical, and these do not overlap with those for the other two types of noun. Rather than recognizing four genders, it appears better to recognize three (as is the tradition in Serbo-Croat grammars). Nouns like *škola* are

Table 6.1 *Attributive agreement in Serbo-Croat*

	ovaj 'this'	*student* 'student'	*zakon* 'law'	*škola* 'school'	*vino* 'wine'
Singular					
Nominative	ovaj	student	ovaj zakon	ova škola	ovo vino
Accusative	*ovog*	studenta	*ovaj* zakon	*ovu* školu	*ovo* vino
Genitive	ovog	studenta	ovog zakona	ove škole	ovog vina
Dative	ovom	studentu	ovom zakonu	ovoj školi	ovom vinu
Instrumental	ovim	studentom	ovim zakonom	ovom školom	ovim vinom
Plural					
Nominative	ovi	studenti	ovi zakoni	ove škole	ova vina
Accusative	ove	studente	ove zakone	ove škole	ova vina
Genitive	ovih	studenātā	ovih zakonā	ovih školā	ovih vinā
Dative	ovim	studentima	ovim zakonima	ovim školama	ovim vinima
Instrumental	ovim	studentima	ovim zakonima	ovim školama	ovim vinima

Table 6.2 *Predicate agreement in Serbo-Croat*

	A	B	C
Singular	Ø	a	o
Plural	i	e	a

traditionally 'feminine', and those like *vino* are neuter; the third main gender, the masculine, is divided into two subgenders: nouns like *student* belong to the masculine animate subgender while nouns like *zakon* are masculine inanimate.

Serbo-Croat provides a particularly clear instance of subgenders. We must now attempt to specify when agreement classes can be analysed as subgenders, rather than as full genders, in more complex cases as well:

> Subgenders are agreement classes which control minimally different sets of agreement, that is, agreements differing for at most a small proportion of the morphosyntactic forms of any of the agreement targets.

Of course, what constitutes a 'small proportion' is a matter of judgement. A part of that judgement rests on the degree of difference between the other agreement classes. In the Serbo-Croat example, there are no gender distinctions in the oblique cases of the plural. Given that, nouns of the *škola* type and of the *vino* type control agreements which are as different as they could be (all seven remaining agreement forms differ). Against that background, a difference in one form indeed appears minimal. But what of the difference between *student* and *zakon* together on the one hand and *vino* on the other. Here we find only four differences. Suppose there were fewer still (as in some other Slavonic languages)? In such instances we must bear in mind the reference to 'any' agreement target in the last part of the definition: thus no agreement target must show more than minimally different agreements. In the Serbo-Croat case, if there was any doubt about separating *vino* from *student* and *zakon* on the evidence of attributive modifiers, the evidence of the predicate (where they differ in both available forms) demonstrates that the agreements are not minimally different.

A useful way of thinking about subgenders is to imagine listing all the separate agreement requirements for members of different agreement classes (including all case/number combinations, and all possible targets). Then the results are compared. For two nouns to be in different agreement classes, then the lists of the agreements they take must of course differ in some way. If comparison of the difference between two agreement classes yields no more than a minimal difference (compared with the general level of differences between other agreement classes) then the two agreement classes in question are subgenders.

We have already said that the use of subgenders allows us to reflect more accurately the relative similarity of *student* and *zakon* in Serbo-Croat as opposed to the others. In particular, some rules can refer to the feature [masculine] without any account of the feature [animate]. There is a second advantage, which is that the assignment rules are rather different for genders and subgenders in Serbo-Croat. For the main genders some nouns are assigned by a semantic rule (basically males are masculine, females feminine); the remaining nouns (not referring to sex-differentiable beings) are assigned according to morphology (the declensional type). On the other hand, the distinction between animates and inanimates is, with a very few exceptions, purely semantic (nouns which denote beings which live and move counting as animate). The subgenders are clearly subsidiary to the main masculine gender, being distinguished only in the accusative case. This relationship represents an inversion of the semantic hierarchy in which male and female are subdivisions of animate.

Table 6.1 reveals a further feature of the subgenders in Serbo-Croat, namely that the agreement forms involved are not independent but syncretic. The question arises as to how we should count the target genders of Serbo-Croat. For this we require the notion of 'dependent target gender'.

> A dependent target gender is a target gender consisting of a set of morphological realizations which mark agreement with members of a given agreement class by an opposition involving only syncretism (and no independent form).

The sets of morphological realizations which mark accusative singular masculine in Serbo-Croat fit this definition. As was illustrated in table 6.1, when, say, the determiner *ovaj* 'this' is in agreement with an accusative singular masculine inanimate noun like *zakon* 'law', its morphological realization is the same as for the nominative singular. This is a systematic syncretism; other agreeing elements take a different ending from *ovaj*, but it is always the same as for the nominative. No target has an independent form for this feature specification. Similarly, the corresponding forms which agree with animates are syncretic with the genitive. The opposition animate/ inanimate is marked only by syncretism and so both sets of morphological realizations, those for animate and those for inanimate, constitute dependent target genders. We can then say that Serbo-Croat has three controller genders, one of which has two subgenders, three (independent) target genders (singular and plural mark the same distinctions) plus two dependent target genders. This situation is presented graphically in figure 6.13.

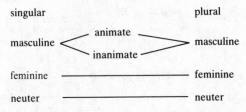

Figure 6.13 *The gender system of Serbo-Croat*

Let us now examine Russian, the language which both Zaliznjak and Gladkij analysed. Agreement of attributive modifiers is exemplified in table 6.3 (we use the irregular determiner *ètot* since it collocates readily with a range of nouns and marks the same distinctions as regular modifiers). The evidence of table 6.3 demonstrates that we have six agreement classes; no two nouns included take identical agreements under all circumstances. Consider first *sestra* 'sister' and *škola* 'school'; the agreements they take differ only in the accusative plural of the attributive modifier (the same is also true of the relative pronoun). Similarly *čudovišče* 'monster' and *vino* 'wine' differ only in one form out of twelve. In both instances we should say that there is one main gender with two subgenders. For *student* 'student' and *dub* 'oak' there are two differing forms (accusative singular and accusative plural) out of twelve. This is not quite so clearly a minimal difference; but when we note that the two differences both involve the same case and the same kind of syncretism it does seem reasonable to recognize two subgenders here. As in Serbo-Croat the subgenders correlate with animacy. And as in Serbo-Croat, predicate agreement reinforces the opposition between the main three genders, while the subgenders are not reflected there. Thus in Russian each of the three controller genders has two subgenders, as shown using the usual names in figure 6.14. (For the assignment of nouns to the subgenders see section 3.1.1; note, too, that most nouns of type III in table 3.3 take agreements as *škola* but a few denote animates and take agreements like *sestra*.)

One might consider an analysis which would involve changing the case of the whole noun phrase from accusative to genitive if it is headed by certain types of animate noun. But this approach would be inadequate, as is shown by masculine nouns ending in *-a*, which take the accusative in *-u* (similar data could be quoted from Serbo-Croat to match these Russian data):

(15) nominative moj   djadja 'my uncle'
     accusative   mojego djadju
     genitive   mojego djadi

Table 6.3 *Attributive agreement in Russian*

	ètot 'this'	*student* 'student'	*dub* 'oak'		*sestra* 'sister'		*škola* 'school'		*čudovišče* 'monster'		*vino* 'wine'	
Singular												
Nominative	ètot	student	ètot	dub	èta	sestra	èta	škola	èto	čudovišče	èto	vino
Accusative	*ètogo*	studenta	*ètot*	dub	èta	sestru	ètu	školu	èto	čudovišče	èto	vino
Genitive	ètogo	studenta	ètogo	duba	ètoj	sestry	ètoj	školy	ètogo	čudovišča	ètogo	vina
Dative	ètomu	studentu	ètomu	dubu	ètoj	sestre	ètoj	škole	ètomu	čudovišču	ètomu	vinu
Instrumental	ètim	studentom	ètim	dubom	ètoj	sestroj	ètoj	školoj	ètim	čudoviščem	ètim	vinom
Locative	ètom	studente	ètom	dube	ètoj	sestre	ètoj	škole	ètom	čudovišče	ètom	vine
Plural												
Nominative	èti	studenty	èti	duby	èti	sestry	èti	školy	èti	čudovišča	èti	vina
Accusative	*ètix*	studentov	*èti*	duby	*ètix*	sester	*èti*	školy	*ètix*	čudovišč	*èti*	vina
Genitive	ètix	studentov	ètix	dubov	ètix	sester	ètix	škol	ètix	čudovišč	ètix	vin
Dative	ètim	studentam	ètim	dubam	ètim	sestram	ètim	školam	ètim	čudoviščam	ètim	vinam
Instrumental	ètimi	studentami	ètimi	dubami	ètimi	sestrami	ètimi	školami	ètimi	čudoviščami	ètimi	vinami
Locative	ètix	studentax	ètix	dubax	ètix	sestrax	ètix	školax	ètix	čudoviščax	ètix	vinax

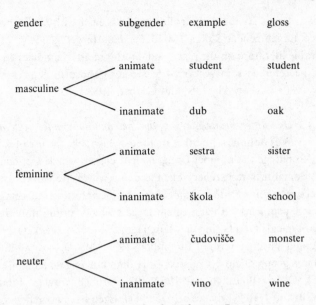

gender	subgender	example	gloss
masculine	animate	student	student
	inanimate	dub	oak
feminine	animate	sestra	sister
	inanimate	škola	school
neuter	animate	čudovišče	monster
	inanimate	vino	wine

Figure 6.14 *Genders and subgenders in Russian*

The form *djadju* is unambiguously accusative; its attributive modifier *mojego* is masculine and is accusative–genitive. Here the noun does not show accusative–genitive syncretism (thus animacy is not simply a morphological problem); nevertheless the fact that it is an animate noun is reflected in the form of the agreeing modifier. Given that the type of syncretism found with the animacy features is always the same in Russian (it is always accusative–genitive syncretism), and that it has a role elsewhere in the grammar (see Corbett 1981a), the subgender analysis is clearly superior to one recognizing six genders. A six-gender scheme would allow agreements for animate masculines to be completely different from other animates, whereas in all examples it is syncretism of accusative and genitive agreeing forms which is involved. We can thus retain the traditional three genders. The system is shown in figure 6.15.

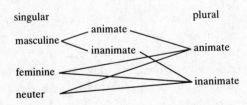

Figure 6.15 *The gender system of Russian*

167

Russian, then, has three controller genders, each with two subgenders. It has three target genders, plus two dependent target genders. (There is a considerable literature on the place and development of animacy in Slavonic; besides the references in section 4.5, see also those in Stankiewicz 1968; Huntley 1980; Laskowski 1986; and Corbett 1988.)

6.4.2 *Overdifferentiated targets and pronominal gender systems*

We continue with other methods which, like the use of subgenders, allow us to reduce the number of agreement classes which are recognized as genders. Sometimes researchers include items which are subject only to co-occurrence restrictions rather than being genuine agreement targets. But there are also real problems with agreement targets which permit more distinctions than do typical targets in the language: we term such targets 'over-differentiated' (using a term of Bloomfield 1933: 223–4). A dramatic example is found in a group of closely related Dravidian languages: Kolami (Emeneau 1955: 56), Ollari (Bhattacharya 1957: 19), Parji (Burrow & Bhattacharya 1953: 9–10) and Naiki (Emeneau 1955: 141). Each has two genders, basically male human and other. Yet some lower numerals ('two', 'three' and 'four' in Kolami) have additional forms for female human, as the following Kolami data show:

(16) iddar ma·sur
     two   men
(17) i·ral pillakul
     two   women
(18) indiŋ siḍl
     two   buffaloes

We should maintain the traditional account that these languages have two genders (as demonstrated by verb agreement and the forms of personal pronouns). The three numerals discussed are overdifferentiated targets; they are exceptional, and should be labelled as such, being the only three targets in the language which have special forms which co-occur with nouns denoting female humans.

It is worth considering the difference between subgenders on the one hand and agreement classes which are induced by overdifferentiated targets on the other. In the former case, agreement classes are separated by a distinction which is widely and consistently marked, but only for a small proportion of the morphosyntactic forms of the target. The distinction is therefore not so significant as that between the main genders. In Serbo-Croat and Russian almost all agreeing attributive modifiers (as well as the relative pronoun) make the animate–inanimate distinction, but, as we saw, this distinction is found only in the accusative case. With overdifferentiated targets, however, taking the Kolami case as illustrative, it is not a whole target type (like attributive modifiers or agreeing predicates) which is involved, nor is it a whole word-class (such as all numerals). There are just three irregular numerals, and these should be lexically marked as such. Thus for targets to be considered overdifferentiated, a specific gender agreement distinction must be restricted to a particular word-class, and even within this word-class it must be restricted to certain lexical items. We met various examples of lexical restrictions on gender agreement in section 5.3.8. Such cases do not necessarily involve overdifferentiated targets, since a distinction may be limited within a particular word-class but be securely distinguished elsewhere. For example, of the Russian numerals only *odin* 'one' distinguishes three genders. This is not an overdifferentiated target because adjectives and verbs regularly distinguish three genders in Russian; the three-way distinction is found in only one of the numerals, but is clearly reflected in other word-classes.

At this point we should consider those languages where gender is reflected only in pronouns; English is an example. We noted earlier that the definition of agreement adopted includes the control of anaphoric pronouns by their antecedents (the arguments for this were considered in section 5.1). It follows from our approach to defining gender in this chapter that pronouns may be the means by which particular languages divide nouns into different agreement classes. Thus languages like English have the category of gender. This conclusion appears justified for two reasons. First, when languages mark gender on pronouns and on some other target type, then typically they require a similar machinery to handle them all. Thus in French, the choice of masculine or feminine for anaphoric pronouns is determined by factors which are essentially the same as for attributive modifiers (though, as we shall see in section 8.2, personal pronouns may be avoided for some antecedents). In languages like French it is natural to treat the gender of pronouns together with that of the other targets. Consequently, it would be strange to treat pronouns differently (as not defining genders), simply because in a given language they were the sole indicators. The second argument is that when pronouns are the only evidence for gender, then the resulting gender system seems to be of the same type as that found in some other, fuller system. For example, the system of Defaka, which has only pronominal gender agreement, was described in section 2.1.2; the assignment system matches that of Tamil (section 2.1.1), which has a much fuller agreement system. There would seem to be no justification for treating languages like Defaka as greatly different in terms of gender system from those like Tamil. Nevertheless, some take a different view (Palmer 1971: 189–90 is an example). Given this other approach, which is generally based on a different view of agreement, we have referred to languages in which pronouns provide the only evidence for gender as having 'pronominal gender systems'. This reflects the fact that gender is less central to the syntactic structure of such languages.

In the case of English the evidence for a gender system is the existence of options such as *he/she/it*. It might be argued that the personal and reflexive pronouns of English are overdifferentiated and that for this different reason English has no gender system. But personal pronouns are central to the syntax in a way which the numerals 'two', 'three' and 'four' are not (as in the Kolami case discussed earlier). Pronouns are the basis of a separate target type. They are also, of course, extremely frequent. Thus some putative genders may be ruled out on the grounds that they are induced by overdifferentiated targets (as in the Kolami case). However, this argument is not appropriate for personal pronouns, given their important status. Whether or not gender is recognized in languages like English, Defaka and Zande depends on a different criterion, namely one's view of agreement. We shall continue to treat them as having gender.

6.4.3 *Inquorate genders*

Inquorate genders are the controller counterpart to over-differentiated targets. While the latter might artificially raise the number of genders on the basis of a small number of targets, inquorate genders are those postulated on the basis of an insufficient number of nouns, which should instead be lexically marked as exceptions. In Lak, as pointed out in section 2.2.5, there is one noun which does not fit into the four-gender system, namely *qaĩa* 'house'. This noun takes gender III agreements in the singular and IV in the plural. We should treat it as an individual exception. In another North-East Caucasian language, Gunzib, we also find one exceptional noun. The word for 'child' takes gender V agreement when singular and gender I/II when plural (Bokarev 1967b: 476). In the closely related Khvarsh, 'child' is also irregular, taking gender III when singular and I/II when plural; in Khvarsh it is joined by two further nouns, the word for 'family', and a borrowing from Avar also meaning 'family' (Bokarev 1967c: 424). Archi has an agreement class with just two nouns ('people' or 'nation', and 'population'), which can be treated as gender III when singular and I/II when plural (Kibrik 1972: 126). In all these cases the nouns should be lexically marked as exceptional. The situation with these nouns is very different from that found in Rumanian (section 6.3); while there are Rumanian nouns which take masculine agreements when singular and feminine when plural, these are counted in hundreds and not in ones and twos.

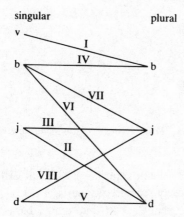

Figure 6.16 *Agreement classes in Tsova-Tush*

While the cases discussed may appear uncontroversial, it is worth pointing out that if the first published analysis of a language takes a different approach, the existence of a larger number of genders can be perpetuated through the literature. Thus it is regularly stated that Tsova-Tush, sometimes called Bats, which is a North-Central Caucasian or Nakh language, has eight genders. Tsova-Tush has an apparently complex crossed system; it has eight agreement classes, which may be represented as in figure 6.16. However, the membership of the agreement classes is unequal. (Information on class membership is given in Dešeriev 1953: 138–45. This has been revised and updated in the light of data kindly provided by Dee Ann Holisky, based on her fieldwork in Zemo-Alvani, on lecture notes from a course by Rusudan Gagua and on Kadagidze & Kadagidze 1984.) Agreement class VIII (*d–j*) contains only four nouns 'lip', 'cheek', 'ear' and 'hand'; we should label them as [V singular/III plural] and not treat agreement class VIII as a gender. This agreement class has insufficient members and so is deemed 'inquorate'. Agreement class IV is also small: it has only one native word, meaning 'a knit slipper', together with the word for 'boot', a borrowing from Russian. These should be labelled as [VI singular/I plural]. There are also some singularia tantum (see section 6.4.4) which Dešeriev treats as members of class IV, but these could equally well be treated as belonging to class VI. The last remnants of agreement class IV (which should not be counted as a gender, being inquorate) appear to be being absorbed by the largest class, VI, which clearly should be recognized as a gender.

Most interesting for our purposes is agreement class VII (*b–j*), which consists of the words for 'wing' (of a bird), 'mouth', 'lung', 'breast', 'rib', 'kidney', 'testicle', 'leg', 'knee', 'arm', 'fist', 'finger', 'nail' (of finger), 'eye'

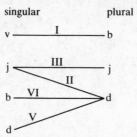

Figure 6.17 *Gender in Tsova-Tush* (*excluding inquorate genders*)

and 'throat'. We find fifteen nouns in all. Like agreement class VIII, class VII is strong on body parts, particularly paired body parts. There appear to be good grounds for declaring agreement class VII inquorate; that is to say, we should mark the nouns listed as lexical exceptions and not recognize a gender VII. The system would then be as shown in figure 6.17 (with the original numbers retained, but with the layout rearranged).

We have noted inquorate genders containing one, two, three, four and now fifteen nouns. This leaves the interesting question as to when an agreement class becomes quorate and so is recognized as a gender. There can be no simple answer: we should look to evidence such as productivity, changes affecting all the nouns involved (rather than individual members) and so on. Such evidence would suggest that the nouns involved share a gender (eventually one assigned by an assignment rule) rather than being individual exceptions. Where there is any doubt, that is, when the number of nouns in an agreement class is known to be small, it is important that this should be stated in descriptive grammars, particularly if it is claimed that the agreement class should be recognized as a gender. Voorhoeve (1968: 587) adopts the useful convention of indicating classes with few members by broken lines, in representations like figure 6.16. Unfortunately the broken line, like the star, has a different meaning in synchronic and diachronic description; De Wolf (1971: 49) uses a broken line to indicate an innovative pairing while a solid line indicates one retained from the parent language.

Though our examples of inquorate genders have so far all been from languages of the Caucasus, the phenomenon is widespread. Even in French, which everyone 'knows' has two genders, there are three nouns (*amour*, 'love', *délice* 'delight' and *orgue* 'organ') which are masculine in the singular and feminine in the plural. These, too, should be marked as lexical exceptions (in any case they are not straightforward singular–plural pairs and there is some variability). Serbo-Croat has several inquorate genders; the nouns in table 6.4 have different genders in the singular and plural (Ivić 1963: 56). In

Table 6.4 *Inquorate genders in Serbo-Croat*

Singular		Plural		Gloss
akt	masculine	akta	neuter	document
oko	neuter	oči	feminine	eye
mače	neuter	mačići	masculine	kitten

these and similar instances, the nouns are morphologically irregular; *akt* 'document' does not decline in the plural in the way one would predict, given the singular. The other two nouns given actually have modified stems in the plural. The gender irregularity follows from the morphological irregularity; thus if the assignment rules were applied separately to singular and plural forms of these nouns, then we would obtain exactly the gender features given above. We are dealing with exceptions whose irregular morphology gives rise to unusual pairings of gender agreements; the numbers of nouns involved are relatively small, and so we can treat them as inquorate genders. (However, the *akt* type is expanding from borrowings and so might eventually constitute a new gender.) A similar situation is found in Noni (a language of the Grassfields Bantu region of Cameroon; data from Hyman 1981: 8). Just six nouns have the irregular pairing 3/13, and we do not recognize them as a gender (they are inquorate). Of these six, four have irregular plurals.

It is important to note that in all the cases discussed the nouns could be given an exceptional marker (for an unusual pairing of singular and plural target gender forms) which would allow the normal agreement rules to determine the required markers. It does not follow that any agreement class with a small number of members is necessarily inquorate, since it may not be possible to give all the nouns an irregular marker in this way. Let us consider the very interesting case of Lelemi (a Togo Remnant language, in turn part of Niger-Kordofanian, spoken in the Volta region of Ghana by 14,900 people at the 1960 census). Heine (1982: 197–8) presents it as an example of a complicated crossed system. There is more information in Heine (1968b: 114–15), and it is that source which we shall follow. There is evidence for ten agreement classes, which Heine labels I–X (see figure 6.18). Agreement classes II and VIII normally both take the plural agreement marker *á-*, but class II has the optional alternative *lέ-* for the demonstrative pronoun *mέ* 'this' only. We should mark this pronoun as overdifferentiated and so not recognize II and VIII as two separate genders, but as one. When we look at the examples given both in the section on Lelemi and in the general word-list (Heine 1968b: 212–57), it is clear that most of the nouns are accounted for by

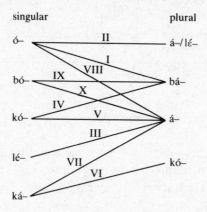

Figure 6.18 *Agreement classes in Lelemi*

Table 6.5 *Main agreement classes in Lelemi*

Agreement class	Agreements Singular	Plural
I	ó-	bá-
II	ó-	á-
III	lé-	á-
V	kó-	á-
VI	ká-	kó-

the agreement classes given in table 6.5 (but note that 'II' here is not strictly an agreement class but the combination of agreement classes II and VIII).

The agreement classes given in table 6.5 should all be recognized as genders. Provided they are as uncommon as appears to be the case, the small sets of nouns in agreement classes IV (*kó-/bá*) and VII (*ká-/á-*) can be treated as inquorate and the nouns can be marked lexically (as V singular and I plural, and as VI singular and II plural respectively). What then of the remaining agreement classes, IX and X? Heine gives just one example in IX (agreements *bó-/bá-*), and two examples in X (agreements *bó-/á-*). Let us assume the worst case, that there are no other nouns in either agreement class. We would like to treat them as inquorate. However, unlike the cases considered so far, there is no exceptional marker available, since no other gender has *bó-* for singular agreement. Furthermore, we cannot look to an irregularity in a particular target, since there are seven possible agreement targets in Lelemi and it appears that all seven take the marker *bó-*. Thus although we do not need to recognize Heine's IV, VII and VIII as genders, we must accept X. This agreement class is not inquorate, since the nouns cannot be lexically marked as exceptional, and they are not induced by overdifferentiated targets since the target gender form *bó-* is found throughout the agreement system. (We could then treat IX as inquorate, and mark the one noun of this type as X singular and I plural.) Lelemi has a genuinely complicated gender system, including a gender which contains very few nouns yet is not inquorate.

6.4.4 *Defective nouns*

There are many instances of nouns which lack certain forms; most commonly they have no singular or no plural. (Nouns with only plural forms are called 'pluralia tantum', while those with only singular forms are called 'singularia tantum'.) Intuitively, where in all the morphosyntactic forms available these nouns take the same agreements as normal nouns (in the forms they share), then they are of the same gender. Thus Russian *razgovorčivost'* 'talkativeness' is found only in the singular. Its agreements are the same as those of the feminine inanimate noun *škola* 'school', when singular. We can therefore label *razgovorčivost'* as feminine inanimate. This will happen automatically if the normal assignment rules operate on its meaning and on its existing forms. There are, similarly, nouns which have no singular. In languages like Russian where gender distinctions are not found in the plural, there is a slight complication (this is considered in detail by Zaliznjak (1964: 32–40), who introduces an additional gender class, which is something we shall avoid). The noun *nožnicy* 'scissors' occurs only in the plural; its agreements match those of *duby* 'oaks' (masculine inanimate), *školy* 'schools' (feminine inanimate) and *vina* 'wines' (neuter inanimate) in table 6.3. Since Russian distinguishes animacy but not the main genders in the plural, it is sufficient that *nožnicy* be marked as plural and inanimate. There are insufficient grounds for creating an extra gender. This much follows from the definition of agreement class given in section 6.2. Whenever nouns like *nožnicy* meet the conditions of the definition, they will be found to be in the same agreement class as inanimate plural nouns. The best solution is therefore to have them underspecified in this way (that is, as inanimate, but with no specification as to main gender). If, however, in a particular theory it was necessary for every noun to have a gender feature, then *nožnicy* could be assigned arbitrarily to any gender, or preferably it could be assigned to the feminine since its morphology is like that of a feminine noun in the plural (other nouns would be masculine or neuter accordingly). Peculiarities of the syntactic behaviour of such nouns, notably with quantifiers, are a problem of

175

number rather than of gender, and so need not concern us. Thus the fact that some nouns lack morphological realizations for particular morphosyntactic specifications does not give rise to new gender categories.

6.4.5 *Consistent agreement patterns*

The question of differences in targets has already been mentioned. In some languages all targets mark the same distinctions; we may then take any one target type and use it to establish the agreement classes. In other languages different targets make a greater or lesser number of distinctions; we noted examples of animacy being reflected in attributive modifiers but not in the predicate (section 6.4.1). In such cases we include the target type which marks most distinctions when we are establishing agreement classes. We will look first at a situation which is relatively unusual, that in which different agreement targets make different distinctions (and where it is not simply that the distinctions made by one are a subset of those made by the other). In such a case it is clear that we need to establish a relationship between the sets of agreement markers found on the different controllers. Then we shall see that in fact we need to do the same even for the apparently simpler cases where the distinctions marked on different targets are identical. In both instances we must establish what we shall call 'consistent agreement patterns'. This analytic step is usually taken without comment, but it crucially determines the analysis of gender systems.

We start with a language where it is necessary to look at two different word-classes in order to establish the number of agreement classes and indeed the number of genders. The Papuan language Yimas, discussed in section 3.2.4, has eleven agreement classes. The ones which concern us here are numbers I, II, III and V. The forms for adjectival and verbal agreement are given in table 6.6 (Foley 1986: 86–7, 89). Note that the agreement markers occur after adjectival stems and before verbal stems. If we considered only adjectival agreement (found in attributive use and in the predicate together with the

Table 6.6 *Agreement forms in Yimas*

| | Adjective | | | Verb | | |
	Singular	Dual	Plural	Singular	Dual	Plural
I	-n	-rim	-um	na-	impa-	pu-
II	-nmaŋ	-nprum	-nput	na-	impa-	pu-
III	-n	-rim	-um	na-	tima-	pu-
V	-n	-rim	-ra	na-	tima-	∅-i-a-

copula) then we would accept the forms in the line labelled 'II' as separating out an agreement class (II); there is ample evidence, since the agreements are distinct in all numbers. Moreover, agreement class V would be no problem, for it has a different plural agreement form from the others. But then agreement classes I (which contains nouns denoting male humans) and III (higher animals) would be indistinguishable. If, conversely, we considered only the forms found on verbal predicates, we could distinguish agreement classes I and II on the one hand from III and V on the other by means of the dual forms. We could further distinguish agreement class III from V by using the plural agreement forms. However, there would be no justification for dividing agreement classes I and II (which contain nouns denoting male humans and female humans respectively).

The evidence from both adjectives and verbs should be accepted, which leads to an analysis in which all these classes are indeed distinct. We therefore have a case, covered by our definition of agreement class, in which different targets have to be considered. These data make it quite clear that we cannot point to a single set of agreement forms to distinguish agreement classes (and from them genders); we need to be able to establish links between target gender forms. Thus agreement class I is defined as taking *-n* on singular adjectives, *-rim* on dual adjectives, and so on. Such sets of target gender forms, shown as horizontal rows in table 6.6, are termed 'consistent agreement patterns'. A definition will be given a little later in the discussion.

It is worth spelling out why the four agreement classes illustrated in table 6.6 are all accepted as genders. It might be suggested that either verbs or adjectives are overdifferentiated targets, but of course we cannot exclude all of a major word-class in this way. Alternatively, it might be claimed that agreement classes I and III should really be seen as subgenders of a single gender, being distinguished only in the dual of the verb. In Yimas, however, this is one morphosyntactic form out of three, hence it is hardly the case that the distinction is restricted to a small proportion of the morphosyntactic forms of the target. Moreover, if we compare with other genders, we find that III and V are distinguished in two forms only, while I and II and I and V differ from each other in three. In comparison, therefore, agreement classes I and III do not control 'minimally different' sets of agreements and so can be recognized as full genders. There are, nevertheless, considerable similarities between genders I, II and III, and Foley suggests (1986: 86–7) that they have developed from a single animate gender, in turn a specialization of gender V.

In Yimas the need for establishing consistent agreement patterns is obvious; it is in fact just as necessary in many other languages, where the need is less immediately obvious. Russian can again serve as an example. We established three main target gender forms. For the attributive adjective we have the nominative singular endings: *-yj*, *-aja* and *-oe*. The past tense verb has three singular endings: *-∅, -a, -o*. The relative pronoun has the same endings as the attributive adjective, and the personal pronouns are *on*, *ona* and *ono*. For the vast majority of nouns, the agreements are as given in table 6.7. This

Table 6.7 *Agreement patterns in Russian*

Attributive adjective	Predicate	Relative pronoun	Personal pronoun	Traditional gender
-yj	-∅	-yj	on-∅	masculine
-aja	-a	-aja	on-a	feminine
-oe	-o	-oe	on-o	neuter

table represents a simplification; the full version would include the other cases, the plural number, and therefore the animate and inanimate subgenders. From the data given, relating to the main genders, the distinctions made by each target gender type are identical. The question is how this analysis is done, particularly in view of the fact that there are nouns which take other combinations of agreements. For example, *vrač* in the meaning 'woman doctor' can occur in the following constructions:

(19) nov-yj   vrač
new-MASC doctor
'the new doctor'

(20) nov-aja   vrač
new-FEM   doctor
'the new doctor'

Examples like (19) are more common than (20). In the predicate, the feminine is somewhat more common:

(21) vrač   rabotal-∅
doctor worked-MASC
'the doctor worked'

(22) vrač   rabotal-a
doctor worked-FEM
'the doctor worked'

The relative pronoun is usually feminine and the personal pronoun is normally feminine (though even here the masculine is possible).

How then is table 6.7 constructed? In this case there are phonological clues (*-a* in the feminines, for example), but this is not always a reliable indicator. There are two important factors. The first is that, as mentioned earlier, the vast majority of nouns which take *-yj*, also take *-∅* and *on*; the second point is that these are nouns for which we can give absolute rules: they always take the same agreements. Each horizontal line of table 6.7 represents a 'consistent agreement pattern', which we define as follows:

> A consistent agreement pattern is a set of target gender forms such that:
>> (i) the agreement class it induces is as large as possible;
>> (ii) agreement rules relating to this agreement class will be simple and exceptionless.

The notion of consistent agreement pattern allows us to separate nouns like *vrač* from ordinary nouns like, say, *ženščina* 'woman' and *mužčina* 'man'; the agreements taken by the latter two each form a consistent agreement pattern while those of *vrač* do not. The other result is that a consistent agreement pattern links all the target gender forms of a given gender. The notion of consistent agreement pattern gives us a principled way of capturing the intuition that, for example, a feminine marker on an attributive modifier is 'the same as' a feminine marker on a verb, even if they are phonologically different. Thus it is needed even for languages where different targets mark similar distinctions, as well as for languages, like Yimas, where they do not.

It seems that the notion of consistent agreement pattern fulfils important functions; before going on, however, we should check that it is indeed necessary, since it might appear to duplicate apparatus already given. In particular, we must consider whether agreement patterns which are not consistent are simply those which induce agreement classes which are inquorate genders. Unfortunately, things are not that simple. The notion of inquorate gender is necessary for cases like Tsova-Tush (section 6.4.3), where there would otherwise be no principled reason for choosing between possible singular–plural pairings. We were able to exclude some, since the classes involved were small and the nouns could be marked as lexical exceptions. But there are over 200 nouns like *vrač* in Russian and so they are too numerous to be simply labelled as exceptional. Given their ability to take two types of agreement, and especially the variability involved, we need the notion of consistent agreement pattern to ensure that such nouns do not form the basis of genders, but that the more straightforward ones do. Furthermore, the notion of inquorate gender does not allow us to link up target gender forms as consistent agreement patterns do (whether linking similar forms as in Russian, or dissimilar ones as in Yimas). If we accept that the notion of consistent agreement pattern fulfils these useful functions, we should still check whether a simpler account would work just as well. Could we not simply say that a consistent agreement pattern is the set of agreements which can occur with one and the same noun (even adding the requirement that they must do so with the same instance of the noun)? Unfortunately not, since Russian nouns like *vrač* '(woman) doctor' can take different agreements at the same time:

(23) nas-∅   vrač   prišl-a
     our-MASC doctor came-FEM

It is the notion of consistent agreement pattern which allows us to differentiate the agreements in (23), and so to give an account of nouns like *vrač* (as we shall see in more detail in section 6.4.5.2).

Of course, the majority of nouns will belong to agreement classes which have a consistent agreement pattern and which are recognized as genders or subgenders. But we must now consider how to treat those which do not. We shall distinguish between nouns which take freely all the agreements of more than one consistent agreement pattern and those for which the possibilities are more restricted than that. An example from the pronominal gender system of English will make the distinction clear. We find three consistent agreement patterns (table 6.8). This simple example illustrates the point that a single form

Table 6.8 *Consistent agreement patterns in English*

who	he	(masculine)
who	she	(feminine)
which	it	(neuter)

(*who*) can appear in more than one consistent agreement pattern. Such syncretisms are considered in detail in sections 7.1.1 and 7.1.2. The important point for the present argument, however, is the difference in behaviour between two types of noun. Those like *baby* can occur with all the forms of all three patterns. They are to be distinguished from those like the so-called 'boat nouns', which are the various expressions denoting ships. These may take the neuter agreement pattern (*which* and *it*):

(24) The Canberra, which has just docked, is a fine ship. It sails
     again on Friday.

Boat nouns can also take the personal pronoun *she*, but not the relative *who*:

(25) I sailed on the Canberra. She's a fine ship.

(26) * The Canberra, who is a fine ship...

Thus *ship* and similar nouns take agreements from two consistent agreement patterns but do not take freely all the forms of both. (For further discussion see Malone 1985 and for data see Marcoux 1973: 102-3.) We shall first consider in more detail nouns comparable to *baby*, and then examine cases like English boat nouns.

6.4.5.1 Double- and multiple-gender nouns

These are nouns, like English *baby*, which can take all the agreements of more than one consistent pattern. Thus the Lak noun *ḣakin* 'doctor' can take the pattern associated with gender I, gender II or gender III, depending on whether the doctor is a man, an older woman or a younger woman (Khaidakov 1963: 50). And in Archi, several nouns like *lo* 'child' and *misgin* 'poor person' can take gender I agreements (when a male is denoted), gender II (female), or gender IV singular and gender I/II plural when the sex is unknown or unimportant (Kibrik 1972: 126); other cases where commitment as to the sex of the referent is avoided are considered further in section 7.3.2. Nouns of the type we have been discussing are often called nouns of common gender. This term is useful, as long as it does not imply the existence of a new gender. The notion of double or mulitiple gender is wider than common gender. Common-gender nouns normally take different agreements for semantic or pragmatic reasons; other nouns may take alternative agreements without such motivation and so still have double gender.

Let us now review more generally the circumstances in which nouns may have, or may be claimed to have, double gender. We should also consider the lexical entries of such nouns (so taking further the brief discussion in section 3.3.3.2). The first diagnostic is whether the difference in gender of the noun in question correlates with some other difference or not. In most cases it does. The correlation may be with a semantic (understood broadly) or a formal factor. Taking correlations with semantic factors first, we can further ask whether the difference in meaning is derivable solely from the meanings of the genders. In the most straightforward examples, like English *doctor*, the different genders correlate with different meanings (male or female), which are the core meanings of the genders. *Doctor* takes *he* when it denotes a male, and *she* when it denotes a female. Given that its semantics allow it to be used to denote males and females, the normal assignment rules will account for the genders. Nouns like *doctor* are nouns of common gender in the narrow sense. The next type is that in which the different genders of the noun correlate with different meanings, but these do not match the gender meanings (the semantic assignment rules). In French we find *la trompette* (feminine) 'the trumpet', and *le trompette* (masculine) 'the trumpeter, soldier who plays the trumpet' (Wienold 1970: 399). While the masculine gender matches the meaning involved, the feminine does not. It appears, then, that we have two separate, though related, nouns, and not a case of double gender. This is even clearer in cases like *le livre* (masculine) 'the book' and *la livre* (feminine) 'the pound'. Here we have a case of homonymy; the two words happen to have the same form, though they are quite distinct in meaning. They are separate words, synchronically and diachronically, and so the difference in their genders is not specially significant. The two nouns require separate lexical entries and so do not constitute a case of double gender.

There remain the cases where nouns have two (or more) genders, and where this difference correlates not with meaning but with form. Now it is sometimes stated that certain Russian nouns like *šampun'* 'shampoo' can be masculine or feminine. But this is only part of the story, since the noun exists in two forms. Normally it declines rather like *zakon* in table 3.3 (strictly its soft variant paradigm) and is masculine according to the normal assignment rules (see section 3.1.1). But it can also in colloquial usage decline like *kost'* 'bone' when, again as expected, it is feminine. Therefore it must be stated in the lexicon that it can belong to two different declensional types; in both cases the gender is derivable from the morphology. Thus the noun has two genders, but this is fully predictable and need not be stated in the lexicon. Its ability to follow two different paradigms must be stated in the lexicon in any case, since it is not predictable, and the genders follow automatically from this.

The last possibility is that a noun has two genders, and that this difference has no other correlate. There are two main sets of circumstances where we might find such examples: during change of gender and in borrowings. A possible case is found in Babanki (one of the Ring languages, which form part of the Western Grassfields group within Bantu, spoken in north-west Cameroon); there are several nouns, including 'branch', 'face' and 'feather', which can take the agreements either of gender 3/13 or of gender 5/13. This forms part of a more general change in which the target gender form labelled class 3 is supplanting class 5 (Hyman 1980b: 231–3, 236); a similar change is discussed in section 7.1.3. There is no indication of any difference apart from that of gender, and nouns in the course of the change are of double gender. However, during the course of such changes, there are often stylistic effects, with the new form being more colloquial and the old being more formal. Thus, while double gender nouns certainly occur during gender change, there may well be other factors which correlate with the use of the different genders.

Another set of circumstances in which double gender occurs, and one in which there may perhaps be no other correlations is in borrowings. If borrowings are not unambiguously assigned to a gender by the prevailing assignment rules, then they may have double gender, if only for an initial period (see section 4.1.2). For example, *interview* was borrowed into French near the end of the last century, and was treated initially both as masculine and as feminine (Grevisse 1964: 211-12); it is now normally feminine.

Before leaving this topic, it is worth pointing out that nouns which are claimed to be of common or double gender sometimes turn out, on closer examination, not to belong fully to the two genders (see, for example, Kopeliovič 1977 for a careful investigation of Russian data). The terms may sometimes be used loosely for hybrid nouns, to which we now turn.

6.4.5.2 Hybrid nouns

These are nouns which neither simply take the agreements of one consistent agreement pattern nor belong to two or more genders. The agreement form to be used depends in part on the type of target involved. English 'boat nouns' meet this definition. Another good example is the German word *Mädchen* 'girl'. *Mädchen* can take agreements exactly as a neuter noun. It may also take the feminine personal pronoun *sie*, but not the other agreements of the consistent agreement pattern associated with feminine nouns. Thus to determine the gender agreement form we need to know the target in question (whether or not it is a personal pronoun). Examples of this type typically arise when assignment rules are in conflict; in this case, nouns denoting females are usually feminine in German, but nouns formed with -*chen* are normally neuter. Such nouns must be lexically marked.

A more complex example is Russian *vrač* 'doctor', which was discussed earlier. When *vrač* denotes a male doctor, then it takes the consistent agreement pattern associated with masculine animate nouns. When it denotes a female doctor it takes both masculine and feminine patterns as follows:

attributive modifiers	usually masculine, feminine possible
predicate	both possible
relative pronoun	normally feminine, masculine rare
personal pronoun	normally feminine (masculine just possible)

In this remarkable case, the agreement required is variable for all the different types of target (there is more detailed discussion in section 8.1.1). Thus *vrač* denoting a female is a 'hybrid' noun, as it does not take consistently feminine agreements, nor consistently masculine agreements, nor both. The choice of form to be used depends in part on the target type. Again this situation results

Table 6.9 *Agreement with* vrač *and similar nouns in Russian*

	Attributive modifiers (% of informants favouring feminine agreement)	Predicate agreement (% of informants favouring feminine agreement)
vrač '(female) doctor'	16.9 (N = 3,835)	51.7 (N = 3,806)
buxgalter '(female) accountant'	25.5 (N = 3,835)	–
upravdom '(female) house manager'	–	60.7 (N = 3,806)

from a conflict of the assignment rules, since the noun denotes a female (and so should be feminine) yet its declensional type is such that it should be masculine (see section 3.1.1 and especially figure 3.3). Taking *vrač* as a whole, it is a curious composite with one half being masculine, apparently half of a double-gender noun (when a male is denoted), while the other half is a hybrid noun (when a female is denoted).

There are several nouns like *vrač*. However, the frequency with which they take the different agreements varies. The Panov survey of some 4,000 speakers (see section 8.1.1 for details) produced the data presented in table 6.9 (we are concerned only with instances in which a female is denoted). It is evident that *vrač* and *buxgalter* do not take exactly the same agreements; no more, we must assume, do other nouns of the same type. Thus each one, strictly speaking, belongs to a different agreement class. This fact leads to an explosive increase in the number of agreement classes (Zaliznjak does not discuss nouns of this type). Naturally we do not wish to propose a separate gender for each noun; rather they must be lexically marked as masculine and feminine, with an indication as to the relative weight of the two features. These data reinforce the need to supplement the agreement class approach with the notion of consistent agreement pattern. While here we have stressed the variability in the behaviour of hybrid nouns, there are also generalizations to be made, which are investigated in chapter 8.

6.4.6 *Combined gender systems*

Particularly interesting problems arise when two different gender systems appear to coexist. This rare situation is found in the Mba group (Ubangian branch of Niger-Kordofanian; data from Tucker & Bryan 1966: 110, 114–23, 131–40; Pasch 1985: 69–71; 1986). Here we find systems similar to the Bantu type (somewhat reduced), and a second system distinguishing up to four members: male human, female human, animal and inanimate. The latter type of system, based on semantic criteria, is a later development. The four languages of the group show four different possibilities. Ndunga has only the Bantu-like system of agreements and so is straight-forward – the new development has not affected it. At the other extreme, Ma has lost the Bantu-type agreement and has only a semantically based system, similar to that of Zande (section 2.2.1); this four-gender system is found in pronouns, and elsewhere there is an animate–inanimate distinction. Ma, too, is therefore unproblematic; the evidence that it once had the earlier system is that the old suffixes are still found on nouns. Dongo, however, has both types of system. For example, verbs agree in animacy (an animate–inanimate distinction), while adjectives preserve a Bantu-like set of agreements. When we look more carefully at adjectival agreement, we find that agreement according to gender as predictable by the morphological class of the noun occurs only with inanimates. Animates, irrespective of their morphology, take the agreements of one specific gender. When we analyse Dongo using the agreement class approach we arrive at precisely the same genders which could be identified by looking solely at the adjectival agreement forms. Within the noun phrase (but not outside it) the development is similar to that in Swahili (sections 3.1.2 and 8.3). Thus, though the gender system of Dongo has two separate origins, the systems have fused and can readily be described using the approach we have developed.

The most interesting of the Mba languages for present purposes is Mba itself. Mba has several inquorate genders, which need not concern us , and one or two whose size is not fully clear. To avoid exaggerating the problem we shall include only those genders which are well established. If we take agreement within the noun phrase (the agreement of demonstratives and interrogatives among others) we can distinguish the following agreement classes, which we label according to the agreements taken in the singular and the plural: 1/2, 3/4, 5/6, 7/2, 9/6, 11/2. There is also a personal pronoun, used only to denote animates, which has the forms shown in table 6.10.

Table 6.10 *Personal pronouns in Mba*

	Singular	Plural
Male human	ndé	
		6έ
Other animate	6i	

185

Most interestingly, these pronouns can be used optionally as agreement markers:

(27) djù (6i) úmà
  woman ANIM 1.one
  'one woman'

Here the numeral is in the class 1 form; the form in parentheses is optional and indicates animacy (animate, excluding male human). For an inanimate noun which takes the same form of the numeral, the optional element is not available:

(28) ŋgbà úmà
  song 1.one
  'one song'

Now compare the following pair:

(29) kíá (6i) k-ímà
  snake ANIM 5-one
  'one snake'
(30) kàsà k-ímà
  leaf 5-one
  'one leaf'

The agreement on the numeral is identical in (29) and (30); both nouns take class 5 agreement (and class 6 when plural). But since *kíá* 'snake' is animate, it can take the optional agreement marker, while *kàsà* 'leaf' cannot.

How then do we determine the number of genders in Mba? Following the approach taken so far, we establish the agreement classes. The question is how many there are. To concentrate on a specific case, we must ask whether *kíá* 'snake' and *kàsà* 'leaf' are in the same agreement class. Let us take the most difficult scenario. The optional agreement markers occur only with animates; it could be argued that for inanimates the optional marker merely takes the null form. Then according to our definition the two nouns in question belong to different agreement classes. More generally, since attributive modifiers require us to divide nouns into six classes, and the optional markers divide nouns into three classes, we would expect to find a total of eighteen agreement classes. However, not all the combinations occur (Pasch 1986: 173). We find the consistent agreement patterns given in table 6.11, which induce eleven agreement classes. In the first two columns we have the attributive agreement markers, which would allow us to set up agreement classes 1/2, 3/4, 5/6, 7/2, 9/6, 11/2. As we have just seen, not all the nouns in these proposed agreement classes behave identically, hence we must take the analysis further. In only two

Table 6.11 *Consistent agreement patterns in Mba*

Singular agreement	Plural agreement	Pronoun/optional agreement	Gender	Combined gender
w	y	ndé	I	1/2 male personal
w	y	ɓi	II	1/2 animate
w	y	∅	III	1/2 inanimate
l	s	∅	IV	3/4 inanimate
k	z	ɓi	V	5/6 animate
k	z	∅	VI	5/6 inanimate
g	y	ndé	VII	7/2 male personal
g	y	ɓi	VIII	7/2 animate
g	y	∅	IX	7/2 inanimate
ny	z	∅	X	9/6 inanimate
m	y	∅	XI	11/2 inanimate

cases, however, classes 1/2 and 7/2, do we find all three possibilities of the optional agreement marker (and this is being further reduced by the transfer of nouns denoting male humans from 1/2 to 7/2; Pasch 1986: 166–72). When the possible combinations are plotted (recall that dubious cases were excluded) we find eleven agreement classes, labelled I–XI in table 6.11; these should all be recognized as genders.

In this difficult case (and we have taken the most problematic interpretation of the data in order to test the procedure), the approach based on agreement classes works satisfactorily, and we find that Mba has eleven genders. However, it is worth asking whether this is the best analysis. There are two different types of agreement involved, and the assignment of nouns is based on two different systems (morphological and semantic). One idea would be to treat the animacy divisions as subgenders, on the Slavonic model. But this is not appropriate, since when we look at the pronoun/optional agreement marker it is clearly not the case that the three types of noun take 'minimally different' agreements: in the singular there are simply three forms (including the null form), and so there is the greatest possible differentiation for this target. An alternative would be to say that in Mba there are two gender systems, and that nouns belong to two genders, one in each system. This would give us the system given on the right of table 6.11. This seems a reasonable account, recognizing the unusual nature of the data. It could be argued, however, that it implies too large a difference between Mba and other gender languages. It is not the case that there are two totally independent gender systems; we do not find the theoretically possible eighteen types of noun but eleven, which shows that in fact animacy is an important factor in the assignment of nouns to the different classes for the purposes of attributive agreement. Thus the straightforward eleven-gender account has a lot to commend it. There is a good compromise solution here. When discussing Bantu languages (section 3.1.2), we noted that labels like 1/2 are a useful mnemonic for genders (nouns in the 1/2 gender take class 1 agreements when singular and class 2 agreements when plural). Similarly labels like 'masculine' are favoured in other traditions (masculine nouns take the same agreements as a typical noun denoting a male). In Mba we could recognize eleven genders, but label them using the description on the right of table 6.11; thus, for example, '7/2 animate' is an alternative to 'gender VIII', and it has the advantage of spelling out the actual agreements involved. It remains to be seen whether any unequivocal examples of languages with two independent gender systems will be found.

6.5 Conclusion

We have seen that in establishing the number of genders in a particular language, Zaliznjak's approach, based on the notion of agreement class, is a useful starting point. It is important to realize, however, that this approach leads us towards controller genders; the other side of the coin is the system of different forms of the agreeing elements: we term these forms target genders. In some languages there are numerous agreement classes, but not every agreement class is necessarily recognized as a gender. Some are subgenders; other agreement classes are based on overdifferentiated targets and so are not accepted as genders; nor indeed are inquorate genders. Nouns belonging to the latter require a feature in their lexical entry, to mark their irregularity, as do defective nouns and nouns with double or multiple gender and hybrid nouns. Thus to find how many genders a language has, we begin with agreement classes but eliminate as many as possible. This minimalist position has been justified at each point. It is interesting to note that in many cases it leads us to traditional analyses. We have now established an analytical basis for the genders whose assignment systems were discussed in chapters 2–4, and we are now in a position to tackle problems of syncretism raised in chapter 5. This we do, together with discussing other target gender problems in chapter 7. Then in chapter 8 we give careful attention to the question of hybrid nouns.

7
Target genders: syncretism and enforced gender forms

We have distinguished the groups into which nouns can be divided (controller genders) from the sets of markers (target genders) which appear on agreeing elements. Nouns are assigned normally to a single gender, while agreeing elements or targets have more than one gender form, and the selection of the appropriate form depends on the gender of the controller. It is interesting topics concerned with target tenders which are the focus of this chapter. First we take up from the preceding chapter the question of the interaction with number, and the types of syncretism which arise (section 7.1). Then we consider the form of gender agreement used when the normal conditions for agreement are not met and so gender agreement becomes a problem. This question is covered in two sections: neutral agreement in section 7.2, and gender agreement with noun phrases involving reference problems in section 7.3. Discussion of inconsistent patterns of agreement is reserved for the following chapter.

7.1 Gender and number

It has already become apparent that number enjoys a special relationship to gender. We saw examples in the last chapter where an agreement class which was based on a difference in agreement in one morphological case was not then recognized as a gender (but as a subgender); on the other hand, agreement classes based on a difference in number were recognized as genders. This apparent inequality was covered by the definition given in section 6.4.1; the subgender examples typically involved one case out of several, whereas the number examples normally involved one number out of two (singular and plural) or three (singular, dual and plural). Thus the sets of agreements involved were not minimally different: they did not differ only for a small proportion of the morphosyntactic forms of any of the targets but for a half or a third of the forms. Number is of more importance for gender also because it is the category most often realized together with gender. It is found together with gender in more different target types than is case, notably in the predicate. Indeed, Greenberg claims that the presence of verbal agreement in gender in a language implies number agreement (1963: 94). It is therefore worth examining more closely the relation of gender to number.

7.1.1 *Syncretism: further examples of convergent and crossed systems*

As we noted in section 5.2.3, 'syncretism' describes the situation in which two or more morphosyntactic forms of the same lexeme have a single morphological realization. In the last chapter we saw the importance of understanding syncretism for the analysis of gender systems, and we shall review the question in more detail here. The more straightforward type of syncretism is found in convergent systems (as discussed in section 6.3.1). Taking Hausa as an example (Parsons 1960; see also section 3.2.2), we find the type of pattern shown in figure 7.1. Similar systems but with three genders differentiated in the singular yet only one set of plural agreement forms are found in languages as diverse as German, Krongo (a Kordofanian language spoken in the Nuba mountains of the Sudan; Reh 1983: 45–7) and Avar (a North-East Caucasian language; Madieva 1967: 259).

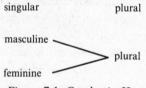

Figure 7.1 *Gender in Hausa*

When a convergent system has more than one plural form, then it can be asked whether the plural target gender forms are used for semantically significant groupings of controller genders (section 6.3.2). Consider Chamalal, a North-East Caucasian language, which shows the pattern given in figure 7.2 (Magomedbekova 1967b: 386–7; see also section 10.2.3). Of the five genders separated in the singular, the first two have a clear semantic base while the other three include a mixture of animates and inanimates. In the plural, the first two genders take the same target form, which therefore is found only with humans; the other three genders have a second form, which is thus restricted to non-humans. In Dido, another North-East Caucasian language, there are four target gender forms in the singular, but two in the plural; the latter split male human from all others. On the other hand, target gender forms which cover a convergence of singular forms may have no semantic significance (as is the case in Slovene, considered in section 6.3.1).

The discrepancy between singular and plural can be even greater; thus Wolof (a West Atlantic language within Niger-Kordofanian) has eight target

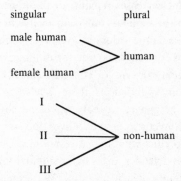

Figure 7.2 Target genders in Chamalal

gender forms in the singular and only two in the plural, one of which is rare (Irvine 1978: 43). One of the languages related to Wolof, Fula, also illustrates this point as well as several other points at issue in this section. Fula is a West Atlantic language, with perhaps 10 million speakers spread widely across West Africa, the largest number being in Nigeria. A simplified picture of the gender system is given in figure 7.3; for more details see Arnott (1967), Koval' (1979), and Koval' & Kubko (1986: 73–96). Fula has about twenty genders, depending on the dialect. There are evident semantic principles involved in

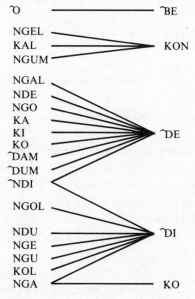

Figure 7.3 Target genders in Fula

191

gender assignment, but many unclear cases remain. In the plural there are many fewer target forms than in the singular, only four or five in fact, again depending on dialect. Here the semantic values are relatively clear; reading from the top in figure 7.3, one is for rationals, one for diminutives, one for countable plurals (especially animates), one for collective plurals (especially inanimates) and in some but not all dialects there is also a plural for augmentatives (*κο*). Unlike the languages we have discussed so far in this section, Fula does not show a convergent system. Given the singular target gender form, we cannot always predict what the corresponding plural would be: for example, a noun taking *NDI* gender forms in the singular might be one which takes *DE* in the plural or one which takes *DI*. We therefore have a 'crossed' system. We shall consider further crossed systems in section 7.1.3 below.

So far in this section we have looked at languages with singular and plural numbers. We should now turn to examples with more complex number systems. Seneca has three numbers (Chafe 1967: 13–14, 16–17): the distribution of allomorphs is complex, so we shall use target gender names in figure 7.4. Here we find a relation of convergence between the singular and dual target gender forms, and one of parallelism between dual and plural (compare Slovene, analysed in section 6.3.1).

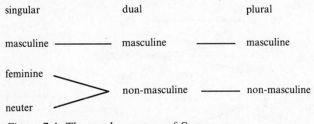

Figure 7.4 *The gender system of Seneca*

For a more difficult case we turn to the West Slavonic language Upper Sorbian, as described by Ermakova (1976) and Fasske (1981: 399–413). In view of its complexity, we give the relevant data in table 7.1. It will also serve as a further illustration of a different aspect of syncretism, namely that of target gender forms which distinguish agreement classes only by means of syncretism, and so will allow us to continue our review of the type of analysis worked out in the last chapter.

The target gender forms illustrated in table 7.1 (selected from Upper Sorbian's three numbers and seven cases) allow us to establish five agreement classes (I–V). The nominative and accusative singular agreement forms

Table 7.1 *Target gender forms in Upper Sorbian*

	I	II	III	IV	V
NOM SG	dobry susod	dobry kóń	dobry štom	dobra žona	dobre słowo
ACC SG	dobreho susoda	dobreho konja	dobry štom	dobru žonu	dobre słowo
ACC DUAL	dobreju susodow	dobrej konjej	dobrej štomaj	dobrej žonje	dobrej słowje
NOM PL	dobri susodźi	dobre konje	dobre štomy	dobre žony	dobre słowa
	'good neighbour'	'good horse'	'good tree'	'good woman'	'good word'
	masculine	masculine	masculine	feminine	neuter
	personal	animate	inanimate		

provide the evidence to separate out agreement class IV (which is the feminine gender) and agreement class V (the neuter). Of the remaining agreement classes, II differs from III only in the accusative singular. Both have dependent target forms (see section 6.4.1), equivalent to the genitive and nominative respectively. They are thus subgenders, masculine animate and inanimate respectively. Agreement class I differs from them both in the accusative dual, a dependent target gender form, and in the nominative plural. (It differs in other forms not included in table 7.1, in the accusative plural, which is a dependent target gender form, and also in the nominative dual, though the data are less clear-cut for this form.) This agreement class (I), the masculine personal, should be treated as a separate gender since it varies in four forms out of twenty-one (seven cases multiplied by three numbers, though there is considerable syncretism), and it has an independent target gender form, the nominative plural (also arguably the nominative dual). This system is presented in figure 7.5. If we now focus on the gender/number relationships, the main point of this section, we see from figure 7.5 that the relation between singular and dual (or singular and plural) is crossed, while that between dual and plural is parallel (as defined in section 6.3.1).

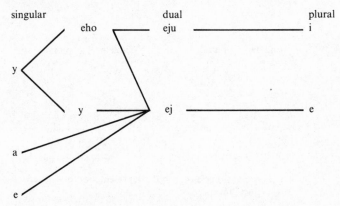

Figure 7.5 The gender system of Upper Sorbian

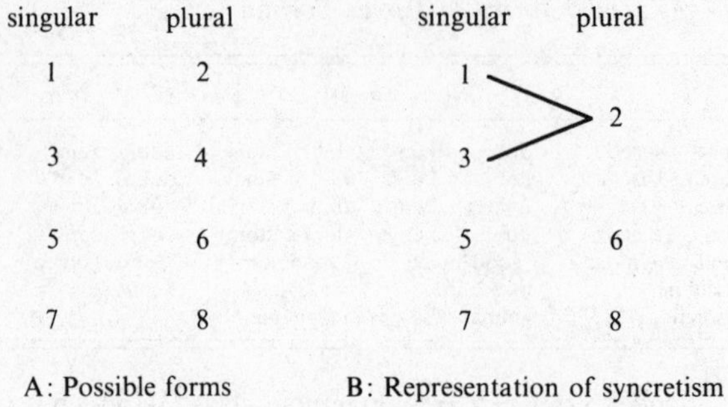

Target genders

singular	plural		singular	plural
1	2		1	
				2
3	4		3	
5	6		5	6
7	8		7	8

A: Possible forms   B: Representation of syncretism

Figure 7.6 Gender syncretism

7.1.2 *Types of syncretism*

Our main interest in syncretism, naturally enough, has been in syncretism of gender, which is presented schematically in figure 7.6. Suppose we have a language with four genders and two numbers; this gives eight theoretically possible target gender forms, as in A in figure 7.6. Suppose further that the forms labelled 2 and 4 are identical; we then have syncretism of the first two genders in the plural, which can be represented as in B. We have already seen many such cases of gender syncretism. But there is a different possibility, namely that, say, 7 should be identical to 8. Consider the target gender forms of Zande, given in figure 7.7 (data from Claudi 1985: 82–91; the assignment rules were discussed in section 2.2.1). Zande shows syncretism in gender: the masculine and feminine forms are identical in the plural (*i*). But it also shows syncretism in number: the singular and plural forms are identical in the neuter (*si*). Syncretism of number is a secondary

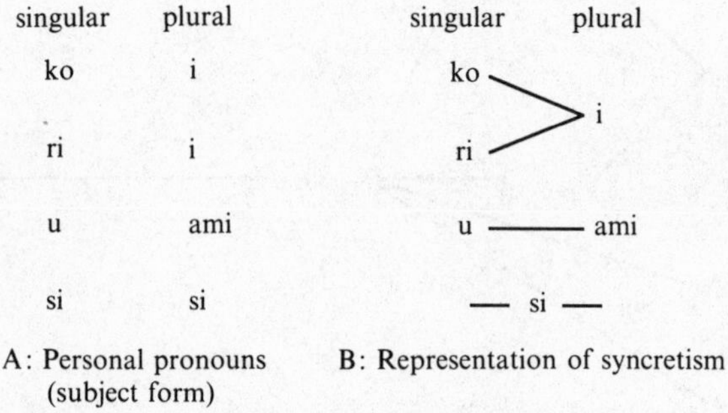

singular	plural		singular	plural
ko	i		ko	
				i
ri	i		ri	
u	ami		u ——— ami	
si	si		— si —	

A: Personal pronouns   B: Representation of syncretism
(subject form)

Figure 7.7 Target genders in Zande

194

Table 7.2 *Verb agreement markers in Qafar*

	Singular	Plural
Masculine	y/∅	t
Feminine	t	t

concern for us, and so it was not pointed out in the earlier analysis. But it deserves attention here because it can occur together with gender syncretism (it will also be considered in section 7.1.3 because of its importance in the development of gender systems).

The co-occurrence of gender and number syncretism is common in Cushitic languages. Take first the situation found in Qafar (see section 3.2.1 for assignment in Qafar); the verb agreement markers are as in table 7.2 (Hayward & Corbett 1988: 265; there is a very small number of irregular nouns whose agreements do not fit these patterns). Here there is one marker for the feminine singular, the feminine plural and the masculine plural. Thus we have syncretism of gender (in the plural) and syncretism of number (in the feminine). Bayso, an East Cushitic language, is more complex (Corbett & Hayward 1987). Nouns distinguish four numbers morphologically: unit reference and singulative reference (which are identical for agreement purposes and take the agreements labelled 'singular' in table 7.3), paucal and plural. The agreement markers are as in table 7.3, where the associative particle is used for illustration. Paucal forms show syncretism of gender. More interestingly, the form *ka* is used for the masculine singular and the masculine and feminine plurals. This is similar to Qafar, but here the masculine and not the feminine is identical to the plural marker. Many more examples could be quoted.

Table 7.3 *The associative particle in Bayso*

	Singular	Plural	Paucal
Masculine	ka	ka	o
Feminine	ta	ka	o

Within Cushitic we may also find a remarkable phenomenon known as 'polarity', a term proposed by Meinhof (1910: 135–6), though the phenomenon had been noted before. Polarity is an unusual occurrence, whose importance should not be over-rated (as argued cogently by Speiser 1938).

The phenomenon is best illustrated by an example, and a standard one is found in the Cushitic language Somali (data from Serzisko 1982: 184–6; see also Bell 1953: 12–13):

(1) ìnan-kii   baa   y-imid
     boy-the.MASC FOCUS.MARKER MASC-came
     'The boy came.'

(2) inán-tii   baa   t-imid
     girl-the.FEM FOCUS.MARKER FEM-came
     'The girl came.'

(3) inammá-dii   baa   y-imid
     boys-the.MASC.PL FOCUS-MARKER PL-came
     'The boys came.'

(4) ináma-hii   baa   y-ìmid
     girls-the.FEM.PL FOCUS.MARKER PL-came
     'The girls came.'

The postposed definite article has various morphophonologically determined variants: for example, after any vowel except *i*, *kii* becomes *hii*, and after any vowel *tii* becomes *dii*. Given this, in the examples above the article used for the masculine plural is really the same as that for the feminine singular, while that for the feminine plural is the same as that for the masculine singular. The underlying forms would be as in table 7.4. This is the situation described by the term 'polarity'. The two markers are exponents of two categories (gender and number in our case) and when the value of one category is changed the marker changes, but if both values are changed the form stays the same. The polar opposites are identical.

Table 7.4 *The definite article in Somali*

	Singular	Plural
Masculine	kii	tii
Feminine	tii	kii

It seems that polarity is never complete. This is illustrated by two facts about the Somali data. First, polarity is found there only in noun-phrase-internal agreement. If we look back to examples (1)–(4) we see that the verbal agreement forms are different: there the plural for both genders is the same as the masculine singular, which is a type of syncretism illustrated earlier with respect to Bayso. So when we say that a language exhibits polarity we should specify which targets are involved. The second restriction in Somali is that not

196

all nouns fall into the pattern shown in (1)–(4). Some masculine nouns take the same article in the singular and the plural, for example *nin-kii* 'the man', *niman-kii* 'the men'. Thus not all targets show polarity, nor are all nouns included in the polarity system. (On the other hand, a small number of nouns is exceptional in taking polarity-type agreements for predicate agreement too: see Hetzron 1972; Zwicky & Pullum 1983.)

Table 7.5 *Agreement markers in the Rendille possessive construction*

	Singular	Plural
Masculine	k	t
Feminine	t	ḥ

There are also languages which show what, following Serzisko, we shall call 'partial polarity'. This, too, is best explained by an example, in this case the agreement forms found in the possessive construction in the Cushitic language Rendille shown in table 7.5 (Serzisko 1982: 186; for a more detailed picture see Oomen 1981). The masculine plural is identical to the feminine singular, but the feminine plural is not identical to the masculine singular; for this reason it is called partial polarity. Such partial polarity is found outside Cushitic too.

Table 7.6 *Predicate agreement markers in Serbo-Croat*

	Singular	Plural
Masculine	∅	i
Feminine	a	e
Neuter	o	a

Consider the predicate gender and number markers of Serbo-Croat (table 7.6). The neuter plural is identical to the feminine singular, but the feminine plural is not identical to the neuter singular. It seems reasonable to treat this as a case of partial polarity, and by doing so we extend the notion to cover two genders within a larger gender system. A particularly interesting example is provided by the agreement markers (second type) in Khinalug, which were discussed earlier (section 5.2.3), and are presented again in table 7.7. Here the plural of gender I is identical to the singular of III and vice versa, so these two genders show full polarity. Moreover, the plural of II is identical to the singular of III, but not vice versa, so these two genders show partial polarity. Note that these correspondences hold for markers of types 1–3, but not for the

Table 7.7 *Agreement markers in Khinalug* (*type* 2)

	Singular	Plural
I	j	v
II	z	v
III	v	j
IV	j	j

pronominal type (section 5.2.3). In cases like this, and equally in the examples of number syncretism examined earlier, we may ask how the hearer knows which number is intended. Typically the number can be determined by other means, such as a marker on the noun itself.

7.1.3 *Diachronic implications*

Our discussion of syncretism provides the background for understanding some of the mechanisms by which genders are gained and lost. The different dialects of the North-East Caucasian language Andi are particularly instructive (Cercvadze 1967: 280; Khaidakov 1980: 57–66). The most conservative dialects, which we shall call 'type A', preserve a very interesting system, which may well be close to the original gender system of North-Central as well as North-East Caucasian (see figure 7.8A).

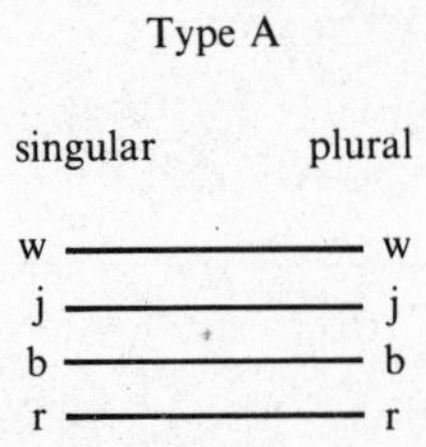

Type A

singular   plural

w ——————— w
j ——————— j
b ——————— b
r ——————— r

Figure 7.8A *Gender in Andi: conservative dialects* (*type A*)

These show total syncretism of number. The gender markers give no indication of number; however, number is marked separately. There are two points to note here: first, the definition of agreement class given in section 6.2 is fully adequate even in these surprising cases; and second, though in Andi the verb marks number, it seems most likely that there have been cases where this was not so. The parent language of the related North-Central Caucasian languages (Chechen, Ingush and Tsova-Tush) had a gender system but probably did not have number marking on verbs. This is relevant to Greenberg's Universal 32: 'Whenever the verb agrees with a nominal subject or nominal object in gender, it also agrees in number' (1963: 94). This claim certainly holds for most cases. It appears, though, that there may have been counter-examples in Caucasian languages at an earlier time, and that it is therefore worth looking for counter-examples elsewhere in the world.

Type B

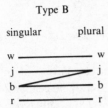

Figure 7.8B Gender in Andi: dialect type B

We should now move on by comparing these conservative dialects with the other types found in Andi. When we turn to type B, the most common type of Upper Andi dialect, we note an apparently minor change; some nouns which earlier took *b* as their sole agreement marker now take *b* only when singular but take *j* when plural (figure 7.8B) As a result of the change described, type B dialects have a crossed rather than a parallel system; furthermore, gender markers in some cases now give information as to number. And these dialects have five genders rather than four. It is interesting to look at the gender assignments involved. The first two genders (taking *w–w* and *j–j*) are for male humans and female humans respectively. The original third gender (*b–b*) included most of the animates together with some inanimates. In type B this gender has been split, the animates forming the new gender (*b–j*) and the inanimates remaining as the (*b–b*) gender.

Type C

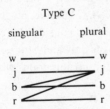

Figure 7.8C Gender in Andi: Rikvani dialect (type C)

Type C, represented only by the Rikvani dialect, has gone a stage further (figure 7.8C). In the Rikvani (type C) dialect, the animates which were left in the original fourth gender (*r–r*), mainly denoting insects, have been separated from the other nouns denoting inanimates to form a sixth gender (*r–j*), mentioned in section 2.2.5. In this dialect, gender markers more often give information on number than in the others.

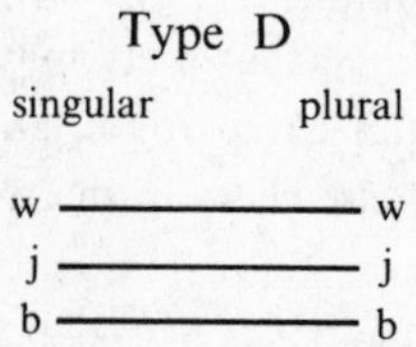

Type D

singular   plural

w ——————— w
j ——————— j
b ——————— b

Figure 7.8D Gender in Andi: dialect type D

Dialects of type D, the Lower Andi dialects, have lost a gender by combining the original *b–b* and *r–r* genders into a single gender for all nouns not denoting humans, as is illustrated in figure 7.8D. This type represents a simplification as compared with the earlier pattern (type A). The 'crossing' mechanism which marks the development from type A to type B and then to type C, is the main source of the larger gender systems found in the Caucasus. In some instances in other languages, only a few nouns are involved, in which case we find inquorate genders, as discussed in the case of Tsova-Tush in section 6.4.3.

Changes in the relations between singular and plural agreement markers continue to be a major mechanism for change even if singular and plural are fully distinct. This can be illustrated from Grebo, a Western Kru language, which has simplified the Proto-Kru gender system (Marchese 1988: 328–9), better preserved in Godie (section 3.2.3). A plausible stage in the process is shown as 'Earlier Grebo' in figure 7.9. Pronominal forms are used for illustration. The earlier system preserved a human gender (*ɔ–o*) and a non-human gender (*ɛ–e*). In Modern Grebo, however, *ɔ* is used for nouns denoting important things (which includes humans) and generally large and valuable things (Innes 1966: 52–3; Marchese 1988: 329). Thus the range of nouns taking *ɔ* and comparable target forms has increased considerably. The plural forms have not been affected: *o* is still for humans only and *e* for non-humans. As a result, we have a new controller gender comprising nouns which denote

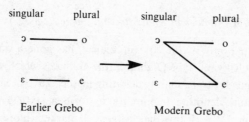

singular   plural   singular   plural

Earlier Grebo   Modern Grebo

Figure 7.9 Development of gender in Grebo

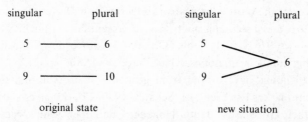

Figure 7.10 *Loss of class ten agreement in the Ngemba group*

important non-human things, large animals for example, which take ɔ when singular (like nouns denoting humans) and e when plural (like nouns denoting non-humans). A new gender has been created, and a parallel system has become a crossed one.

Changes in the singular–plural pairings we have looked at so far have mostly had the effect of expanding the system. Comparable changes can also lead to a reduction, as in the case of Andi dialect type D. The progress of contraction can be seen clearly in eight of the closely related Ngemba group of the Grassfields Bantu languages. The marker for class 6 (the plural for gender 5/6 nouns) is taking over from other plural markers, including that for gender 9/10. Schematically the change is as shown in figure 7.10 (for the relevant part of the gender system). This part of the system is changing from being parallel to convergent. The progress of the change is made clear in table 7.8, which gives for each language investigated the number of nouns belonging to gender 9/10, those which vary between taking the class 6 and the class 10 marker in the plural, and those which have moved to the new combination of 9 (singular) and 6 (plural). The data are from Leroy (1980: 127).

Table 7.8 *Loss of class ten agreement in the Ngemba group*

Language	Number of nouns in 9/10	Number of nouns in 9/6 ~ 10	Number of nouns in 9/6
Mankon	29	1	1
Bafut	20	5	0
Mundum I	22	3	1
Nkwen	21	2	3
Bambui	9	0	12
Pinyin	5	3	11
Bagangu	3	1	23
Awing	0	0	23

Direction of change →

Mankon is the most conservative: only one noun has moved from gender 9/10 to 9/6, and a second is on its way, at present fluctuating between the two (indicated as 9/6 ~ 10 in table 7.8). As we move down the list we find increasing numbers of nouns which have made the transition. Finally in Awing all nouns have moved from gender 9/10 to 9/6, and the class 10 agreement marker has been lost. Schaub (1985: 171–85) gives statistical data on another Grassfields Bantu language, Babungo, which indicates how genders may be lost, and Kadima (1969: 100–29) documents examples of similar developments from other Bantu languages, and suggests that the most common cause is phonetic similarity resulting from sound changes in which various consonants were lost.

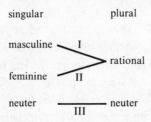

Figure 7.11 *Gender in Tamil*

An example of the complete loss of a gender through changes in the singular–plural pairings can be found in the Dravidian languages. The earliest establishable system appears to be that still found in languages like Tamil, shown in figure 7.11 (we shall simplify the account by considering only verbal agreement). Nouns denoting male rationals (I) take masculine forms in the singular, and rational in the plural; nouns denoting female rationals (II) take feminine and rational forms, while nouns denoting non-rationals (III) take neuter agreement in both numbers. Languages like Telugu show a system one stage on from this (figure 7.12). As compared with Tamil, Telugu has the same three controller genders (I male rational; II female rational; and III neuter), but it has one fewer target gender forms (in verbs). The loss of this target

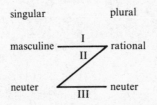

Figure 7.12 *Gender in Telugu*

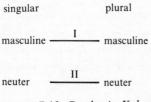

Figure 7.13 *Gender in Kolami*

gender form has changed a convergent system into a crossed one. The last stage is found in languages like Kolami (figure 7.13). In the Kolami development, all nouns taking neuter agreement in the singular take neuter agreement in the plural. This means that we now have a parallel system, and one with only two controller genders: I – male rational, and II – all others.

It is interesting to note again, that, from a single starting point, change in gender systems can proceed in opposite directions. This was the case with the Andi dialects examined earlier, and we can observe it again in Dravidian languages. We have already seen how a convergent system in Dravidian (preserved in standard Tamil) developed into a crossed system, as found in Modern Telugu, and from that type into a parallel system in languages like Kolami, with the loss of a complete gender. But in a Tamil dialect spoken in the region of Nagercoil (southern Tamil Nadu) the opposite development has occurred: this dialect had developed separate masculine and feminine third person plural pronouns and corresponding verb endings (Shanmugam Pillai 1965: 11, 71). There are therefore three target genders in both singular and plural and the convergent system of Tamil has been converted into a parallel one.

In this section we have been concerned primarily with target genders and with problems arising from their relation with number. We have assumed that the controllers involved are straightforward. We now move to instances where less standard controllers create difficulties as far as target genders are concerned.

7.2 **Neutral agreement**

If a particular target type can mark agreement in gender then in many languages it must. A Latin adjective, which distinguishes masculine, feminine and neuter (in a given case and number combination), must do so: the ending cannot simply be omitted. This may be called 'enforced' gender agreement. Such enforced gender can give rise to two sorts of problem. The first is that there may be constructions in which the target has to agree in gender with a controller which is not specified for gender. This is the problem tackled in this section; an example in many languages is agreement with an infinitive phrase. The second type of problem involves cases where the choice of gender agreement in the normal way would force greater specificity than is possible (or perhaps desirable) for the speaker. A speaker may wish to refer to a child but be unable to select gender agreement based on sex. Problems of this type will be considered in section 7.3. In both these areas there is more than one strategy for resolving the difficulty.

7.2.1 *The problem*

The basic problem of agreement with non-prototypical controllers (like clauses and infinitive phrases) is outlined in this section. We shall see that languages may adopt two strategies for solving it: the use of already available agreement forms (section 7.2.2) or the use of special forms (section 7.2.3). And sometimes the forms appropriate for non-prototypical controllers are extended to ordinary controllers (section 7.2.4).

In a nutshell, if an agreement target *can* agree then typically it *must* agree, even if the agreement controller lacks the appropriate features. Consider the following Russian example:

> (5) dozvonit′sja   byl-o   problemoj
> to.ring.through was-NEUT.SG problem
> 'To ring through was a problem.'

The subject is the infinitive phrase *dozvonit′sja* 'to ring through'. This is a non-prototypical controller; among other characteristics, it lacks the normal gender and number features. Nevertheless, past tense verbs (and predicative adjectives) must agree in gender and number in Russian, and in fact we find the neuter singular. We shall term this enforced agreement 'neutral agreement'. The idea of 'neutral agreement' can be seen as a development of Jespersen's 'conceptional neuter' (1924: 241–3); the wider term is preferred since the phenomenon is found in gender systems other than the Indo-European type, to which Jespersen restricted himself. The range of non-prototypical controllers varies from language to language, as some of our examples will illustrate. It may include clauses, infinitive phrases, nominalizations, interjections and other quoted phrases, noun phrases in particular cases (for example, subject noun phrases in an oblique case), dummy elements and certain null elements. The last type deserves illustration, again from Russian:

> (6) byl-o   xolodn-o
> was-NEUT.SG cold-NEUT.SG
> 'It was cold.'

Here there is no overt subject, but the verb and adjective must still take a particular agreement form. An especially interesting type is found in the following Serbo-Croat sentence from Klajn (1984-5: 351), who gives examples of non-prototypical controllers from various Indo-European languages (see also Priestly 1983: 349–50):

(7) kod njih čovek mora biti lukav, a ja
    with them person must be cunning but I
    to   nisam
    that.NEUT.SG am.not
    'With them a person must be cunning,
    but I am not (that).'

Here the antecedent of *to* 'that' is *lukav* 'cunning'. Though *lukav* is in fact masculine singular (agreeing with *čovek* 'person'), a predicative adjective in Serbo-Croat is not itself a prototypical controller and so *to* stands in the neutral form, the neuter singular. As discussed in section 5.1, we understand agreement in the wider sense, which includes the selection of the appropriate forms of pronouns. The data analysed here help to confirm the validity of this approach, since pronouns whose antecedents are not prototypical antecedents normally take the same agreement form as other agreement targets with non-prototypical controllers, and the factors involved in the choice of form usually appear to be the same. Non-prototypical controllers often have morphological and syntactic peculiarities distinguishing them from prototypical controllers (regular noun phrases). They tend to be indeclinable and to be restricted as to the configurations in which they can occur. Thus infinitive phrases do not normally take inflectional affixes, nor in many languages can they occur directly following a preposition. There is nevertheless a need for agreement targets to agree with such controllers. There are two strategies, which we shall consider in turn. The problem affects gender and number, and we shall naturally concentrate on gender.

7.2.2 *Strategy 1: the use of a regular gender/number form*

Not surprisingly, many languages solve the problem of agreement with non-prototypical controllers by pressing one of the regular gender/ number forms into service. The form may be termed the 'neutral agreement form' or the 'default agreement form'. The first problem which arises is the motivation for the selection of a particular form.

7.2.2.1 The selection of the neutral agreement form

In the Russian examples (5) and (6) and the Serbo-Croat example (7), we find that in these three-gender systems it is the neuter which is used for neutral agreement. We might expect markedness theory to predict the choice of form, and indeed it is often claimed that it makes the right prediction for neutral agreement. But it is not at all clear that the neuter is the unmarked gender. If, however, we consider the semantics of the genders in these languages we find that almost all nouns denoting humans are in the masculine and feminine genders, while inanimates are distributed across all three genders. The use of the neuter for neutral agreement could be understood as the selection of the gender which is most appropriate in semantic terms (thereby avoiding the semantic clash of neutral with human, which would arise with the other genders).

The same consideration may apply in a two-gender system. In Algonquian languages there is an animate and an inanimate gender; the animate gender includes all notional animates, and some notional inanimates too (mainly in specific categories with special significance), while the inanimate gender contains only notional inanimates (section 2.2.4). It is the inanimate gender which serves for neutral agreement, as in this Menominee example (Bloomfield 1962: 27):

> (8) eneh   sa   se:hkas-e-yan
> that.INAN.SG PARTICLE hate-1ST.OBJ-1ST/2ND.SG
> 'the fact that you hate me'

The suffix complex -*e-yan* indicates a second person singular acting on a first person singular; more important here is the demonstrative *eneh*, which is inanimate singular, since 'Reference to indifferent objects, gestures, events, circumstances, and the like is made in inanimate gender' (Bloomfield 1962: 26). The semantics of the genders would lead us to expect the use of the inanimate: since animates are in one gender, rather than being split, it is understandable that non-prototypical controllers should take the agreements of the inanimate gender. (On the other hand, there would be no obvious morphological reason which would lead us to expect the use of the inanimate gender.) Similar reasoning may be applied to the Omotic language Zayse, which, unusually for Omotic, has in the masculine gender only nouns denoting the male sex-differentiables; all other nouns are feminine. And it is the agreement found with the feminines which is used for neutral agreement (Hayward 1989). Clearly, in Zayse, the feminine gender is more compatible semantically with non-prototypical controllers. In Fula there are about twenty genders, according to the particular dialect (see figure 7.3 above), and animates are found in several of them. For neutral agreement, the agreement of the *ÐUM* class is used; this class comprises mainly abstracts and stands largely outside the singular–plural opposition (Koval' 1979: 28–9, 84–5). And in the Mon-Khmer language Khasi, which has a two-gender system, abstract nouns are feminine and it is the feminine agreements that are used for neutral agreement (Rabel-Heymann 1977: 247, 249).

The situation found in two languages of the North-East Caucasian family, Archi and Khinalug, can be understood in a similar way. Both have four genders. The first two are for male humans and female humans. The assignment of nouns to the other two genders is complex, and differs between the two languages. But in both, most non-human animates are found in the third gender, and abstracts belong to the fourth (section 2.2.5). And it is the fourth gender forms which are used for neutral agreement. For example when an infinitive phrase is the controller (sometimes they are 'transparent' and allow an associated noun phrase to act as controller), then in both languages the fourth gender agreement forms are used (A. E. Kibrik, personal communication). Ungarinjin, an Australian aboriginal language of north-west Australia, shows a rather similar picture to that we have seen in North-East Caucasian languages. There are two genders strictly for nouns with human referents, and two genders for other nouns. The assignment of non-human nouns is not clear. As we would expect, it is one of these two non-human genders (the *w*-gender) which is used for neutral agreement. According to Rumsey (1982: 36–41, 150–1), it is significant that this is the gender which includes nouns referring to language itself; Rumsey claims that this explains why forms of this gender are used to refer to stretches of discourse, such as clauses.

In the languages investigated so far the choice of the neutral form can be understood in terms of the semantics of the controller genders. The fact that this approach works for examples which are so diverse genetically (from Indo-European, Algonquian, Afro-Asiatic, Niger-Kordofanian, North-East Caucasian and Australian) might make us expect it to apply without exception. Nevertheless, we now move to languages for which the semantic criterion fails. In some we find that a different criterion is at work, but we leave others as perplexing problems. Lak is a language which, though related to Archi and Khinalug, differs from them in an interesting way. Again there are four genders, and nouns are assigned to them as follows (section 2.2.5): I male humans; II some female humans (older females); III remaining female humans, most other animates, some inanimates; IV a very few animates, some inanimates. Again we would expect gender IV to be used for neutral agreement, as in Archi and Khinalug; in fact gender III is used (Kibrik 1979: 13):

(9) g₀aniša d-uč'an b-uqIʰlaj b-u-r
    she   II-come III-can   III-AUX-3RD
    'She can come.'

Table 7.9 *Gender agreement in Lak*

	Singular	Plural
Gender I (male humans)	Ø/w	b/w
Gender II (some female humans – older)	d/r	b/w
Gender III (most remaining animates, some inanimates)	b/w	b/w
Gender IV (residue – largely inanimates)	d/r	d/r

The gender II agreement marker *d-* on the infinitive *d-uč'an* is controlled by a deleted subject noun phrase *g₀a*, coreferential with *g₀aniša*. The point of interest is the agreement on the modal and on the auxiliary; both have a gender III prefix, since they are controlled by the infinitive. Thus gender III is used for neutral agreement and there is no evident explanation in terms of the semantics of the controller genders as to why this should be (gender IV would be expected). However, as A. E. Kibrik points out (personal communication), an explanation is available if we take into account the pattern of the target gender forms, which were discussed in section 6.3.1 and which are given again in table 7.9. Forms before the slash are prefixal, those after it are internal or suffixal. As can be seen in table 7.9, the forms for gender IV and gender II are identical in the singular. The use of the gender IV marker *d/r* for neutral agreement is ruled out by the fact that this marker is also the marker for gender II, which contains only nouns denoting females. This leaves *b/w*, the gender III agreement form as the only possibility for neutral agreement. This particular syncretism is not found in Archi and Khinalug, and so in those languages the gender IV forms are available for neutral agreement.

A more perplexing choice is found in the Bantu language Chichewa. In Bantu languages infinitives do not constitute a problem: they usually have a special form of agreement (class 15) and a special prefix:

(10) kuthamanga ku-ma-pweteka
to.run   15-HABITUAL-hurt
'Running hurts.'

We might anticipate that this *ku* would serve for neutral agreement, but it is not used for non-prototypical controllers, such as interjections:

(11) 'aaa' a-na-mv-eka
'aaa' 1-PAST-hear-PASSIVE
'An "aaah" was heard.'

Remarkably, class 1 agreement (as for humans) is used, as the agreement marker prefixed on the verb suggests; to demonstrate this conclusively requires an example with object agreement (Corbett & Mtenje 1987: 14):

(12) a-na-mu-mva   'mayo'
1.SUBJ-PAST-1.OBJ-hear crying-sound
'He heard a crying sound.'

The combination of *a* as subject agreement marker in (11) and *mu* as object agreement marker in (12) means that we are dealing with class 1 markers. The same agreement is found with, for example, *meee*, the sound a sheep makes, and *gugululu*, the noise of thunder (Francis Moto, personal communication). Similarly in Loko, a Cross River language of eastern Nigeria (and so distantly related to Chichewa), we find the class marker for the singular of the human gender being used for impersonals. The gender is not exclusively for nouns denoting humans; it includes among others the word for 'thing', which Winston (1962: 67–8) suggests may be connected with its use for impersonals. It is worth returning to Bantu data, in order to illustrate the variation in the range of non-prototypical controllers which can be found between languages of the same group. In Kinande, a Bantu language spoken in eastern Zaire, we find a picture different from that observed in Chichewa (data from Ngessimo Mutaka and Larry Hyman):

(13) e-'a'   yo   Kambale owa (< a-a-owa)
9.AUGMENT-'a' 9.FOCUS.MARKER Kambale 1.heard
'It is "a" that Kambale heard.'

Here the interjection is given an augment (or pre-prefix), as though it were a normal noun. The augment is that of class 9, and the focus marker *yo* (< *yi-o*) shows agreement in class 9. Thus in Kinande, interjections can be integrated into the gender system if required: the degree of integration is shown by the fact that when conjoined they take plural agreement:

(14) e-'a'   n'e-'o'
9.AUGMENT-'a' and.9.AUGMENT-'o'
syo   Kambale owa
10.FOCUS.MARKER Kambale heard
'It is "a" and "o" that Kambale heard.'

The focus marker is class 10, the plural for class 9. (Note in passing that in Kinande infinitives have lost their special marker and are found in class 5.)

While these examples demonstrate the difficulty of predicting the gender form to be used, the number selection has been as might be expected: in all instances the form chosen has been one which is either indisputably singular

Table 7.10 *Personal pronouns in Godie*

	Singular	Plural
Human	ɔ	wa
Non-human	ɛ	
	a	ɩ
	ʋ	

or one which could reasonably be interpreted as such (though neutral forms normally lack a plural counterpart). This much would be predicted by markedness considerations. However, the Kru language Godie demonstrates that there can be problems with number too, and although this is not our primary concern it deserves brief consideration. Godie distinguishes human from non-human in both singular and plural, and in the singular, non-human divides into three (section 3.2.3). The system can be illustrated by the personal pronoun (see table 7.10). Of these it is the plural pronoun *ɩ* which is used as the neutral pronoun, the appropriate pronoun for nominalized verbs, whole phrases and longer discourse units (see Marchese 1986: 239–40 for examples).

Thus far we have found an explanation for the choice of neutral form in several languages, according to the semantics of the controller genders, but in others the choice remains unexplained. We now turn to cases which are initially surprising and for which the semantics of the controller genders appears to provide no help. But in these cases we find an explanation available in terms of the target gender forms. For example, the East Cushitic language Bayso has two genders, masculine and feminine, and uses the masculine agreement forms for neutral agreement (Corbett & Hayward 1987: 11n.):

(15) ibaaddo boçaano
    person to.beat
    ka-meelan-ya
    PARTICLE.MASC-bad-COPULA.3RD.SG.MASC
    'To beat people is bad.'

In the last item, *ka-* is the associative particle in the masculine form and *-ya* is the clitic copula, third singular masculine. In Qafar, another Cushitic language, it is the feminine which is used. This can be shown with the so-called '*m*-nominalization'. The clitic element *-m* attaches to a wide range of items, and the resulting form takes feminine agreement, despite ending in a consonant and so being of a phonological shape associated with masculines (section 3.2.1):

(16) gaddàli   kinnim   yòt   celta
wealthy.man is.3RD.SG + m to.me seems.3RD.SG.FEM
'He seems to me to be a wealthy man.'

Here the -*m* is attached to the phrase 'is a wealthy man' and this new element is a non-prototypical controller; as a result, the verb *celta* stands in the neutral form, which is the feminine (Hayward & Corbett 1988: 266–8).

There are no obvious differences in the semantics of gender in the two languages to explain the different choice of neutral form (R. J. Hayward, personal communication). However, if we look at the morphology of agreeing forms there is a ready explanation. Table 7.11 gives the forms of the associative particle for the two of the four numbers of Bayso which are significant for differentiating gender, and the verbal agreement markers of Qafar which are found in agreement with simple noun phrases (from tables 7.2 and 7.3 above). As discussed in section 7.1.2, there is considerable syncretism: one form covers three of the four theoretical slots, being used for the singular of one gender and the plural of both. And in each case it is this form, the one with the wider range of use, which is the neutral agreement form.

Table 7.11 *Patterns of syncretism in Bayso and Qafar*

	Bayso		Qafar	
	Singular	Plural	Singular	Plural
Masculine	ka	ka	y/∅	t
Feminine	ta	ka	t	t

It is worth clarifying the criteria we have employed so far. In the first languages discussed it was the semantics of the controller genders – the genders into which nouns are divided – which provided the reason for the choice of neutral agreement form. In these languages there is a gender for abstracts or inanimates, or at least one containing few, if any, nouns denoting humans, which appeared an appropriate gender for non-prototypical controllers to attach themselves to. Yet in Chichewa, such a gender exists but it is not the one used for non-prototypical controllers. In Godie, the 'right' gender is used, but the choice of number is surprising. In the case of Bayso and Qafar, however, there is no obvious choice in terms of the semantics of the controller genders, since humans and other animates are found in both of the

211

available genders, as are inanimates. Here a second criterion comes into play: the choice of the neutral form can be understood in terms of the morphology of the agreeing elements (target gender forms). Lak can be seen as an intermediate type, in which the semantics of the controller genders and the pattern of syncretism of the target gender forms interact to determine the neutral agreement form.

7.2.2.2 Unusual properties of neutral agreement forms

A major peculiarity of neutral agreement forms is that they normally stand outside the number system. Although these forms appear identical to singular markers in the main (Godie is an exception, as noted above), they lack plural counterparts. This can be illustrated by conjoining; if in Chichewa we conjoin interjections, the neutral form remains unchanged:

(17) 'mayo'   ndi 'aaa' wa-ke
     crying.sound and aaa   1-his
     ti-na-mu-mva   kutali
     1ST.PL-PAST-1.OBJ-hear far.away
     'We heard his crying sound and "aaah" far away.'

The *wa* ($< u + a$) of *wa-ke* is a marker of class 1 (human singular), while *-mu-* is the objective concord of the same class. The fact that 'singular' agreement is *possible* would not necessarily be significant: there are numerous examples from other languages of agreement with just one conjunct, especially with nouns denoting inanimates (section 9.2.1). What is significant is that the plural is quite unacceptable in (17). This adds weight to the view that neutral agreement is really a failure to agree: controllers which lack the necessary features still lack them when conjoined.

A second unusual feature of neutral agreement forms is that certain target types may be avoided. We have, in fact, already seen an example in the Serbo-Croat sentence (7), where, instead of the personal pronoun, we found the neuter demonstrative *to* 'that'. Similarly, in Russian for non-prototypical controllers the pronoun used is *èto* 'this' (in the neuter singular form) rather than *ono* 'it':

(18) Sereža ne xočet naprasno trevožit' ženu i
     Serezha not want in.vain   to.alarm wife and
     ja èto ponimaju
     I this understand
     'Serezha does not want to alarm his wife
     unnecessarily and I understand that.'

As is suggested by the gloss to (18) (from Channon 1983: 60), in English *that* replaces *it*. In these examples an already existing form is used for neutral agreement, but not that of the ordinary pronoun.

A third and particularly interesting feature of neutral agreement is that the form to be used can vary according to the target type. This situation is found in Rumanian, whose complex gender system was examined in section 6.3. Agreement targets distinguish only two agreeing forms, masculine and feminine, in the singular and plural. However, nouns can be divided into three controller genders: masculine, feminine and neuter. We can now examine the agreements found with non-prototypical controllers (data from Donka Farkas):

(19) e evident   că   a   venit, şi
     is clear.MASC.SG that has come and
     asta   o   ştie   toată lumea
     this.FEM.SG it.FEM.SG knows all   world.the
     'It is clear that s/he came and everyone knows this.'

Here we have a clause as subject (some might prefer to say there is no subject); the predicative adjective, which has to mark agreement, is masculine (the feminine *evidentă* is unacceptable). *Asta* 'this' can stand for 'that s/he came' or 'it is clear that s/he came'. What concerns us is that it must be feminine (the masculine *ăsta* is unacceptable). Since the form used for neutral agreement in Rumanian varies according to the type of target involved, we should try other possibilities, such as attributive modifiers:

(20) un   bum   puternic   a
     a.MASC.SG 'boom' strong.MASC.SG has
     fost   auzit
     been heard.MASC.SG
     'A loud boom was heard.'

Here *un* 'a' is masculine, like the agreeing predicate. We now try the relative pronoun:

(21) a   admis   că   a   venit, ceea ce
     has admitted that has come which.FEM.SG
     nu   e surprinzător
     not is surprising.MASC.SG
     'S/he admitted that s/he came, which is not
     surprising.'

Ceea ce is a complex relative, the first part of which shows feminine gender agreement. We thus have masculine agreement for attributive modifiers and the predicate, and feminine for the relative pronoun and the demonstrative

213

(which replaces the personal pronoun here). This split is consistent with the positions of the Agreement Hierarchy, which we consider in section 8.1.1. But there is more to example (21); though *ceea ce* is feminine, its predicate *surprinzător* is masculine (** surprinzătoare* feminine). This shows that *ceea ce* is a remarkable neutral form: though morphologically feminine, it must carry a feature to distinguish it from ordinary feminines. The reason for this is the fact that its antecedent is a clause, and the evidence for the special feature is that *ceea ce* controls masculine predicate agreement (as clauses do). Let us try the demonstrative in a similar environment:

(22) asta   e uluitor
this.FEM is amazing.MASC

Here *asta* denotes a situation, not a specific object. While it is morphologically feminine, its predicate is masculine. Thus *asta*, too, is a special neutral form, since it controls a different agreement from the *asta* which can stand for a noun of feminine gender.

So far we have seen that languages may press a regular gender/number form into service for neutral agreement, but that the choice of form is sometimes hard to predict and that, though it may look like an ordinary agreement form, it is likely to have some unusual properties.

7.2.3 *Strategy 2: the use of a unique neutral agreement form*

Some languages use a neutral form which has only this function. (Such forms are generally called 'neutral agreement forms'; the other term, 'default agreement forms', is an alternative only when regular gender/number forms are involved.) Spanish is a good example of a language with unique agreement forms. It has two genders, masculine and feminine. Consider now this sentence (Spanish data from Joseph Clements and Almerindo Ojeda):

(23) antes me gustaba   mucho ir   a los
before me was.pleasing much   to.go to the
partidos de fútbol,   pero todo ello ya
games   of football, but all   it   any.more
no me interesta
not me interests
'I used to be very keen on going to football
matches, but all that doesn't interest me any more.'

The relevant form is the pronoun *ello* 'it, that', which is neither masculine (*él*) nor feminine (*ella*). In Spanish grammar it is termed neuter; it is a neutral form in our terminology. There is no set of nouns for which *ello* would be the normal antecedent – there are no neuter nouns in Spanish. In (23) *ello* refers

214

to 'going to football matches'. There are a few more neutral forms, like *lo*, which can function as a pronoun or as an article:

(24) lo curioso de   esa situación
the curious about that situation
'the curious thing about that situation'

The masculine form of the article is *el*, which could similarly be used with an adjective and no noun. *El curioso* would mean 'the curious man', or 'the curious one' provided a nominal of masculine gender had occurred in the preceding discourse. Note that here and in (24) *curioso* has the form of the masculine; there is no special form for adjectives. Other Spanish neutral forms are *esto* 'this', *eso* 'that' and *aquello* 'that' (more distant): see Ojeda (1984) for further examples and Ojeda (1989) for dialectal data.

The likely explanation of the origin of these special neutral forms is that Spanish has reduced the three genders of Romance to two, and remnants of the neuter gender survive as neutral forms. Not surprisingly, Portuguese shows the same phenomenon, though the inventory of neutral forms is slightly different: *tudo* 'everything', *isto* 'this', *isso* 'that', *aquilo* 'that' (more distant). A similar explanation appears likely for data from the Surselvan dialect of Romansh (Haiman 1974: 130–2). The nouns are divided into two genders, but predicative adjectives and participles have three agreement forms: *-s* (masculine), *-a* (feminine) and $\emptyset$ (neutral). This latter form is reserved for the following non-prototypical controllers: sentential subjects (the example Haiman gives is of an infinitive phrase), the demonstrative pronoun *quei* 'that' and the impersonal pronoun *igl* 'there', as in this example (discussed in section 6.3.3):

(25) igl   ei sesalzau   in urezi
there is arisen.NEUTRAL a storm

The masculine form *sesalzaus* 'arisen' would occur if *in urezi* 'a storm' were the subject. A further example of a unique neutral form, again in predicative adjectives, is found in the East Slavonic language Ukrainian (Shevelov 1963: 128–33; see also Sobin 1985; note that the verb 'be' has the null form in the present tense):

(26) v odnij simji nam žyty i   lehko
in one family us.DAT to.live both easy
i   prekrasno
and wonderful
'For us to live in one family is both easy
and wonderful.'

The adjectival forms in *-o* represent neutral agreement; the neuter form is in *-e*, for example *prekrasne* 'wonderful'. The earlier neuter form was in *-o*, and it appears that the ending has been changed for neuter agreement, leaving the older ending for neutral agreement only. It is worth mentioning that the forms in *-o* used for neutral agreement in Ukrainian's close relative Russian in earlier examples above are usually formally identical to neuters but that they show considerable differences from normal neuters (Corbett 1980: 165–6). Also in Slavonic, the Sele Fara dialect of Slovene has lost the neuter gender, but some original neuter forms survive only in impersonal predicatives (Priestly 1983: 355).

In view of the peculiarities of some neutral agreement forms, despite their identity to regular gender/number forms, we should not make too much of the distinction between the two strategies. Furthermore, the languages which have unique neutral forms do not, in the languages identified so far, have a full set. That is, regular gender/number forms are used for some targets.

7.2.4 *Extension of use of neutral agreement forms*

An interesting development occurs when neutral forms are used when the controller is an apparently straightforward noun phrase. This phenomenon is well attested in Scandinavian languages (Faarlund 1977; Hellan 1977: 102–8; Eriksson 1979; Nilsson 1979). Our examples are Norwegian, taken from Faarlund (1977). Norwegian predicative adjectives distinguish singular from plural and, in the singular, neuter from common (for neuter versus common compare the Swedish examples in section 5.3.1); the verb does not distinguish number or gender. The sentences of interest are of the following type:

(27) pannekaker er godt
     pancakes   is good.NEUT.SG
(28) grammatikk er morosamt
     grammar   is fun.NEUT.SG

The noun in (27) is plural and in (28) it is of common gender, but in both we find neuter agreement (in fact neutral agreement). For such examples there is an intuition that something is missing: in (27) it is eating pancakes which is good, not any specific pancakes. The difference is particularly clear in this sentence:

(29) ein ny   utanriksminister ville   ikkje vere
     a   new foreign.secretary would not   be
     so dumt
     so stupid.NEUT.SG

The interpretation is that having a new foreign secretary would not be a bad idea. If the adjective were in the common gender form *dum*, then it would agree directly with the subject noun phrase and the interpretation would be less complimentary.

Similar constructions have been identified elsewhere, though these cases are limited to the spoken language and are not so well documented. Spoken Hebrew allows the following (data from Ruth Berman):

> (30) ha-samin ze bəˈaya
> the-drugs.MASC.PL this.MASC.SG problem
> 'Drugs is a problem.'

This structure may be analysed as a grammaticalized left-dislocation construction; the dummy pronoun *ze* occurs, just as it would with an infinitive phrase. And the interpretation is that it is drugs and the things that go with them which are a problem. In colloquial Russian too we find (Zemskaja 1973: 258):

> (31) les/ prijatn-o//
> forest.MASC.SG pleasant-NEUT.SG
> 'Forest is pleasant.'

Here it is being in a forest which is pleasant. Similarly:

> (32) matematika/ tjaˇzel-o//
> mathematics.FEM.SG difficult-NEUT.SG
> 'Mathematics is difficult.'

Example (32) suggests that doing or studying mathematics is what is considered difficult. In these Russian examples the slashes indicate intonational contours, and the fact that the initial noun phrase is marked off intonationally lends support to the suggestion (A. E. Kibrik, personal communication) that this noun phrase is a topic which is outside the main syntactic structure of the sentence. The sentences are subjectless (hence the appearance of neutral agreement). Under this analysis, Russian illustrates the first step on the way to constructions like that of English *drugs is a problem*, where the syntactic structure and intonation are as for sentences with normal subject–verb agreement.

7.2.5 *Neutral agreement: summing up*

We have seen that agreement with non-prototypical controllers is a significant problem. We left to one side the question of the possible sets of non-prototypical controllers for a given language, since this is of secondary importance for gender agreement. It appears likely that there are general-izations of the type 'if infinitive phrases are non-prototypical then so are clauses'. A hierarchy of these controllers can probably be constructed, starting from the notion of 'nouniness' (Ross 1973). For agreement with such controllers we noted that two strategies are adopted: either a regular gender/number form or a unique neutral agreement form will be used. But, given the peculiarities of regular forms when pressed into service as neutral forms, the difference between the two strategies is not great. When a regular gender/number form is used for neutral agreement, the choice may be determined by the semantics of the controller genders. When there is no obvious choice in terms of controller genders, then the choice may be made in terms of the target gender forms (as in the Cushitic examples involving syncretism). We also found some exceptional cases. And we observed that the use of neutral forms may be extended to constructions with normal controllers, though the conditions under which this can occur are not clear. To make further progress we shall need detailed information on a wide range of languages.

7.3 **Gender agreement with noun phrases involving reference problems**
        If a language has targets which distinguish gender, then typically they *must* distinguish gender. As we saw in the previous section, this creates problems with non-prototypical controllers since these do not have the necessary features. Another type of problem also arises: even if the controller is a noun phrase headed by a noun or pronoun, the speaker may not be able to ascertain the sex of the referent. There are three types of problem. Suppose we ask *Who said that*? in a language which requires agreement in gender on the verb. In this first type we cannot determine the gender, since we cannot identify the referent of *who* – finding out is precisely the point of the question. As a variant of this type we may have a noun, like English, *manager* or *friend*, which can be used of a person of either sex. Again we may not know the sex of the referent: *In that case I'd like to speak to the manager and we'll see what he/she/he or she says*. This problem may be played upon since we may actively wish to avoid gender forms: *I'm back late because I met a friend. Who was it? Oh, just a friend.* Second, there are cases where the sex cannot be ascertained because the referent is non-specific: *If a patient wishes to change doctors, he/she/he or she should advise the receptionist.* A third area of difficulty here is agreement with a noun denoting a group of people of both sexes (*villagers, athletes*). Here again the sex cannot be uniquely determined, but if the language distinguishes gender in the plural, then clearly one form must be selected for agreement purposes.

218

We shall see that there are four approaches to dealing with these problems: one of the possible alternative agreement forms may be used by convention (section 7.3.1), an 'evasive' form may be used (section 7.3.2), a special form may be used (section 7.3.3), or there may simply be no general strategy (section 7.3.4). It is often assumed that in a single language, all problem types are dealt with in the same way (for example, it may be stated or implied that a particular gender is the unmarked one and so used in all these cases). But in fact languages may handle the three parts of the problem differently. This is an area where there has been a good deal of research on one small part of the topic but where much of the problem is only poorly understood.

7.3.1 *Use of one possible form by convention*

Suppose we have a language in which there is at least a masculine gender (containing nouns denoting males, and other nouns) and a feminine gender (for females and other nouns). For the problem cases above, one set of target gender forms, say the masculine set, could be used by convention. The situation is found in many Indo-European languages. Let us take Russian examples:

(33) kto èto sdelal-∅?
who this did-MASC
'Who did this?'

The speaker does not know the sex of the person responsible, but the masculine is used. Surprisingly, even in a setting in which the person must be one of a group of women, masculine agreement is still normal. Similarly, with nouns which can denote a male or a female, like *vrač* 'doctor', masculine agreements are used if the sex is not known. In Russian there is no agreement problem when mixed groups are involved, since genders are neutralized in the plural. But in the related language Serbo-Croat, we find the masculine plural *oni* 'they' in such cases. We may take the problem back into derivational morphology: *Amerikanac* (masculine) is a male American, while *Amerikanka* (feminine) is a female American in Serbo-Croat. To refer to Americans in general, the plural of the masculine noun is used, that is, *Amerikanci*, and it takes masculine plural agreements. This instance of the way in which gender is assigned to nouns denoting mixed groups links directly to the analysis of agreements used with conjoined noun phrases, which we undertake in chapter 9.

We have seen that the masculine may be used as the chosen form for reference to both females and males. This is a common situation which has given rise to a great deal of discussion. The problem is normally discussed in the context of sex differences in language and of the extent of sexism in language. A great deal has been written in this area (Thorne & Henley 1975; Froitzheim & Simons 1981; McConnell-Ginet 1983; Sullivan 1983; Thorne, Kramarae & Henley 1983; Cameron & Coates 1985; Silverstein 1985; Coates 1986; and Graddol & Swann 1989). A good overview of work on sex differences and language can be found in Smith (1985); see also the references in section 5.3.3, Bodine's (1975a) survey and McConnell-Ginet (1988). While work on English has tended to predominate, Philips, Steele & Tanz (1987) include studies of non-English-speaking cultures; Brown (1980) reports on speakers of Tzeltal, a Mayan language, Herbert & Nykiel-Herbert (1986) analyse Polish data and Alpher (1987) considers mainly Australian aboriginal data. Our concern being primarily linguistic, we shall concentrate on this side of the problem, which is the less well-studied; results from this type of study should, of course, contribute to the more general debate. From a linguistic point of view, two questions arise. First, there is the typological question: in systems based at least in part on sex, is it always the masculine which is used when reference problems occur? And second, does the use of the masculine work, that is, does the hearer understand that the referent may be a woman as well as a man?

Though the literature might suggest otherwise, it is not the case that the masculine is always used. In the Nilotic language Maasai, we find the following possible questions:

(34) aiŋai   o-ewuo?
    it.is.who who.MASC-has.come
    'Who has come?'
(35) Aiŋai   na-ewuo?
    it.is.who who.FEM-has.come
    'Who has come?'

The masculine form, as in (34), is used only when it is known that a male is involved. The feminine, as in (35), is used both when a female is involved and also when the sex of a person is unknown. In Seneca the feminine is used for indefinite reference to people in general – 'people', 'they', 'one' – and this extends to other Iroquoian languages (Chafe 1967: 13; 1977: 519–22). A similar situation is found in Goajiro, an Arawakan language of the Goajiro peninsula (Columbia and Venezuela). According to Holmer (1949: 110) Goajiro has two genders, one for male humans (with a few 'leaks' into this gender including 'sun' and 'thumb') and the other for all remaining nouns. It is this second gender which is used when the sex of a person is not known. And in the Khoisan language Dama, spoken in northern Namibia, mixed groups of people are referred to using the feminine pronouns (J. R. Payne, personal communication).

While the use of feminine is possible, it is nevertheless the masculine which occurs in most of the languages reported on. Thus in English *he/his* is said to be used 'generically' in examples like *Everyone loves his mother*. It is suggested that *he* is used both to denote males, and in cases where either sex (or both) can be denoted. The question, then, is whether the convention actually works: whether hearers consistently understand the pronoun generically. The experimental evidence suggests that they do not. For example MacKay & Fulkerson (1979) showed that the use of generic *he* frequently leads to a male-referent interpretation of antecedents such as *student*, *dancer* and *musician* (see also Bendix 1979; Martyna 1980; MacKay 1983; and Crawford & English 1984; for a related cross-linguistic experiment see Batliner 1984).

Given that the evidence indicates that generic *he* is often interpreted as not including females, it is worth asking why it fails to work. The obvious reason is that the normal use of *he* is to denote a male and this carries over into the less common generic usage. But there is a secondary, more disturbing reason. Yokoyama (1986: 156) draws attention to relevant statistical data in the Brown corpus, which consists of just over 1 million words of American English (Kučera & Francis 1967). There were 9,543 occurrences of *he* in all functions to only 2,859 of *she*; that is, *he* occurred over three times more frequently than *she*; a similar imbalance is reported by Graham (1975: 58). Generics do not account for the discrepancy; the conclusion must be that, in the sources scanned, men are referred to considerably more frequently than women (figures from Russian are almost as one-sided). Therefore the hearer has a second reason to treat generic *he* as denoting a male: even when reference could be to a male or to a female, the pattern of the other (non-generic) pronouns would lead the hearer to conclude that the actual person involved is more likely to be male. But whatever the reasons, the main point is that the use of generic *he* seems not to work in English.

It should be noted that actual usage in English is more varied than is suggested by the simple claim that *he* is used as the generic; in situations where women are particularly visible *she* can function generically (see McConnell-Ginet 1979 for interesting examples and discussion). A second type of departure from what is increasingly only a prescriptive rule is illustrated in the next section.

7.3.2 *Use of an 'evasive' form*

In view of the difficulties associated with generic *he* in English, speakers often replace it by *they*. We term this and similar forms 'evasive'

221

forms. While, say, the use of masculine for masculine or feminine represents a choice between possible appropriate forms, the forms we term 'evasive' are those with a different role in the system. Thus *they* is primarily for plural reference: when it is drafted in to replace the singular pronouns (because it does not mark gender), thus avoiding the gender choice, this is its 'evasive' role. The relevant usage is shown in this example:

    (36) When a person eats too much, they get fat.

The example is from McConnell-Ginet (1979: 76), who points out that *they* is less readily accepted in certain contexts, for example when relating anaphorically to a singular noun with the definite article. According to Bodine (1975b) the use of *they* is not new; it was accepted and widespread before the beginning of the upsurge in prescriptive grammar. From the end of the eighteenth century prescriptivists found fault with the use of *they* and recommended the use of *he*. In recent times the pressure has been against generic *he* and it has been claimed that its use is declining in American English (Cooper 1984); it is almost certainly declining in other varieties too.

Polish also has an evasive form, but instead of using the plural it uses the neuter singular. This usage is described by Gotteri (1984), from whom we take the term 'evasive'. An example of the Polish neuter in evasive use is the following:

    (37) któr-eś   z   małzonków jest winn-e
          one-NEUT from spouses   is   guilty-NEUT
          zarzucanej mu   zbrodni
          imputed   it.DAT crime
          'One of the spouses is guilty of the crime he
          or she has been accused of.'

Małzonkówie is masculine personal and means 'husband and wife'; when either the husband or the wife is potentially the referent, then the evasive neuter is used. The neuter cannot be used in all the situations we have considered; in most the masculine is used (for examples see Herbert & Nykiel-Herbert 1986: 67). Most interestingly, the evasive neuter seems to be used in the sort of contexts which also preclude the use of generic *he* in English:

    (38) If either of my parents comes, he or she (*he) will bring a
          friend.

In this example (McConnell-Ginet 1979: 75), there are implied disjuncts, one of which is specifically female. In these circumstances, in Polish as in English, the generic masculine is avoided.

The evasive neuter is found also in Serbo-Croat but in rather limited use as in Polish. An evasive gender form with more widespread use is found in Archi. Recall that Archi has four genders, I and II for humans, male and female, III and IV less clearly defined semantically but with the larger animates in III and most abstracts in IV (section 2.2.5). In Archi, nouns like *lo* 'child', *adam* 'person', *c'ohor* 'thief', *misgin* 'poor person' take gender IV agreements in the singular if the sex of the referent is unimportant or unknown (Kibrik 1972: 126). (If the sex is known they can take gender I or II agreements as appropriate; in the plural, genders I and II share the same form, as discussed in section 6.3.2, and this form is used in all circumstances as it does not specify sex.) Archi shows a particularly clear example of an evasive form, since gender IV does not contain any nouns denoting humans.

7.3.3 *Use of a special form*

Given the difficulties that can arise when the sex of the referent is unknown, a reasonable strategy would appear to be to have a special form precisely for that purpose. Baron (1986: 190–216) documents over eighty proposals made since the eighteenth century for pronouns that would fit the bill in English, such as *thon*, *heesh* and *herm*; none has caught on. This is not surprising, since this strategy is rare in the languages of the world. Zande, however, has a pronoun *ni*, distinct from the normal personal pronouns, which is used if no specific individual is intended or if the individual is unknown (Claudi 1985: 95–6). It seems that an additional pronoun is possible, but it is unlikely that a language with extensive agreements would have a full extra set merely for referents of unknown sex.

7.3.4 *No strategy*

In some or all of the circumstances described, languages may have no set strategy favouring a particular gender. For example, R. M. W. Dixon (personal communication) has spent considerable time trying to establish whether gender I (male humans) or gender II (female humans) is unmarked in Dyirbal and has concluded that neither is. When referring to a group of mixed sex, either *bayi* (gender I) or *balan* (gender II) may be used. If the most senior person is a woman, or if most of the members of the group are women, then *balan* might be preferred; similarly, in the case of the senior or the majority being male, *bayi* might be used.

7.4 **Conclusion**

We have reviewed problems associated with gender agreement. First we looked at the relationship with number and found numerous examples of syncretism. We also saw that gender is not always subservient to

223

number; indeed the data from the Caucasus included cases where it is gender rather than number which is clearly indicated. We also analysed situations in which the existence of gender agreement creates problems: first, when the controller does not carry the required gender specification (it is a non-prototypical controller); and second, when the controller denotes a human or group of humans, whose sex is unknown, unclear or unimportant. In the next chapter we tackle a different, but related, problem: the question of nouns which take more than one set of gender agreement forms.

8

Hybrid nouns and the
Agreement Hierarchy

In this chapter we tackle a most interesting problem, namely that of hybrid nouns. As early as Chapter 3 we noted cases where the meaning and the form of nouns conflict in terms of gender assignment. Normally semantic criteria overrule formal considerations. In some instances, however, the conflict of criteria is not settled in this unambiguous way, and a hybrid noun results. The specific nature of hybrid nouns was identified in section 6.4.5.2. Like nouns of double (or multiple) gender, hybrid nouns take more than one set of agreements, that is, they take forms from more than one consistent agreement pattern. But unlike nouns of double gender, hybrid nouns do not simply belong to two genders. The crucial point about hybrid nouns is that the form of gender agreement used with them depends in part on the type of agreement target involved. Thus, while we can say of a normal noun simply that it takes, for example, feminine agreement, for a hybrid noun we can specify the agreement only provided we know the agreement target in question. Given this, the range of possible inventories of agreements taken by hybrids would appear to be extensive. However, we shall see that there are generalizations to be made about such agreement options; they are constrained by the Agreement Hierarchy (section 8.1). It turns out that pronouns have a special importance for hybrid nouns, which is examined in section 8.2. Finally we consider the sources, development and loss of hybrid nouns (section 8.3); in doing so, we shall take up issues raised in chapters 4 and 5.

8.1 The Agreement Hierarchy

'Ordinary' nouns can be assigned to a gender, and any agreement target which they control will show this same gender. Hybrid nouns on the other hand take agreement in more than one gender, depending on the target. To refer to these different possibilities we shall use the well-established terms 'semantic' and 'syntactic' agreement. Semantic agreement (or agreement *ad sensum*) is agreement consistent with the gender assigned by semantic assignment rules. In the case of Russian *vrač* '(female) doctor', this would be feminine agreement. Note that the factors involved may be pragmatic as well as strictly semantic, as will be discussed later in this section. Syntactic agreement (or agreement *ad formam*, or 'grammatical' agreement) is agreement consistent with form, that is, agreement consistent with the gender as it would be assigned by morphological or phonological assignment rules. For *vrač* '(female) doctor', this would be the masculine.

As we shall see from the data which follow, four types of agreement targets can be distinguished:

> The Agreement Hierarchy
> attributive < predicate < relative pronoun < personal pronoun

These four positions make up the Agreement Hierarchy. Possible agreement patterns are constrained as follows:

> As we move rightwards along the hierarchy, the likelihood of semantic agreement will increase monotonically (that is, with no intervening decrease).

We shall consider the data which give rise to this claim (section 8.1.1) and then discuss the wider aspects of the hierarchy (section 8.1.2).

8.1.1 *Data*

In looking at examples we shall begin with instances where syntactic agreement is dominant and then progress to those where semantic agreement has a greater role. With French titles, now largely obsolete, feminine agreements are usually found. This is surprising because they can and frequently do refer to men. *Sa Sainteté* 'His Holiness' has only ever had a male referent. Yet the agreements with this and similar titles are feminine, as (1) illustrates for the attributive modifier *sa* and the agreeing predicate *ombrageuse*:

(1) Sa   Sainteté n'est   pas si ombrageuse
    his.FEM holiness NEG.is not so touchy.FEM
    de s'en   formaliser
    of REFL.of.it to.offend
    'His Holiness is not so touchy as to
    take offence.'

(Hermant, quoted by Grevisse 1964: 314)

Why should we find feminine agreement? The point is that *Sainteté* 'Holiness' (like similar titles) is established as a noun, and by the normal assignment rules its form requires that it should be feminine. This assignment normally holds even when the noun is used as a title. Like the targets already discussed, the agreeing relative pronoun is also feminine:

> (2) Sa Sainteté, avec laquelle je viens
> his.FEM holiness with whom.FEM I come
> de parler...
> from to.speak
> 'His Holiness, with whom I have just been speaking...'
>
> (informant)

and the personal pronoun is normally feminine:

> (3) Votre Majesté partira quand elle voudra
> your majesty leave.FUT when she wish.FUT
> 'Your Majesty will leave when he (literally 'she') wishes.'
>
> (Voltaire, quoted by Grevisse 1964: 406)

Example (3), with the feminine pronoun *elle* even though the king is addressed, represents normal usage; but examples with a masculine pronoun also occur:

> (4) Sa Majesté fut inquiète, et de nouveau
> his.FEM majesty was worried.FEM and of new
> il envoya La Varenne à son ministre
> he sent La Varenne to his minister
> 'His Majesty was worried, and again he sent La Varenne to his minister.'
>
> (J. & J. Tharaud, quoted by Grevisse 1964: 405)

Here we find a masculine pronoun *il*, which would not, of course, be possible with *sainteté* 'holiness' or *majesté* 'majesty' in their normal use. So when used as titles they are hybrid nouns because the form of gender agreement depends on the target; for these examples the degree of variation is severely restricted since it involves only the personal pronoun, and even here syntactic agreement is usual. We shall see instances which involve a more even balance of syntactic and semantic agreement later in the section.

A frequently quoted example of a hybrid noun is German *Mädchen* 'girl'. Like similar nouns in several other languages, this case arises from a complex conflict of the assignment rules. Many Indo-European languages assign sex-differentiable nouns to the masculine or feminine gender as appropriate, while the young of sex-differentiables – typically young animals which are treated as not yet sex-differentiable – are neuter. With a noun denoting a human, like *Mädchen*, there is a sharp conflict; it denotes a female so should be feminine, yet denotes a young being and so should be neuter. Crucially, the last factor is supported by the morphology: the diminutive suffix *-chen* ensures that a noun will be neuter. In the case of *Mädchen* agreements are neuter in all positions except the personal pronoun:

> (5) das   Mädchen, das   ich gesehen habe...
> the.NEUT girl   that.NEUT I seen   have
> 'the girl I saw...'

Here the attributive modifier and the relative pronoun are neuter. This is the position in Modern German, particularly in formal Standard German; for the earlier situation see Batliner (1984: 850). The personal pronoun is different:

> (6) Schau dir dieses   Mädchen an, wie gut
> look   you this.NEUT girl   at how good
> sie/es Tennis spielt
> she/it tennis plays
> 'Do look at this girl, see how well she plays tennis.'

The personal pronoun allows a choice of form – both neuter and feminine are possible (Batliner 1984: 849). There is a further point of interest: Manfred Kripka suggests (personal communication) that the older the girl in question, the more likely the feminine becomes (and conversely for the neuter). Limited informant work supports this view.

There are many more examples of hybrid nouns which allow a choice of agreement form in the personal pronoun only (the importance of the personal pronoun is discussed further in section 8.2). For example, Czech *děvče* 'girl' (colloquial) takes neuter agreements of attributive modifiers, the predicate and the relative pronoun, while the personal pronoun can be neuter or feminine (Vanek 1970: 87–8; Corbett 1983a: 11–12). Dutch has various diminutives like *jongetje* 'little boy' and *vrouwtje* 'little woman', which take neuter agreements, except of the personal pronoun, which normally appears in the semantic form, that is, masculine for *jongetje* and feminine for *vrouwtje*. French *sentinelle* 'sentry, guard' takes only feminine agreements, except of the personal pronoun which can be masculine or feminine. And *ministre* 'minister', when a female is denoted, takes masculine agreements except for the personal pronoun, which can be masculine or feminine (Boel 1976: 66–7; Tasmowski & Verluyten 1985: 352–3, 366–7; Cornish 1986: 160–4; 1988: 240–1, 251–4; with *ministre* feminine agreements have started to extend their range, Francis Cornish, personal communication). German has words like *Memme* 'coward' and *Drachen* 'dragon, shrew' which take syntactic agreement except of the personal pronoun, which can take syntactic or semantic agreement. Thus for *Memme* agreements are feminine, except that when the noun denotes a male the personal pronoun may be masculine or feminine. And *Drachen* takes masculine agreements, except that when used of a woman the pronoun may be masculine or feminine (Batliner 1984: 849). And Polish *ofiara* 'victim' takes feminine agreements, except of the personal pronoun; if the noun denotes a male, then the pronoun can be masculine or feminine (Herbert & Nykiel-Herbert 1986: 66–7 and informants).

Our examples so far have all been from Indo-European languages. This is because the very detailed information required is available for relatively few languages, and those which have been most intensively studied are Indo-European languages in the main. But data from other families can be found, as the following examples from Landuma show. Landuma is a member of the Temne cluster, which in turn comes within the Southern Branch of the West Atlantic group of Niger-Congo; it is spoken by a small tribe in the northern part of southern Guinea. It has a gender system similar to that of some southern Bantu languages (Welmers 1973: 278). The data are from Wilson (1962: 28–9; supplemented by Wilson 1961: 53; and personal communication); unfortunately, there is information on only some of the relevant agreements:

>   (7) abil ŋŋe, i-nəŋk ŋi lɛ
>   boat this I-see it FOCUS.MARKER
>   'This boat, I have seen it.'
>   (8) abok ŋŋe, i-nəŋk kɔ lɛ
>   snake this I-see him FOCUS.MARKER
>   'This snake, I have seen it.'
>   (9) oteem   uwe, i-nəŋk kɔ lɛ
>   old.man this I-see him FOCUS.MARKER
>   'This old man, I have seen him.'

In all three examples, the attributive modifier agrees syntactically with the head noun. *Abil* 'boat' in (7) and *abok* 'snake' in (8) are in the same morphological class (3/4) and take the appropriate gender form of the demonstrative, namely, *ŋŋe* 'this'. *Oteem* 'old man' in (9) is in gender 1/2 and so takes *uwe*. When we turn to the personal pronoun, we find that *abil* 'boat' in (7) takes *ŋi*, which is consistent with its membership of gender 3/4 (assigned on the basis of its morphological class). Similarly *oteem* 'old man' in (9) takes *kɔ*, the normal pronoun for nouns of gender 1/2. The interesting case is *abok* 'snake' in (8), where we find the same pronoun *kɔ* as with *oteem* 'old man'.

Abok 'snake' is in the same morphological class as *abil* 'boat' and, as we have already noted, takes the same form of the attributive modifier. The pronoun is different; nouns which, like *abok* 'snake', denote animates take *kɔ*, the pronoun of gender 1/2, irrespective of the agreements they take with other targets. Thus *abok* 'snake' and similar nouns are hybrids. The attributive modifier stands in the syntactically agreeing form, as in example (9), and according to Wilson (1962: 28) most other targets also take syntactic agreement; but the personal pronoun shows semantic agreement.

We now move on to cases where semantic agreement plays a larger role. Spanish titles, like French titles, involve abstract nouns of feminine gender. But the agreements are rather different from French (data from J. England, personal communication). Attributive modifiers take feminine agreement:

> (10) Su Majestad suprema
> his majesty supreme.FEM
> 'His Supreme Majesty.'

However, the predicate shows masculine agreement:

> (11) Su Majestad está contento
> his majesty is happy.MASC

The next example includes relative and personal pronouns:

> (12) A Su Majestad suprema, el cual está
> to his majesty supreme the.MASC which is
> muy contento aquí en Valencia, le
> very happy here in Valencia OBJECT-CLITIC
> recibieron con muchos aplausos. Él se mostró
> they.received with much applause He self showed
> muy emocionado.
> very moved
> 'His Supreme Majesty, who is very happy here in Valencia, was received with much applause. He showed himself very moved.'

Both the compound relative *el cual* and the personal pronoun are masculine. Thus only the attributive modifier shows syntactic agreement, all the other targets show semantic agreement. A similar situation is found with titles in Polish, and in Russian, though the latter allows some variation (Corbett 1983a: 23–4).

In Konkani a particularly interesting change has occurred, whereby neuter agreements are used for nouns denoting females who are young, or young relative to the speaker (see section 4.5). For some nouns the change is not complete, and hybrids result, taking neuter and feminine agreements. In the new gender system, the use of the neuter represents semantic agreement, provided, of course, a young or relatively younger female is denoted. In such cases *awoy* 'mother' takes neuter agreements for all targets, except attributive modifiers, where the feminine persists (Miranda 1975: 211):

(13) jɔniči   awoy aylḕ
John's.FEM mother came.NEUT

The possessive adjective in (13) shows syntactic (feminine) agreement and the verbal predicate (like other agreeing targets) shows semantic agreement.

We have so far considered hybrids for which the agreement facts are relatively straightforward, normally involving two agreement possibilities for one target only. We now turn to more complex cases. Russian *vrač* '(female) doctor' has been mentioned several times. Like the numerous nouns of the same type it can take both masculine (syntactic) and feminine (semantic) agreements. There is a considerable amount of information about attributive and predicate agreement with such nouns. In the early 1960s, a team led by M. V. Panov carried out a large-scale survey of Russian usage, involving a questionnaire to which over 4,000 replies were received (Panov 1968). Certain questions relate to the problem in hand, for example the following examples were included (figures are taken from the account in Kitajgorodskaja 1976; details are given in Corbett 1983a: 30–9):

(14) Ivanova – xoroš-ij   vrač
Ivanova   good-MASC doctor
'Ivanova is a good doctor.'
(15) Ivanova – xoroš-aja   vrač
Ivanova   good-FEM doctor
'Ivanova is a good doctor.'

The inclusion of the name *Ivanova* makes it clear that the doctor is a woman. As reported earlier, in table 6.9, of the 3,835 who answered this question, 16.9 per cent chose the feminine form. (It does not follow that the remainder chose the masculine, since some were undecided; though the figures are not given for this question, other responses suggest 5–10 per cent as a likely proportion for the undecided respondents.)

The informants were also asked to choose between the following (they were told that a woman doctor was intended):

(16) vrač   prišel-∅
doctor came-MASC
'The doctor came.'

(17) vrač   prišl-a
doctor came-FEM
'The doctor came.'

Of 3,806 respondents, 51.7 per cent chose the feminine (just under 10 per cent were undecided). Thus there is a choice in both positions, but the likelihood of semantic agreement is considerably higher in the position further to the right on the hierarchy (the predicate). Informant judgements of this type must be viewed with caution; it is likely that some chose the form they believed to be correct, the masculine, and that the feminine is more frequent, certainly in speech, than these results suggest. Nevertheless, it is significant that there was a substantial difference between the predicate and the attributive modifier (even if both figures for semantic agreement are underestimates).

For the relative pronoun, data are much less extensive. However, Janko-Trinickaja (1966: 193–4) studied women's journals of the 1920s and reports that feminine (semantic) agreement of the relative pronoun is found with nouns like *vrač* more frequently than it is found in the predicate. (Of the six examples with relative pronouns which she cites, five have feminine agreement.) For the personal pronoun, the feminine *ona* would be normal, but the masculine *on* 'he' is possible even here. On Red Square in May 1988, the organizer of guided tours round the Kremlin said:

(18) Èkskursovod pered vami. On podnjal ruku.
guide   before you   he lifted   hand
'Your guide is in front of you. He has lifted his hand.'

The guide was a woman (as was the speaker). Informants agree that in certain settings *on* 'he' could similarly be used with *vrač* '(woman) doctor'; nevertheless, the feminine is what we would normally expect. Remarkably, then, we find a choice of agreement at all four positions on the Agreement Hierarchy, and we do indeed find a monotonic increase in the likelihood of semantic agreement as we move from left to right along it.

Another complex case involves Serbo-Croat nouns like *gazda* 'landlord, master, boss'. These denote males, but are declined according to a pattern which includes mainly feminine nouns. When the noun is singular, the semantic criterion overrides the morphological, as expected, and masculine agreements are found. But when the noun is plural then feminine as well as masculine agreements are found. Feminine agreement is syntactic agreement (according to form) while the masculine is semantic agreement. The following examples are from the novelist Ivo Andrić:

(19) Mlad-e   kalfe   su se   uozbiljil-e...
young-FEM.PL journeymen are selves made.serious-FEM.PL
'The young journeymen became serious...'

Here both attributive modifier and predicate are feminine. But in both positions masculine agreement is possible, as in this example with a preposed predicate:

(20) jednog i   drugog su podstical-i   moćn-i
one.OBJ and other.OBJ are goaded-MASC.PL Powerful -MASC.PL
paše...
pashas
'Powerful pashas goaded both of them.'

Information on the relative frequency of the options is patchy and depends on small samples (see Corbett 1983a: 14–17). It seems that masculine (semantic) agreements are found in somewhat less than half the cases in attributive position, while in the predicate they are the more common. The relative pronoun, too, occurs in both forms, with the masculine apparently more frequent here than in the predicate. What data there are on the personal pronoun suggest that it is normally masculine in the contemporary language. These data are fully consistent with the Agreement Hierarchy. In the last century, semantic agreement was less common, but the pattern which was found then was also in accord with the hierarchy. We must hope that a proper study will provide more complete data; even so, these nouns deserve a mention here because the agreement choice involved occurs in the plural only.

The Polish example which we consider next is also complex. The literature on gender in Polish is extensive (see Corbett 1988: 3 for references). In essence the gender system is similar to that of Upper Sorbian, described in section 7.1.1, though Polish has only two numbers, singular and plural. As with the Serbo-Croat example just discussed, we are concerned only with the plural. Plural agreements in Polish distinguish between masculine personal and other. In the straightforward cases, a masculine personal noun denotes a male person, it forms its plural in a different way from other nouns (including other masculine nouns) and it takes different agreements. Thus *Polak* 'Pole' has a plural form involving consonant alternation *Polacy*, and takes masculine personal agreements (for example *mili Polacy* 'nice Poles'), while *Polka* 'Polish woman' has the plural *Polki* and, like all remaining types of noun, takes non-masculine personal agreements (for example *miłe Polki* 'nice Polish women'). However, in some instances the consistent matching of meaning, morphology and agreements is not maintained. Some nouns which denote male humans do not have the morphology typical of masculine personal nouns, or they may have both the masculine personal and the non-masculine personal morphological forms. The nouns involved are derogatory: 'ruffian', 'boor', 'scoundrel' and so on. The cases which concern us are those which show non-masculine personal morphology. What agreements will they take? *Łajdak* means 'scoundrel, wretch' and can take the non-masculine personal plural form *łajdaki*. This form takes non-masculine personal agreements in attributive and predicate positions (the following judgements are those of Ewa Jaworska):

(21) te   łajdaki   znowu
     those.NON_MASC_PERS wretches again
     mnie oszukały!
     me   cheated.NON_MASC_PERS
     'Those wretches have cheated me again!'

Similarly the relative pronoun was accepted only in the non-masculine personal form:

(22) te   łajdaki które   mnie oszukały...
     those wretches who.NON_MASC_PERS me   cheated
     'those wretches who cheated me...'

The personal pronoun, however, in anaphoric use is masculine personal:

(23) te   łajdaki zepsuły   mi   radio
     those wretches damaged.NON_MASC_PERS me.DAT radio
     do reszty!
     to rest
     Oni   już   ci   kiedyś
     they.MASC_PERS already you.DAT some.time
     zepsuli telewizor.
     damaged television.
     'Those wretches have ruined my radio!'
     'They have already damaged your television.'

This is a familiar pattern: the personal pronoun shows semantic agreement, while we find syntactic agreement in the other positions. Other informants have given similar judgements. However, there is variation both from speaker to speaker, and when different nouns are used. The variation found to date has shown patterns consistent with the Agreement Hierarchy. The agreements found change considerably when we turn to evidence from written sources (Rothstein 1976: 248–50; 1980: 85–6, reported in Corbett 1983a: 21–3). According to Rothstein, in attributive position in written sources the non-masculine personal form is found (with an occasional exception); in the

Table 8.1 *Evidence for the Agreement Hierarchy*

	Attributive	Predicate	Relative pronoun	Personal pronoun
French titles	fem	fem	fem	fem/(MASC)
German *Mädchen*	neut	d.n.a.	neut	neut/FEM
Polish *lajdaki* (plural, spoken language)	non-masc_pers	non-masc_pers	non-masc_pers	MASC_PERS
Spanish titles	fem	MASC	MASC	MASC
Konkani young females	fem	NEUT	n.a.	NEUT
Russian *vrač* (female)	masc/(FEM)	masc/FEM	(masc)/FEM	(masc)/FEM
Serbo-Croat *gazde* (plural)	fem/(MASC)	fem/MASC	(fem)/MASC	MASC

Notes: within the table lower case signifies syntactic agreement and capitals signify semantic agreement; parentheses indicate a less frequent variant; d.n.a. = does not apply (no agreement); n.a. = not available.

predicate, both forms are well attested; the relative and personal pronouns normally occur in the masculine personal forms (those in the non-masculine personal form make up a trifling percentage of the total). Thus the written sources show a considerable shift in favour of semantic agreement as compared to informant responses, but they again show a pattern fully in accord with the Agreement Hierarchy.

Let us now review the evidence in summary form. Where very similar patterns are found in different languages we will consider only one of them. The data are presented in table 8.1, where the complex data from spoken Polish have been put in their logical place. We see that there is considerable variety: first in the types of gender choices, and second in the relative frequency of syntactic and semantic agreement. With French titles semantic agreement is all but excluded, while with Serbo-Croat *gazde* semantic agreement is dominant. Yet all the agreement patterns considered are consistent with the Agreement Hierarchy; we do, indeed, observe a monotonic increase in the likelihood of semantic agreement as we move rightwards along the hierarchy. This can be seen even more clearly if we abstract away from the particular genders involved and examine the data in the form given in figure 8.1. When seen in this form, the pattern is absolutely clear. The remarkable variety of agreements which we find with hybrid nouns is indeed constrained by the Agreement Hierarchy.

8.1.2 *Wider considerations*

We should now consider the scope of the hierarchy. We have seen that it constrains the patterns of agreement of individual lexical items like German *Mädchen*; it also limits the idiosyncratic usage of an individual author (see Corbett 1981b). On the other hand, it constrains the agreement possibilities of large groups of nouns like Russian *vrač* '(woman) doctor'. We shall consider further the different types of hybrid noun in section 8.3. Naturally we have concentrated on instances where the complete hierarchy is involved and so its relevance is most obvious. But there are also instances where only a part is invoked. In German there is no agreement in gender in the predicate, hence only three positions of the hierarchy can be demonstrated to affect the agreements with *Mädchen* 'girl'. In section 6.4.5 we met English 'boat nouns', and noted that with such nouns two forms of the personal pronoun (*she* and *it*) are possible, but that the relative pronoun is *which* (not *who*); this is a pattern allowed for by the Agreement Hierarchy. The other two positions on the hierarchy are not relevant to English in this instance, since agreement in gender is not found there. (For a case of agreement in animacy which involves only the relative pronoun and

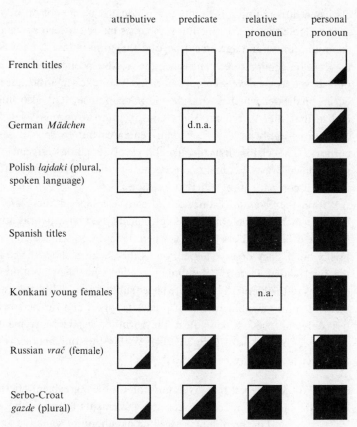

Figure 8.1 *Evidence for the Agreement Hierarchy*

Notes: 1. the blacker the square, the greater the likelihood of semantic agreement; 2. d.n.a. = does not apply (no agreement); 3. n.a. = not available.

attributive position see Melčuk 1985: 467.)

The scope of the hierarchy extends considerably beyond the problem of agreement in gender with hybrid nouns. First, it covers number just as it covers gender (Corbett 1979; for additional evidence see Huntley's 1989 analysis of Old Church Slavonic). Second, it constrains agreement in particular constructions (rather than just with specified lexical items). The best-documented construction is conjoined noun phrases, which we shall examine in the next chapter. Beyond this, it accounts for the surprising data found in the control possibilities of possessive adjectives (Corbett 1987). Thus, although the Agreement Hierarchy is well motivated by the gender facts we have discussed, it is required for quite independent reasons, not directly involving gender. Note that the distinction sometimes made between agreement within the noun phrase and agreement beyond the noun phrase cannot account for the data on gender agreement, since the relative pronoun is within the noun phrase, yet, as we have seen, it is more likely to take semantic agreement than is the predicate, which is outside the noun phrase. It is also important to realize that the Agreement Hierarchy operates at corpus level; that is, its predictions apply not to individual sentences but to sets of sentences or corpora. The claim that the likelihood of semantic agreement increases monotonically as we compare targets moving rightwards along the hierarchy implies a comparison of different examples.

Within the essential framework already established there are subsidiary factors which help determine the agreements used with hybrid nouns. These have been described elsewhere (Corbett 1983a) and will be considered only briefly here. They deserve a mention as they help to show the complexity of the interrelated factors determining gender agreement. Within the major divisions of the hierarchy there are lesser subdivisions. Thus the predicate can be divided into a subhierarchy of predicate types; and the personal pronoun has different uses, which affect the form of gender agreement (Corbett 1983a: 42–59; Cornish 1986: 203–14). Within the four major divisions, too, the effect of case may be observed:

> Whenever, in a given position on the Agreement Hierarchy there is a difference between the agreements found in the nominative and in the oblique cases, the likelihood of semantic agreement in the nominative will be as high as or higher than the likelihood of semantic agreement in the oblique cases.

For example, we have seen that Russian *vrač* '(woman) doctor' can take masculine (syntactic) and feminine (semantic) agreement:

(24) ona xoroš-ij/xoroš-aja   vrač
she good-MASC/good-FEM doctor
'She is a good doctor.'

Here, as in the cases quoted earlier, the agreeing modifier is in the nominative case. If we take an example of an oblique case, then syntactic agreement is normally found:

(25) k xoroš-emu   vraču
to good-MASC.DAT doctor
'to a good doctor'

It is sometimes stated that the feminine (semantic) form is quite impossible in the oblique cases; however, examples have begun to occur (Švedova 1980: 57), though they are certainly less common than in the nominative.

There are two further effects observable within the main four divisions of the hierarchy but these operate at sentence level. One may be observable with 'stacked' agreement targets; for example, we may have an attributive modifier, which forms a phrase with the noun it modifies and this larger phrase may be modified in turn. Some languages allow the stacked modifiers to show different agreement forms, as in this Serbo-Croat example:

(26) nijihov-i   stran-e   voďe
     their-MASC.PL foreign-FEM.PL leaders
     'their foreign leaders'

                 (Oslobođenje, 27 February 1953, quoted by Marković 1954: 96)

Voďe 'leaders' behaves like *gazde* 'landlords'; it may take masculine (semantic) and feminine (syntactic) agreements. In this example it takes both. The pattern is this:

> When stacked targets of a given controller stand in different agreement forms, the further target will show semantic agreement.

The same effect can be seen in these data from Chichewa. *Ngwazi* 'hero' has the morphology of gender 9/10, and can take 9/10 agreements (syntactic); it can also take gender 1/2 agreements (semantic) because it denotes a human. Mixed agreements are possible and so, given two stacked modifiers, we might expect four possible combinations (data from Sam Mchombo):

(27) ngwazi   y-athu   y-oyamba
     hero   9-our   9-first
     'our first hero'

(28) ngwazi   w-athu   w-oyamba
     hero   1-our   1-first
     'our first hero'

In (27) and (28) we have consistent syntactic and consistent semantic agreements, which are acceptable. We now try the mixed possibilities:

(29) ngwazi   y-athu   w-oyamba
     hero   9-our   1-first
     'our first hero'

(30) *ngwazi   w-athu   y-oyamba
     hero   1-our   9-first
     'our first hero'

Example (29) with the further target showing semantic agreement is acceptable, while the reverse combination (30) is not, which is the situation allowed for by our constraint.

The second constraint concerns parallel targets, that is targets which fill a single syntactic slot, as in this example from Serbo-Croat:

(31) Sarajlije   su igral-e   bolje i   gotovo
     Sarajevans are played-FEM.PL better and almost
     potpuno   dominiral-i   terenom
     completely dominated-MASC.PL field
     'The Sarajevans played better and dominated the field almost
     completely.'

(Oslobođenje, 27 February 1953, quoted by Marković 1954: 96)

In (31) the two verbal predicates are parallel. The controller is *Sarajlije* 'Sarajevans', which is another noun like *gazde* 'landlords'. The nearer target shows feminine, syntactic agreement while the further shows masculine, that is semantic, agreement. The following constraint applies:

> If parallel targets show different agreement forms, then the further target will show semantic agreement.

The latter two constraints must operate at sentence level; they refer to the simultaneous presence of two targets. They are, however, linked to a more general corpus-level regularity which is the effect of 'real' distance:

> For any particular target type, the further it is removed from its controller, the greater the likelihood of semantic agreement.

Thus, for example, the further the personal pronoun is removed from German *Mädchen* 'girl', the more likely the feminine (semantic) form *sie* 'she' becomes. This point will be illustrated from Old English in section 8.2 (example (33)).

The Agreement Hierarchy and associated constraints, which are grammatical factors, do not completely determine the choice between syntactic and semantic agreement. There are three other types of factor involved: register, sociolinguistic variables and pragmatic considerations. Register often affects the choice of agreement form. We have already seen examples from Polish and Russian of differences between the spoken and written registers. It is interesting to note that in the Polish case (agreement with *lajdaki*) semantic agreement was more likely in the written language, while with Russian *vrač* semantic agreement was more likely in the spoken language. Considerations of register merge into sociolinguistic matters. And similarly, given a choice of form, sociolinguistic variables frequently have an influence. In the case of Russian *vrač* it has been shown that the likelihood of semantic agreement being chosen is increased if the speaker is less well educated, lives in a particular part of the Soviet Union, is an industrial worker and is young (see Corbett 1983a: 30–9 for details). A change is in progress in favour of semantic agreement with such nouns and the different parameters are measures which distinguish conservative and innovative speakers (see also section 8.3, concerning the effect of age). There is also some evidence that females choose the feminine (semantic) form more readily than males; a similar situation appears to hold for German *Mädchen* 'girl' (Mills 1986: 52).

The pragmatic factors involved fall mainly under the notion of 'referential perspective' (Cornish's term). While several writers have claimed that referential perspective has an effect, relatively few data have been put forward (but see Kopeliovič 1977: 181–6; Cornish 1986: 160–6). Informally, the more clearly that reference is to a specific individual and the more directly reference is to the individual (rather than via some property or function), the more likely semantic agreement will be. Using a familiar example, consider again Russian *vrač* '(female) doctor'. It is suggested than when the context makes it clear that reference is to, say, Anna Ivanovna, semantic (feminine) agreement is more likely than when reference is less specific. Similarly, if the doctor is described as 'young', 'old', 'short' or 'tall', that is, in terms of properties of the person independently of being a doctor, this makes semantic agreement more likely than if the description focusses on the function or status of a doctor (for example, using terms like 'competent' or 'pediatric').

8.2 **Personal pronouns**

The items we have been referring to for convenience as personal pronouns deserve further attention. It is the third person pronouns which are of interest. As their name implies, they can be used of persons; in some languages this function is fulfilled by demonstrative pronouns (as mentioned at the end of section 5.3.3), and such pronouns are included in what follows. In many languages the pronouns we are calling 'personal' are not restricted to persons but can be used of non-persons as well as of persons. Of the possible functions they can fulfil, the one which primarily concerns us is anaphoric use, as shown by *she* in this sentence:

(32) Mary buys a lot of books because she enjoys reading.

Personal pronouns have other uses in addition, notably deictic use, to which we shall return shortly. Personal pronouns occupy a special position in the

Agreement Hierarchy. The question of whether they should be considered to agree or not (and hence whether they can be included in the hierarchy) has already been discussed (section 5.1). The evidence of the previous section indicates that there is no good reason for splitting the hierarchy at the point between relative and personal pronouns, nor indeed at any other point. This is a further argument to support the view that personal pronouns are involved in agreement. Furthermore, attempts to divide agreement into two different types, local and anaphoric, are unsatisfactory (as shown by Barlow 1988: 134–52). While personal pronouns are less subject to strict control than are other target types, this is a matter of degree since, as we have seen, even attributive modifiers may show agreement forms which are not determined by the formal properties of the controller. The personal pronoun is also of special importance because it is a major source of agreement morphology (section 5.5). And, as we shall see, it is the major initiator of changes in the balance between syntactic and semantic gender.

A special feature of the behaviour of personal pronouns, which will help us to understand their role, is the fact that they can be widely separated from their antecedent. (Other agreement targets normally occur in the same sentence as the controller.) This feature can be seen from a segment of Old English text (from the Preface to the *Cura Pastoralis*, quoted by Dekeyser 1980: 101):

> (33) ...þæt þu þone wisdom þe   þe   God sealde,
> that you that wisdom which to.you God gave,
> þær þær þu hiene befæstan mæge, befæste.
> there where you it.MASC implant may, implant
> Geþenc hwelc witu   us   þa becomon
> think what punishments to.us then came
> for þisse worulde, þa þa we hit   nohwæþer
> for this world   when we it.NEUT neither
> ne selfe   ne lufodon, ne eac oþrum
> NEG ourselves NEG loved   NEG also other
> monnum ne lefdon...
> men   NEG allowed...
> '...that wisdom which God gave to you, where you may
> implant it, there implant it. Think what punishments would
> come to us for this world if we did not love it nor allowed
> others to do so...'

In this example *wisdom*, which was formerly of masculine gender, as shown by the attributive modifier *þone* 'that', acts as antecedent for two anaphoric pronouns. The first, *hiene* 'him, it', is in the same sentence and is masculine; the second is further separated and is neuter (*hit* 'it'). As we noted in the last section, the further the target is distanced from the controller, the more likely semantic agreement becomes. Even in systems where strict syntactic agreement is the norm, there may be a chance of semantic agreement occurring when a personal pronoun is very far from its antecedent (a Chichewa example (46) is given in section 8.3 below). The fact that there is no determinable maximum distance between antecedent and pronoun means that sometimes it is not fully clear which noun phrase is the antecedent of a particular pronoun. And when a pronoun is widely separated from possible antecedents it may be being used deictically rather than anaphorically. This highlights the complex nature of the pronouns we are discussing (for anaphora and deixis see Lyons 1977: 646–77). It is worth considering deictic use briefly; the following example is taken from an account of the role of pronouns in discourse by Brown & Yule (1983: 214–22). It is uttered on the approach of a large dog:

(34) I hope it's friendly.

Frequently some physical indication is required to make clear the intended referent of a deictic pronoun (like *it* in (34)). At this point we should note an intriguing problem concerning gender, raised by Tasmowski-De Ryck & Verluyten (1981, 1982). They give examples like the following, from French. The situation is that John is trying to get a large table into the boot of his car. Mary says:

(35) tu   n'arriveras   jamais à la   faire
     you NEG.will.manage never to it.FEM make
     entrer dans la   voiture
     enter in   the car
     'You'll never get it into the car.'

Here the pronoun must be in the feminine form *la* (** le* is unacceptable); *table* 'table' is feminine in French. However, if John is trying to get a desk into his car, then the pronoun must be masculine (*bureau* 'desk' is masculine):

(36) tu   n'arriveras   jamais à le   faire
     you NEG.will.manage never to it.MASC make
     entrer dans la   voiture
     enter in   the car
     'You'll never get it into the car.'

The point is that the pronoun must be in the appropriate gender; since there is no antecedent present, the question is the source of the gender of this deictic pronoun. These data have been one of the stimulants to an interesting debate on the nature of deixis and anaphora (Bosch 1987, 1988; Tasmowski & Verluyten 1985; Cornish 1986: 167–70; 1988; see also Pollard & Sag 1988: 249–50; Dowty & Jacobson 1989: 98–101). A view found in most of these papers is that the gender of the pronoun in examples like (35) and (36) is determined by that of the default description of the referent in question. Normally this default description will be the basic-level term, a notion which comes from Rosch (see, for example, Rosch 1978; and for discussion see Pulman 1983: 83–106). The basic level is the appropriate level for naming an object in most situations in which it occurs. Thus *dog* would be a basic-level term, rather than *animal* (the superordinate) or *golden retriever* (a sub-ordinate). In (35) above, the basic-level term for the object in question is *table*, which is feminine, hence the use of *la*. The fact that it is a piece of furniture (*meuble*, masculine) and indeed an object (*objet*, masculine) does not affect the gender since neither are basic-level terms. The use of pronouns without an overt antecedent works well in languages with large gender systems. One such is Fula, which has around twenty genders, according to dialect, and uses pronouns without overt antecedents frequently (Koval' 1987). Given the large number of genders, the number of possible referents for a pronoun is more limited. As an extreme case, one gender is so restricted that the use of the appropriate pronoun unambiguously indicates that the intended referent is denoted by the noun *nagge* 'cow'.

Let us now return to anaphoric use, as in the example already given:

(37) Mary buys a lot of books because she enjoys reading.

Anaphora is a complex problem, on which a great deal of work is being done at present. Here we can give only a simplified account of these difficult issues. For an introduction to recent work see Cornish (1988) and Kempson (1988). The more traditional formulation of the link between a pronoun and its antecedent (which we shall call 'alternative A') is to say that *she* refers to its antecedent, the expression *Mary*. The other position ('alternative B') is to say that the pronoun *she* refers to what its antecedent refers to, that is, the person called Mary (Lyons 1977: 659–60). In terms of identifying the referent of *she*, the two alternatives reach the same result. However, alternative B has the advantage that it brings the anaphoric use of pronouns closer to their deictic use, which helps to explain the relationship between deixis and anaphora. In alternative B the gender of the anaphoric pronoun is determined, just as in deictic use, by the gender of the noun which conceptualizes the referent. Some take this position and argue from it that anaphoric pronouns are outside the scope of agreement. This brings us back to the earlier debate as to whether pronouns agree (section 5.1). Suffice it to say that some others would extend the argument even further, and consider verb agreement to be controlled by discourse referents, rather than by a syntactic controller. There is no consensus as to where the cut-off point should be, if there is one. There is, however, a major problem with this approach, which occurs in languages with formal gender assignment rules. If, rather than *Mary*, we have a noun phrase headed by an inanimate noun whose gender is assigned by a formal rule (such as French *bâtiment* 'building'), then alternative B will not explain why the gender of an anaphoric pronoun must match that of the antecedent. (Naturally, we should try the explanation just given to account for the gender of deictic pronouns, namely that the gender will be that of the appropriate basic-level term; however, if the antecedent does not include a basic-level term, as in the case of *bâtiment*, which is not a basic-level term, then this approach will fail.) And there is a second problem, namely our prime concern here, hybrid nouns. Suppose this time that the antecedent is not *Mary* but a noun phrase headed by German *Mädchen* 'girl'. If alternative A were correct, we would expect that the pronoun would take the same gender (neuter) as that shown by the article within the noun phrase, and that only the syntactically agreeing *es* (literally 'it') would be possible. If alternative B were right, so that the link was more directly from the pronoun to the referent, then the only form would be *sie* 'she', derived from the default description of the referent (which for humans in German is according to sex); the referent is a female and there is no way for the anomalous noun to interfere. In fact, pronouns of both genders occur, *es* 'it' as predicted by alternative A and *sie* 'she' as predicted by alternative B. This shows that the determination of the form of the pronoun can involve both the referent and the form of the antecedent (compare Karmiloff-Smith 1979: 49–50). There is no simple choice between A and B. This explains why two forms are found, and the fact that the pronoun is the agreement target most likely to agree semantically. The relevance of hybrid nouns to the anaphora debate is that the agreement options of hybrid nouns are not necessarily restricted to the pronoun but often extend to other targets. This makes it difficult to justify treating pronouns separately as far as gender agreement is concerned.

A slightly different approach to the status of the personal pronoun is to look at its possible meaning, or semantic content: what Bosch (1988: 214–15) calls its 'descriptive content' (compare Wiese (1983: 394), who distinguishes 'conceptual meaning' from 'associative potential'). The semantic content of pronouns is most easily identified when they are used without antecedents, that is, deictically. If we take an Indo-European-type three-gender system (as in German, Polish or Russian, ignoring subgenders), we find that the main meanings we can identify for the personal pronouns are 'male', 'female' and 'neither male nor female'. Thus the meaning of the pronouns matches part of the meaning of prototypical nouns of the corresponding genders; it reflects the core meaning of the genders. More specifically, the meaning of the personal pronouns matches the semantic assignment rules; these languages have, for example, a rule that states that nouns denoting females are assigned to the feminine gender and there is a matching personal pronoun, for referring to females.

In straightforward anaphoric use, the semantic content of the pronoun need not come into play (as when the antecedent denotes an inanimate). But there are interesting cases where a clash with the potential semantic content of the pronoun is sufficient to make a sentence unacceptable, as in the following German example (Bosch 1988: 225):

> (38) Wenn du die   Mutter von dem   Bolzen
> if   you the.FEM nut   from the.MASC bolt
> lösen   willst, musst du *IHN   festhalten
> to.loosen want must you IT.MASC hold
> und *SIE   nach rechts drehen.
> and IT.FEM to   right to.turn
> 'If you want to loosen the nut from the bolt you must hold IT and turn IT to the right.'

If the pronouns are stressed, as in this example (indicated by capitals), they must denote male and female, as in the following similar example, which is therefore fully acceptable:

> (39) Der Mann stritt   sich mit seiner Freundin,
> the man   argued self with his   girl.friend
> weil   SIE   noch in ein anderes Lokal
> because SHE yet   in an other   pub
> wollte   und ER keine Lust mehr hatte
> wanted and he no   desire more had
> 'The man had a row with his girl friend, because SHE wanted to go on to another pub and HE didn't feel like it any more.'

Clearly then, semantic considerations are of greater importance for the personal pronoun than for any other target.

We saw earlier that personal pronouns are the targets most likely to take semantic agreement, and we have just observed how the clash with the semantic content of personal pronouns can make sentences unacceptable. Furthermore, the distribution of possible forms of the personal pronoun when compared with other targets reveals differences which favour semantic criteria in the case of the personal pronoun. A clear example is Amo, a Niger-Congo language of Nigeria. According to Anderson (1980), there is a set of personal pronouns which can be used only for reference to humans. There is a second set of pronouns with a full set of gender distinctions. For referring to humans, both sets are available, but for non-humans only the second set can be used. And in Qafar the personal pronouns are used only for humans and sometimes for named domestic animals; otherwise a different, gender-neutral pronoun must be used. A clear case of the personal pronoun following semantic criteria, and to a greater extent than other targets, was examined in Mba (section 6.4.6). There the pronoun had fewer forms than certain other targets; on the other hand, several languages make more gender distinctions in the personal pronoun than elsewhere. Telugu is a clear case (section 6.3), and there are several further instances in Germanic languages. While English is an obvious example, more interesting systems are found in other Germanic languages like Swedish and Danish (Royen 1929: 328–9; Bechert 1982: 27–8). In attributive position two forms are distinguished: the article *det* for the neuter gender, and *den* for the other nouns, in what is somewhat confusingly called common gender (see section 5.3.1); nouns denoting humans are in this common gender, but so are some nouns which denote non-humans. The pronoun, however, distinguishes four forms; Danish has *han* 'he' for male persons, *hun* 'she' for female persons, *den* 'it' for remaining nouns of common gender and *det* 'it' for neuter nouns. Thus the choice of pronoun is more firmly based on semantic considerations than is the choice of article. And in Romance, we find that French, at least in the colloquial register, is increasingly using *ce* and *ça* 'that' for non-human referents (Harris 1978: 120–2). The result is that the normal pronouns *il* 'he' and *elle* 'she' are specialized for humans and hence the choice of pronoun is a more semantic choice than is the case for other agreement targets. The fact that demonstratives may become anaphoric pronouns, but with restrictions in their use to, say, humans, is a possible source for gender systems. We return to this point in section 10.2.1.

We have seen that the personal pronoun has a special place in the Agreement Hierarchy. This is because there is, as mentioned earlier, no definable limit for its separation from the antecedent. Its form can be determined both by the antecedent and by the referent; given that the referent may be denoted by nouns of different genders, there is pressure towards personal pronouns being determined semantically; their use as deictics creates a similar pressure, since here their semantic content comes to the fore. Moreover, as Givón (1976: 171–2) suggests, the agreement features of pronouns represent just the most general semantic features of nouns. The fact that pronoun systems are of this type, he claims, allows the antecedent to be identified without the great proliferation of pronouns which would result if, instead, the more specific features were used. We turn next to the role of the Agreement Hierarchy in gender change and we shall see again the special importance of the personal pronoun.

8.3 Diachrony

We should now consider how the Agreement Hierarchy helps us to understand the way in which nouns can change their gender; if small numbers of nouns are involved the effect on the system will be negligible, but if several nouns follow the same path then the assignment system itself may change. We have already noted the importance of the personal pronouns, and indeed gender change regularly starts from the rightmost position on the Agreement Hierarchy. This is because a personal pronoun used deictically may take a gender form which differs from that which it would take if used anaphorically, in a similar external context but after the introduction into the linguistic context of a noun whose semantic and formal features are not fully consistent. The discrepancy between the two gender forms of the pronoun becomes sharper in situations where it is not clear whether the pronoun is being used anaphorically or deictically (for example, when a possible antecedent has become remote in the discourse).

We begin with a situation where semantic agreement is extremely restricted, but where the very first stage in gender change can be observed. In the Bantu language Chichewa strict syntactic agreement is the norm; there are several nouns which denote humans, yet take agreement according to the gender assigned from their morphological class, rather than taking 1/2 agreement as do most nouns denoting humans. Thus there are a few nouns which denote humans but which have the morphological form of gender 9/10, and these normally take gender 9/10 agreements. Similarly, there are nouns denoting humans with the prefixes *chi/zi* (the morphological form of gender 7/8) which normally take gender 7/8 agreements; there are also diminutives formed from nouns denoting humans, which normally take the agreements of gender 12/13. Let us begin with the diminutives. *Kamwana* 'small child' or 'infant' takes agreements of gender 12/13 (data from Corbett & Mtenje 1987: 11–13):

> (40) kamwana ko-kongola ka-ku-gona
> small.child 12-pretty   12-PRES-sleep
> 'The pretty small child is sleeping.'

Gender 1/2 agreements are ungrammatical:

(41) *kamwana a-kongola a-ku-gona
     small.child 1-pretty   1-PRES-sleep
     'The pretty small child is sleeping.'

Similarly with the relative pronoun, gender 12/13 agreements are found:

(42) kamwana ka-mene ka-ku-gona
     small.child 12-who 12-PRES-sleep
     'The small child who is sleeping.'

(43) *kamwana a-mene a-ku-gona
     small.child 1-who 1-PRES-sleep
     'The small child who is sleeping.'

Subject pronouns are normally dropped in Chichewa; however, the form of emphatic pronouns, and of the subject agreement marker when no pronoun is included, are both normally of gender 12/13. Yet gender 1/2 agreements are also possible, when the target is sufficiently separated from the controller:

(44) kamwana ka-mene ka-ma-gona   mu-nyumba
     small.child 12-who 12-HABIT-sleep in house
     umu ka-mene ka-ma-pita ku sukulu ku London,
     this 12-who 12-HABIT-go to school in London

$$\text{mai} \quad \text{ake a-ma-} \begin{Bmatrix} \text{ka} \\ \text{mu} \end{Bmatrix} \text{-konda} \begin{Bmatrix} \text{iko(ko)} \\ \text{iye(yo)} \end{Bmatrix}$$

     mother its 1-HABIT-AG-love   it
     'The small child who sleeps in this house who goes to school in London – its mother loves it.'

In (44), the object pronoun *iko* (which has the optional extension *ko*) and the object marker *ka* show agreement as for gender 12/13, while *iye(yo)* and *mu* are gender 1/2 forms. When we substitute the word *chitsilu* 'fool' (morphologically gender 7/8), then the switch to semantic agreement is not possible in an example similar to (44):

(45) chitsilu chi-mene chi-ma-gona mu-nyumba umu
     fool   7-who   7-HABIT-sleep in-house   this
     chi-mene chi-ma-pita ku sukulu ku London, galu
     7-who   7-HABIT-go to school in London dog
     wa-ke a-ma-chi-konda icho(cho) /
     1-his 1-HABIT-7-love 7.him
     *a-ma-mu-konda iye(yo)
     *1-HABIT-1-love   1.him
     'The fool who sleeps in this house who goes to school in London – his dog loves him.'

However, when the pronoun is yet further removed from the antecedent, semantic agreement becomes a possible alternative:

(46) chitsilu chi-mene chi-ma-gona mu-nyumba umu
     fool   7-who   7-HABIT-sleep in-house   this
     chi-mene chi-ma-pita ku sukulu ku London, galu
     7-who   7-HABIT-go to school in London dog
     wa-ke a-ma-chi-konda ndipo mai   a-ke
     1-his 1-HABIT-7-love and   mother 2-his
     a-ma-bvomera-di   kuti a-na-chi-ona
     2-HABIT-agree-indeed that 2-past-7-see
     icho(cho) chi-ku-yenda ndi galu yo
     7.him   7-PRES-walk with dog that
     (*or* a-na-mu-ona iye(yo) a-ku-yenda ndi galu yo)
        2-past-1-see 1.him 1-PRES-walk with dog that
     'The fool who sleeps in this house, who goes to school in
     London – his dog loves him and indeed his mother agrees that
     she saw him walking his dog.'

Here a switch to semantic agreement is possible: *iye(yo)* may be used in the last part of the sentence, and then, of course, the following verb is also in the semantic (gender 1/2) form. (The class 2, plural, agreements with *mai* 'mother' indicate respect.) Not surprisingly, the switch to semantic agreement in longer sentences is also possible with *kamwana* 'small child'. With a noun like *nkhalamba* 'old person', the switch from gender 9/10 to gender 1/2 is acceptable in sentences similar to (46), and is marginally possible in sentences like (44), but the result in the latter is less good than with *kamwana*. Thus the switch is easiest with *kamwana* (gender 12/13) 'small child', less so with *nkhalamba* (gender 9/10) 'old person' and most difficult with *chitsilu* (gender 7/8) 'fool'.

These examples provide interesting support for the claim of the Agreement Hierarchy. Semantic agreement (gender 1/2 agreement with nouns which belong in other genders but which denote humans) is only a marginal phenomenon with these particular nouns (unlike *ngwazi* 'hero' discussed earlier). Nevertheless, the one position in which semantic agreement is possible is in the (emphatic) personal pronoun (and, of course, in agreements dependent on it or on a dropped pronoun). In Chichewa we can observe the very beginning of a possible change. Noun phrases headed by nouns like *kamwana* 'small child' can take agreement in a gender which differs from their normal gender, provided there is a target which is sufficiently removed from them. (A comparable example from the Kru language Godie is quoted by

Marchese (1988: 332–3).) Such nouns may function as 'Trojan horses' (discussed in section 4.5), and give rise to more dramatic realignments of genders. Other cases where semantic agreement is possible only for the personal pronoun were considered in section 8.1.1; they included French titles and German *Mädchen* 'girl'. In such circumstances there is the potential for further change, but it is not inevitable that semantic agreement will spread into other target types.

In some instances further change does occur: Serbo-Croat nouns like *gazda* 'landlord' and Russian *vrač* '(woman) doctor', which we analysed in section 8.1.1, are just such examples. In the case of *gazda*, semantic agreement is now normal in the singular and it is the plural which is of interest. There semantic agreement is possible in all positions on the hierarchy, and there is evidence that it has become more dominant since the last century. But it has some way to go in order to take over completely. With Russian *vrač*, too, semantic agreement is possible at all four positions, and there is evidence that it has become more frequent in the recent past. However, it also is far from having taken over completely. This is a change that we can observe in mid-course. If we plot the year of birth of Panov's informants (from the survey quoted in section 8.1.1), we obtain the picture in figure 8.2 (Corbett 1983a: 36).

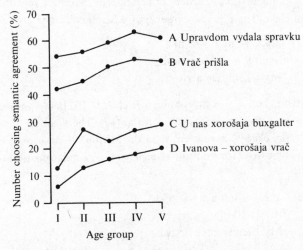

Figure 8.2 *Agreement with Russian hybrid nouns (by age of speaker)*

Glosses: A *Upravdom vydala spravku* 'the house manager issued a certificate'; B *vrač prišla* 'the doctor came'; C *u nas xorošaja buxgalter* 'we have a good accountant'; D *Ivanova – xorošaja vrač* 'Ivanova is a good doctor'.

Sentences A and B show predicate agreement, and, as expected, semantic agreement is found considerably more frequently here than when attributive modifiers are involved (C and D). We see a fairly steady rise in the acceptability of semantic agreement as we consider increasingly younger informants. However, the youngest group was slightly less ready to accept semantic agreement in the predicate than the older group. It has been suggested, quite plausibly, that this may result from schooling (Panov 1968: 31). These were the speakers who might still remember the normative rules learned at school. These two cases, from Serbo-Croat and Russian, show gender change near the middle point. Semantic agreement is common overall, but syntactic agreement is common too (their relative distribution being constrained by the Agreement Hierarchy). We now go on to examples where gender change is near the end point.

There is considerable evidence for the last stages of gender change from Bantu languages. Data are from Wald (1975), who investigated various Bantu languages spoken on the coast of Kenya and northern Tanzania, and in neighbouring areas (over thirty languages in all). The dominant language of the area is Swahili, commonly used as a lingua franca. Our account of Swahili in section 3.1.2 included a slight oversimplification when we stated that nouns denoting animates take gender 1/2 concords irrespective of their morphological class. There is one target type where exceptions are found:

> (47) rafiki y-angu a-mefika
>   friend 9-my   1-arrived
>   'My friend has arrived.'

Rafiki 'friend' belongs in morphological class 9/10. Being animate, it takes 1/2 agreements, as in the predicate verb in (47). The position in which it can take syntactic, class 9, agreement is in the attributive position, provided the target is a possessive, for example *y-angu* 'my'. A similar possibility occurs in the plural:

> (48) rafiki   z-angu wa-mefika
>   friends 10-my 2-arrived
>   'My friends have arrived.'

Gender 9/10 nouns do not mark plurality. However, the verb shows class 2 concord (as expected for an animate) but the attributive possessive stands in the syntactically agreeing class 10. Similar examples exist with nouns denoting humans in morphological class 5/6. Note, however, that if another modifier intervenes between the noun and the possessive, then animate concord is required (Zawawi 1979: 89):

(49) rafiki mw-ema w-angu
     friend 1-good   1-my
     'my good friend'

(50) *rafiki mw-ema y-angu
     friend 1-good   9-my
     'my good friend'

This conforms with our account of stacking in section 8.1.2. With non-human animates in gender 9/10, syntactic agreement remains *possible* only in the plural (for reasons for this discrepancy see Wald 1975: 284–5):

(51) ng'ombe z-angu wa-mefika
     cows   10-my 2-arrived
     'My cows arrived.'

Note that the syntactically agreeing form *z-angu* in (51) is acceptable but not preferred in urban Swahili; *w-angu* (class 2, identical to class 1) is the preferred form there (Wald 1975: 285, 290, 299 and especially page 311). For speakers who accept only *w-angu*, nouns like *ng'ombe* are in gender 1/2 (as our account in section 3.1.2 suggested); they are assigned to that gender by the semantic assignment rule, which overrides the fact that they are morphologically in class 9/10. For those for whom *z-angu* is still possible, *ng'ombe* and similar nouns are hybrids, taking almost all their agreements as gender 1/2 nouns but having 9/10 still possible in certain attributive modifiers.

Wald gives data from different languages on the last five stages in the loss of the old syntactic agreement in such cases. All the languages in question have gone well beyond the Chichewa situation, described earlier, in that semantic agreement is possible in the predicate. There are languages which allow semantic agreement provided it is not in attributive position. One such is Kimbundu (Mbaka dialect) spoken in northern Angola, and so outside the coastal area on which Wald concentrated. *Kilumba* 'girl' must take syntactic agreement in attributive position:

(52) kilumba ki-na (*u-na)
     girl   7-that (1-that)
     'that girl'

In the predicate, syntactic and semantic agreement are both acceptable:

(53) kilumba ki-na ki-amwiza/u-amwiza
     girl   7-that 7-come   1-come
     'That girl is coming.'

In Sambaa and Zigua too (both languages of northern coastal Tanzania) semantic agreement is tolerated but not in attributive position. Moving on a stage, we find that in Chonyi (Northern Miji Kenda group of Kenya), semantic agreement has reached the attributive position. Then in Kami (mid-coastal area of Tanzania) semantic agreement has become obligatory (rather than just possible) in the predicate:

> (54) mbudzi dz-angu wa-gomba ng'ombe dz-ako
> goats 10-my 2-attacked cows 10-your
> 'My goats attacked your cows.'

Syntactic agreement of the predicate (*dzi-gomba*, class 10) was not accepted. For attributives (other than the possessive), both forms were accepted:

> (55) ng'ombe dz-angu n-hulu/wa-kulu
> cows 10-my 10-big 2-big
> 'my big cows'

The next stage again is that found in urban Swahili, where semantic agreement is obligatory in all target positions, except in attributive possessives (as illustrated in sentence (48)). This is evidence for a finer division of the Agreement Hierarchy since attributive possessives are being treated differently from other attributives (a point reinforced by (55) above). The final stage is that in which gender 1/2 concords are obligatory in all positions including the attributive possessive. This situation is found in Bondei (a language of northern coastal Tanzania). Thus *mbuzi* 'goat', once a 9/10 gender noun, now takes exclusively 1/2 gender agreements, just like nouns denoting humans. It is remarkable to be able to identify such small stages in a linguistic change still evident in neighbouring languages. And, what is even better, the stages just described can be identified geographically: semantic agreement in these cases originated in the coastal area and spread further inland, with Swahili bilingualism being the main stimulus (Wald 1975: 312).

Once semantic agreement has reached all agreement targets, then the nouns involved take a consistent agreement pattern, that of gender 1/2. They are therefore established as members of gender 1/2 and so the question of semantic agreement disappears. Nevertheless, their morphology does not match that of the majority of nouns in gender 1/2; nouns originally from 9/10 do not take prefixes, while those in gender 1/2 typically have distinct singular and plural prefixes. This situation is not uncommon and appears to be quite stable: in Latin we find nouns like *agricola* 'farmer', which decline exactly like nouns which are feminine, but which take consistent masculine agreements. Similarly Russian *djadja* 'uncle' and several other nouns are morphologically like feminines but are consistently masculine in gender. Thus it is perfectly possible for nouns to belong to a morphological class which is out of step with their gender, and this situation may remain unchanged. There are cases, however, where such nouns adjust their morphology to become more like the majority of nouns in their new gender. In languages of southern coastal Tanzania and extending into Mozambique, nouns which were formerly in gender 9/10 but which now take 1/2 agreements take the class 2 prefix in the plural; the following example is from Makonde, Mawia dialect, spoken in northern Mozambique (Wald 1975: 277–9):

(56) βa-ng′ombe a-βa
2-cows   2-these
'these cows'

It is understandable that this change should occur in the plural first since by adding a plural prefix such nouns mark number (like gender 1/2 and unlike their original gender 9/10); it would be unusual to have a prefix for the singular but not for the plural. The final stage is for the class 1 prefix to be adopted in the singular. This has occurred in Luguru; this is the majority language of Morogoro in Tanzania and it is in close contact with the coast, where Swahili in spoken (Wald 1975: 277). In this language there are forms such as *yu-mbwa* 'dog' and *a-mene* 'goats' which were once in gender 9/10 and had the morphology associated with that gender, but which now are in gender 1/2 and have the same morphological behaviour as that of the other 1/2 gender nouns. They are fully integrated with gender 1/2 and, were it not for comparative and historical evidence, there would be no way of telling that they had ever had a different gender affiliation. Further examples of changes in agreement being followed by morphological adjustment are documented from other Bantu languages in Kadima (1969: 101–21).

It is tempting to suggest that morphological adjustment to the new gender comes *only* after agreement has been made consistent. The evidence for this claim is that we find the following three situations. First, we observe nouns which take consistent agreements in a gender which is not in harmony with their morphology and yet which do not adjust their morphology. This seems to be the case with Bondei *mbuzi* 'goat', and is certainly so with Russian *djadja* 'uncle'. And second, we find cases like Makonde *ng′ombe* 'cow' (and like Polish *poeta* 'poet'), where there are consistent agreements and where the morphology has been partly adjusted to fit with the gender. And third, we find complete morphological adjustment as in the Luguru case above. This would suggest that morphological adjustment is a possible consequence of agreement being made consistent. But it may be that in some cases the morphology changes at a stage when the noun is still a hybrid in terms of agreement (a possible though unclear Swahili case is cited by Zawawi 1979: 86, 91). Once, however, the morphology has been fully adjusted then we would expect consistent agreements to occur, since then both the semantic and the morphological assignment rules will assign the noun to the same gender and so there is no source for hybrid status.

We noted that when semantic agreement has spread along the hierarchy but has not taken over completely, the hybrid nouns involved may take a surprising set of agreements during the last stage of the process. The Swahili nouns discussed have syntactic agreement of attributive possessives only. Another example of a relic of syntactic agreement can be seen in French, where the noun *gens* 'people' retains feminine (syntactic) agreement, but only when its target is in attributive position, and only there provided a further set of rather remarkable conditions are fulfilled: the modifier must stand before the noun, and must not be separated from it by an adjective whose gender marking is ambiguous (Corbett 1979: 221–3); elsewhere the masculine is used.

Though the most detailed data on the stages of change come from Bantu languages, it is worth considering another group of languages which illustrate the place of the Agreement Hierarchy in gender change, namely the Temne cluster (data from Wilson 1962). In two of the languages of the group, Baga Maduri and Baga Sitemu, animacy plays no part; we assume this to be the original situation. In Landuma, as we saw in section 8.1.1, animate nouns which are not in morphological class 1/2, which is mainly associated with animates, take animate (semantic) agreement of the personal pronoun while preserving syntactic agreement elsewhere. This is the first stage in the change. In Temne and Baga Koba semantic agreement has spread to all agreement targets for animate nouns; irrespective of their morphology (class prefixes), animate nouns take 1/2 agreements. In these languages it is no longer necessary to talk of semantic agreement – these nouns have completely changed gender and are now in the 1/2 (animate) gender.

Change in gender caused by a conflict between semantic and formal gender assignment is usually initiated, as in the Temne cluster, by the personal pronoun. However, there is a case which appears to have resulted from the reverse development. We noted in section 4.5 that in some southern Polish dialects hypocoristics and patronymics used for girls and unmarried women (like *Zusię* 'Zuzia') follow a declension whose nouns are usually neuter (Zaręba 1984–5). A dramatic change resulted. A plausible scenario for it (though in this case the different stages cannot be documented) is that such nouns took neuter attributive modifiers and from there neuter agreements spread rightwards along the hierarchy. These nouns now take consistently neuter gender agreements. Furthermore, reference, including self-reference, to girls and unmarried women, is in the neuter gender. Hence, in these dialects the core meanings of the genders have changed, the feminine being for nouns denoting married women and the neuter for unmarried and young females. In a small dialect area a similar change has occurred, but starting this time from derivational forms which followed a typically masculine pattern; the result is that masculine agreements are now used for agreement with nouns and pronouns denoting girls and unmarried women.

Having charted these developments primarily in terms of the agreements at different positions on the hierarchy, that is, in terms of target genders, we will now look for the source of change from the point of view of controller genders; we must investigate the sources of hybrid nouns. While in section 8.1.1 we categorized hybrids according to the degree to which they permitted semantic agreement, we now consider their types and origins. Hybrid nouns may result from a conflict of different semantic assignment rules. In German, nouns denoting females are feminine and diminutives are neuter. Normally only one of these rules can apply; but in the case of *Mädchen* 'girl' both apply, and a hybrid results. Or the clash may be between old and new, in other words the assignment rule may change. We saw how in Bantu the rule that nouns denoting humans will be in gender 1/2 is being extended in several languages to include all animates (human and non-human). Such a change is likely to be set off by a 'Trojan horse' (section 4.5). Swahili had in gender 1/2 two exceptional nouns *mnyama* 'animal' and *mdudu* 'insect' (Wald 1975: 271–2); it is clear that such important nouns could attract others into the same gender. Personification may be another route. A similar change from human to animate as the criterion for a gender is also found in the Temne group. And in Konkani the change in meaning of *čeḍū* from 'child' to 'girl' might have produced an isolated hybrid noun. Instead, this noun retained its original neuter gender, but a new assignment rule was added, namely that nouns denoting young or relatively younger females are assigned to the neuter gender. This has produced several hybrid nouns like *awoy* 'mother'. More generally, transferred use is a frequent source of hybrid nouns. We saw cases where abstract nouns, like French *sainteté* 'holiness', are used as titles for humans. Less respectfully, nouns normally denoting non-humans may be employed for humans, like German *Drachen* 'dragon' hence 'shrew'. And conversely, as already mentioned, animals may be personified (notably in folk tales). In each case there is a potential conflict between the gender of the noun in its normal use and the gender expected in view of what it denotes in the transferred use. A more subtle effect can be observed in examples where a change in society leads to a change in usage of groups of nouns. Suppose we have nouns for professions whose members are exclusively or almost exclusively open to one sex. Such nouns will tend to include this restriction as part of their meaning. Thus French *ministre* 'minister', Russian *vrač* 'doctor' and similar nouns previously *de facto* denoted males engaged in the particular profession. What, then, when social conditions change, and women enter these professions? In some instances a new noun may be formed, by derivational means, which will be feminine (see Rothstein 1973 for some examples). But if this does not occur, then new hybrid nouns may emerge, as happened in the cases just mentioned.

Given that there are these various sources for hybrid nouns, it is worth asking why some nouns go on to change gender and so to cease being hybrids, sometimes relatively quickly, while others do not and remain as hybrids. There are two types of factors which can inhibit the change, semantic and formal. The semantic restraining factor is the retention by the noun in question of a meaning which is not involved in the change. Thus French *sainteté* 'holiness' still retains the original abstract meaning, which impedes change of the masculine/feminine hybrid title to masculine gender. Konkani *awoy* 'mother' is a hybrid when used of a young or relatively younger female. But this noun is by its nature frequently used also of an older female and in this use it retains its feminine gender, which hinders the progress of the hybrid towards neuter gender. And Russian *vrač* 'doctor' continues to denote male as well as female doctors, which holds back the move to feminine gender when denoting females. Contrast these with the change we observed in various Bantu languages. As nouns denoting animals move from their original gender to the gender previously for nouns denoting humans, there is no conflict of meaning within the individual lexical items. Thus Bondei *mbuzi* 'goat', now in the animate gender (which was previously the human gender), did not have to compete with some other meaning of the noun. Rather, the meaning of the genders changed and this noun, like several others, moved completely into the newly appropriate gender.

The other type of hindrance to gender change is formal. If the noun has a morphological or phonological marker according to which it should be assigned to the 'old' gender, it will transfer less readily than a similar noun without. For example, German *Mädchen* 'girl' has the diminutive suffix *-chen*, which is a marker of neuter gender. Russian *vrač* '(woman) doctor' belongs to declensional type I, whose nouns are normally masculine. And French *sainteté* 'holiness' is feminine by the regular phonological assignment rules. A helpful comparison is provided by Algonquian languages. There is a shared myth, that of the Rolling Skull, in which the Skull shows certain human behaviour, such as talking. In Fox, the form of the noun for 'head' used in the myth indicates an inanimate. When used in its special role in the myth, agreements are inanimate, except for anaphoric reference. But in Cree, gender is not evident from the singular form of most nouns (including 'head'), and so switching in gender to animate agreement occurs more readily (Ives Goddard, personal communication; for Cree examples see Straus & Brightman 1982: 116). Of course, the two types of hindering factor may interact; in both the Algonquian cases, gender change is hampered by the existence of the normal meaning of the word for 'head', while in Fox it is additionally restrained by the formal factor.

A final aspect of gender change, which links back to our discussion of the personal pronoun, is the situation in which gender agreement is in decline. We saw in section 5.5 that the partial loss of gender agreement can lead to quite variegated pictures. However, it seems that as long as gender agreement is retained in some targets, the personal pronoun will be one of them. An obvious example is English, where the personal pronoun retains three gender forms, and the only other forms are the animate/inanimate forms of the relative pronoun. When we examined the loss of gender markers in section 5.5, we noted how in various Indo-European languages and in some Niger-Kordofanian languages (Cross River and Kru languages), while gender agreement has been lost to varying degrees, it is generally retained in pronouns. Also within Niger-Kordofanian, Wilson (1971) shows the effect of gender loss in certain Gur languages. The process has gone further than in the previous examples and in some languages the pronouns no longer show all the original gender distinctions. The result is that the semantic criteria for use of these pronouns are clearer than in the original system (compare section 8.2). Thus, while Naudem preserves seven genders, in some other languages the system has been drastically reduced. In Dagbani the pronoun distinguishes (besides number) only animate from inanimate; in Dagaari there is an additional form for liquids. Mampruli has these distinctions and also a pronoun for neutral use (compare section 7.2.3). For additional data see Naden (1982).

8.4 Conclusion

We have seen that agreement with hybrid nouns depends in part on the particular target involved, and that variation in gender agreement is constrained by the Agreement Hierarchy. Within the hierarchy the personal pronoun has a special place, which is particularly evident when we look at language change. The personal pronoun initiates changes involving semantic agreement, while in cases of gender loss it is normally the last target to mark gender. We now turn to gender resolution, where the Agreement Hierarchy also has a role, since it helps to determine whether or not resolution will occur.

9

Gender resolution rules

Gender resolution is an area in which the data are often surprising and interesting, yet the topic is frequently left out of account. The term 'resolution rule' is taken from Givón (1970), and it refers to a rule which specifies the form of an agreeing element (or target) when the controller consists of conjoined noun phrases. If we have a sentence like *Mary and John are happy*, it is the number resolution rule which specifies the use of the plural *are*, rather than *is*. If we translate this sentence into a language like French, where predicative adjectives agree in gender, we need a gender resolution rule to establish the gender of the adjective, since one conjunct is feminine and the other is masculine. We shall also meet more complex cases: in Slovene, if a neuter singular and a feminine singular are conjoined, it is the gender and number resolution rules which specify the form of the target, say the verbal predicate, as masculine dual. This example, like the English one, illustrates the point that resolution rules do not operate only to resolve feature clashes but can also operate when conjuncts share features (singular in this example). It also suggests that this topic draws together problems connected with controller genders and target genders. While gender resolution will be our main concern, we should see it in the wider context of feature resolution (section 9.1). It is important to realize that resolution is generally not obligatory; instead agreement is often with one conjunct only, and so resolution is not involved. The question of when resolution occurs is therefore considered in section 9.2. Then we shall turn to the different types of gender resolution: some languages have rules which are basically semantic (section 9.3), others rely on a syntactic principle (section 9.4), and yet others show interesting combinations of the two principles (section 9.5). While gender resolution rules show considerable differences from language to language they are, nevertheless, determined by common semantic and functional considerations (section 9.6). The degree to which these common requirements can be met depends on the morphological possibilities of the given language. Finally, in section 9.7, we see how resolution rules can change over time.

261

9.1 **Features requiring resolution**

The features which most commonly require resolution are person, number and gender. These will be discussed in turn.

9.1.1 *Person resolution*

In person resolution the first person takes precedence over the second, and the second over the third, as we see in the following examples from Czech, a West Slavonic language (Trávníček 1949: 433; Bauernöppel, Fritsch & Bielefeld 1976: 164):

(1) já a   ty   zůstan-eme   doma
     I   and you will.stay-1ST.PL at.home
     'You and I will stay at home.'

In (1), one of the conjuncts is first person and this takes precedence over the second person, so that the verb is in the first person. In (2) it takes precedence over the third:

(2) bratr   a   já se   uč-íme
     brother and I   REFL teach-1ST.PL
     hrát   na klavír
     to.play on piano
     'My brother and I are learning to play the piano.'

In (3) there is no first person conjunct and so the presence of a second person determines the agreement form:

(3) tvůj otec   a   ty   jste
     your father and you are.2ND.PL
     si   podobni
     REFL.DAT alike
     'Your father and you are alike.'

The resolution rules may be stated as follows:

1. if the conjuncts include a first person, first person agreement forms will be used;
2. if the conjuncts include a second person, second person agreement forms will be used.
   (The default condition is that third person agreement forms are used.)

These rules are ordered, the second applying only when the first fails to apply. It has been claimed that rules equivalent to those given above are universal. The suggestion appears well founded, not only because such rules are reported frequently, but also because they match the hierarchy of reference which constrains pronominal systems independently of the resolution rules (see Zwicky 1977: 718, 725). First person pronouns can be used to refer to 'speaker plus listener' or 'speaker plus another person'. These meanings are matched by the resolution rule which determines that a first person conjoined with a second or third person is resolved as a first person. Similarly, second person pronouns can be used on their own to indicate 'listener plus other person'; this is reflected in the rule which resolves second and third persons conjoined into the second person. Thus the person resolution rules have a clear semantic basis. While it may be possible to maintain that person resolution always takes the form given above, it may be optional, like other types of resolution.

9.1.2 *Number resolution*

The typical number resolution rule can be stated simply: conjoined elements require a plural. The rules are a little more complicated in the case of languages with more than two grammatical numbers. Slovene, a South Slavonic language, has singular, dual and plural. If two singulars are conjoined, then the verb stands in the dual (examples from Lenček 1972):

(4) Tonček in   Igor sta   prizadevn-a
    Tonček and Igor are.DUAL assiduous-DUAL

However, if there are more than two nouns, as in (5), or if one of the nouns is in the dual (6), or with any other combination, then a plural predicate results:

(5) Tonček, Igor in   Marina so   prizadevn-i
    Tonček Igor and Marina are.PL assiduous-PL
(6) Marta   in   njegova brat-a
    Marta.FEM and his   brother-DUAL
    bodo   prišl-i
    will.PL come-PL
    'Marta and his (Igor's) two brothers will come.'

The number resolution rules are as follows:

1. if there are two conjuncts only, both of which are in the
   singular, then dual agreement forms will be used;
2. in all other cases, provided there is at least one non-plural
   conjunct, plural agreement forms will be used.

Of course, for languages with no dual category the first rule is not required. At first sight the restriction on the second rule appears superfluous; why should not instances where all the conjuncts are plural be covered by this rule? There is no need for a resolution rule in such instances and, as we shall see below, in some languages it is important to ensure that no resolution rule operates in these cases (see discussion of examples (39)–(42) and (54)). The second complication with number resolution is that it frequently does not apply. We discuss this problem in section 9.2. When it does apply, as was the case with person resolution, it produces forms which are semantically justified, that is, consistent with the meaning of the grammatical numbers.

9.1.3 *Gender resolution*

While person and number resolution rules produce forms which are semantically justified, gender resolution rules often do not. Take the case of a language with two genders, masculine and feminine, in which inanimates are distributed between the two genders. If two inanimates are conjoined, one masculine and one feminine, neither resolution will be semantically justified. As might be expected, therefore, gender resolution rules show great diversity. We shall describe the possibilities in the central sections of the chapter; but first it is essential to distinguish genuine cases of resolution from instances where the problem is simply avoided (because agreement is with one conjunct only).

9.2 **The application of resolution rules**

Not all languages with gender systems have gender resolution rules. There are languages where conjoining is severely limited. In Yimas, discussed in section 6.4.5, conjoined heads of noun phrases are prohibited (William Foley, personal communication); there is thus no place for any resolution rules. Then there are languages in which conjoining is generally unproblematic, but which have convergent gender systems (section 6.3.1) with only one target gender form in the non-singular number or numbers. German has three genders, but in the plural there is only one agreement form. It has person and number resolution but there is no need for gender resolution. Where different gender forms do exist in the plural, gender resolution may still not be required if a single form is used for all cases of conjoining. This is what happens in Lama, a Gur language of northern Togo, according to Yu (1988). And even in languages where conjunction is generally acceptable, agreement with conjoined structures may be barred under specific conditions. In Luganda, as we shall see in section 9.3, agreement with conjoined structures is possible provided all the conjuncts denote humans or none denote humans. Conjoining noun phrases headed by nouns denoting humans and non-humans produces unnatural forms, and the comitative construction is preferred. The same appears to be true of Temne (Delisle 1972: 132–5). Similarly in Ojibwa, conjoining animates and inanimates appears problematic (section 9.7). And in many languages where gender resolution occurs readily, particular sentences may cause difficulty when unlikely combinations of nouns are involved.

In languages which have no constraints on agreement with conjoined noun phrases, the application of the resolution rules may still not be automatic. Instead, it is usually possible for agreement to occur with one conjunct only, thus avoiding the resolution rules. The terminology has become confused here; we shall use 'resolution rule' to imply that feature computation (or equivalent) is involved; agreement with a single noun phrase means that no resolution has occurred. In the latter case, there is the question of which conjunct will control agreement (section 9.2.1). We must also investigate the factors which favour resolution as opposed to agreement with one conjunct only (section 9.2.2).

9.2.1 *Agreement with one conjunct*

When the resolution rules do not operate there is normally full agreement with one of the conjuncts. This can be illustrated from Swahili (Bokamba 1985: 45):

(7) ki-ti   na   m-guu wa meza u-mevunjika
    7-chair and 3-leg of table 3-be.broken
    'The chair and the leg of the table are broken.'

The verb agrees just with the nearer conjunct, headed by *m-guu* 'leg', which is a gender 3/4 noun; this noun and the verb are in the singular, so a literal translation would be 'is broken'. If we reverse the order of conjuncts, the agreement changes:

(8) m-guu wa meza na ki-ti   ki-mevunjika
    3-leg   of table and 7-chair 7-be.broken
    'The leg of the table and the chair are broken.'

Again agreement is just with the nearer conjunct. This situation may be represented schematically as follows:

(9)

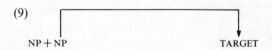

    NP + NP   TARGET

If resolution were to occur, then the 8 form (the plural used with the 7/8 gender) would be found.

265

Gender resolution rules

For resolution to fail to apply, and so for agreement to be with the nearest conjunct, is even more likely when the target precedes its controller. This can be illustrated from Serbo-Croat:

(10) toj službi   su   bil-e   posvećen-e   njene
     this job.DAT are been-FEM.PL devoted-FEM.PL her
     misli   i   njena osećanja...
     thoughts.FEM.PL and her feelings.NEUT.PL
     'To this job were devoted her thoughts and her feelings.'

(Andrić, Travnička Hronika)

This example, in which the verb agrees just with the nearer conjunct, may be represented as (11):

(11)

     TARGET   NP + NP

If gender resolution occurred in a similar sentence, the resolved form would be the masculine (as we shall see in section 9.7 below).

While agreement with the nearest conjunct is the most frequent result when resolution does not operate, this is not the only possible outcome. Agreement may also be with the first conjunct, which, when the subject precedes the verb, is not the nearest; this type of agreement can be found in Slovene, which is a close relative of Serbo-Croat (example quoted by Lenček 1972: 59):

(12) groza   in   strah   je
     horror.FEM.SG and fear.MASC.SG is
     prevzel-a   vso vas
     seized-FEM.SG whole village
     'Horror and fear seized the whole village.'

Here neither gender nor number resolution has operated (the resolved form would be the masculine dual) and the gender of the predicate indicates clearly that agreement is with the first conjunct, as shown in (13):

(13)

    NP + NP   TARGET

Note, however, that agreement with the nearer conjunct, as in (11), is much more common. Other languages which, like Slovene, allow the possibility of

266

agreement with a more distinct conjunct include Serbo-Croat (Corbett 1983b: 180) and Latin (Kühner & Stegmann 1955: 53, 55, 58–9). We conclude that, when the resolution rules do not apply, agreement is normally with the nearest conjunct, but that this is not the only possibility.

9.2.2 *Factors favouring resolution*

Our main interest is in what occurs when resolution takes place. But it is important to consider the factors which favour or inhibit it, to establish which types of sentence are most appropriate to use when investigating gender resolution. The factors which make resolution more likely to operate are of two types: those which involve the agreement controller and those which concern the agreement target. Controllers which denote animates, and controllers which precede their targets, are more likely to take resolved agreement forms than those which do not. Table 9.1 provides convincing evidence to substantiate this claim, which comes from number resolution in the predicate (number resolution occurs more frequently than gender resolution in running text in the languages which have been studied in the required detail). Data on Spanish (thirteenth to fifteenth centuries) have been derived from England (1976: 813–20); statistics on German are calculated from figures in Findreng (1976: 145, 165–6, 197); the Russian and Serbo-Croat data are taken from modern literary texts (Corbett 1983a: 105–35, 139–40). In each category we give the total number of examples and the percentage in which number resolution was found. For example, in the Medieval Spanish texts there were 288 examples of conjoined noun phrases which denoted animates and which preceded the predicate; of

Table 9.1 *Agreement with conjoined noun phrases* (*controller factors*)

| | Animate | | Inanimate | |
	N	% plural	N	% plural
Subject–predicate				
Medieval Spanish	288	96	243	31
German	1,095	96	1,702	67
Russian	115	100	67	85
Serbo-Croat	21	100	35	91
Predicate–subject				
Medieval Spanish	318	69	239	6
German	379	93	925	40
Russian	89	84	114	28
Serbo-Croat	23	70	62	26

these 96 per cent had a plural predicate (thus number resolution occurred in 96 per cent of the cases).

It is evident from table 9.1 that if the controller stands before the target, and if it denotes animates, these conditions indeed favour resolution. When both factors are present, all four languages give overwhelming preference to the resolved form. When either one is present, the resolved form is found in a significantly higher proportion of the cases than when neither is present. In Medieval Spanish and German the animacy of the subject exerts a stronger influence than its position, while in Russian the two factors are of about equal weight, and in Serbo-Croat precedence appears to be the more important factor. (In Spanish and German there is also evidence showing that concrete subjects take plural predicates more often than abstract subjects do.)

So much for controller factors; let us now consider the target. Resolution as opposed to non-resolution is a particular case of semantic versus syntactic agreement. It is therefore subject to the Agreement Hierarchy, discussed in chapter 8. As we move rightwards along the hierarchy, the likelihood of resolved (semantic) agreement increases monotonically. Data on number resolution in modern literary Russian are given in table 9.2 (derived from data in Corbett 1983a: 158). It can be seen that resolved forms show a monotonic increase. The fit is actually better than figures from this corpus indicate, for singular relative pronouns occur, if infrequently, and even a singular personal pronoun is possible, though exceptionally rare. For a confirming case, an account of how the Agreement Hierarchy constrains gender resolution in Serbo-Croat, see Corbett (1983a: 209–10). We have talked of resolution versus non-resolution as a single choice, and this can be justified as follows. When conjoined noun phrases show features which could trigger more than one of the types of resolution rules (for example, person and number), then the normal choice is either to apply all the appropriate resolution rules, or to apply no resolution rules and so for agreement to be with one conjunct only. Exceptions are rare (see Corbett 1983b: 182–3), and they all involve person resolution; no examples have been found of number or gender resolution failing to apply when another resolution rule has operated.

Table 9.2 *Agreement with conjoined noun phrases (target factors)*

Attributive		Predicate		Relative pronoun		Personal pronoun	
N	% plural	N	% plural	N	% plural	N	% plural
34	12	230	70	10	100	26	100

In this section we have investigated the application of the resolution rules – whether they apply, the factors influencing their application and the possibility of the operation of one resolution rule independently of the others. For the rest of the chapter we shall give most of our attention to those instances where the resolution rules do operate (and as a set), in order to establish what the resolved forms are and what rules are required to specify them. We have seen that in the case of person and number these are relatively straightforward. With gender resolution the situation is much more complex.

9.3 Semantic gender resolution

Gender resolution may follow two distinct principles: the semantic principle or the syntactic principle. Gender resolution by the semantic principle involves reference to the meaning of the conjoined elements even if this implies disregard for their gender. The syntactic principle operates according to the gender of the conjoined items, irrespective of their meaning. In this section we shall look at examples of semantic gender resolution. Here the meaning of the nouns which head the co-ordinated noun phrases determines the agreement form to be used. We find this type in Dravidian languages. Recall that in Tamil there are three genders, masculine (for nouns denoting male rationals), feminine (for female rationals) and neuter (for non-rationals), as described in section 2.1.1. In the plural, however, there are only two agreement forms, the rational (for masculines and feminines) and the neuter (see figure 7.11). When all conjuncts denote rationals (whether masculine, feminine or a mixture), the rational agreement form is used (Asher 1985: 67, 69, 72–3):

(14) raaman-um murukan-um va-nt-aaŋka
      Raman-and Murugan-and come-PAST-3RD.PL.RATIONAL
      'Raman and Murugan came.'

(15) akkaa-vum   taŋkacci-yum   iṇṇekki
      elder.sister-and younger.sister-and today
      kooyilukku poo-r-aaŋka
      temple.DAT go-PRES-3RD.PL.RATIONAL
      'Elder sister and younger sister are going to the temple today.'

(16) akkaa-vum   aṇṇan-um   neettu
      elder.sister-and elder.brother-and yesterday
      va-nt-aaŋka
      come-PAST-3RD.PL.RATIONAL
      'Elder sister and elder brother came yesterday.'

The conjunction is added to each conjunct. In (14) we have two masculines, in (15) two feminines, and in (16) one of each; in every case the rational form is used. When all conjuncts are neuter, then neuter agreement is found:

(17) naay-um puune-yum va-nt-atuŋka
     dog-and cat-and   come-PAST-3RD.PL.NEUT
     'The dog and the cat came.'

In this example we find the neuter plural (for many speakers the form would be *vantatu* 'came', with the neuter plural identical to the singular). The remaining possibility is the conjoining of a rational (masculine or feminine) with a neuter:

(18) *raaman-um naay-um va-nt-aaŋka
     Raman-and   dog-and come-PAST-3RD.PL.RATIONAL
     'Raman and the dog came.'

It is generally stated that such sentences are quite unacceptable (Arden 1942: 184–5; Asher 1985: 73, 185). Thus the system is entirely based on semantics:

1. if all conjuncts denote rationals the rational form is used;
2. if all conjuncts denote non-rationals the neuter form is used.

We do not need to specify that the plural is used since that will result from the number resolution rules. The rules as given do not allow for the combining of rationals and non-rationals; an alternative must be used, such as 'Raman came and the dog came' or 'Raman came, with the dog.' Sentences like (18) are unacceptable in the written language, and for some informants in colloquial use too. There is, however, a little evidence that for some speakers such sentences are possible in colloquial use (with rational plural agreement). Normally, however, an alternative is used. Speakers who allow (18) have a more permissive form of the resolution rules with an additional rule, which may apply when neither of the others can apply, that is for rationals conjoined with non-rationals:

3. otherwise the rational plural may be used (although an alternative construction is preferred).

It is interesting to compare the situation in Tamil with that found in Telugu. The latter is also a Dravidian language, with a gender assignment system extremely close to that of Tamil; but the morphology of target gender forms differs in that the feminine and neuter are not distinguished in the singular (figure 7.12). This morphological difference does not affect the gender resolution rules, as the following data show (Malathi Rao, personal communication). Again when all conjuncts denote rationals we find rational

270

plural agreement:

(19) tallii kuuturuu vaccaeru
  mother.and daughter.and came.3RD.PL.RATIONAL
  'Mother and daughter came.'

(20) tanDrii koDukuu vaccaeru
  father.and son.and came.3RD.PL.RATIONAL
  'Father and son came.'

(21) aayanaa aaviDaa vaccaeru
  he.and she.and came.3RD.PL.RATIONAL
  'He and she came.'

With neuters we find neuter agreement:

(22) kukkaa pillii vaccaeyi
  dog.and cat.and came.3RD.PL.NEUTER
  'A dog and a cat came.'

Let us now consider examples with rationals and non-rationals together:

(23) aaviDaa kukkaa vaccaeru
  she.and dog.and came.3RD.PL.RATIONAL
  'She and the dog came.'

According to Malathi Rao (personal communication), it is not uncommon to hear such sentences in colloquial speech (in spite of the views of grammarians). However, it is more common to use a different construction; alternatives would be, literally, 'she with dog came', 'she dog bringing came'. Thus the rules are as in Tamil: if all conjuncts denote rationals, the rational form is used, and if none denote rationals the neuter is used. For a mixture, a different construction is preferred, but if conjoining is employed then the rational agreement forms will be selected.

 While the resolution rules we have just examined are clearly based on semantics, this is hardly surprising since the gender of nouns in Dravidian languages is intimately linked with their meaning (their assignment systems are of the strict semantic type). We now move on to languages where meaning and gender are not so tightly linked but where we still find semantic resolution rules. One such is the North-East Caucasian language Archi. Of all the Caucasian languages, Archi is the only one on which details of gender resolution are available (data from Kibrik 1977b: 186–7, superseding Kibrik 1972: 128). As described in section 2.2.5, Archi has four genders: I male rational; II female rational; III some animates and some (larger) inanimates; IV residue. There is a handful of nouns which do not fit into the main genders (belonging to inquorate genders or having multiple gender). The situation is slightly complicated by the fact that agreement in person uses the same markers as agreement in gender. If we accept the analysis given in section 5.3.3, which recognizes the category of person in Archi, then person resolution is standard and, as we shall see, the account of gender resolution is simple (which is certainly not the case unless person is separated out). In the first example we have nouns from genders I and II:

> (24) dija-wu x̄ₒonnōl-u x̄ₒak b-i
> father.I-and mother.II-and near I/II.PL-are
> 'Father and mother are near.'

The conjunction *-u* 'and' (or *-wu* after a vowel, as in *dija-wu*) is added to each conjunct, as was the case in Dravidian languages. The verb has the agreement marker *b-* which serves as the plural for both gender I and gender II. The other agreement marker is Ø-, for genders III and IV (section 6.3.2). Since both conjuncts in (24) are headed by nouns in genders I and II it is not surprising to find the I/II plural form. Let us now include a conjunct from a different gender:

> (25) dija-wu dogi-wu x̄ₒak b-i
> father.I-and donkey.III-and near I/II.PL-are
> 'Father and the donkey are near.'

The presence of a gender III noun does not affect the agreement; the same can be observed with a gender IV noun:

> (26) dija-wu motōl-u x̄ₒak b-i
> father.I-and kid.IV-and near I/II.PL-are
> 'Father and the kid are near.'

Motol 'kid' denotes a young animal and so is in gender IV, but we still find gender I/II agreement. It must be asked, however, whether it is significant that all the examples so far have involved animates exclusively. It is not, as shown by an example including an inanimate noun:

> (27) dija-wu marzi-k'olōr-u x̄ₒak b-i
> father.I-and loom.IV.PL-and near I/II.PL-are
> 'Father and the loom are near.'

Marzi-k'olor 'loom' always takes plural agreement. It denotes an inanimate, and so the fact that we still find gender I/II agreement suggests that the significant factor in the examples so far is the presence of at least one conjunct denoting a rational. To demonstrate that the distinction is rational versus non-rational rather than animate versus inanimate, we take examples where we have an animate but no rational (all conjuncts are from genders III and IV):

(28) dogi-wu   motōl-u   x̄₀ak ∅-i
donkey.III-and kid.IV-and near III/IV.PL-are
'The donkey and the kid are near.'
(29) dogi-wu   marzi-k'olōr-u   x̄₀ak ∅-i
donkey.III-and loom.IV.PL-and near III/IV.PL-are
'The donkey and the loom are near.'

Thus III/IV agreement is found when there are no conjuncts denoting rationals. It could be argued that the rules should refer to genders (I, II, III and IV), rather than to the semantic distinction rational/non-rational. The analysis based on the latter distinction is shown to be simpler by examples like the following:

(30) xalq'-u   dogi-wu   x̄₀ak b-i
people.III-and donkey.III-and near I/II.PL-are
'The people and the donkey are near.'

Xalq' 'people' is one of only two nouns which take gender III agreement when singular, and gender I/II agreement when plural. If the resolution rules referred to gender, a special stipulation would be required for this small group of nouns. The significant point is that they denote rationals, and so follow the general rule, provided this is formulated in semantic terms:

1. if there is at least one conjunct denoting a rational or rationals, then gender I/II agreements will be used;
2. otherwise gender III/IV agreements will be used.

We have then a language with predominantly semantic gender assignment rules (though not strictly semantic), and its resolution rules are most simply stated purely in semantic terms.

The most familiar examples of semantic resolution are found in Bantu languages. These usually have several genders, which correspond to semantic classifications only partially: nouns of the 1/2 gender are human, but not all nouns denoting humans belong to the 1/2 gender (see sections 3.1.2 and 5.2.2). For gender resolution, the important thing is whether a noun denotes a human or a non-human, irrespective of its gender. This point is illustrated in data from Luganda, presented by Givón (1970: 253–4; 1971: 38–9).

(31) omu-kazi, es-sajja   ne   olu-ana
1-woman 5-fat.man and 11-thin.child
ba-alabwa
2-were.seen
'The woman, the fat man and the thin child were seen.'

Recall that the Bantu genders are given labels such as '1/2', which means 'takes class 1 agreements when singular and class 2 when plural'. In labelling nouns in these examples, where the prefix clearly indicates the gender, we give the appropriate class number. Agreement targets are also marked according to the class shown. Odd numbers usually indicate a singular and even numbers typically indicate a plural marker (but not always: 12 is a singular in example (32)). The resolved form for conjoined nouns denoting humans is the class 2 marker – the one used for agreement with plural nouns of the 1/2 gender. In (31) only one of the conjuncts belongs to that gender. In (32) none of the conjuncts belongs to the 1/2 gender, but as all denote humans the resolved form is again the class 2 marker:

> (32) ek-kazi,   aka-ana   ne olu-sajja
>   5-fat.woman 12-small.child and 11-tall.man
>   ba-alabwa
>   2-were.seen
>   'The fat woman, the small child and the tall man were seen.'

Example (32) proves that the use of the class 2 form as the resolved form is motivated by semantic considerations. If none of the conjuncts denotes a human, then the class 8 form is used, as in (33):

> (33) en-te, omu-su, eki-be ne
>   9-cow 3-wild.cat 7-jackal and
>   ely-ato bi-alabwa
>   5-canoe 8-were.seen
>   'The cow, the wild cat, the jackal and the canoe were seen.'

As was mentioned in section 9.2, conjoining nouns denoting a human and a non-human produces an unnatural result:

> (34) ?omu-sajja ne   em-bwa-ye bi-agwa
>   1-man   and 9-dog-his 8-fell
>   'The man and his dog fell down.'

The result is unnatural provided the class 8 (non-human plural) form is used; if the class 2 (human plural) form is used, an unacceptable sentence results:

> (35) *omu-sajja ne   em-bwa-ye ba-agwa
>   1-man   and 9-dog-his 2-fell
>   'The man and his dog fell down.'

The preferred alternative is the comitative construction:

> (36) omu-sajja y-agwa ne   em-bwa-ye
>   1-man   1-fell with 9-dog-his
>   'The man fell down with his dog.'

In Luganda, and widely in Bantu, the conjunction glossed 'and' in previous examples also means 'with' (its earlier meaning). As a result, the distinction between co-ordinate and comitative constructions is not always clear cut, and in practical terms great care must be taken in informant work. Example (36) has a simple subject, with which the verb can agree fully (in the singular) and the problem of resolution is avoided. The resolution rules can be stated as follows:

1. if all the conjuncts are semantically human, then the 1/2 form is used;
2. if none of the conjuncts is semantically human, the 7/8 form is used;
3. otherwise (that is, if the conjuncts are semantically mixed) the comitative construction is preferable; if gender resolution is forced, the form will be as in rule 2.

In these rules we specify the gender of the target as, for example, 1/2. This allows easy comparison with the sources quoted and with other languages for which we have given a gender name like masculine as the output. The point is that it is the number resolution rules which determine that the plural will be used, hence the 2 form (or the masculine plural, if masculine is determined by the gender resolution rules). The rules as stated allow for the 7/8 form to be used for mixed conjuncts if rule 2 is ignored. The same rules account for the Chibemba data given by Givón (1972: 82):

(37) im-fumu na i-shilu   ba-aliile
     9-chief and 5-lunatic 2-left
     'The chief and the lunatic left.'
(38) ici-tabo, ubu-sanshi na   ulu-balala fi-li kuno
     7-book   14-bed   and 11-peanut 8-be here
     'The book, the bed and the peanut are here.'

It is worth reviewing work on other Bantu languages. While it was Givón who highlighted the interest of the data, Horton (1949: 189) had earlier discovered similar data in Luvale. He gives rules like those of Givón, except that he does not report any problem about conjoining animates with inanimates. Voeltz (1971) found that for some speakers of Xhosa conjoining is severely limited. His analysis is discussed by Roberts & Wolontis (1974), who also give data on Tswana, and discuss Zulu briefly; more recently, Pullum & Zwicky (1986) have reviewed the Xhosa data. Bokamba

275

(1985: 38–44) claims that rules like those for Luganda also operate in Dzamba, Likila, Lingala and Swahili (except that in Swahili the first rule must refer to animate rather than human; see Brauner 1979: 423–5 for textual examples). In almost all the Bantu languages investigated we find evidence for semantic resolution rules based on the human/non-human distinction. Frequently there are problems, however. Judgements may be uncertain with particular sentence types, as already indicated, and it is important to bear in mind the possibility of comitative constructions and cases of agreement with the nearest conjunct. Corbett & Mtenje (1987) undertook a detailed analysis of Chichewa, and considered problems which are often ignored. First, there is the question of agreement with conjoined elements which individually take neutral agreement. As we saw in section 7.2.2.2, neutral agreement will still normally result. When infinitive phrases are conjoined they may retain the agreement as for an infinitive (class 15) or they may take the form for agreement with conjoined inanimates (class 8, which is identical to class 10 in Chichewa). Then there is the question of conjoined locative gender nouns (see section 6.3.3). Here the possibilities are very restricted; locatives conjoin only with other locatives and locative agreement is obligatory (thus these instances fall outside the general scheme). The most important cases to consider are those involving conjoined noun phrases headed by plural nouns, which are often left out of account. Consider the following Chichewa data:

(39) ma-lalanje ndi ma-samba a-kubvunda
    6-orange   and 6-leaf   6-are.rotting
    'The oranges and leaves are rotting.'

Here we find two nouns of the same gender, both plural, and the verb takes the same plural form. This was found fully acceptable, though it is not the form which would be predicted by the rules above. The nouns in (39) are from the 5/6 gender. Consider now a similar example but with nouns from the 1/2 gender: while most denote humans, just a few do not, as in this example:

(40) a-mphaka ndi a-galu a-kuthamanga
    2-cat   and 2-dog 2-are.running
    'The cats and dogs are running.'

Again there are two plural nouns and the verb takes the same gender. There are two different hypotheses which cover the data so far:

    A. If noun phrases headed by plural nouns of the same gender are conjoined they take the plural agreement form of that gender.

Clearly this is based on the controller gender. The second hypothesis refers to target genders:

> B. If noun phrases headed by plural nouns which would take the same target gender form are conjoined, then that target gender form will be used.

This hypothesis too covers the data. To choose between them we need to examine plural nouns which are of different genders but which take the same agreement form. This we can do taking nouns from (39) and (40); note that the target gender forms 2 and 6 can be distinguished elsewhere, but are identical in subject agreement:

> (41) a-mphaka ndi ma-lalanje a-li   uko
>   2-cat   and 6-orange AG-be there
>   'The cats and the oranges are there.'

The agreement marker on the verb is that corresponding to the plural both of gender 1/2 and of gender 5/6. This example demonstrates that the formulation of the rule given as B above is the correct one: when noun phrases headed by plural nouns which take the same target gender form are conjoined, that form will be used (the form zi-, which would be predicted by the usual rules, may be an alternative). This regularity holds, somewhat surprisingly, even when noun phrases denoting humans and non-humans are conjoined:

> (42) a-na   ndi ma-lalanje a-kusowa
>   2-child and 6-orange AG-be.missing
>   'The children and the oranges are missing.'

We started from the assumption that examples all of whose conjuncts denoted non-humans would take the agreement zi- (class 8, identical to class 10 in Chichewa). But the situation turns out to be considerably more complex; there are instances where zi- is not possible or is not the preferred form. The most consistent cases are those involving plural conjuncts: if each individually would take the same target gender form, then this will be preferred. Of course, this is a case of agreement with the nearest conjunct; gender resolution is avoided. We can say, then, that in Chichewa gender resolution can be triggered in two ways:

> 1. by the operation of number resolution (which can operate provided there is at least one singular conjunct);
> 2. by the presence of conjuncts which would require different target gender forms.

This has a somewhat surprising consequence. If conjuncts are plural and take the same target gender form, this will be used (though in some instances gender resolution is a less good alternative). Thus this purely syntactic strategy (which involves agreement with the nearer conjunct) prevents the (semantically based) gender resolution rules from operating in appropriate sentences. While these data show how complex the area is, they in fact concern the conditions – more restricted than usually believed – under which gender resolution operates. The actual rules of gender resolution are not affected (for very interesting relevant data from Kikuria see Gould 1988; see also Steinberg & Caskey 1988: 301–2). There is no doubt about the resolution rules being semantic, but the syntactic restrictions on their operation are more severe than was believed. We see now the justification for the restriction on number resolution (the requirement for a non-plural conjunct, section 9.1.2), since we can now claim that in examples like (42) no resolution applies, and agreement is with the nearest conjunct. If number resolution could apply, then gender resolution would also have to apply.

Shona, the last Bantu language we shall consider here, provides a different picture. Here semantic conflicts are not problematic, according to Hawkinson & Hyman (1974: 148–50). Conjoining noun phrases headed by nouns denoting humans and non-humans is acceptable, and class 2 forms are used (as for the plural of nouns denoting humans, contrary to the rules found for other Bantu languages). Given no noun denoting a human, but at least one denoting an animal, any conflict is resolved in favour of that noun (class 10 is the class used for the plural of nouns in the animal class); this leaves class 8 for conflicts involving inanimates only. These rules are very different from those of Luganda, both in the direction in which conflicts are resolved and in the fact that human, non-human animate and inanimate are distinguished; Shona certainly deserves further study. On the other hand, as in Luganda, a semantic principle is part of the solution.

The Bantu examples, like the Tamil, Telugu and Archi examples, show that resolution may operate according to the meaning of the conjuncts. While in the first cases semantic rules covered the data fully, in some of the Bantu languages, like Chichewa and Shona, there are syntactic restrictions which partially mask the semantic principle. There is challenging research to be done here. We now turn to examples where semantic considerations are apparently irrelevant.

9.4 **Syntactic gender resolution**

Gender resolution according to the syntactic principle means that the gender of the nouns involved is what counts, rather than their meaning. In French there are two genders; if conjoined noun phrases are headed by nouns of the same gender then that gender will be used (examples from Grevisse 1964: 306–7):

(43) un livre   et   un cahier
a   book.MASC and an exercise-book.MASC
neuf-s
new-MASC.PL
'a new book and exercise book'

(44) la misère   et   la ruine
the poverty.FEM and the ruin.FEM
général-es
general-FEM.PL
'the general poverty and ruin'

When the conjuncts are headed by masculine and feminine nouns, then a masculine form is used:

(45) un père   et   une mère
a   father.MASC and a   mother.FEM
excellent-s
excellent-MASC.PL
'an excellent father and mother'

(46) un savoir   et   une adresse
a   knowledge.MASC and a   skill.FEM
merveilleux
marvellous.MASC.PL
'a marvellous knowledge and skill'

Here the rules apply with the same effect to animate and inanimate nouns (though the relative frequency with which they apply may differ as discussed in section 9.2.2). The rules are evidently of the syntactic type; however, they can be stated in two different ways:

A: 1. if at least one conjunct is masculine, the masculine form is used;
2. otherwise the feminine is used.

Alternatively:

B. 1. if all the conjuncts are feminine, the feminine form is used;
2. otherwise the masculine is used.

Languages with resolution rules like those of French are common; they include Spanish, Latvian (Veksler & Jurik 1978: 351–2), Hindi (Černyšev 1965: 138), Panjabi (Tolstaya 1981: 67–8) and modern Hebrew (informants). For languages like these either set of rules is adequate; indeed, the two formulations are logically equivalent in cases where there are exactly two genders. However, we shall see that some other languages require rules of type A, in which one conjunct of a particular gender is sufficient to determine the agreement form, while others use type B, in which homogeneous controllers are distinguished.

Table 9.3 *Predicate agreement forms in Slovene*

	Singular	Dual	Plural
Masculine	bil	bila	bili
Feminine	bila	bili	bile
Neuter	bilo		bila

An example of a language for which one rule type is clearly preferable (type B in fact) is Slovene, which has three genders and three numbers. The predicate agreement forms are given in table 9.3 (compare figure 6.11; *bil* is the past active participle of the verb 'be'). The dual number forms can result from the operation of the resolution rules only if two noun phrases headed by singular nouns are conjoined (section 9.1.2), as in the following sentences (from Lenček 1972):

(47) Tonček   in   Marina
Tonček.MASC and Marina.FEM
sta prizadevn-a
are assiduous-MASC.DUAL

(48) Tonček   in   to   dekletce
Tonček.MASC and that little.girl.NEUT
sta prizadevn-a
are assiduous-MASC.DUAL

A masculine noun conjoined with a feminine, as in (47), or with a neuter, as in (48), requires a masculine dual predicate. When a feminine and a neuter are conjoined, the masculine dual is still found:

(49) ta   streha   in   gnezdo   na njej
that roof.FEM and nest.NEUT on it

mi   bosta ostal-a   v spominu
me.DAT will   remain-MASC.DUAL in memory

'That roof and the nest on it will remain in my memory'.

Similarly, two neuter singulars take a masculine dual:

(50) to   drevo   in   gnezdo   na njem
that tree.NEUT and nest.NEUT on it

mi   bosta ostal-a   v spominu
me.DAT will   remain-MASC.DUAL in memory

'That tree and the nest on it will remain in my memory'.

(We follow Lenček here, who gives the fullest and clearest account. For a
possible complication with examples like (50) see Corbett 1983a: 212, n. 6.)
The way in which the feminine/neuter dual form can result from the
resolution rules is if two feminines are conjoined:

(51) Marina   in   Marta   sta prizadevn-i
Marina.FEM and Marta.FEM are assiduous-FEM.DUAL

The most economical way to write the gender resolution rules is to use the
type B formulation:

1. if all conjuncts are feminine, then the feminine form is used;
2. otherwise the masculine is used.

The number resolution rules determine when the dual and when the plural
form are to be used. As this is so, the rules just given will also account for
gender resolution when the plural results. Thus in (52), all the conjuncts are
neuter, but the masculine plural form is required:

(52) to   okno,   drevo   in   gnezdo
that window.NEUT tree.NEUT and nest.NEUT

v njem mi   bodo ostal-i   v spominu
in it   me.DAT will   remain-MASC.PL in memory

Again, the feminine is possible only if all the conjuncts are feminine:

(53) Marina,   Marta   in   Marjanca
Marina.FEM Marta.FEM and Marjanca.FEM

so   prizadevn-e
are assiduous-FEM.PL

Note that in the rules given there is no recourse to semantic factors – gender is the determining factor.

The fact that rules given for gender resolution apply equally well for the dual and the plural suggests an interesting paradox. On the one hand, the resolution rules – specifically here the gender resolution and the number resolution rules – are independent of each other. Thus we have no rules which refer, say, to feminine plurals or neuter singulars. On the other hand they are interrelated in that if one type of resolution rule operates then all must operate where possible (compare section 9.2.2). Given a subject consisting of a feminine singular and a neuter singular noun, it is not possible to apply gender resolution (to give a masculine) but at the same time to fail to apply number resolution, and so to have a masculine singular predicate. This interrelation of the resolution rules helps explain the particularly interesting situation seen in (52), where gender resolution has applied, giving a masculine predicate, even though all the nouns are of the same (neuter) gender. Here number resolution is triggered by the presence of singular conjuncts; if one resolution rule operates then all must operate where possible; gender resolution does not include the possibility of assigning neuter plural endings in Slovene, but specifies the masculine (we discuss why this should be so in section 9.6.2 below).

Similar gender resolution rules are found in Serbo-Croat (though there the position is somewhat simpler, as Serbo-Croat has lost the dual; at the same time, there is an added complication in that the first rule allows interesting leaks, which we discuss in section 9.7 below). Consider now the situation when the subject consists of neuter plurals only, as in this Serbo-Croat example:

> (54) ta sećanja i razmatranja
> those memories.NEUT.PL and reflections.NEUT.PL
> sve su više ustupal-a mesto novim
> ever are more yielded-NEUT-PL place new.DAT
> utiscima
> impressions.DAT
> 'Those memories and reflections increasingly gave way to new impressions.'
>
> (Andrić, *Travnička Hronika*)

In sentences like this, we do not find the resolved form (the masculine plural *ustupali*) but the neuter plural. Here number resolution does not apply since all conjuncts are plural (this again is the reason for the restriction on number resolution in section 9.1.2) and so it does not trigger gender resolution.

Agreement is therefore with the nearer conjunct. However, it would be incorrect to claim that gender resolution can be triggered only by number resolution, as the following example shows:

(55) sve njegove molbe   i   uveravanja
     all his   prayers.FEM.PL and assurances.NEUT.PL
     ni-su   pomagali   ništa
     NEG-are helped-MASC.PL nothing
     'All his prayers and assurances did not help at all.'

(Andrić, Anikina Vremena)

Here we find feminine and neuter conjuncts and a masculine predicate, as required by the gender resolution rules. The correct generalization appears to be as follows. Gender resolution in Serbo-Croat can be triggered in two ways: either by the operation of number resolution (if one resolution rule operates, all must operate where applicable), or by the presence of conjuncts which would require different target gender forms. Sentence (54) does not meet either condition, and so gender resolution does not operate (and the neuter plural results from agreement with the nearer conjunct). These data are strikingly similar to the Chichewa data discussed earlier.

Serbo-Croat discriminates against the neuter plural, as it can arise only by agreement with the nearest conjunct and not from the operation of the resolution rules. Icelandic, however, favours it: the neuter plural is used for any mixture of genders (example (56) is from Jónsson 1927: 14, and (57) from Einarsson 1949: 133; the straightforward cases will not be illustrated):

(56) þau   (drengurinn og telpan)
     they.NEUT.PL (boy.MASC   and girl.FEM)
     eru þreytt
     are tired.NEUT.PL
     'They (the boy and the girl) are tired.'
(57) ég sá   á   og lamb,
     I saw ewe.FEM and lamb.NEUT
     bœði   svort
     both.NEUT.PL black.NEUT.PL
     'I saw a ewe and a lamb, both black.'

The resolution rules required for Icelandic are as follows:

1. if all conjuncts are masculine, the masculine is used;
2. if all conjuncts are feminine, the feminine is used;
3. otherwise the neuter is used.

In this section we have considered languages where the principle behind gender resolution appears to be purely syntactic; we shall see in section 9.6 that, while in cases such as these the mechanism is syntactic, the motivation is semantic and functional. Let us first consider cases where the syntactic and semantic principles are found together.

9.5 Mixed semantic and syntactic gender resolution

In this section we analyse three languages in which the semantic and the syntactic principles of gender resolution coexist. The first is Polish, a West Slavonic language; the possibilities for predicate agreement are given in table 9.4. *Był* is the past tense of the verb *być* 'be'.

Table 9.4 *Predicate agreement forms in Polish*

		Singular	Plural
Masculine	personal	był	byli
	non-personal		
Feminine		była	były
Neuter		było	

Polish has three forms for gender agreement in the singular; in the plural there is a division into masculine personal and the remainder. The masculine personal category comprises nouns which are of masculine gender and which denote humans: it does not coincide completely with the semantic criterion of male human but its relation to semantics is much closer than that of the genders in the singular. When in conjoined structures none of the conjuncts is headed by a masculine personal noun, then the non-masculine personal/feminine/neuter form is used (Kulak, Łaciak & Żelezkiewicz 1966: 249):

(58) siostry   i   matka   czytał-y
sisters.FEM and mother.FEM were.reading-NON_MASC_PERS.PL

If a masculine personal noun is present then the masculine personal form is used:

(59) brat,   siostry   i
brother.MASC_PERS, sisters.FEM and
matka   czytal-i
mother.FEM were.reading-MASC_PERS.PL

The resolution rules required appear to be as follows:

1. if at least one conjunct is masculine personal, then the masculine personal form is used;
2. otherwise the non-masculine personal form is used.

These rules are of the form labelled type A in section 9.4: the first rule picks out conjoined structures which include one conjunct of a particular type (and therefore 'mixtures' will be included); in type B rules, structures with homogeneous conjuncts are isolated. Unlike the French situation, we cannot rewrite these rules in the other form (1. if all nouns are non-masculine personal...) because there is no other motivation for labelling nouns as non-masculine personal in Polish.

Rules like those given above can be found in numerous sources; they also operate in other West Slavonic languages (Corbett 1983a: 193–6). However, Polish shows interesting exceptions. Consider the following example (Doroszewski 1962: 237):

(60) Hania   i   Reks
Hania.FEM and Rex.MASC
bawil-i   się piłką
played-MASC_PERS.PL REFL ball.INS
'Hania and Rex were playing with a ball.'

Reks is a dog (masculine but not personal). There is no masculine personal conjunct in (60), but the predicate is masculine personal. The status of sentences like (60) has been the subject of considerable debate. The most informative study of the question available, that of Zieniukowa (1979), describes responses to a questionnaire by thirty-one young people in their upper teens. For a sentence comparable to (60), only two informants used the non-masculine personal form (and one used a different construction). The masculine personal form, as in (60), is obviously the usual form. It cannot result simply from the presence of the noun *Hania* denoting a person, because in (58) both conjuncts denoted humans but a non-masculine personal form was used.

We must check whether the presence of a masculine animate is sufficient: in the following example both conjuncts are masculine animate:

(61) pies   i   kot
dog.MASC and cat.MASC
jedl-i   na podwórzu
were.eating-MASC_PERS.PL on yard
'The dog and the cat were eating in the yard.'

The masculine personal form (as in the example) was the majority choice in Zieniukowa's study, but seven informants chose the non-masculine personal form. Thus masculine animates are less likely to produce a masculine personal form than masculine animate plus feminine denoting a human. Feminine denoting a human conjoined with masculine inanimate can also result in a masculine personal form:

(62) mama,   córeczka   i   wózek
     mother.FEM daughter.FEM and pram.MASC
     ukazal-i   się nagle
     showed-MASC_PERS.PL REFL suddenly
     'The mother, daughter and pram appeared suddenly.'

In this example informants were equally divided between the masculine personal and the non-masculine personal *ukazały* (one informant chose neither).

The rules required to cover these examples (and other types described in Corbett 1983a: 197–200) are as follows:

1. if the subject includes a masculine personal conjunct, the predicate will be in the masculine personal form;
2. (optional) if the subject includes the features masculine and personal, whether these are syntactic or semantic, the predicate may be in the masculine personal form;
3. (optional) if the subject includes a masculine animate conjunct, the predicate may be in the masculine personal form;
4. otherwise the predicate will be in the non-masculine personal form.

The first rule, which accounts for the form used in (59), requires no further comment. The optional rules 2 and 3 both represent plausible weakenings of rule 1: in rule 2 the conditions apply to the subject as a whole rather than to a single conjunct and, more surprisingly, they allow semantic or syntactic (grammatical) features or a combination of these. Rule 3, on the other hand, retains the restrictions to a single conjunct but reduces the requirement from personal to animate. Rule 2 accounts for the form in sentence (62), while rule 3 has operated in (61). It is significant that when both rule 2 and rule 3 can apply, as in (60), then for Zieniukowa's informants the masculine personal form is almost obligatory. When none of these rules apply, the non-masculine personal form is assigned by rule 4, as in sentence (58). The rules refer both to gender and to semantic criteria. Thus Polish stands between the clearly semantic gender resolution found in languages like Tamil and the syntactic type found in languages like Slovene. It is perhaps worth noting that resolution operates also in quasi-comitative constructions in Polish (Dyła 1988: 385–6).

Latin shows a mixture of syntactic and semantic criteria of a different type. Always provided resolution occurs (in many instances it does not), conjuncts of the same gender take agreeing forms of that gender. This is resolution by straightforward syntactic rules and need not be illustrated again. However, when conjuncts are of different genders, then the resolved form to be used depends on whether the nouns denote persons or not. For persons the masculine is used:

(63) quam pridem   pater   mihi   et
     how   long.ago father.MASC me.DAT and
     mater   mortu-i   essent
     mother.FEM dead-MASC.PL were
     'How long ago my father and mother had died.'

For other conjoined elements the neuter is used:

(64) murus   et   porta   de   caelo
     wall.MASC and gate.FEM from sky
     tact-a   erant
     struck-NEUT.PL were
     'The wall and the gate have been struck by lightning.'

These examples are from Kühner and Stegmann, who state that when humans and non-humans are conjoined agreement is usually with the nearer noun, but resolution to the neuter plural is possible (1955: 44–52). The resolution rules are as follows:

1. if all conjuncts are masculine, then the masculine is used;
2. if all conjuncts are feminine, then the feminine is used;
3. if all conjuncts denote humans, then the masculine is used;
4. otherwise the neuter is used.

These rules are ordered; there is no need, therefore, to stipulate that the conjuncts in rule 3 are of mixed gender. Similarly, rule 4 will automatically cover cases of mixed gender and those where all the conjuncts are neuter. Thus Latin has two resolution rules based on the syntactic principle and one on the semantic principle.

Gender resolution rules

Rumanian exhibits a resolution system which is mixed in a similar way to that of Latin. It is of special interest because its gender pattern is a crossed three-gender system (figure 6.1). There are two sets of agreement markers, but three genders, the neuters or ambigenerics taking the same agreements as the masculine when singular and as the feminine when plural. How will resolution operate in these circumstances? It must be said that the position is far from clear, and conflicting statements can be found in the literature. In part, this is due to normative influence; in addition, certain combinations are generally avoided and sometimes agreement with the nearest conjunct is normal. The important point is that animates are treated differently from inanimates (a semantic distinction) while other (syntactic) rules refer to gender. For animates the position looks familiar (Mallinson 1984: 445–6):

> (65) fata   şi   femeia   sînt fericite
> girl.the and woman.the are happy.FEM.PL
> 'The girl and the woman are happy.'
>
> (66) băiatul şi   bărbatul sînt fericiţi
> boy.the and man.the are happy.MASC.PL
> 'The boy and the man are happy.'
>
> (67) acest băiat şi   această fată sînt frumoşi
> this boy and this   girl are happy.MASC.PL
> 'This boy and this girl are happy.'

With inanimates the picture is more interesting. Gruiţă (1981: 26–7) avoids some of the complications concerned with agreement with one conjunct by giving examples involving the personal pronouns. For all cases of mixed genders involving inanimates, the feminine is used:

> (68) uşa   şi   peretele...   ele...
> door.FEM.the and wall.MASC.the they.FEM.PL
> 'The door and the wall...they...'
>
> (69) peretele   şi   scaunul...   ele...
> wall.MASC.the and chair.NEUT.the they.FEM.PL
> 'The wall and the chair...they...'
>
> (70) scaunul   şi   masa...   ele...
> chair.NEUT.the and table.FEM.the they.FEM.PL
> 'The chair and the table...they...'

Now consider examples with inanimates where the conjuncts are headed by nouns of the same gender:

(71) nucul   şi   prunul…
     walnut.tree.MASC.the and plum.tree.MASC.the
     ei…
     they.MASC.PL
     'The walnut tree and the plum tree…they…'

(72) frigiderul   şi   televizorul…
     refrigerator.NEUT.the and television.NEUT.the
     ele…
     they.FEM.PL
     'The refrigerator and the television…they…'

(73) uşa   şi   masa…   ele…
     door.FEM.the and table.FEM.the they.FEM.PL
     'The door and the table…they…'

These examples show that the feminine is used (with inanimates) unless all conjuncts are masculine. We could give separate rules for animates and inanimates as follows:

1. if all conjuncts denote female animates the feminine is used;
2. otherwise if conjuncts denote animates the masculine is used.
3. if all conjuncts are of masculine gender the masculine is used;
4. otherwise the feminine is used.

Here the first two rules cover the animate cases, leaving the inanimates for rules 3 and 4. This set of rules can be collapsed as follows:

1. if one conjunct denotes a male animate then the masculine is used;
2. if all conjuncts are masculine, the masculine is used;
3. otherwise the feminine is used.

Rule 1 covers mixed animates and male plus male; rule 2 covers masculine inanimates (as in example (71)), and rule 3 the rest, that is, examples where all conjuncts denote female animates, where all are feminine and where the various mixtures of inanimates are found. There is some evidence that rule 2 is being lost; some find feminine agreement acceptable for conjoined masculines denoting inanimates. For further data and discussion see Windisch (1973: 34–46), Mallinson (1984: 445–9) and references there. The important thing is that when resolution occurs (and it is frequently avoided) both the semantic factor of animacy and gender have a role, as they did in Latin. The details are complex and deserve careful empirical study.

9.6 Strategies for gender resolution

In section 9.4 we observed that gender resolution rules may either specify that at least one conjunct be of a particular sort (type A), or that all the conjuncts be of a particular sort (type B). We found no examples of the logically possible type which would refer to the majority of the conjuncts being of a certain sort. One reason is that conjoining most often involves just two conjuncts; for example, Findreng (1976: 196) gives separate figures for the conjoining of two abstract nouns or more than two in German: 87 per cent of the cases (total 2,277) involved conjoining two elements only. Furthermore, the distinction between type A and type B rules is not a major one: while type A rules were postulated for Polish and type B for Slovene, the effect was the same: in both languages the masculine or masculine personal form is used as the dominant resolution form. We should therefore address the more basic question of why it is that different languages favour particular forms in their resolution rules. We shall see that there are two factors involved. First a particular form may be justified in semantic terms (compare 6.3.2 on target gender forms). That is, the form is simply the most appropriate in terms of its meaning. And second, forms may be favoured because they mark number (usually the plural number) clearly. Here there is a functional motive, but one which also stems from a semantic source, since in the languages in question number is generally more clearly related to meaning than is gender. Before examining how these two factors help us to understand the forms used in gender resolution (9.6.2), we should first consider an account which has been proposed more than once but which is inadequate (9.6.1).

9.6.1 *Markedness: an inadequate motivation*

Markedness has been invoked on several occasions to explain gender resolution, notably by Schane (1970), who attempted to extend markedness from phonology into French morphology and syntax. The claim is that the unmarked gender will be used as the resolved form. It is significant that such claims about markedness often relate to two-gender languages like French; given only two genders it is not surprising that various properties are found with a single gender (compare Roca 1989 on Spanish). Once we move to systems with three and more genders the clustering of properties no longer obtains. The phenomena discussed by Schane are taken from morphology, syntax and semantics; in each case the form considered unmarked according to the different criteria is claimed to correspond to the form used for gender resolution. We will attempt to relate these claims to the other languages we have investigated.

The morphological argument runs as follows: the masculine singular form of the adjective in French consists of the stem only: the feminine singular is the stem plus feminine marker /ə/; for the masculine plural the plural marker /z/ is added, while for the feminine plural /ə/ and /z/ are both added (various deletion rules then apply). Thus the masculine plural form is unmarked for gender in the most literal sense. In cases where gender resolution is required, the form used is equivalent to the morphologically unmarked form (Schane 1970: 291). Let us consider Slovene in these terms (table 9.3). Here the masculine singular is signalled by the stem only, but the plurals cannot be derived from the singulars by the addition of a plural marker as in French. If we try to substitute a more general claim, that the least complex form will be used (compare Schane 1970: 292) then Polish is a counter-example: the masculine personal form, used for resolution, frequently requires a mutation of a consonant, which is not found in the other forms.

Schane also considers phenomena which are syntactic in nature. Impersonal pronouns, which are neither masculine nor feminine, take masculine agreements. It may be added that elements such as infinitives, which do not bear a gender specification, take masculine agreements in French. However, in three-gender systems, like that of Slovene, such items are typically assigned to the neuter gender (unless there is a special neutral form, see section 7.2). Schane includes discussion of interrogative and indefinite pronouns, which require masculine agreements in French. In a three-gender system like that of Slovene, these also require masculine agreement forms when they denote humans, but neuter for inanimates. Thus the three-gender system does not have a single gender which is unmarked according to the different criteria.

Schane draws attention to a different phenomenon, concerning nouns and nominal adjectives referring to humans, and this proves significant. He points out that in French *les Américains* (masculine plural) 'the Americans' is unmarked in that it can denote both sexes, while *les Américaines* (feminine plural) denotes only female Americans (see section 7.3.1). It is not difficult to find similar examples in Slovene, and other languages under discussion, of masculine nouns which may denote people of both sexes. Examples like these had already been noted by Greenberg (1966: 30–1), who took from the Arab grammarians the notion of 'dominance', the use of one gender in place of both. We shall not use this term, since it covers only the most common of the means used to meet the situation which interests us. It is not necessary for one gender to dominate the other: as we shall see when we consider Icelandic, a third gender may be used. However, the relation of these cases to gender resolution certainly holds. If we discover the gender to which the gender assignment rules allot nouns which denote pairs or larger groups of both sexes, this will reveal the information we need about the semantics of gender, in a given language. In French, *les Américains* 'the Americans' is used to denote both males and females and is assigned to the masculine gender. (This was not spelled out in section 3.2.5, where the semantic assignment rules of French were of secondary interest. The first rule 'sex-differentiable nouns denoting males are masculine' should be interpreted as including nouns, such as *Américains*, which denote males, but not exclusively males.) This is a language-specific fact (though some will wish to relate it to more general questions of markedness). It is this specific semantic choice which is of help in understanding gender resolution. The gender required by the assignment rules will be favoured in gender resolution. This is one type of (language-specific) semantic justification for the use of a particular gender form in resolution. In the case of French, we observed that the masculine is used to denote humans of both sexes and that this is the resolution form for conjuncts of different genders. Note that it is semantically justified only for nouns denoting humans; when inanimates are conjoined we cannot make the same claim. However, in such cases gender has little or no semantic justification in any case. We claim, therefore, that it is the instances where a semantically justified form is possible which determine the resolution form. The remainder, for which neither form is semantically justified, merely conform with the semantically justified cases.

This appeal to a semantically justified form means that we do not have to try to identify an unmarked gender in each language and expect it to be used for gender resolution (we have seen that this approach fails). We shall discuss semantically justified forms for the different languages in turn. While we may view French examples like *les Américains* as instances of semantic neutral-ization, the important thing is simply that there are cases where the masculine refers to both sexes. The resolution form is established on that basis (the role of markedness is at best an indirect one). This view enables us to avoid a contradiction inherent in Schane's approach: if it is claimed that the form used for gender resolution will be the unmarked form, we would expect the same to be the case for person and number resolution. Yet in person resolution the first person is the favoured form, and this is a marked form. Similarly, the plural is the marked number in a two-number system but it is the resolved form. As the unmarked form and the resolved form coincide neither for person nor for number, it is not surprising that there is no direct correspondence between the unmarked gender and the gender resolution form. With person and number we saw that the forms used for resolution are semantically justified. It is wholly consistent, therefore, that semantic justification is the main factor in determining the form to be used for gender resolution.

9.6.2 *Semantic justification and clear marking of plurality*

We have claimed that the forms used for gender resolution are those which have semantic justification in a given language. While this is indisputable in the case of Dravidian languages, which have semantic-type gender resolution, how does it apply to languages of the syntactic type? The division into syntactic and semantic types of gender resolution refers to a difference in the way the rules operate in particular languages. This division refers to the nouns heading the conjuncts; it is concerned therefore with the syntactic and semantic properties of the controllers. In this section, however, we are concerned with the 'right-hand side' of the rule. Why is it that, given certain controllers, particular target gender forms are used? Here, I suggest, in all instances the first motivating factor behind the choice of the target form to be favoured by the resolution rules is semantic; this factor is the use of semantically justified target gender forms. In instances such as the use of the masculine in French, this basic principle of semantic justification has already been established: it depends upon the normal agreement with nouns which denote mixed groups (and so upon the assignment of such nouns). There is a second motivating factor at work, namely that the resolved form should bear a clear indication of number. This factor, clear marking of number, is a functional one. But it is also based on semantics because, as we discussed above, the use of a dual or plural with conjoined elements is semantically justified (while it may be that none of the gender forms would have any semantic backing). A form may be favoured either because it is at least partially justified in semantic terms or because it is a clear marker of number. Thus gender may be made subservient to number (a category which generally corresponds more closely to the real world). The extent to which these two principles are observed depends on the morphological possibilities of a given language. We will reconsider each of the languages analysed (though varying the order somewhat), bearing in mind that we must explain not only why certain forms are favoured for resolution but also why the others are used or are excluded.

Let us start with Tamil. As was shown in figure 7.11, there are two target gender forms in the plural: the rational (used for all nouns which denote rationals whether they take masculine or feminine agreements when singular) and the neuter (corresponding to the neuter in the singular number). Given that there are just two sets of markers available, and that their semantics are quite clear, it is natural that the rational form will be used for rationals (including masculine and feminine conjoined) and the non-rational form for others. A similar argument is appropriate for Telugu. When we turn to Archi, we note that though it has four genders, it also has only two target gender forms in the plural (see figure 6.12). Again it is no surprise that the one for controllers denoting humans is used (for conjuncts denoting males, females and mixed cases) and the marker for non-humans is used for cases where non-humans are involved (including cases of mixed gender). The use of gender I/II (human) markers for mixed human/non-human conjuncts is not quite so self-evident; there are, as we saw in example (30) and in section 7.3.2, nouns which denote humans yet which take gender III or IV agreements when singular and I/II when plural. This provides a model for the use of the I/II target gender forms (plural) with nouns of the other genders. The I/II gender is also a somewhat better marker of plurality since the III/IV target gender has null as one of its forms. When we move to Bantu languages the picture is almost as clear cut. The morphological resources are considerable, but of the various plural markers normally only two are used in resolution. The one selected for conjoined noun phrases denoting humans (class 2) is easy to understand: the 1/2 gender is largely restricted to nouns denoting humans in most of the languages analysed. The use of the 7/8 gender for remaining conjoined noun phrases also make good sense, in that its corresponding gender is the most general gender for inanimates. If we consider clear marking of plurality, we find that of the plural predicate agreement forms in Chibemba, for example (see figure 6.9), all except one are uniquely plural. Provided this form is avoided, then any resolution rule will mark plurality clearly. Bantu can follow both principles absolutely: the gender forms used are semantically justified (based on the human/non-human distinction) and they mark plurality unambiguously. The rules given for Bantu follow both our proposed principles and are relatively simple. In most of the remaining languages analysed there is not the same lack of ambiguity in morphology. For this reason the two principles cannot operate with the same consistency.

Let us consider how they apply to Slovene: in this language the masculine is the favoured form, the feminine is used provided all conjuncts are feminine, and the neuter is excluded in the variety described by Lenček. As mentioned above, the use of the masculine is semantically justified when humans are involved (the masculine gender is the one used for reference to both sexes). When inanimate nouns are involved, then no gender would be semantically justified and so these follow the animates. When the subject consists of two

Table 9.5 *Agreement markers in Slovene*

	Singular	Dual	Plural
Masculine	∅	a	i
Feminine	a	i	e
Neuter	o/e		a

nouns denoting females, the use of the feminine is semantically justified, and this form is also used by inanimates when all are of feminine gender. How, then, is the exclusion of the neuter to be explained? For this it is necessary to examine again the possible forms for predicates which show gender agreement in Slovene, as given in table 9.5. (Table 9.5 is slightly more complex than table 9.3 above as we include the neuter ending -e, which is taken by certain adjectives but which did not appear in any of our examples.) Suppose the subject consists of two inanimate singular nouns; the number resolution rules specify the dual. The gender resolution rules cannot specify a form which would be semantically justified in terms of gender; we claim, therefore, that they will mark number as clearly as possible. Neither dual ending is unambiguously dual: the -a ending is found also in the singular, and the -i ending in the plural. However, the finite verb forms end in -a for all genders; for this reason -a is a clearer marker of duality than -i. Now let us consider instances where the gender resolution rules are to mark the predicate clearly as plural. Then the neuter ending -a would not be favoured because it coincides with the feminine singular and, though this is probably of less importance, with the masculine dual. Of the remaining alternatives, the feminine plural -e also occurs in the singular while the masculine -i is found in the dual as well as in the plural. In terms of marking plurality, a case can be made for the masculine and for the feminine, but the neuter ending would be avoided. We can now assess the relative merits of the different forms. The masculine forms (dual and plural) are semantically justified in some cases (when the conjuncts denote male persons or persons of both sexes). In the dual, the masculine marks number more clearly than the alternative, and in the plural it marks number as clearly as or more clearly than the alternatives. As a result of these two factors, the masculine is favoured by the resolution rules. The feminine is also semantically justified in some instances (when the conjuncts denote female persons); the feminine/neuter dual form marks number less clearly than the masculine, but in the plural, the feminine form marks number more distinctly than the neuter would. The feminine occurs as a resolution form, but is more restricted than the masculine. The neuter has no semantic backing and does not mark number clearly; it is therefore excluded from the resolution rules.

In Polish there are only two agreement forms in the plural; both are used in gender resolution, the masculine personal being the favoured form as it is used when the conjuncts contain a mixture of masculine personal and non-masculine personal forms. The use of the masculine personal as the semantically justified gender can be explained on the same semantic grounds as for French and Slovene. For example, the word *państwo* 'Mr and Mrs, ladies and gentlemen', which refers to both sexes, takes masculine personal agreement forms. Similarly, the use of the non-masculine personal forms is semantically justified when the conjuncts denote female humans. The forms used, therefore, are semantically justified in some cases. The principle of clear marking of number also operates, though this is not immediately evident from the table 9.6 (which includes alternative forms which did not occur in our examples).

Table 9.6 *Agreement markers in Polish*

		Singular	Plural
Masculine	personal	$\emptyset$/y/i	i/y
	non-personal		
Feminine		a	y/e
Neuter		o/e	

Table 9.6 shows that the available plural endings are found in the singular as well. However, the masculine personal ending is distinguished in an important way: a mutation of consonant is required in the case of many adjectives and in the past tense (*byli* as opposed to *były* and all the singulars; see table 9.4). Thus the masculine personal form is clearly marked for plurality; again our two principles point to the same form. The West Slavonic languages are at different stages of losing gender forms in the plural; in each case, the form which is gaining ascendancy is also the form favoured by the resolution rules (Corbett 1983a: 191–6, 206). It is unlikely that conjoined

structures are a sufficiently frequently occurring construction to be the motivation for the change. It is more likely that gender differentiation is being lost in the plural for independent reasons; the form to survive is that which marks plurality clearly, which is partly for that reason the one favoured by the resolution rules.

We have already discussed the semantic justification for the use of masculine forms for gender resolution in French. The principle of marking plurality also points to the masculine form, though the motivation is less strong than in Polish. In French, singular and plural agreeing forms are usually indistinguishable in speech. Some masculines are distinguishable, for example, adjectives of the type *loyal* 'honest, loyal', plural *loyaux*. Once again the principle of using the gender form which is semantically justified (even though not in all cases) and the principle of using forms which are clearly marked as plural indicate the same form. In Rumanian we have an interesting situation with three controller genders but two sets of target gender forms. Nouns denoting humans of both sexes are again assigned to the masculine, so this form has a semantic factor in its favour. On the other hand, the feminine/neuter form also has a semantic factor backing it; since there is an animate/inanimate split in the resolution rules, the fact that the neuter gender contains almost exclusively inanimates makes the feminine/neuter agreement form appropriate when the conjuncts denote inanimates. Then the agreement markers *-i* (masculine) and *-e* (feminine) both mark plurality clearly. Thus both forms are supported by both principles and indeed both plural forms are used.

We now turn to two examples in which the two principles do not concur. In the case of Latin we find the now familiar semantic justification for the use of the masculine (thus the masculine plural *liberi* 'children' can denote children of both sexes) and for the feminine plural when all conjuncts denote females. There is, however, semantic justification for the use of the neuter plural for inanimates: the neuter plural is used for abstract nominals, for example, *incerta* 'fickle things'. Our first principle would allow the use of all three forms. To investigate the second, we must consider the actual forms available, as given in table 9.7. The masculine and feminine plural forms are unambiguously plural; in most instances the neuter plural coincides with the feminine singular, though for some agreeing elements it is clearly marked as plural. As we observed above, all three forms are used in gender resolution. While the neuter plural is not favoured by the principle of clear marking of number, it is a semantically justified gender in Latin; this ensures that it is used as a resolution form in Latin, unlike Slovene (and Serbo-Croat), where it has no semantic justification and is excluded.

Table 9.7 *Agreement markers in Latin*

	Singular	Plural
Masculine	us/∅/is	i/es
Feminine	a/∅/is	ae/es
Neuter	um/∅/e	a/ia

In Icelandic the neuter plural is the major resolution form, used for all gender clashes. This choice is semantically justified. First the neuter is used for beings of unknown sex: *afkvæmi* 'offspring', *barn* 'child', *fólk* 'people, household', *kyn* 'kin, kindred', *goð* '(heathen) god, idol', *folald* 'foal'. So the neuter does not exclude humans. The most significant examples involve the assignment of these nouns: *hjón* 'man and wife' and its derivative *bóndahjón* 'peasants (husband and wife)'. Both these nouns denote persons of both sexes and both require neuter plural agreement forms. There is evident semantic justification for the use of the neuter plural to denote humans of both sexes. Let us now consider the neuter plural in terms of clear marking of number.

Table 9.8 *Agreement markers in Icelandic*

	Singular	Plural
Masculine	ur/r/inn/ill	ir/nir/lir/dir
Feminine	∅/in/il	ar/nar/lar/dar
Neuter	t/tt/ið	∅/in/il

Table 9.8 shows that for agreeing predicates the neuter plural always coincides with the feminine singular (it is, however, distinct in the personal pronoun). On the other hand, the masculine and feminine are clearly marked as plural. In this instance our two principles are in direct conflict: the neuter plural is semantically justified while the masculine and feminine are clearly marked as plural. The neuter plural is the favoured form, but all three forms are used in gender resolution.

When the two principles are in harmony, this leads in larger gender systems to a restriction of the resolution forms used. In Slovene, according to Lenček, and, as we shall see, in Serbo-Croat, the neuter plural is excluded, while in Polish we observed that the favoured resolved form is extending its scope. More dramatically, in Bantu the majority of the target gender forms are excluded from the output of the resolution rules. When the two principles conflict, this leads to the use of different forms, supported by one principle or the other. The more significant factor is that of semantic justification: the favoured resolution form is always the semantically justified gender for conjuncts of at least one type (normally those referring to humans). When this principle is supported by that of clear marking of number, this may lead to a restriction of the forms available for gender resolution. Thus gender resolution employs semantically justified forms, as far as the morphology of a given language permits.

9.7 **Diachrony**

The evidence on how gender resolution systems change is still relatively slight; Polish provided a preview, since it is undergoing change in this area. We shall consider two more cases here, to gain an impression of the possibilities. The first is particularly interesting in that it appears to be a counter-example to the claims just made. We have a case where it seems at first that there is a morphological principle involved in gender resolution; we must consider whether our typology needs to be extended and we must demonstrate that even here there is a semantic motivation behind the resolution rules. The language involved is Serbo-Croat which, as we noted earlier, has rules similar to its South Slavonic neighbour, Slovene. It differs from Slovene in having lost the dual, so there are fewer agreement forms available. These are illustrated by the past active participle of *biti* 'be' in table 9.9.

Table 9.9 *Predicate agreement forms in Serbo-Croat*

	Singular	Plural
Masculine	bio	bili
Feminine	bila	bile
Neuter	bilo	bila

The resolution rules appear to be as in Slovene, that is to say: if all the conjuncts are feminine then the feminine form is used and otherwise the masculine form is used. When there is at least one non-feminine conjunct there is no problem – the masculine form is the resolved form. In our first example feminine and neuter are conjoined:

(74) znanje   i   intuicija   su kod njega
      knowledge.NEUT and intuition.FEM are in   him
      sarađival-i   i   dopunjaval-i   se
      worked.together-MASC.PL and supplemented-MASC.PL REFL
      'Knowledge and intuition worked together in him and
      supplemented each other...'

(Andrić, *Travnička Hronika*)

Similarly, when neuters are conjoined we find a masculine plural predicate:

(75) njegovo mesto   u razvitku   kasabe
his   place.NEUT in development town.GEN
i   njegovo značenje   u životu
and his   importance.NEUT in life
kasabalija   bil-i   su onakv-i
inhabitants.GEN been-MASC.PL are such-MASC.PL
kako smo ih   napred ukratko opisali
as   are them before briefly   described
'His place in the development of the town and his
importance in the life of the inhabitants were such as we
described them briefly before.'

(Andrić, *Travnička Hronika*)

When all the conjuncts are feminine, then we would expect feminine
agreements, as we find in the following example:

(76) opreznost,   suptilnost   i
discretion.FEM subtlety.FEM and
pedanterija   tih   bezbrojnih   poruka
pedantry.FEM these innumerable assignments.GEN
zbunjivale   su mladića
perplexed.FEM.PL are young.man
'The discretion, subtlety and pedantry of these innumerable
assignments perplexed the young man...'

(Andrić, *Travnička Hronika*)

So far the position is as in Slovene. The simple set of rules, still found in
Slovene (if all conjuncts are feminine, agreements will be feminine, otherwise
masculine) represents an earlier situation in Serbo-Croat. The complication
found in Serbo-Croat involves the use of masculine agreements in instances
not sanctioned by the old rules. If we look again at example (76) we see that
the feminine nouns in it are of two different types. *Pedanterija*, like the
majority of feminine nouns in Serbo-Croat, ends in -*a* in the nominative
singular. There is also a sizable group of nouns like *opreznost* and *suptilnost*
which have no inflection in the nominative singular (the -∅ declension). These
decline rather differently from nouns like *pedanterija* (they also decline
differently from masculine nouns, the majority of which also have no
inflection in the nominative singular). Nominal morphology is thus somewhat
akin to that of Russian, described in section 3.1.1. Though the two types of

feminine noun are morphologically dissimilar, they behave in the same way for agreement purposes, which is, of course, why they are assigned to the same gender. However, they have led to a complication of resolution rules, according to Gudkov (1965). A masculine predicate is possible, even though all the conjuncts are feminine, provided that at least one of them is headed by a noun which belongs to the -∅ declension, as does *lakomislenost* 'capriciousness' in (77):

(77) vređal-i   su ga nebriga
offended-MASC.PL are him carelessness.FEM
i   lakomislenost   Tahir-beg-ov-a.
and capriciousness.FEM Tahir-beg-POSS.FEM
'Tahir-beg's carelessness and capriciousness offended him.'

(Andrić, *Travnička Hronika*)

Agreement of this type is not obligatory, as example (76) shows: masculine and feminine agreements are both found.

The gender resolution rules are similar to those required for Slovene, but we must allow for the first rule to be optional. The main question is the nature of the condition which allows it to be optional. The examples so far suggest a morphological condition:

1. if all conjuncts are feminine, then the feminine form will be used (if at least one of the conjuncts is a noun of the -∅ declension, then this rule is optional);
2. otherwise the masculine will be used.

If this formulation were correct, it would be quite remarkable, because agreement rules normally refer to syntactic or semantic categories. The condition referring to a noun of a particular declensional type is of a different sort. It appears at first sight that the condition could be given in phonological terms, referring to the presence of a noun which ends in a consonant (since the nouns of the -∅ declension typically end in a consonant, and this phonological similarity may be a contributory factor). But this approach fails, since there are nouns like *misao* 'thought' which belong to the -∅ declension yet end in a vowel, and although this vowel alternates with a consonant, this alternation is not fully predictable (see Corbett 1983a: 190 for details). We cannot therefore replace the morphological condition with a phonological one. Whether or not the morphological condition marks a genuine stage in development, it does not cover all the present 'leaks'. There are other examples in which the first rule is not applied. Gudkov subsequently found

occasional examples in which subjects consisting entirely of feminine nouns in
-*a* take masculine agreements (1974: 61):

(78) štula   i   štaka   bili
      wooden.leg.FEM and crutch.FEM been-MASC.PL
      su sve što je tadašnja   medicina mogla
      are all that is of.that.time medicine could
      da mu   pruži
      that him.DAT offer
      'A wooden leg and a crutch were all that medical science of
      that time could offer him.'

(Popović)

Examples like this show that the first rule is optional in cases beyond that
covered by the morphological condition. The significant point is that in all the
examples with feminine conjuncts but masculine agreement, the noun phrases
denote inanimates. I have found no examples of masculine agreement with
feminine nouns denoting persons. Therefore the condition can and should be
stated as a semantic one (and not as a morphological one):

1. if all conjuncts are feminine, then the feminine form will be
    used (if the conjuncts denote inanimates, then this rule is
    optional);
2. otherwise the masculine will be used.

But there is still the difficulty that the majority of examples with feminine
conjuncts and masculine agreements involve a noun of the -∅ declension. The
explanation is that this declension includes a large proportion of abstract
nouns, and practically no animates. When one collects examples of conjoined
noun phrases it is striking that the overwhelming majority involve the
conjoining of nouns of the same semantic type (all animate or all inanimate).
Thus, when a feminine noun of the -∅ declension is one of the conjuncts, then
there will normally be no animates in the subject. This means, in turn, that the
use of the feminine agreement form will have no semantic justification (unlike
its use with animate conjuncts which denote females). What is happening, I
suggest, is that Serbo-Croat is moving from gender resolution rules operating
on syntactic conditions towards a semantic system. We may chart the
development as follows:

        Stage 1 (as still in Slovene)
        1. all feminine   →   feminine
        2. otherwise   →   masculine

This is a simple syntactic system.

Stage 2 (present Serbo-Croat)
1. all feminine   →   feminine
  (optional for inanimates)
2. otherwise   →   masculine

It is not clear whether the option should relate to inanimates or non-humans. In either case the crucial point is that we now have a reference to semantics, and so have moved from a syntactic to a mixed system. These rules can be formulated in a different way:

Stage 2 (alternative formulation)
1. all female   →   feminine
2. all feminine   →   feminine (optional)
3. otherwise   →   masculine

A possible development is for the optional rule to be dropped.

Stage 3 (hypothetical)
1. all female   →   feminine
2. otherwise   →   masculine

If this were to occur, and it seems plausible though it is only speculation, then we would have had the development from a syntactic system, through a mixed system, to a semantic system.

For a second case which may provide clues as to how gender resolution rules change over time we turn to a quite different family. In Algonquian languages, as we saw in section 2.2.4, there are animate and inanimate genders. For most nouns assignment is straightforward. But there is a minority of nouns which are grammatically but not biologically animate; some claim that these instances can be explained by reference to the world view of the speakers. The data on conjoining are rather patchy. In Algonquian languages it is generally the case that noun phrases headed by animates can be conjoined, giving animate agreement, as can inanimates, with inanimate agreement (Ives Goddard, personal communication). However, conjoining animate with inanimate can be problematic. This situation can be illustrated from Ojibwa. When two straightforward animates are conjoined we find animate agreement. The same holds for animates which are not biologically animate (these examples are from Delisle 1972: 130):

(79) akik   mi:nawa: bikwak
    pail.ANIM and   arrow.ANIM
    indaya:wa:g
    I.have.ANIM.PL
    'I have a pail and an arrow.'

With conjoined inanimates, inanimate agreement is found:

    (80) ji:ma:n   mi:nawa: abwi
           boat.INAN and   paddle.INAN
           indaya:nan
           I.have.INAN.PL
           'I have a boat and a paddle.'

However, animate and inanimate may not be conjoined, irrespective of the verb form:

    (81) *akik   mi:nawa: ji:ma:n
           pail.ANIM and   boat.INAN
           indaya:nan
           I.have.INAN.PL
           'I have a pail and a boat.'
    (82) *akik   mi:nawa: ji:ma:n
           pail.ANIM and   boat.INAN
           indaya:wa:g
           I.have.ANIM.PL
           'I have a pail and a boat.'

Changing the order of the constituents does not alter the judgements. Thus the rules are simple:

    1. if all conjuncts are animate, animate agreements are used;
    2. if all conjuncts are inanimate, inanimate agreements are used.

According to Delisle, animates and inanimates may not be conjoined (and so another construction is used). We therefore have simple rules, which could be viewed as semantic or syntactic, depending on whether we accept the cultural–semantic hypothesis for the assignment of nouns like *opwa:gan* 'pipe' to the animate gender.

    The bar on conjoining animate with inanimate strongly suggests that the rules are semantic. However, Linda Schwartz and Timothy Dunnigan (personal communication) report cases where mixed conjuncts were accepted, but only for subject agreement (not for object agreement):

    (83) mo:koma:n mi:nawa: opwa:gan
           knife.INAN and   pipe.ANIM
           atewan   ado:powining
           be.PL.INAN table.LOC
           'The knife and the pipe are on the table.'

In this sentence *opwa:gan* 'pipe' is grammatically animate while *mo:koma:n* 'knife' is not, and the verb is in the inanimate form (the order of conjuncts may be reversed without affecting the agreement). This possibility is found only with nouns which are grammatically animate but which do not denote a biological animate. The informant who accepted (83) and similar examples was younger than Delisle's main informant. It may be, therefore, that the younger speaker had less access to the world view which has been claimed to underlie the apparently anomalous animate gender nouns (detailed in section 2.2.4), so that for her nouns like *opwa:gan* 'pipe' are no more than exceptions. If the rules given earlier are treated as semantically based, such nouns are, therefore, treated as inanimate. (This type of account gains some support from the development in Dyirbal, where younger speakers have lost access to their mythology and have gone further than is suggested here by reallocating nouns whose gender depended on mythological associations, section 2.2.2.) The rules for this speaker are not a simple semantic set, however; when all conjuncts are grammatically animate but biologically inanimate, it is the grammatical gender which counts:

> (84) opwa:gan mi:nawa: asema:
> pipe.ANIM and tobacco.ANIM
> abiwag ado:powining
> be.PL.ANIM table.LOC
> 'The pipe and the tobacco are on the table.'

The resolution rules required for such speakers are still predominantly semantic, but they require a complication in the form of a reference to grammatical gender:

1. if all conjuncts are animate, animate agreements are used. (This rule applies whether the conjuncts are all animate semantically or whether they are all animate only grammatically.)
2. if all conjuncts are (semantically) inanimate, inanimate agreements are used. (This rule applies even if one but not all conjuncts is grammatically but not semantically animate.)

Note that it is still impossible to conjoin items which for the speaker count as semantically animate (like humans) with others which are semantically inanimate (like utensils), and an alternative construction must be used.

Thus the system is still predominantly a semantic one; the evidence is sketchy (since, for example, we lack information on subject agreement from Delisle's informant) but it suggests that the anomalous status of nouns like *opwa:gan* 'pipe' has led to a complication in the resolution rules. We have a picture of how a semantic set of resolution rules can acquire a syntactic restriction and so become a mixed system. If the assignment system moved further towards becoming a formal system then the resolution system might become fully syntactic.

9.8 **Conclusion**

Agreement with conjoined noun phrases is a complex and interesting problem. Gender resolution rules are of different types and allow various conditions on their operation. While they are language-specific, this does not mean that there is no pattern. We saw that they may refer to the meaning or to the gender of the conjuncts of the controller (or there may be a mixture of semantic and syntactic stipulations). The type of gender resolution system found is constrained by the assignment system of the language. Languages with strict semantic assignment systems (like Tamil and Telugu) have semantic resolution systems, as do those with predominantly semantic systems (like Archi). Languages with formal assignment systems may have semantic resolution (Bantu languages), syntactic (= formal) resolution (as in the case of Slovene, French and Icelandic), or mixed resolution (Latin, Polish and Rumanian). Informally speaking, gender resolution may be 'more semantic' but not 'less semantic' than gender assignment. The rather scanty diachronic data support this view. Serbo-Croat has formal assignment and has moved from syntactic resolution to mixed resolution; Ojibwa has predominantly semantic assignment, becoming less so, and its resolution appears to be becoming less strictly semantic than was the case. A further regularity is that it is the languages with semantic resolution systems which are most likely to have restrictions as to the type of noun phrases which can be conjoined (as with Dravidian and Bantu languages).

When we turn to the output of the gender resolution rules (the target gender forms selected) we find that the principles involved here are semantic (use of the semantically justified form) and functional (clear marking of plurality). When these principles coincide, then in larger gender systems we find that only a proportion of the target gender forms are used in gender resolution. Once again we have seen the interplay of semantic and formal factors in gender systems, and the way in which different parts of the system (notably assignment and resolution) are related to each other.

10
Generalizations and prospects

In this concluding chapter we draw out and develop some general themes which have emerged in our study of gender; we will also take a look backwards at earlier work and forwards to what may be achieved by future research. The notions of meaning and form provide an entry point for reviewing parts of our study and some previous research (section 10.1). The review of earlier work leads us to a discussion of the development and loss of gender systems (section 10.2). Finally, we look at the prospects in this area, both for understanding major questions of the function of gender and for feasible shorter-term projects (section 10.3).

10.1 Meaning and form

The relationship between meaning and form is central to linguistics and, not surprisingly, the theme runs through our investigation of gender (section 10.1.1), and through earlier work on the subject (section 10.1.2).

10.1.1 *A perspective on gender systems*

We saw in chapter 6 how establishing the existence of a gender system and determining the number of genders requires evidence from agreement (that is, evidence concerned with form). At the same time, gender always has a semantic core: there are no gender systems in which the genders are purely formal categories. As shown in chapters 2 and 3, nouns are assigned to gender according to semantic and formal criteria. At one end of the range we find languages like Tamil, in which the meaning of a noun is sufficient to assign it to a gender. At the other extreme are languages like Qafar, in which the form of the noun would be sufficient to determine its gender in almost all cases. But there is an imbalance here, in that even in the systems nearest to the formal end of the spectrum there is a considerable overlap with semantic criteria and, when the two are in conflict, it is typically the semantic criterion which dominates. Hence formal assignment systems are really semantic plus formal systems. The same tension between form and meaning is found when nouns are borrowed from another language and must be assigned to a gender (section 4.1).

While semantic criteria typically outweigh formal factors in assignment, in some instances the conflict is not settled unambiguously in favour of one factor. Then a hybrid noun results, taking agreements from more than one consistent agreement pattern. It may take agreements according to its meaning (semantic agreement) or according to its form (syntactic agreement). The possible patterns of such agreements are severely constrained by the Agreement Hierarchy (chapter 8). The opposition between meaning and form turns up in a slightly different guise in gender resolution (chapter 9). There we saw how the sets of rules for resolution in different languages may be based on the meaning of the nouns heading the conjuncts or on their formal gender (or on both in mixed systems). The type of resolution system found in a given language is related to the assignment system: a semantic assignment system implies a semantic resolution system (provided, of course, that gender resolution is required in the language), while a formal assignment system permits any type of resolution system. When we add in the evidence from assignment systems which are predominantly semantic, we see that resolution is never less dependent on meaning than is assignment in a given language.

10.1.2 *Earlier research on gender*

An interest in gender goes back at least to Greek writers of the fifth century BC such as Protagoras, and at that time meaning and form were already being discussed:

> The fifth-century discussions on gender show that two facts
> were discovered with regard to this category, firstly, its formal
> character as a marker of agreement between words in certain
> syntactic groupings, and secondly, the correlation in part
> between masculine and feminine forms and male and female
> sex. (Robins 1951: 15)

Aristotle developed the topic in the next century (Robins 1979: 27). Discussion of the subject was taken up again during the Renaissance, notably by Sanctius (1523–1600), for which see Breva-Claramonte (1983: 105–9).

It is not our purpose here to survey the vast amount which has been written on gender since then. In a book of this type attempting to convey the breadth of the subject, a good deal depends on the best of earlier research, which has been noted on our way through. However, for those who would like to investigate the history of the study of gender, the major sources will be provided. It should be noted that, until relatively recently, Indo-European dominated discussion (though the contributions of Bleek, de la Grasserie and Meinhof were noted earlier, and work on Semitic languages is reported by Ibrahim 1973: 39–50). The question everyone wanted to answer was what was the origin of gender. Given the overwhelming concentration on Indo-European, this was not a particularly good question to ask, since it involved hypothesizing about the remote past, working on a yet earlier stage of a language which is itself a reconstruction. And so there was a good deal of speculation. The last century saw a lively debate on the origin of grammatical gender, mainly concerned with Indo-European. The opposing views were associated with the names of Grimm and Brugmann. Grimm, who acknowledged the influence of Humboldt, started from the semantic link of gender to sex; gender was extended to inanimate nouns by the working of human imagination (1831: 311–59). Brugmann (1889) rejected this view; he took the origin of gender to be formal, the starting point being particular suffixes which were used for sex-differentiable nouns; other nouns with these suffixes were treated identically for adjectival agreement purposes; this account relies heavily on the working of analogy. Again in this discussion we recognize the themes of meaning and form. A detailed account of the debate is given by Royen (1929: 42–141). Other surveys of earlier work with references to the sources include Wheeler (1898), Lehmann (1958) and Fodor (1959). A more recent attempt to answer the old question is that of Wienold (1967), which also has an extensive bibliography (see also Wienold 1989).

A new perspective on Indo-European gender has been provided by the discovery and decipherment of Hittite texts (of the second millennium BC). Hittite had two genders, common (or animate) and neuter (or inanimate). Nouns assigned to the neuter gender were almost exclusively semantically inanimate. There was also a close correlation between gender and morphology (that is, Hittite had straightforward morphological assignment rules – see Brosman 1979). As a result of the Hittite evidence, many now accept Meillet's view (1931) that Indo-European (before the split of Anatolian, which included Hittite), once had two genders, common and neuter, and that the former later split into masculine and feminine (see discussion in Brosman 1982). The debate on the origin of gender was widened, as Royen (1929: 141–270) shows, as more information became available on non-Indo-European languages; these included the languages of Africa (especially through the work of Carl

Meinhof) and of the Caucasus (Adolf Dirr). An amusing suggestion made early in this century (by Jules Torrend) was that Bantu noun classes divided objects into the days on which they were created according to Genesis.

10.2 **Diachrony**

Here we shall consider the way in which gender systems change, looking not only at their origins but also at their development and decline. We have already examined these topics in the appropriate parts of the book, when concrete evidence was available. Now we shall try to piece the story together.

10.2.1 *The rise of gender systems*

We are still some way from understanding how gender systems arise. What follows is not the whole story, nor the only story. But we now have sufficient evidence for the different stages in the rise of gender systems to be able to offer a plausible account.

Let us begin with a mature system, like that of, say, Swahili. Where did agreement in gender come from? As we saw in section 5.5, Givón demonstrates how verb agreement develops from subject pronouns which become obligatory even with a normal noun phrase as subject, and which later become reanalysed as a part of the verb (*the man, he came* becomes *the man he-came*). For this process to result in gender agreement requires that the subject pronouns already distinguish gender (that is, that there was already a pronominal gender system). So we must ask how the personal pronouns acquire gender. They inherit it from their source, which is the demonstrative pronoun. Demonstratives are central to the story. They may simply serve as the source for personal pronouns (to which we return below). But they may contribute more than this. As we saw in chapter 5, they occur not only in pronominal use but also in attributive use (as in English *this* and *this book*). This second use is also relevant to gender. In their use within the noun phrase, demonstratives become articles. At first they function as a definite article, but typically their range gradually extends to all but generic use. Finally, a stage is reached in which nouns always occur with the article (whose meaning and original function is not completely lost). If the original demonstrative distinguished two or more genders, then the nouns will now be marked for these genders. Thus it will be possible to tell the gender of a noun from its form and we have an overt gender system (section 3.3.1); for a full account see Greenberg (1978).

Whether or not this last development occurs, we still have to demonstrate how it is that a gender distinction arises at all. The main source of the distinction would seem to be a demonstrative pronoun which inherits more than one gender form (and which may then develop into a personal pronoun). And so, going a further step back, we must look for the source for such a demonstrative pronoun. A demonstrative pronoun which makes gender distinctions is likely to have gained the different forms from a classifier system (section 5.4). Classifier systems distinguish different groups of nouns, and when they spread, they first extend to demonstratives (Greenberg 1978: 78). Classifier systems appear to be the main source for gender-distinguishing demonstratives; we saw the example of Dyirbal in section 5.5. There is, however, a second possible source for the distinction, which is hinted at by Greenberg (1978: 78–9) and which has been taken further more recently (Greenberg, personal communication). He observes that in a number of languages we find an anaphoric pronoun (derived from a demonstrative) which is restricted to animates or persons, while another demonstrative fills the remaining gap (we noted in the latter part of section 8.2 that personal pronouns often have such restrictions). Thus in Latvian, the personal pronouns *viņš* 'he', *viņa* 'she' are normally used for animates, *tas* (feminine *tā*) 'that' is used in the same role for inanimates, and for all nouns when a normal demonstrative is required. Now Latvian already has an inherited gender system and its evidence is of a secondary nature; but there are also cases where a similar development could signal the start of a new gender system, for example in Persian. What all this suggests is that the specialization of a personal pronoun (originally a demonstrative) could give rise to an animate/inanimate (or personal/non-personal) gender system. In this scenario the distinction between two sets of nouns arises at the stage when a demonstrative extends to being used as a third person pronoun (an earlier personal pronoun having become specialized for use with persons or animates).

Let us return to classifiers since, like demonstratives, they may play more than one role in the development of gender. Classifiers can be used anaphorically, without a head noun, and it is in this use that they could give rise to demonstratives (and hence to gender systems). But classifiers can also be repeated within the noun phrase (with adjectives, for example) and can give rise to gender agreement within the noun phrase (as we saw in the Daly languages of Australia, section 5.5). Where, in turn, do classifiers come from? This is one of the easier questions, since there is ample evidence that they come from nouns. This is shown by the fact that frequently some classifiers are identical to nouns (as in Ami, section 5.5). Some languages allow a noun to classify itself; thus in addition to constructions like 'woman Mary', we may find 'woman woman'. In the Meso-American language Jacaltec (Craig

1986b, c), *ix* is the noun for 'woman' and is also the classifier for female non-kin. 'The woman' is *ix ix*, with the classifier followed by the noun. Jacaltec also shows the next stage of development, in that *ix* can also be used anaphorically, meaning 'she'.

Thus the ultimate source of gender systems is nouns, more specifically nouns with classificatory possibilities such as 'woman', 'man' and 'animal'. This view is reinforced by recent evidence from different continents. In Australian languages the development from nouns to the use of generic nouns or classifiers and from there to agreement in gender is clear. And there are African languages where the etymological link between pronouns (which are giving rise to agreement) and their noun sources is still apparent. Thus in Zande (whose assignment system we analysed in section 2.2.1) some of the gender pronouns can be traced to noun sources meaning 'man', 'animal, meat', 'thing' and 'person' (Claudi 1985: 127–37; Heine & Reh 1984: 220–5). In Eastern Nilotic languages like Ongamo, which is spoken near Mount Kilimanjaro in south-west Kenya, but not in the other branches of Nilotic, there are two genders, masculine and feminine (some have a third gender, as we shall see below). Agreement is found within the noun phrase, on different items in different languages, and it is suggested that two demonstratives **lo* (masculine) and **na* feminine became proclitics, giving rise to agreement, and sometimes to overt gender marking on nouns. The origin of these demonstratives can be traced back to nouns, one meaning 'person' and the other meaning 'girl, daughter' (Heine & Vossen 1983). It is interesting to note that gender agreement in Eastern Nilotic does not extend to the verb nor to the personal pronoun. The development thus recalls that seen in Daly languages in that it occurred within the noun phrase. Unlike the Daly languages, however, there is the puzzle of how inanimate nouns acquired masculine or feminine gender.

It is worth mentioning that the processes described can occur repeatedly, and so the picture may become far from clear in a given language. Furthermore, the attrition of affixes means that similarities which were once obvious may become obscured.

10.2.2 *The development of gender systems*

There is a good deal of evidence about how, once a gender system has arisen, it can grow and develop. At different stages the forms on which it depends may be renewed. In section 5.2.3 we examined Khinalug, which has a four-gender system. The agreement markers are subject to complex phonotactic constraints and the null form is found frequently. All this suggests that the markers are rather old. There is also a new set of agreement markers, which are regular, and which have clearly developed relatively recently from the demonstrative pronoun. In a sense the system is unchanged; however, it is much more secure, since gender is now extremely well marked on the verb.

Markers on nouns, which produce overt systems (and add to the 'security' of the gender system) may also be renewed. We saw this happening in Godie (section 3.2.3). It is also widely found in Bantu languages which have pre-prefixes (Greenberg 1978: 66–7). These pre-prefixes typically function as articles, but are well on the way to becoming obligatory markers on the noun, thus making the gender system highly overt. The new affixes may not be of the same type as the old; thus suffixes may succeed earlier prefixes, as is happening in Southern West Atlantic languages like Gola and Kisi (Childs 1983).

Gender systems may expand by adding new genders; this is generally done using existing morphological material. The dialects of Andi which have gained one or two additional genders have done so according to a semantic basis of assignment, using new singular–plural pairings of agreements. The agreement markers were already available but the pairing was new. Similarly Grebo has added a third gender in this way (section 7.1.3). The rise of subgenders in Slavonic languages (sections 3.1.1, 4.5 and 6.4.1) was also based on existing morphological material; here existing markers for agreement in case were reallocated (on a semantic basis) to give new agreement classes, which are the basis for the new subgenders, which can, in turn, develop into new genders. And Chafe (1977) shows how in Iroquoian languages existing agreement markers were reanalysed to give gender markers.

A common source of a new gender or genders is locative expressions. If a language has overt gender, then preposition plus noun combinations may be reassessed as marker plus noun, and hence the nouns involved may be reanalysed as belonging to a new gender (Givón 1976: 173–5; Greenberg 1978: 70–1). Such a gender will at least start out as a non-lexical gender (section 6.3.3). Non-lexical genders of other types (for example, for diminutives) may provide another means of expanding the number of genders (Greenberg 1978: 79).

A slightly different way in which locative expressions can give birth to a new gender is shown dramatically by various Nilotic languages (Nilotic languages form a group within Nilo-Saharan). Maasai has the masculine and feminine genders of Eastern Nilotic, whose origin was considered in the last section, plus a third 'place' gender. This third gender contains just one noun *e-wwéji* 'place', though place gender agreements are taken also by the interrogative *aji* 'where' (Heine & Claudi 1986: 43–51, following Tucker & Mpaayei

1955: 15–33). Not all agreement targets have special 'place' forms. A suggested source is in phrases like

(1) *ene ŋoji
     here place
     'Here it is, the place.'

Ene 'here' was a demonstrative in origin, and so was similar to other (gender-distinguishing) demonstratives. The phrase could therefore be reanalysed as 'this place', with 'this' agreeing in gender, and showing a place gender form. Originally, the demonstrative would be an overdifferentiated target (section 6.4.2). But the distinction has spread to other targets. Those that do not distinguish a place gender use the feminine form, the reason being that the word for place was of feminine gender. Here, then, we can see the very beginning of a new gender. Its position is precarious, having not separated itself fully from the feminine and having only one noun. But it may well survive, since in the related Teso-Turkana group there is also a third gender which had a similar source. Thus in Turkana (Dimmendaal 1983: 218–19) the position of the third gender has improved considerably. Targets generally distinguish three agreement forms (though only in the singular). Second, it has acquired more nouns, though it is still small in comparison to the other two genders. It has done so by extending its semantics to include particular instances of larger groups and also diminutives. Most importantly, it is used in the derivation of nouns; this latter fact suggests that it has a safe future.

Changes in gender systems need not affect the number of genders; instead, the composition of the genders may change. At the lowest level the change may affect a single noun. For example, if a language has a gender for nouns denoting humans and another for diminutives then the noun for a child, a small human, may move from one gender to the other (or may stay in between as a hybrid noun). Or else a small anomalous group may change gender (like the fourteen nouns like *imja* 'name' in some Russian dialects, section 4.5). But small numbers of nouns may serve as Trojan horses and lead to dramatic changes in the gender system. Thus the human gender of Bantu has been invaded by nouns denoting non-human animates to different degrees in different languages; in some, like Lunda, the change is complete and the previous human gender is now an animate gender (section 4.5). Such changes affect the different agreement targets in turn (see section 8.3), but the result is that the assignment rules change without any effect on the gender agreement forms. Other dramatic changes which we observed involved changes in the semantics of the neuter gender in Konkani and Polish dialects.

The composition of the genders can also be affected by borrowing. If we have a language with overt gender, borrowed nouns will normally not carry appropriate markers. If they are assigned to a gender on semantic grounds, this makes the system 'less overt' and so weakens it slightly (as has happened in Lelemi; section 4.1.2). There may already be a gender which differs from the others by the absence of an affix. This will therefore be an obvious place for borrowings assigned by a morphological rule. If there are substantial numbers of borrowings this may affect the balance of the genders dramatically, as we saw in Kikuyu (section 4.1.1); in this language the 9/10 gender had around 30 per cent of the native nouns but has taken 73 per cent of borrowings (all sources).

10.2.3 *The decline of gender systems*

The major cause of the decline of gender systems is attrition, that is, the partial or complete loss of the formal markers on which the system depends. We can see its effects clearly in Modern French. The loss of final -*e*, that is /ə/, the marker of the feminine gender, has left gender agreement in a confused state, with some targets marking gender by the presence or absence of various final consonants and many targets not marking gender at all (section 5.3.7). The effect of the same change on nouns has been to make the system much less overt; the assignment rules are now complex (section 3.2.5), particularly when contrasted with other Romance languages like Spanish. We noted further examples in section 5.3.8 of strange distributions of gender agreement, where chaos seems to have resulted from attrition. However, the loss of gender agreement is not totally random; for example, there is evidence that gender agreement lasts longest in the pronoun (section 5.5).

In some cases phonological change can lead more directly to a decline in the gender system. This can be clearly seen by a comparison of the dialects of Chamalal (North-East Caucasian). In table 10.1 we have the forms for the conservative Gigatl' dialect (compare figure 7.2). The innovating Gakvarin dialect has undergone a sound change *r* > *j*. The effect on the gender system

Table 10.1 *Target gender forms in Chamalal (Gigatl' dialect)*

	Singular	Plural
I (male human)	w	b
II (female human)	j	b
III (non-human)	b	r
IV (non-human)	l	r
V (non-human)	r	r

is considerable. In most instances, the agreements for gender II (female human) cannot be distinguished in the singular from one of the non-human genders, gender V, though some targets take different markers which still distinguish II and V. However, the two genders are separate because they take different agreement forms in the plural, *b* versus *j*, so we still have five agreement classes. The details need not concern us (see Khaidakov 1980: 66–79); the important point is that a specific phonological change has weakened the gender system and the loss of a gender could be the final result. Developments of this type may well leave overdifferentiated targets (section 6.4.2), if a small number of targets maintains a distinction which is lost by the majority as a result of phonological change.

It is worth stressing that when two sets of agreement forms coalesce completely, this does not necessarily involve the loss of a gender, since the genders may be separated in a different grammatical number. We observed this situation in Chamalal and it is also found in Telugu, where the feminine and neuter forms are identical in the singular, but different in the plural. The crossed system which results can, however, lead to the loss of a gender if the forms in the other number fall together, as happened in Kolami (figures 7.12 and 7.13).

When the phonological form of the agreement marker is affected, then all nouns in the corresponding controller are likely to be affected equally. But a different type of change is possible, in which nouns 'transfer their allegiance' by changing from using one target gender form to another. As shown in table 7.8, in the Ngemba group nouns from the 9/10 gender are moving to the 9/6 gender. This is happening gradually, through a stage of vacillation between genders 9/10 and 9/6. In one language, Awing, there is no target form 10 remaining since no nouns take this form. A change of this type with gradual transfer of nouns from one gender to another implies that a controller gender will become an inquorate gender (section 6.4.3) before finally being lost; if no other controller gender takes the target form involved, then that target form will disappear too.

It is not unusual for a gender to be lost completely. Many members of the Indo-European family have reduced its three genders to two. In Romance languages like French we find masculine and neuter have combined. In some Scandinavian languages masculine and feminine have combined, although the pronouns distinguish additional genders (section 8.2); the conflict of different resulting systems gives rise to a complex sociolinguistic situation in Norwegian (Flydal 1975). The loss of a gender may result from a conspiracy of contributing factors. In Russian, for example, there is considerable pressure on the neuter gender. A major factor is phonological change. In unstressed syllables *a* and *o* are pronounced identically in the dominant dialects. This means that for many agreement targets the feminine and neuter forms are identical. Similarly, the nominative singular form of many nouns no longer gives a clue as to gender. Added to this, there is the statistical factor: the neuter gender has about 13 per cent of the nouns (see table 4.1). It has little support in derivational morphology; almost all the productive formations produce new masculine or feminine nouns. And loanwords entering the language go primarily to the masculine gender, with substantial numbers also going to the feminine; the neuter is falling further behind in this regard. For all these reasons the position of the neuter is difficult. Elsewhere in Slavonic, in the Sele Fara dialect of Slovene, the neuter has actually been lost, and that since 1935, with most neuter nouns joining the masculine (Priestly 1983: 353–5). Some neuter target gender forms survive as neutral forms (section 7.2.3).

When a gender is lost this may well make the assignment system for the remaining genders less clear in terms of semantics. Specifically, the rule assigning nouns denoting males to the masculine gender accounted for a smaller proportion of the masculine nouns in the Sele Fara dialect after the neuters had joined the masculine. This helps us to answer a difficult problem. The plausible suggestions for the rise of gender base it on a semantic classification. And the rise of new subgenders is equally based on semantics. The question then is why gender systems should be anything but semantic; we might expect them all to remain like that of Tamil. As we have just noted, however, the fusion of genders may blur an earlier distinction. Thus in Kolami (as a result of the loss of a gender) the second gender is for nouns denoting female humans, animates and inanimates, a less clear system than that of Tamil. And if the change in Chamalal discussed earlier were to lead to the complete fusion of genders II and V, the semantics of the system would be much less clear. This, then, is a first mechanism which can lead to the weakening of semantic systems; there are several others. A second mechanism depends on the fact that the semantic criteria cannot be absolutely clear cut. If the division is human/non-human where do gods fit in? And what if gods are represented as animals or inanimates? If the division is animate/inanimate what is the lower boundary? Is an animal killed for food animate or inanimate? Some of these potential triggers of change can be illustrated from Nunggubuyu, whose gender system includes a human/non-human division. In Nunggubuyu nouns denoting babies and ghosts vary in the gender assigned to them, as does the noun meaning 'dog', dogs being the only traditional domesticated animal. Gender may also vary in instances of personification (Heath 1984: 178–9). The areas of doubt in a given language may appear small in relation to the whole, but we saw in section 4.5 how a small number of Trojan horses can lead to major changes. A third, related mechanism depends on changes in the world view of the speakers. We saw clear examples of the weakening of semantic systems in the Algonquian languages (section 2.2.4). While the assignment of nouns to the animate gender may have been fully explicable according to the world view of the speakers, when the world view changes, numerous nouns are left stranded with their gender predictable from their morphology but no more from their meaning. The fourth mechanism is based on cross-classification. Some languages have size – large/small – as a semantic criterion. Such relative criteria invite problems in any case, but particularly since they can cross-clarify with other criteria. Thus a child could be classified as small or human. The examples available show that even one or two problem nouns of this type can lead to widespread change, but it is difficult to say when they will do so and when, instead, they will simply remain as isolated hybrid nouns. A final but important factor in the equation is derivational morphology. If we have a derivational affix with a particular meaning, which is therefore also tied to a particular gender, and this affix extends its meaning, then this may affect the distribution of nouns. For example, an affix with the meaning 'agent', whose derivatives were all in the human gender, might extend to cover tools (like English *cutter*, *trimmer*) and could lead to a conflict of assignment criteria.

We have looked at the loss of individual genders and have noted that such a loss may affect the nature of the assignment system. It is also possible for all genders to be lost so that a genderless language results. In Indo-European, for example, most Iranian languages have lost gender (Persian, Sarikoli, Beludzhi and Ossete) as have many Indic languages (Assamese, Bengali, Nepali, Oriya) (Priestly 1983: 345–6). In its decline, a gender system, if overt, may leave its trace in different morphological classes (perhaps marking only singular versus plural). This has happened in Ma, though a new semantic gender system has arisen (see section 6.4.6, and compare Wurzel 1986). Finally, we may find no more than relatively small groups of nouns with a phonological similarity, which is the last remnant of a prefix or suffix, which in its day was a clear indication of gender.

10.3 Prospects

Here we review three areas in which we can hope for progress: descriptive studies, work on the function of gender and collaborative projects.

10.3.1 *Descriptive studies*

While the literature on gender is considerable, there are many languages for which we have no adequate account of the gender system; in some cases, there is little time left, since languages are disappearing at an alarming rate. And even for well-studied languages, the accounts are often only partial.

Ideally a description should include the types of agreement in gender found in a language, that is the evidence which demonstrates the presence of a gender system. Then we would expect an account of the number of genders and of any problem cases (inquorate genders, overdifferentiated targets, hybrid nouns). Given the number of genders, there should be a set of rules for assigning nouns to these genders. If gender resolution occurs, then there should be an account of the rules. In the cases where historical data are available a description of changes in any of these parts of the gender system may prove revealing. Several aspects of such descriptions are suitable project or dissertation topics, though they vary considerably in difficulty according to the language. In some languages, for example, the number of genders can be demonstrated quickly and definitely. In others, establishing the number of genders would be a suitable topic in itself. Gender assignment is a particularly interesting area for project work; however, here again, the problems involved are considerably more complex in some languages than in others. If the language being investigated has a predominantly semantic assignment system, then a useful approach is to collect all the nouns which are not covered by the main semantic rules and to look for explanations for these apparent exceptions (perhaps in the cultural setting, as in the cases of Dyirbal and Ojibwa). If a morphological or phonological system is found, then writing the basic assignment rules may be a sufficient project in itself. For suffixing languages a reverse dictionary, if one exists, can be useful (since, for example, if all the words ending in -*a* are listed together, one can more easily check the hypothesis that all words ending in -*a* are feminine). Of course, it is not sufficient merely to suggest rules and find examples corroborating the rules proposed. Ideally, the rules should be checked against all the nouns in the language. This is not a practical possibility; however, if a frequency dictionary is available, it is worth checking the rules against the most common 1,000, 2,000 or 5,000 nouns (since difficult cases are more likely to be found in common items). In languages where all types of assignment rule operate, it is useful to try to determine the overlap between them – the extent to which the rules predict the same gender for different nouns as compared to the cases where the factors conflict and one rule overrides another.

Proposing a set of assignment rules on the basis of the linguistic evidence may provide a considerable challenge. If this stage has already been carried out, however, then the results can be verified by investigating the assignment of invented words (if native speakers are available) by observing gender assignment by children (again provided this is practicable) or by studying the allocation of borrowings to gender. In the last case, it is best to select nouns borrowed within a specified period. For certain languages, dictionaries of new words are available, which contain only words which appeared after a certain date (though not all will be borrowings). Alternatively, both period and subject area can be limited by examining, for example, all loans relating to a specific technology or activity. As examples, one could look at loanwords relating to railways, the internal combustion engine, the microchip or those to do with windsurfing or jazz. In each case, looking at the appropriate specialist journals and magazines will increase the examples found considerably. And the aim should be to examine all the loans found within the defined area.

Work on hybrid nouns (in relation to the Agreement Hierarchy) may require careful informant work. It is an area in which speakers are often conscious of the issues involved and so it may prove difficult to obtain spontaneous judgements. For finding textual examples it is again profitable to choose the source carefully (for example, Janko-Trinickaja 1966 used women's journals, which provided numerous examples of Russian nouns which were masculine in form but had female referents). There is also a great deal to be discovered about gender resolution. Here it is important to be sure that cases where agreement is with just one conjunct are distinguished from genuine resolution. And it may take considerable ingenuity to construct plausible sentences with the combinations of nouns one wishes to test. When historical evidence is available then it may help fill one of the gaps in the story of the development of gender systems. There are fascinating possibilities in gender systems for students looking for a dissertation topic, for those embarking on fieldwork, for philologists working on ancient texts and for linguists working in the traditional core areas of linguistics.

10.3.2 *The function of gender*

We have concentrated on *what* gender systems are; given the confusion in some previous work, this has been essential. But it is also a prerequisite for the *why* question: why do languages have gender systems? Several writers give a vague response along the lines that they serve to disambiguate various constructions. However, as Claudi (1985: 33–45) demonstrates neatly, in most instances, in German at least, gender agreement does not do this. Many examples which show gender agreement other than of pronouns are equally ambiguous when translated, say, into English. It is mainly in the case of third person pronouns that a disambiguating role is found. As Heath (1975: 91–7) points out, the referent of first and second persons is easily established and it is the third person where difficulty is likely to arise (compare section 5.3.3). Consider this German example involving third person pronouns (Mills 1986: 38):

(2)° Maria fotografierte Tobias vor dem
Maria photographed Tobias in.front.of the
Haus, als sie/er/es zehn Jahre alt war
House when she/he/it ten years old was
'Maria photographed Tobias in front of the house when
he/she/it was ten years old.'

Here gender distinctions allow the pronoun to distinguish between three potential antecedents. It is clear how this can work when the assignment is based on semantics, but less so for formal systems. If we have a comparable German sentence with all inanimate objects will the gender system help in disambiguation? Zubin & Köpcke (1986: 173–5) claim that it does:

(3) der Krug fiel in die Schale, aber
the jug.MASC fell into the bowl.FEM but
er zerbrach nicht
it.MASC broke not
'The jug fell into the bowl, but it (the jug) didn't break.'

The German sentence is unambiguous because the two nouns are of different genders. They claim that for the optimal use of this function of gender, basic-level terms whose referents tend to be found in the same context should be of different gender, as far as is possible. And of fifty-nine kitchen implements, they found 41 per cent denoted by masculine gender nouns, 42 per cent by feminine gender and 17 per cent by neuter gender. Koval' (1979: 97–8) claims that domestic animals are found in different genders in Fula for the same reason. Heath (1975: 95–6) also almost makes a virtue of the semantic opacity of the gender system of Nunggubuyu because of its use for his purpose. The data are intriguing: if gender is to be used for differentiation in this way, then nouns with similar meaning must be of different genders (which is what formal assignment provides). Yet we noted at the end of section 3.3.2 how even in formal assignment systems there tend to be clusters of nouns of similar meaning being found in the same gender. Here we need detailed study of large subsets of the lexicon of languages with formal systems, to establish how clustering and dispersal coexist; at the same time we should look at authentic spoken language to establish the extent to which this potential function of gender is actually utilized.

There are two studies where short texts are indeed provided, which demonstrate that gender has a major role in the languages described. The first concerns the Australian language Nunggubuyu, just mentioned. In terms of the syntactic structures with which most of us are familiar, Nunggubuyu is remarkably simple: subject and object are usually not differentiated whether by word order or case marking and there is almost no cross-clause relational syntax. In this language the gender system 'appears to constitute the glue which holds the system together' (Heath 1983: 139). A text is provided which gives an idea of how the verb, by indexing the different participants according to the seven genders, allows the language to function without many of the syntactic devices which are sometimes believed to be essential. In the second study, Foley & Van Valin give an account of Yimas (see section 3.2.4). They claim that the gender system 'carries most of the load of referential tracking in Yimas', and they continue: 'An NP whose referent is known or given does not normally appear overtly: it is simply represented by the cross-referencing affix on the verb' (1984: 327). The gender affixes play a similar role to anaphoric pronouns in other examples we have considered. Foley & Van Valin also provide a text to illustrate their claim. It may be significant that Yimas also has a large gender system with eleven genders (section 6.4.5), and so can take this major role.

We have seen how gender may have a central role. In some languages the reference-tracking role depends largely on gender, while in others it is shared with other devices, and in some, of course, gender has no place. Heath (1975) suggested that there is an inverse relation between switch reference and gender in fulfilling this function. There is interesting work to be done here, based on authentic language, examining how different devices interact in different languages.

Besides this major function of gender, namely reference tracking, gender has other secondary functions in showing the attitude of the speaker. It may be used to mark status, to show respect or a lack of it and to display affection. The use of a particular gender may be fixed, or it may be available for 'switching' in particular circumstances according to the speaker's attitude. We have already seen how in some Polish dialects the feminine gender is used only for women of married status. The neuter (or masculine, according to dialect) is used of unmarried women (section 4.5). Ferguson reports (1964: 106) that in baby talk in Arabic, affection can be shown by shifting gender (masculine for a girl, feminine for a boy). It is not just masculine and feminine which may be involved. In Tsova-Tush, nouns denoting men and women are in genders I and II. But humans can also be referred to using genders V or VI to show scorn; these are genders for non-human nouns (Dešeriev 1953: 138–9).

Similarly in Grebo the use of non-human agreements for humans is insulting (Innes 1966: 53). For other comparable examples see Head (1978: 175–7).

10.3.3 *Collaborative work*

It is already clear that gender offers exciting research prospects for linguists of various types. Added to this are fascinating opportunities for collaborative work. Anthropologists and ethnographers have already contributed to our understanding of assignment systems, notably those which are predominantly semantic but where the semantic criteria are not fully clear (chapter 2). Joint work on such languages is still possible, though time is running out. Assignment systems offer scope also for collaboration with psycholinguists and psychologists. For many languages, especially those with formal systems, we can now describe the assignment of nouns quite accurately. There is then the question as to how this information is represented in the brain. Work in this area was described in parts of sections 4.2, 4.3 and 4.4. The goal here must be to come to an understanding of how the internal lexicon is structured. When we consider work with sociolinguists and sociologists, where the concern is the link between language and society, we find the problems are more challenging than might have been expected. Provided we examine a wide range of languages, we discover that it is not at all straightforward to establish links between grammatical gender and the relative status and treatment of those classified by the different genders (notably men and women, though the other classifications also deserve study). In Polish we find a distinction male human versus all other in the plural, which appears to be a particularly sexist division. Russian, which is related to Polish, has no such feature; however, this does not reflect any obvious difference in the relative status of Polish and Russian women and men. Archi, in contrast, has a remarkably equitable gender system: there is a single plural form corresponding to masculine singular and feminine singular and nouns whose human referent is unknown are assigned to a non-human gender (section 7.3.2). Such equity does not appear to extend fully into society; thus, for example, it is the women who carry all the heavy weights. This is an area where cross-linguistic work must be combined with cross-cultural research. A fourth type of collaboration is with computational linguists. We have seen how gender can provide the major means for reference tracking in a language, yet it may also be absent. If this is so, then the strategies for parsing must reflect this difference. And we should be able to implement parsers to demonstrate how the different strategies work in different languages. Thus gender offers a large number of worthwhile projects, both in the core areas of linguistics and in a whole range of cross-disciplinary fields.

323

REFERENCES

Aksenov, A. T. 1984. K probleme èkstralingvističeskoj motivacii grammatičeskoj kategorii roda. *Voprosy jazykoznanija* no. 1: 14–25.

Allan, E. J. 1976. Dizi. In M. L. Bender (ed.) *The Non-Semitic Languages of Ethiopia*, 377–92. East Lansing: African Studies Center, Michigan State University.

Alpher, B. 1987. Feminine as the unmarked grammatical gender: buffalo girls are no fools. *Australian Journal of Linguistics* 7: 169–87.

Anderson, S. C. 1980. The noun class system of Amo. In L. M. Hyman (ed.) *Noun Classes in the Grassfields Bantu Borderland* (Southern California Occasional Papers in Linguistics, 8), 155–78. Los Angeles: Department of Linguistics, University of Southern California.

Anderson, S. R. 1985. Inflectional morphology. In T. Shopen (ed.) *Language Typology and Syntactic Description*, III: *Grammatical Categories and the Lexicon*, 150–201. Cambridge: Cambridge University Press.

Andronov, M. S. 1966. *Grammatika tamil'skogo jazyka*. Moscow: Nauka.

1969. *The Kannaḍa Language*. Moscow: Nauka.

Applegate, J. R. 1958. *An Outline of the Structure of Shilḥa*. New York: American Council of Learned Societies.

Arden, A. H. 1873. *A Progressive Grammar of the Telugu Language: With Copious Examples and Exercises*. Madras: Society for Promoting Christian Knowledge.

1942. *A Progressive Grammar of Common Tamil*. Madras: Christian Literature Society for India. (Fifth edition, revised by A. C. Clayton: first edition 1891.)

Arndt, W. W. 1970. Nonrandom assignment of loanwords: German noun gender. *Word* 26: 244–53.

Arnott, D. W. 1967. Some reflections on the content of individual classes in Fula and Tiv. *La Classification nominale dans les langues négro-africaines*, 45–74. Paris: Centre national de la recherche scientifique.

Asher, R. E. 1985. *Tamil*. London: Croom Helm. (Reprinted 1989, London: Routledge.)

Austin, P. 1981. *A Grammar of Diyari, South Australia*. Cambridge: Cambridge University Press.

Bani, E. 1987. Garka a ipika: masculine and feminine grammatical gender in Kala Lagaw Ya. *Australian Journal of Linguistics* 7: 189–201.

Barkin, F. 1980. The role of loanword assimilation in gender assignment. *Bilingual Review* 7: 105–12.

Barlow, M. 1988. A situated theory of agreement. Unpublished PhD dissertation, Stanford University.

Baron, D. 1986. *Grammar and Gender*. New Haven: Yale University Press.

Baron, N. S. 1971. A reanalysis of English grammatical gender. *Lingua* 27: 113–40.

Batliner, A. 1984. The comprehension of grammatical and natural gender: a cross-linguistic experiment. *Linguistics* 22: 831–56.

Bauernöppel, J., H. Fritsch & B. Bielefeld 1976. *Kurze tschechische Sprachlehre*. Berlin: Volk und Wissen. (Third edition: first edition 1968.)

Beardsmore, H. B. 1971. A gender problem in a language contact situation. *Lingua* 27: 141–59.

Bechert, J. 1982. Grammatical gender in Europe: an areal study of a linguistic category. *Papiere zur Linguistik* (Tübingen) 26: 23–34.

Becker, A. L. 1975. A linguistic image of nature: the Burmese numerative classifier system. *Linguistics* 165: 109–21.

Beito, O. T. 1976. Zum Wechsel des Nominalgeschlechts in den nordischen Sprachen: eine kurze Übersicht. *Zeitschrift für Dialektologie und Linguistik* 43: 11–21.

Bell, C. R. V. 1953. *The Somali Language*. London: Longmans, Green.

Bendix, E. H. 1979. Linguistic models as political symbols: gender and the generic 'he' in English. In J. Orasanu, M. K. Slater & L. L. Adler (eds.) *Language, Sex and Gender: Does* La Différence *Make a Difference?* (Annals of the New York Academy of Sciences, volume 327), 23–39. New York: New York Academy of Sciences.

Bennis, H. & L. Haegeman 1984. On the status of agreement and relative clauses in West-Flemish. In W. de Geest & Y. Putseys (eds.) *Sentential Complementation: Proceedings of the International Conference held at UFSAL, Brussels: June, 1983* (Linguistic Models, 5), 33–53. Dordrecht: Foris.

Berman, R. A. 1985. The acquisition of Hebrew. In D. I. Slobin (ed.) *The Crosslinguistic Study of Language Acquisition*, 255–371. Hillsdale, NJ: Lawrence Erlbaum.

Bhattacharya, S. 1957. *Ollari: A Dravidian Speech*. (Department of Anthropology, Government of India, memoir no. 3, 1956). Delhi: Manager of Publications.

1976. Gender in the Munda languages. In P. N. Jenner, L. C. Thompson & S. Starosta (eds) *Austroasiatic Studies: Part I* (Oceanic Linguistics Special Publication, 13), 189–211. Honolulu: University Press of Hawaii.

Bidot, E. 1925. *La Clef du genre des substantifs français* (*Méthode dispensant d'avoir recours au dictionnaire*). Poitiers: Imprimerie nouvelle.

Bing, J. M. 1987. Phonologically conditioned agreement: evidence from Krahn. In D. Odden (ed.) *Current Approaches to African Linguistics*, IV (Publications in African Languages and Linguistics, 7), 53–60. Dordrecht: Foris.

Black, M. B. 1969. A note on gender in eliciting Ojibwa semantic structures. *Anthropological Linguistics* 11: 177–86.

References

Black-Rogers, M. B. 1982. Algonquian gender revisited: animate nouns and Ojibwa 'power' – an impasse? *Papers in Linguistics* 15, 1: 59–76.

Bleek, W. H. I. 1862–9. *A Comparative Grammar of South African Languages*, I: *Phonology* (1862), II: *The Concord*, section I: *The Noun* (1869). London: Trubner. (Republished 1971 in one volume, Farnborough: Gregg.)

Bloomfield, L. 1933. *Language*. New York: Holt, Rinehart and Winston.

1946. Algonquian. In H. Hoijer (ed.) *Linguistic Structures of Native America* (Viking Fund Publications in Anthropology, 6), 85–129. (Reprinted by Johnson Reprint Corporation, New York.)

[1957] *Eastern Ojibwa: Grammatical Sketch, Texts and Word List*. Ann Arbor: University of Michigan Press.

1962. *The Menomini Language*. New Haven: Yale University Press.

Bodine, A. 1975a. Sex differentiation in language. In B. Thorne & N. Henley (eds.) *Language and Sex: Difference and Dominance*, 130–51. Rowley, MA: Newbury House.

1975b. Androcentrism in prescriptive grammar; singular 'they', sex-indefinite 'he', and 'he or she'. *Language in Society* 4: 129–46.

Boel, E. 1976. Le Genre des noms désignant les professions et les situations feminines en français moderne. *Revue romane* 11: 16–73.

Bokamba, E. G. 1985. Verbal agreement as a noncyclic rule in Bantu. In D. L. Goyvaerts (ed.) *African Linguistics: Essays in Memory of M. W. K. Semikenke* (Studies in the Sciences of Language, 6), 9–54. Amsterdam: Benjamins.

Bokarev, E. A. 1967a. Cezskij jazyk. In E. A. Bokarev & K. V. Lomtatidze (eds.) *Jazyki narodov SSSR*, IV: *Iberijsko-kavkazskie jazyki*, 404–20. Moscow: Nauka.

1967b. Gunzibskij jazyk. In E. A. Bokarev & K. V. Lomtatidze (eds.) *Jazyki narodov SSSR*, IV: *Iberijsko-kavkazskie jazyki*, 472–87. Moscow: Nauka.

1967c. Xvaršinskij jazyk. In E. A. Bokarev & K. V. Lomtatidze (eds.) *Jazyki narodov SSSR*, IV: *Iberijsko-kavkazskie jazyki*, 421–35. Moscow: Nauka.

Bosch, P. 1987. Pronouns under control? A reply to Liliane Tasmowski and Paul Verluyten. *Journal of Semantics* 5: 65–78.

1988. Representing and accessing focussed referents. *Language and Cognitive Processes* 3: 207–32.

Braine, M. D. S. 1987. What is learned in acquiring word classes – a step toward an acquisition theory. In B. MacWhinney (ed.) *Mechanisms of Language Acquisition*, 65–87. Hillsdale, NJ: Lawrence Erlbaum.

Brauner, S. 1979. Aktuelle Tendenzen der Entwicklung der Konkordanzbeziehungen im Swahili. *Zeitschrift für Phonetik, Sprachwissenschaft und Kommunikationsforschung* 32: 422–8.

Bresnan, J. & J. M. Kanerva 1989. Locative inversion in Chicheŵa: a case study in factorization in grammar. *Linguistic Inquiry* 20: 1–50.

Bresnan, J. & S. A. Mchombo 1986. Grammatical and anaphoric agreement. In A. M. Farley, P. T. Farley & K.-E. McCullough (eds.) *CLS 22*, part 2: *Papers from the*

Parasession on Pragmatics and Grammatical Theory at the Twenty-Second Regional Meeting, Chicago Linguistic Society, 278–97. Chicago: Chicago Linguistic Society.

1987. Topic, pronoun, and agreement in Chicheŵa. *Language* 63: 741–82.

Breva-Claramonte, M. 1983. *Sanctius' Theory of Language: A Contribution to the History of Renaissance Linguistics* (Amsterdam Studies in the Theory and History of Linguistic Science, series III: Studies in the History of Linguistics, volume 27). Amsterdam: Benjamins.

Brosman, P. W. 1979. The semantics of the Hittite gender system. *Journal of Indo-European Studies* 7: 227–36.

1982. The development of the PIE feminine. *Journal of Indo-European Studies* 10: 253–72.

Brown, G. & G. Yule 1983. *Discourse Analysis*. Cambridge: Cambridge University Press.

Brown, P. 1980. How and why are women more polite: evidence from a Mayan community. In S. McConnell-Ginet, R. Borker & N. Furman (eds.) *Women and Language in Literature and Society*, 111–36. New York: Praeger.

Bruce, L. 1984. *The Alamblak Language of Papua New Guinea (East Sepik)* (Pacific Linguistics, series C, no. 81). Canberra: Department of Linguistics, Research School of Pacific Studies, Australian National University.

Brugmann, K. 1899. Das Nominalgeschlecht in den indogermanischen Sprachen. *Internationale Zeitschrift für allgemeine Sprachwissenschaft* 4: 100–9.

Burquest, D. A. 1986. The pronoun system of some Chadic languages. In U. Wiesemann (ed.) *Pronominal Systems* (Continuum, 5), 71–101. Tübingen: Narr.

Burrow, T. & S. Bhattacharya 1953. *The Parji Language: A Dravidian Language of Bastar*. Hertford: Austin.

Burton, M. & L. Kirk 1976. Semantic reality of Bantu noun classes: the Kikuyu case. *Studies in African Linguistics* 7, 2: 157–74.

Byarushengo, E. R. 1976. Strategies in loan phonology. *Proceedings of the Second Annual Meeting of the Berkeley Linguistics Society*, 78–88.

Bybee, J. L. 1985. Diagrammatic iconicity in stem-inflection relations. In J. Haiman (ed.) *Iconicity in Syntax: Proceedings of a Symposium on Iconicity in Syntax, Stanford, June 24–6, 1983* (Typological Studies in Language, 6), 11–47. Amsterdam: Benjamins.

Bynon, T. 1977. *Historical Linguistics*. Cambridge: Cambridge University Press.

Cameron, D. & J. Coates 1985. Some problems in the sociolinguistic explanation of sex differences. *Language and Communication* 5: 143–51.

Capell, A. & H. H. J. Coate 1984. *Comparative Studies in Northern Kimberley Languages* (Pacific Linguistics, series C, no. 69). Canberra: Department of Linguistics, Research School of Pacific Studies, Australian National University.

Carstensen, B. 1980. The gender of English loan-words in German. *Studia Anglica Posnaniensia* 12: 3–25.

Castellino, G. R. 1975. Gender in Cushitic. In J. Bynon & T. Bynon (eds.) *Hamito-Semitic: Proceedings of a Colloquium held by the Historical Section of the*

References

Linguistics Association (Great Britain) at the School of Oriental and African Studies, University of London, on the 18th, 19th and 20th of March 1970, 333–59. The Hague: Mouton.

Cercvadze, I. I. 1967. Andijskij jazyk. In E. A. Bokarev & K. V. Lomtatidze (eds.) *Jazyki narodov SSSR*, IV: *Iberijsko-kavkazskie jazyki*, 276–92. Moscow: Nauka.

Černyšev, V. A. 1965. *Sintaksis prostogo predloženija v xindi*. Moscow: Nauka.

Chafe, W. L. 1967. *Seneca Morphology and Dictionary* (Smithsonian Contributions to Anthropology, 4). Washington: Smithsonian Press.

1977. The evolution of third person verb agreement in the Iroquoian languages. In C. N. Li (ed.) *Mechanisms of Syntactic Change*, 493–524. Austin: University of Texas Press.

Champagnol, R. 1982. Représentation en mémoire de mots et de leurs morphèmes de genre et de nombre. *L'Année psychologique* 82: 401–19.

1984. Représentation lexicale du genre et de ses transformations. *Revue canadienne de psychologie* 38: 625–44.

Channon, R. 1983. A comparative sketch of certain anaphoric processes in Russian and English. In M. S. Flier (ed.) *American Contributions to the Ninth International Congress of Slavists, Kiev, September 1983*, I: *Linguistics*, 51–69. Columbus, OH: Slavica.

Chastaing, M. 1973. Le Genre grammatical, symbole de grandeur. *Journal de psychologie normale et pathologique* 70: 427–51.

Chiat, S. 1986. Children's pronouns. In U. Wiesemann (ed.) *Pronominal Systems* (Continuum, 5), 381–404. Tübingen: Narr.

Childs, T. 1983. Noun class affix renewal in Southern West Atlantic. In J. Kaye, H. Koopman, D. Sportiche & A. Dugas (eds.) *Current Approaches to African Linguistics*, II (Publications in African Languages and Linguistics, 5), 17–29. Dordrecht: Foris.

Clark, E. V. 1985. The acquisition of Romance with special reference to French. In D. I. Slobin, (ed.) *The Crosslinguistic Study of Language Acquisition*, 687–782. Hillsdale, NJ: Lawrence Erlbaum.

Clarke, M. A., A. Losoff, M. D. McCracken & J. Still 1981. Gender perception in Arabic and English. *Language Learning* 31: 159–67.

Classification nominale 1967. *La Classification nominale dans les langues négro-africaines*. Paris: Centre national de la recherche scientifique.

Claudi, U. 1985. *Zur Entstehung von Genussystemen: Überlegungen zu einigen theoretischen Aspekten, verbunden mit einer Fallstudie des Zande: Mit einer Bibliographie und einer Karte*. Hamburg: Buske.

Coates, J. 1986. *Women, Men and Language: A Sociolinguistic Account of Sex Differences*. London: Longman.

Comrie, B. S. 1978. Genitive–accusatives in Slavic: the rules and their motivation. *International Review of Slavic Linguistics* 3: 27–42.

1981. *The Languages of the Soviet Union*. Cambridge: Cambridge University Press.

Connell, B. 1987. Noun classification in Lower Cross. *Journal of West African Languages* 17: 110–25.

Cooper, R. 1983. *Quantification and Syntactic Theory* (Synthese Language Library, 21). Dordrecht: Reidel.

Cooper, R. L. 1984. The avoidance of androcentric generics. *International Journal of the Sociology of Language* 50: 5–20.

Corbett, G. G. 1978. Universals in the syntax of cardinal numerals. *Lingua* 46: 355–68.

1979. The agreement hierarchy. *Journal of Linguistics* 15: 203–24.

1980. Neutral agreement. *Quinquereme – New Studies in Modern Languages* 3: 164–70.

1981a. Syntactic features. *Journal of Linguistics* 17: 55–76.

1981b. A note on grammatical agreement in *Šinel'*, *Slavonic and East European Review*, 59: 59–61.

1982. Gender in Russian: an account of gender specification and its relationship to declension. *Russian Linguistics* 6, 2: 197–232.

1983a. *Hierarchies, Targets and Controllers: Agreement Patterns in Slavic*. London: Croom Helm.

1983b. Resolution rules: agreement in person, number and gender. In G. Gazdar, E. Klein & G. K. Pullum (eds.), *Order, Concord and Constituency* (Linguistic Models, 4), 175–206. Dordrecht: Foris.

1986. Gender in German: a bibliography. *Linguistische Berichte* 103: 280–6.

1987. The morphology/syntax interface: evidence from possessive adjectives in Slavonic. *Language* 63: 299–345.

1988. Gender in Slavonic from the standpoint of a general typology of gender systems. *Slavonic and East European Review* 66: 1–20.

1989. An approach to the description of gender systems. In D. Arnold, M. Atkinson, J. Durand, C. Grover & L. Sadler (eds.) *Essays on Grammatical Theory and Universal Grammar*, 53–89. Oxford: Clarendon Press.

forthcoming a. Agreement with non-prototypical controllers. In C. V. Chvany, S. P. Dimitrova & C. E. Gribble (eds.) *Volume in Memory of V. A. Zvegintsev*. (Special issue of *International Journal of Slavic Linguistics and Poetics*.)

forthcoming b. Research into syntactic change: agreement. In J. Jacobs, A. v. Stechow, W. Sternefeld & T. Vennemann (eds.) *Syntax: An International Handbook of Contemporary Research*. Berlin: de Gruyter.

Corbett, G. G. & R. J. Hayward 1987. Gender and number in Bayso. *Lingua* 72: 195–222.

Corbett, G. G. & A. D. Mtenje 1987. Gender agreement in Chichewa. *Studies in African Linguistics* 18, 1: 1–38.

Cornish, F. 1986. *Anaphoric Relations in English and French: A Discourse Perspective*. London: Croom Helm.

1988. Anaphoric pronouns: under linguistic control or signalling particular discourse

References

representations? A contribution to the debate between Peter Bosch, and Liliane Tasmowski and Paul Verluyten. *Journal of Semantics* 5: 233–60.

Cosmas, N. 1981. Grammatical gender in Modern Greek. *Revue romaine de linguistique* 26: 549–57.

—— 1982. Grammatical gender in Ancient Greek. *Revue romaine de linguistique* 27: 47–50.

Craig, C. G. (ed.) 1986a. *Noun Classes and Categorization: Proceedings of a Symposium on Categorization and Noun Classification, Eugene, Oregon, October 1983* (Typological Studies in Language, 7). Amsterdam: Benjamins.

—— 1986b. Jacaltec noun classifiers: a study in language and culture. In C. G. Craig (ed.) *Noun Classes and Categorization: Proceedings of a Symposium on Categorization and Noun Classification, Eugene, Oregon, October 1983* (Typological Studies in Language, 7). 263–93. Amsterdam: Benjamins.

—— 1986c. Jacaltec noun classifiers: a study in grammaticalization. *Lingua* 70: 241–84.

Craik, B. 1982. The animate in Cree language and ideology. In W. Cowan (ed.) *Papers of the Thirteenth Algonquian Conference*, 29–35. Ottowa: Carleton University.

Crawford, M. & L. English 1984. Generic versus specific inclusion of women in language: effects on recall. *Journal of Psycholinguistic Research* 13: 373–81.

Darnell, R. & A. L. Vanek 1976. The semantic basis of the animate/inanimate distinction in Cree. *Papers in Linguistics* 9, 3–4: 159–80.

De Houwer, A. 1987. Gender marking in a young Dutch–English bilingual child. In P. Griffiths, J. Local & A. Mills (eds.) *Proceedings of the Child Language Seminar*, 53–64. York: University of York.

De Wolf, P. 1971. *The Noun Class System of Proto-Benue-Congo*. The Hague: Mouton.

Dekeyser, X. 1980. The diachrony of the gender systems in English and Dutch. In J. Fisiak (ed.) *Historical Morphology* (Trends in Linguistics: Studies and Monographs, 17), 97–111. The Hague: Mouton.

Delisle, G. L. 1972. Universals and person pronouns in Southwestern Chippewa. PhD dissertation, University of Minnesota. (Distributed by University Microfilms, Ann Arbor, reference 73–10, 541.)

Demuth, K. 1988. Noun classes and agreement in Sesotho acquisition. In M. Barlow & C. A. Ferguson (eds.) *Agreement in Natural Language: Approaches, Theories, Descriptions*, 305–21. Stanford: Center for the Study of Language and Information.

Demuth, K., N. Faraclas & L. Marchese 1986. Niger-Congo noun class and agreement systems in language acquisition and historical change. In C. G. Craig (ed.) *Noun Classes and Categorization: Proceedings of a Symposium on Categorization and Noun Classification, Eugene, Oregon, October 1983* (Typological Studies in Language, 7), 453–71. Amsterdam: Benjamins.

Denny, J. P. & C. A. Creider 1976. The semantics of noun classes in Proto-Bantu. *Studies in African Linguistics* 7, 1: 1–30. (Reprinted in C. G. Craig (ed.) 1986. *Noun Classes and Categorization: Proceedings of a Symposium on Categorization and Noun Classification, Eugene, Oregon, October 1983* (Typological Studies in Language, 7), 217–39. Amsterdam: Benjamins.)

Dešeriev, Ju. D. 1953. *Bacbijskij jazyk: fonetika, morfologija, sintaksis, leksika.* Moscow: AN SSSR.

1967. Naxskie jazyki: vvedenie. In E. A. Bokarev & K. V. Lomtatidze (eds.) *Jazyki narodov SSSR*, IV: *Iberijsko-kavkazskie jazyki*, 184–9. Moscow: Nauka.

Desrochers, A. 1986. Genre grammatical et classification nominale. *Revue canadienne de psychologie* 40: 224–50.

Desrochers, A., A. Paivio & S. Desrochers 1986. *L'effet de la fréquence d'usage des mots inanimés et de la valeur prédictive de leur terminaison sur l'identification du genre grammatical* (Research report 21). Ottowa: University of Ottowa, Psychology Laboratory.

Deutsch, W. & F. Wijnen 1985. The article's noun and the noun's article: explorations into the representation and access of linguistic gender in Dutch. *Linguistics* 23: 793–810.

Dietze, J. 1973. Die Entwicklung der altrussischen Kategorie der Beseeltheit im 13 und 14 Jahrhundert. *Zeitschrift für Slawistik* 18: 261–72.

Dimmendaal, G. J. 1983. *The Turkana Language* (Publications in African Languages and Linguistics, 2). Dordrecht: Foris.

Dixon, R. M. W. 1972. *The Dyirbal Language of North Queensland.* Cambridge: Cambridge University Press.

1982. *Where Have All the Adjectives Gone? and other essays in Semantics and Syntax.* Berlin: Mouton.

Dorian, N. 1976. Gender in a terminal Gaelic dialect. *Scottish Gaelic Studies* 12: 279–82.

1981. *Language Death: the Life Cycle of a Scottish Gaelic Dialect.* Philadelphia: University of Pennsylvania Press.

Doroszewski, W. 1962. *O kulturę słowa: Poradnik językowy.* Warsaw: PIW.

Dowty, D. & P. Jacobson 1989. Agreement as a semantic phenomenon. In J. Powers & J. de Jong (eds.) *ESCOL '88: Proceedings of the Fifth Eastern States Conference on Linguistics*, 95–108. Columbus, OH: Ohio State University.

Drossard, W. 1982. Nominalklassifikation in ostkaukasischen Sprachen. In H. Seiler & F. J. Stachowiak (eds.) *Apprehension: Das sprachliche Erfassen von Gegenständen*, II: *Die Techniken und ihr Zusammenhang in Einzelsprachen*, 155–78. Tübingen, Narr.

Dul'zon, A. P. 1964. *Očerki po grammatike ketskogo jazyka*, I. Tomsk: Izdatel'stvo Tomskogo Universiteta.

Duranti, A. & E. Ochs 1979. Left-dislocation in Italian conversation. In T. Givón (ed.) *Discourse and Syntax* (Syntax and Semantics, 12), 377–416. New York: Academic Press.

Dyła, S. 1988. Quasi-comitative coordination in Polish. *Linguistics* 26: 383–414.

Efimov, V. A. 1975. Kategorija roda. In V. S. Rastorgueva (ed.) *Opyt istoriko-tipologičeskogo issledovanija iranskix jazykov*, II: *Èvoljucija grammaticeskix kategorij*, 7–116. Moscow: Nauka.

Einarsson, S. 1949. *Icelandic: Grammar, Texts, Glossary.* Baltimore: Johns Hopkins.

References

Emeneau, M. B. 1955. *Kolami: A Dravidian Language*. (University of California Publications in Linguistics, 12). Berkeley and Los Angeles: University of California Press.

England, J. 1976. 'Dixo Rachel e Vidas': Subject–verb agreement in Old Spanish. *Modern Language Review* 71: 812–26.

Eriksson, O. 1979. Scandinavian gender agreement revisited. *Journal of Linguistics* 15: 93–105.

Ermakova, M. I. 1976. Sopostavitel'noe opisanie sistem soglasovatel'nyx klassov i morfologičeskaja klassifikacija suščestvitel'nyx v sovremennom serbolužickom jazyke. In E. I. Demina (ed.) *Slavjanskoe i balkanskoe jazykoznanie: Problemy morfologii sovremennyx slavjanskix jazykov*, 40–63. Moscow: Nauka.

Ervin, S. M. 1962. The connotations of gender. *Word* 18: 249–61.

Faarlund, J. T. 1977. Embedded clause reduction and Scandinavian gender agreement. *Journal of Linguistics* 13: 239–57.

Faris, J. C. 1978. Nominal classes of the Southeastern Nuba: implications for linguistic science. In R. Thelwall (ed.) *Aspects of Language in the Sudan* (Occasional Papers in Linguistics and Language Learning, 5) 97–113. Coleraine: The New University of Ulster.

Fasske, H. 1981. *Grammatik der obersorbischen Schriftsprache der Gegenwart: Morphologie*. Bautzen: VEB Domowina.

Ferguson, C. A. 1964. Baby talk in six languages. *Language* 66: 103–14.

Findreng, Å. 1976. *Zur Kongruenz in Person und Numerus zwischen Subjekt und finitem Verb im modernen Deutsch*. Oslo: Universitetsforlaget.

Fisher, R. L. 1973. Gender variation in Indo-European. PhD dissertation, University of California, Los Angeles. (Distributed by University Microfilms, Ann Arbor, reference 74–11, 524.)

Fisiak, J. 1975. Some remarks concerning the noun gender assignment of loanwords. *Bulletin de la Société polonaise de linguistique* 33: 59–63.

Flydal, L. 1975. Un Problème social: le conflit des genres en dano-norvégien. *Linguistique* 11: 17–29.

Fodor, I. 1959. The origin of grammatical gender. *Lingua* 8: 1–41, 186–214.

Foley, W. A. 1986. *The Papuan Languages of New Guinea*. Cambridge: Cambridge University Press.

   1988. Language birth: the processes of pidginization and creolization. In F. J. Newmeyer (ed.) *Linguistics: The Cambridge Survey*, IV: *The Socio-Cultural Context*, 162–83. Cambridge: Cambridge University Press.

Foley, W. A. & R. D. Van Valin 1984. *Functional Syntax and Universal Grammar* (Cambridge Studies in Linguistics, 38). Cambridge: Cambridge University Press.

Forchheimer, P. 1953. *The Category of Person in Language*. Berlin: de Gruyter.

Froitzheim, C. & B. Simons 1981. *Sprache und Geschlecht: Bibliographie*, II (series B, paper no. 72). Trier: Linguistic Agency, University of Trier.

Gazdar, G., E. Klein, G. Pullum & I. Sag 1985. *Generalized Phrase Structure Grammar*. Oxford: Blackwell.

Gimpelevič, V. 1982. Svjaz' leksičeskogo i grammatičeskogo osvoenija inojazyčnyx slov v russkom jazyke. *Russian Language Journal* 36, 125: 85–93.

Givón, T. 1970. The resolution of gender conflicts in Bantu conjunction: when syntax and semantics clash. *Papers from the Sixth Regional Meeting, Chicago Linguistic Society, April 16–18, 1970*. Chicago: Chicago Linguistic Society, 250–61.

1971. Some historical changes in the noun-class system of Bantu, their possible causes and wider implications. In C.-W. Kim & H. Stahlke (eds.) *Papers in African Linguistics* (Current Inquiry into Language and Linguistics, 1), 33–54. Edmonton: Linguistic Research.

1972. *Studies in ChiBemba and Bantu grammar* (Studies in African Linguistics, 3, supplement 3). Los Angeles: Department of Linguistics and African Studies Center, University of California.

1976. Topic, pronoun and grammatical agreement. In C. N. Li (ed.) *Subject and Topic*, 149–88. New York: Academic Press.

1979. *On Understanding Grammar*. New York: Academic Press.

1984. *Syntax: A Functional-Typological Introduction*, I. Amsterdam: Benjamins.

Gladkij, A. 1969. K opredeleniju ponjatij padeža i roda suščestvitel'nogo. *Voprosy jazykoznanija* no. 2: 110–23.

1973a. Popytka formal'nogo opredelenija ponjatij padeža i roda suščestvitel'nogo. In A. A. Zaliznjak (ed.) *Problemy grammatičeskogo modelirovanija*, 24–53. Moscow: Nauka.

1973b. An attempt at the formal definition of case and gender of the noun. In F. Kiefer (ed.) *Mathematical Models of Language*, 159–204. Stockholm: Skriptor.

Gotteri, N. 1984. The evasive neuter in Polish. In F. E. Knowles & J. I. Press (eds.), *Papers in Slavonic Linguistics*, II, 1–8. Birmingham: Department of Modern Languages, University of Aston in Birmingham.

Gouffé, C. 1971. Observations sur les emprunts au français dans les parlers haoussa du Niger. *Actes du huitième congrès international de linguistique africaine: Abidjan 24–8 mars 1969*, II, 443–80. Abidjan: University of Abidjan.

Gould, L. J. 1988. Coordination and gender resolution in Kikuria. Paper presented at the Nineteenth Annual African Linguistics Conference, Boston, April 1988.

Graddol, D. & J. Swann *Gender Voices*. Oxford: Blackwell.

Graham, A. 1975. The making of a nonsexist dictionary. In B. Thorne & N. Henley (eds.) *Language and Sex: Difference and Dominance*, 57–63. Rowley, MA: Newbury House.

de la Grasserie, R. 1898. La Catégorie psychologique de la classification revelée par le language. *Revue philosophique de la France et de l'étranger* 45: 594–624.

Graudina, L. K., V. A. Ickovič & L. P. Katlinskaja 1976. *Grammatičeskaja pravil'nost' russkoj reči: opyt častotno-stilističeskogo slovarja variantov*. Moscow: Nauka.

Graur, A. 1937. Sur le genre neutre en roumain. *Bulletin linguistique publié par A. Rosetti* 5: 5–11.

Greenberg, J. H. 1954. Concerning inferences from linguistic to nonlinguistic data. In

References

H. Hoijer (ed.) *Language in Culture: Conference on the Interrelations of Language and Other Aspects of Culture*, 3–19. Chicago: University of Chicago Press.

1962. The study of language contact in Africa. *Symposium on Multilingualism: Second Meeting of the Inter-African Committee on Linguistics: Brazzaville 16–21 VII 1962* (CCTA Publication, 87), 167–75. London: Committee for Technical Cooperation in Africa.

1963. Some universals of grammar with particular reference to the order of meaningful elements. In J. H. Greenberg (ed.) *Universals of Language*, 73–113. Cambridge, MA: MIT Press. (Paperback edition published 1966; page references are to this edition.)

1966. *Language Universals: with Special Reference to Feature Hierarchies.* The Hague: Mouton.

1978. How does a language acquire gender markers? In J. H. Greenberg, C. A. Ferguson & E. A. Moravcsik (eds.) *Universals of Human Language*, III: *Word Structure*, 47–82. Stanford: Stanford University Press.

Gregersen, E. A. 1967. *Prefix and Pronoun in Bantu* (memoir 21 of the *International Journal of American Linguistics*). Bloomington: Indiana University.

Gregor, B. 1983. *Genuszuordnung: Das Genus englischer Lehnwörter im Deutschen* (Linguistische Arbeiten, 129). Tübingen: Niemeyer.

Grevisse, M. 1964. *Le Bon Usage.* Gembloux: J. Duculot. (Eighth edition.)

Grimm, J. 1831. *Deutsche Grammatik*, III. Göttingen: Dieterich.

Gruiță, G. 1981. *Acordul în limba română.* Bucharest: Editura științifică și enciclopedică.

Gudkov, V. 1965. Dodatak pravilima slaganja predikata sa više subjekata. *Književnost i jezik* 12: 60–1.

1974. Prilog o pravilima kongruencije. *Književnost i jezik* 21: 58–61.

Guiora, A. Z., B. Beit-Hallahmi, R. Fried & C. Yoder 1982. Language environment and gender identity attainment. *Language Learning* 32: 289–304.

Gumperz, J. J. & R. Wilson 1971. Convergence and creolization: a case from the Indo-Aryan/Dravidian border. In D. Hymes (ed.) *Pidginization and Creolization of Languages: Proceedings of a Conference held at the University of the West Indies, Mona, Jamaica, April 1968*, 151–67. Cambridge: Cambridge University Press. (Also in *Language in Social Groups: Essays by John J. Gumperz*, selected and introduced by Answar S. Dil, 1971, pp. 251–73. Stanford: Stanford University Press.)

Guthrie, M. 1948. Gender, number and person in Bantu languages. *Bulletin of the School of Oriental and African Studies* 12: 847–56.

Gvozdev, A. N. 1949. *Formirovanie u rebenka grammatičeskogo stroja russkogo jazyka*, I and II. Moscow: APN RSFSR. (Both volumes reprinted in A. N. Gvozdev, 1961, *Voprosy izučenija detskoj reči.* Moscow: APN RSFSR.)

Haas, M. R. 1944. Men's and women's speech in Koasati. *Language* 20: 142–9.

Haiman, J. 1974. *Targets and Syntactic Change.* The Hague: Mouton.

Hall, R. A. 1965. The 'neuter' in Romance: a pseudo-problem. *Word* 21: 421–7.

Hallowell, A. I. 1955. *Culture and Experience*. Philadelphia: University of Pennsylvania Press. (Paperback edition published in 1967 by Schocken; page references are to the paperback edition.)

1960. Ojibwa ontology, behavior, and world view. In S. Diamond (ed.) *Culture in History: Essays in Honor of Paul Radin*, 19–52. New York: Columbia University Press.

Harris, A. C. 1986. Commensurability of terms. In W. P. Lehmann (ed.) *Language Typology 1985: Papers from the Linguistic Typology Symposium, Moscow, 9–13 December 1985* (Current Issues in Linguistic Theory, 47), 55–75. Amsterdam: Benjamins.

Harris, M. 1978. *The Evolution of French Syntax: A Comparative Approach*. (Longman Linguistics Library, 22). London: Longman.

Haugen, E. 1969. *The Norwegian Language in America: A Study in Bilingual Behavior*. Bloomington: Indiana University Press. (Second edition: first edition 1953.)

1976. *The Scandinavian Languages: An Introduction to their History*. London: Faber and Faber.

Hawkinson, A. K. & L. M. Hyman 1974. Hierarchies of natural topic in Shona. *Studies in African Linguistics* 5: 147–70.

Hayward, R. J. 1989. The notion of 'default gender': a key to interpreting the evolution of certain verb paradigms in East Ometo, and its implications for Omotic. *Afrika und Übersee* 72: 17–32.

forthcoming. An analysis of tone and accent in the Qafar noun. To appear in *York Papers in Linguistics* 15.

Hayward, R. J. & G. G. Corbett 1988. Resolution rules in Qafar, *Linguistics* 26: 259–79.

Head, B. F. 1978. Respect degrees in pronominal reference. In J. H. Greenberg, C. A. Ferguson & E. A. Moravcsik (eds.) *Universals of Human Language*, III: *Word Structure*, 151–211. Stanford: Stanford University Press.

Heath, J. 1975. Some functional relationships in grammar. *Language* 51: 89–104.

1978. *Ngandi Grammar, Texts and Dictionary*. Canberra: Australian Institute of Aboriginal Studies.

1983. Referential tracking in Nunggubuyu (Australia). In J. Haiman & P. Munro (eds.) *Switch-Reference and Universal Grammar: Proceedings of a Symposium on Switch Reference and Universal Grammar, Winnipeg, May 1981* (Typological Studies in Language 2), 129–49. Amsterdam: Benjamins.

1984. *Functional Grammar of Nunggubuyu*. Canberra: Australian Institute of Aboriginal Studies.

Heine, B. 1968a. The allocation of loan-words within the nominal class systems of some Togo Remnant languages. *Journal of African Linguistics* 7, 2: 130–9.

1968b. *Die Verbreitung und Gliederung der Togorestsprachen*. (Kölner Beiträge zur Afrikanistik, 1). Berlin: Reimer.

1982. African noun class systems. In H. Seiler & C. Lehmann (eds.) *Apprehension:*

References

Das sprachliche Erfassen von Gegenständen, I: *Bereich und Ordnung der Phänomene*, 189–216. Tübingen: Narr.

Heine, B. & U. Claudi, 1986. *On the Rise of Grammatical Categories: Some Examples from Maa* (Kölner Beiträge zur Afrikanistik 13). Berlin: Reimer.

Heine, B. & M. Reh 1984. *Grammaticalization and Reanalysis in African Languages*. Hamburg: Buske.

Heine, B. & R. Vossen 1983. On the origin of gender in Eastern Nilotic. In R. Vossen & M. Bechhaus-Gerst (eds.) *Nilotic Studies: Proceeding of the International Symposium on Languages and History of the Nilotic Peoples, Cologne, January 4–6, 1982*, part II (Kölner Beiträge zur Afrikanistik, 10), 255–68. Berlin: Reimer.

Hellan, L. 1977. X̄-syntax, categorial syntax and logical form. In T. Freitheim & L. Hellan (eds.) *Papers from the Trondheim Syntax Symposium 1977*, 85–135. Trondheim: University of Trondheim, Department of Linguistics.

Henzl, V. M. 1975. Acquisition of grammatical gender in Czech. *Reports on Child Language Development* 10: 188–200.

Herbert, R. K. 1985. Gender systems and semanticity: two case histories from Bantu. In J. Fisiak (ed.) *Historical Semantics: Historical Word-Formation* (Trends in Linguistics: Studies and Monographs, 29), 171–97. Berlin: Mouton.

Herbert, R. K. & B. Nykiel-Herbert 1986. Explorations in linguistic sexism: a contrastive sketch. *Papers and Studies in Contrastive Linguistics* 21: 47–85.

Hetzron, R. 1972. Phonology in syntax. *Journal of Linguistics* 8: 251–65.

Hewitt, B. G. 1979. *Abkhaz* (Lingua Descriptive Studies, 2). Amsterdam: North Holland.

Hinnebusch, T. J. 1979. Swahili. In T. Shopen (ed.) *Languages and Their Status*, 209–93. Cambridge, MA: Winthrop.

Hockett, C. F. 1958. *A Course in Modern Linguistics*. New York: Macmillan.

1966. What Algonquian is really like. *International Journal of American Linguistics* 32: 59–73.

Holmer, N. M. 1949. Goajiro (Arawak) II: Nouns and associated morphemes. *International Journal of American Linguistics* 15: 110–20.

Hooper, J. B. 1980. Child morphology and morphophonemic change. In J. Fisiak (ed.) *Historical Morphology* (Trends in Linguistics: Studies and Monographs, 17), 157–87. The Hague: Mouton.

Horton, A. E. 1949. *A Grammar of Luvale*. Johannesburg: Witwatersrand University Press.

Huntley, D. 1980. The evolution of genitive–accusative animate and personal nouns in Slavic dialects. In J. Fisiak (ed.) *Historical Morphology* (Trends in Linguistics: Studies and Monographs, 17), 189–212. The Hague: Mouton.

1989. Grammatical and lexical features in number and gender agreement in Old Bulgarian. *Paleobulgarica* 13, 4: 21–32.

Hurford, J. R. 1987. *Language and Number: The Emergence of a Cognitive System*. Oxford: Blackwell.

Hyman, L. M. (ed.) 1980a. *Noun Classes in the Grassfields Bantu Borderland* (Southern

California Occasional Papers in Linguistics, 8). Los Angeles: Department of Linguistics, University of Southern California.

1980b. Babanki and the Ring group. In L. M. Hyman & J. Voorhoeve (eds.) *Les Classes nominales dans le bantou des grassfields* (vol. I of L'Expansion bantoue: Actes du Colloque International du CNRS: Viviers (France) – 4–16 avril 1977), 225–58. Paris: Société d'études linguistiques et anthropologiques de France.

1981. *Noni Grammatical Structure: With Special Reference to Verb Morphology* (Southern California Occasional Papers in Linguistics, 9). Los Angeles: Department of Linguistics, University of Southern California.

Hyman, L. M. & A. Duranti 1982. On the object relation in Bantu. In P. J. Hopper & S. A. Thompson (eds.) *Studies in Transitivity* (Syntax and Semantics, 15), 217–39. New York: Academic Press.

Ibrahim, M. H. 1973. *Grammatical Gender*. The Hague: Mouton.

Ickovič, V. A. 1980. Suščestvitel'nye oduševlennye i neoduševlennye v sovremennom russkom jazyke (norma i tendencija). *Voprosy jazykoznanija* no. 4: 84–96.

Ilola, E. & A. Mustajoki 1989. *Report on Russian Morphology as it Appears in Zaliznyak's Grammatical Dictionary* (Slavica Helsingiensia, 7). Helsinki: Department of Slavonic Languages, University of Helsinki.

Innes, G. 1966. *An Introduction to Grebo*. London: School of Oriental and African Studies, University of London.

Irvine, J. T. 1978. Wolof noun classification: the social setting of divergent change. *Language in Society* 7: 37–64.

Ivić, M. 1963. Relationship of gender and number in Serbocroatian substantives. *International Journal of Slavic Linguistics and Poetics* 6: 51–7.

Jakobson, R. 1966. On linguistic aspects of translation. In R. A. Brower (ed.) *On Translation*, 232–9. New York: Oxford University Press.

1971. On the Rumanian neuter. *Selected Writings*, II: *Word and Language*, 187–9. The Hague: Mouton.

Janko-Trinickaja, N. A. 1966. Naimenovanie lic ženskogo pola suščestvitel'nymi ženskogo i mužskogo roda. In A. E. Zemskaja & D. N. Šmelev (eds.) *Razvitie slovoobrazovanija sovremennogo russkogo jazyka*, 167–210. Moscow: Nauka.

Jenewari, C. E. W. 1983. Defaka, Ijo's closest linguistic relative. In I. R. Dirhoff (ed.) *Current Approaches to African Linguistics*, I (Publications in African Languages and Linguistics, 1), 85–111. Dordrecht: Foris.

Jespersen, O. 1924. *The Philosophy of Grammar*. London: Allen and Unwin.

Jones, C. 1967a. The functional motivation of linguistic change: a study of the development of the grammatical category of gender in the late Old English period. *English Studies* 48: 97–111.

1967b. The grammatical category of gender in early Middle English. *English Studies* 48: 289–305.

1988. *Grammatical Gender in English: 950 to 1250*. London: Croom Helm.

Jónsson, S. 1927. *A Primer of Modern Icelandic*. London: Oxford University Press.

References

Joseph, B. D. 1979. On the animate–inanimate distinction in Cree. *Anthropological Linguistics* 21, 7: 351–4.

Kadagidze, D. & N. Kadagidze 1984. *Cova-tušinsko-gruzinsko-russkij slovar'*. Tbilisi: Mecniereba.

Kadima, M. 1969. *Le Système des classes en bantou*. Leuven: Vander.

Karmiloff-Smith, A. 1979. *A Functional Approach to Child Language: A Study of Determiners and Reference*. Cambridge: Cambridge University Press.

Kaye, J. D. 1981. La Sélection des formes pronominales en vata. *Revue québecoise de linguistique* 11: 117–34.

Keenan, E. L. 1978. On surface form and logical form. In B. B. Kachru (ed.) *Linguistics in the Seventies: Directions and Prospects: Forum Lectures Presented at the 1978 Linguistic Institute of the Linguistic Society of America (= Studies in the Linguistic Sciences* 8, no. 2), 163–203. Urbana, Illinois: Department of Linguistics, University of Illinois, Urbana.

Kempson, R. M. 1988. Logical form: the grammar cognition interface. *Journal of Linguistics* 24: 393–431.

Khaidakov, S. M. [Xajdakov, S. M.] 1963. Principy raspredelenija imen suščestvitel'nyx po grammatičeskim klassam v lakskom jazyke. *Studia Caucasica* 1: 48–55.

1966. The dialect divisions of Lak. *Studia Caucasica* 2: 9–18.

1980. *Principy imennoj klassifikacii v dagestanskix jazykax*. Moscow: Nauka.

Kibrik, A. E. 1972. O formal'nom vydelenii soglasovatel'nyx klassov v arčinskom jazyke. *Voprosy jazykoznanija* no. 1: 124–31.

1977a. *Opyt strukturnogo opisanija arčinskogo jazyka*, II: *Taksonomičeskaja grammatika*. (Publikacii otdelenija strukturnoj i prikladnoj lingvistiki, 12). Moscow: Izdatel'stvo Moskovskogo universiteta.

1977b. *Opyt strukturnogo opisanija arčinskogo jazyka*, III: *Dinamičeskaja grammatika*. (Publikacii otdelenija strukturnoj i prikladnoj lingvistiki, 13). Moscow: Izdatel'stvo Moskovskogo universiteta.

1979. *Materialy k tipologii èrgativnosti*, II: *Lakskij jazyk*, III: *Čiragskij jazyk* (Predvaritel'nye publikacii 127). Moscow: Institut russkogo jazyka AN SSSR.

Kibrik, A. E., S. V. Kodzasov & I. P. Olovjannikova 1972. *Fragmenty grammatiki xinalugskogo jazyka* (Publikacii otdelenija strukturnoj i prikladnoj lingvistiki, 9). Moscow: Izdatel'stvo Moskovskogo universiteta.

Kibrik, A. E., S. V. Kodzasov, I. P. Olovjannikova & D. S. Samedov 1977. *Opyt strukturnogo opisanija arčinskogo jazyka*, I: *Leksika, fonetika* (Publikacii otdelenija strukturnoj i prikladnoj lingvistiki, 11). Moscow: Izdatel'stvo Moskovskogo universiteta.

Kitajgorodskaja, M. V. 1976. Variativnost' v vyraženii roda suščestvitel'nogo pri oboznačenii ženščin po professii. In L. P. Krysin & D. N. Šmelev (eds.), *Social'no-lingvističeskie issledovanija*, 144–55. Moscow: Nauka.

Klajn, I. 1984–5. On conceptual neuter. *Zbornik Matice Srpske za filologiju i lingvistiku* (Novi Sad) 27–8: 347–54.

Klenin, E. 1983. *Animacy in Russian: A New Interpretation* (UCLA Slavic Studies, 6). Colombus, OH: Slavica.

Köhler, C. 1971. Noun classes and grammatical agreement in !Xũ (zû-/hoà dialect). *Actes du huitième congrès international de linguistique africaine: Abidjan 24–8 mars 1969* II, 489–522. Abidjan: University of Abidjan.

Köpcke, K.-M. 1982. *Untersuchungen zum Genussystem der deutschen Gegenwartssprache* (Linguistische Arbeiten, 122). Tübingen: Niemeyer.

Köpcke, K.-M. & Zubin, D. A. 1984. Sechs Prinzipien für die Genuszuweisung im Deutschen: Ein Beitrag zur natürlichen Klassifikation. *Linguistische Berichte* 93: 26–50.

Kopeliovič, A. B. 1977. K voprosu o kodifikacii imen suščestvitel'nyx obščego roda. In V. A. Ickovič, G. I. Mis'kevič & L. I. Skvorcov (eds.) *Grammatika i norma*, 178–92. Moscow: Nauka.

Koval', A. I. 1979. O značenii morfologičeskogo pokazatelja klassa v fula. In N. V. Oxotina (ed.) *Morfonologija i morfologija klassov slov v jazykax Afriki*, 5–100. Moscow: Nauka.

——— 1987. O nekotoryx osobennostjax povedenija pokazatelja klassa v jazyke s gromozdkoj klassnoj sistemy. In N. V. Oxotina (ed.) *Imennye klassy v jazykax Afriki*, 204–15. Moscow: Nauka.

Koval', A. I. & G. V. Zubko 1986. *Jazyk fula.* Moscow: Nauka.

Krejnovič, E. A. 1961. Imennye klassy i grammatičeskie sredstva ix vyraženija v ketskom jazyke. *Voprosy jazykoznanija* no. 2: 106–16.

——— 1968a. Ketskij jazyk. In P. Ja Skorik (ed.) *Jazyki narodov SSSR*, V: *Mongol'skie, tunguso-man'čžurskie i paleoaziatskie jazyki*, 453–73. Leningrad: Nauka.

——— 1968b. O grammatičeskom vyraženii imennyx klassov v glagole ketskogo jazyka. In V. V. Ivanov, V. N. Toporov & B. A. Uspensky (eds.) *Studia Ketica: Linguistics*, 139–95. Moscow: Nauka.

——— 1968c. *Glagol ketskogo jazyka.* Leningrad: Nauka.

Krishnamurti, B. & P. Sivananda Sarma 1968. *A Basic Course in Modern Telugu.* Hyderabad: B. Krishnamurti.

Kučera, H. & W. N. Francis 1967. *Computational Analysis of Present-Day American English.* Providence: Brown University Press.

Kühner, R. & C. Stegmann 1955. *Ausführliche Grammatik der lateinischen Sprache: Satzlehre: Erster Teil.* Leverkusen: Gottschalksche Verlagsbuchhandlung. (Third edition.)

Kuiper, A. & V. Pickett 1974. Personal pronouns in Diuxi Mixtec. *Summer Institute of Linguistics: Mexico Workpapers* 1: 53–8.

Kulak, J., W. Łaciak & I. Żelezkiewicz 1966. *Język polski (Skrypt dla cudzoziemców).* Warsaw: PWN. (Fourth edition.)

Kunene, E. C. L. 1986. Acquisition of siSwati noun classes. *South African Journal of African Languages* 6: 34–7.

Kutik, E. J. 1983. Noun class assignment of English loanwords in Kikuyu. In J. Kaye, H. Koopman, D. Sportiche & A. Dugas (eds.) *Current Approaches to African*

References

Linguistics, II (Publications in African Languages and Linguistics, 5), 345–59. Dordrecht: Foris.

Lakoff, G. 1986. Classifiers as a reflection of mind. In C. G. Craig (ed.) *Noun Classes and Categorization: Proceedings of a Symposium on Categorization and Noun Classification, Eugene, Oregon, October 1983* (Typological Studies in Language, 7), 13–51. Amsterdam: Benjamins. (This material is discussed in a fuller context in Lakoff 1987.)

—— 1987. *Women, Fire and Dangerous Things: What Categories Reveal about the Mind.* Chicago: University of Chicago Press.

Lapointe, S. G. 1988. Toward a unified theory of agreement. In M. Barlow & C. A. Ferguson (eds.) *Agreement in Natural Language: Approaches, Theories, Descriptions*, 67–87. Stanford: Center for the Study of Language and Information.

Laskowski, R. 1986. The development of the category of gender in the Slavic languages. In D. Kastovsky & A. Szwedek (eds.) *Linguistics across Historical and Geographical Boundaries*, I: *Linguistic Theory and Historical Linguistics*, 459–72. Berlin: Mouton de Gruyter.

Leakey, L. S. B. 1959. *First Lessons in Kikuyu.* Nairobi: Eagle Press.

Leeding, V. J. 1989. Anindilyakwa phonology and morphology. Unpublished PhD dissertation, University of Sydney.

Lehmann, C. 1982. Universal and typological aspects of agreement. In H. Seiler & F. J. Stachowiak (eds.) *Apprehension: Das sprachliche Erfassen von Gegenständen*, II: *Die Techniken und ihr Zusammenhang in Einzelsprachen*, 201–67. Tübingen: Narr.

Lehmann, W. P. 1958. On earlier stages of the Indo-European nominal inflection. *Language* 34: 179–202.

Lenček, R. 1972. O zaznamovanosti in nevtralizaciji slovnične kategorije spola v slovenskem knjižnem jeziku. *Slavistična revija* 20: 55–63.

Leroy, J. 1980. The Ngemba group: Mankon, Bagangu, Mundum I, Bafut, Nkwen, Bambui, Pinyin, Awing. In L. M. Hyman & J. Voorhoeve (eds.) *Les Classes nominales dans le bantou des grassfields* (vol. I of L'Expansion bantoue: Actes du Colloque International du CNRS: Viviers (France) – 4–16 avril 1977), 111–41. Paris: Société d'études linguistiques et anthropologiques de France.

Levy, Y. 1983. It's frogs all the way down. *Cognition* 15: 75–93.

Luckov, A. D. 1987. Grammatičeskoe oformlenie zaimstvovanij v jazykax sona i ndebele. In N. V. Oxotina (ed.) *Imennye klassy v jazykax Afriki*, 190–203. Moscow: Nauka.

Luxt, L. I. 1970. *Sravnitel'no-sopostavitel'naja grammatika romanskix jazykov: rumynskij jazyk.* Moscow: Nauka.

Lyons, J. 1977. *Semantics*, II. Cambridge: Cambridge University Press.

McConnell-Ginet, S. 1979. Prototypes, pronouns and persons. In M. Mathiot (ed.) *Ethnolinguistics: Boas, Sapir and Whorf Revisited* (Contributions to the Sociology of Language, 27), 63–83. The Hague: Mouton.

—— 1983. Review article on J. Orasanu, M. K. Slater and L. L. Adler (eds.) *Language*,

Sex and Gender; M. Vetterling-Braggin (ed.) *Sexist Language. Language* 59: 373–91.

1988. Language and gender. In F. J. Newmeyer (ed.) *Linguistics: The Cambridge Survey*, IV: *The Socio-Cultural Context*, 75–99. Cambridge: Cambridge University Press.

MacKay, D. G. 1983. Prescriptive grammar and the pronoun problem. In B. Thorne, C. Kramarae & N. Henley (eds.) *Language, Gender and Society*, 38–53. Rowley, MA: Newbury House.

MacKay, D. G. & D. C. Fulkerson, 1979. On the comprehension and production of pronouns. *Journal of Verbal Learning and Verbal Behavior* 18: 661–73.

McKay, G. R. 1979. Gender and the category *unit augmented*. *Oceanic Linguistics* 18: 203–10.

Madieva, G. I. 1967. Avarskij jazyk. In E. A. Bokarev & K. V. Lomtatidze (eds.) *Jazyki narodov SSSR*, IV: *Iberijsko-kavkazskie jazyki*, 255–75. Moscow: Nauka.

Magnan, S. S. 1983. Age and sensitivity to gender in French. *Studies in Second Language Acquisition* 5, 2: 194–212.

Magomedbekova, Z. M. 1967a. Karatinskij jazyk. In E. A. Bokarev & K. V. Lomtatidze (eds.) *Jazyki narodov SSSR*, IV: *Iberijsko-kavkazskie jazyki*, 323–35. Moscow: Nauka.

1967b. Čamalinskij jazyk. In E. A. Bokarev & K. V. Lomtatidze (eds.) *Jazyki narodov SSSR*, IV: *Iberijsko-kavkazskie jazyki*, 384–99. Moscow: Nauka.

Magometov, A. A. 1976. Sistema grammatičeskix klassov v xinalugskom jazyke. *Annual of Ibero-Caucasian Linguistics* 3: 232–59.

Mallinson, G. 1984. Problems, pseudo-problems and hard evidence – another look at the Rumanian neuter. *Folia Linguistica* 18: 439–51.

Malone, J. L. 1985. On the feminine pronominalization of Irish and English boat nouns. *General Linguistics* 25: 189–98.

Maratsos, M. P. & M. A. Chalkley 1980. The internal language of children's syntax: the ontogenesis and representation of syntactic categories. In K. E. Nelson (ed.) *Children's Language*, II, 127–214. New York: Gardner Press.

Marchese, L. 1986. The pronominal system of Godié. In E. Wiesemann (ed.) *Pronominal Systems* (Continuum, 5), 217–55. Tübingen: Narr.

1988. Noun classes and agreement systems in Kru: a historical approach. In M. Barlow & C. A. Ferguson (eds.) *Agreement in Natural Language: Approaches, Theories, Descriptions*, 323–41. Stanford: Center for the Study of Language and Information.

Marcoux, D. R. 1973. Deviation in English gender. *American Speech* 48: 98–107.

Marcus, S. 1962. Le Genre grammatical et son modèle logique. *Cahiers de linguistique théorique et appliquée* 1: 103–22.

1963. A synchronic analysis of the grammatical gender. *Revue de linguistique* (Bucharest) 7, 1: 99–111.

1967. *Algebraic Linguistics: Analytical Models*. New York: Academic Press.

1970. Les Modèles mathématiques et l'opposition romane-slave dans la typologie du

341

References

genre grammatical. In A. Rosetti (ed.) *Actele celui de-al XII-lea Congres internaţional de lingvistică şi filologie romanică*, I, 247–52. Bucharest: Editura Academiei Republicii Socialiste România.

Marković, S. V. 1954. O kolebljivosti slaganja u rodu kod imenica čiji se prirodni i gramatički rod ne slažu (i o rodu ovih imenica). *Pitanja književnosti i jezika* (Sarajevo) 1: 87–110.

Martyna, W. 1980. The psychology of the generic masculine. In S. McConnell-Ginet, R. Borker & N. Furman (eds.) *Women and Language in Literature and Society*, 69–78. New York: Praeger.

Martysiuk, M. 1970. Rodovaja assimiljacija nemeckix zaimstvovanij v russkom jazyke. *Studia Rossica Posnaniensia* 1: 173–81.

Mathiot, M. & M. Roberts 1979. Sex roles as revealed through referential gender in American English. In M. Mathiot (ed.) *Ethnolinguistics: Boas, Sapir and Whorf Revisited* (Contributions to the Sociology of Language, 27), 1–47. The Hague: Mouton.

Meillet, A. 1931. Essai de chronologie des langues indo-européennes: la théorie du féminin. *Bulletin de la Societé de linguistique de Paris* 32: 1–28.

Meinhof, C. 1899. *Grundriss einer Lautlehre der Bantusprachen nebst Anleitung zur Aufnahme von Bantusprachen*. Leipzig: Brockhaus. (Second edition 1910, English edition *Introduction to the Phonology of the Bantu Languages*, translated by N. J. van Warmelo published 1932. Berlin: Dietrich Reimer.]

1906. *Grundzüge einer vergleichenden Grammatik der Bantu-sprachen*. Berlin: Dietrich Reimer. (Second edition 1948.)

1910. *Die moderne Sprachforschung in Afrika: Hamburgische Vorträge*. Berlin: Buchhandlung der Berliner evangelischen Missionsgesellschaft.

Mel'čuk, I. A. 1958 [1974]. Statistika i zavisimost' roda francuzskix suščestvitel'nyx ot ix okončanija. *Bjulleten' ob''edinenija po problemam mašinnogo perevoda* 7: 13–40. (Revised version, same title, also published 1958, in the collection *Voprosy statistiki reči*, 112–30, Leningrad: Izdatel'stvo Leningradskogo Universiteta. English version: Statistics and the relationship between the gender of French nouns and their endings. In V. Ju. Rozencvejg (ed.) 1974 *Essays on Lexical Semantics*, I, 11–42. Stockholm: Skriptor. Page references are to the 1974 English translation.)

1985. *Poverxnostnyj sintaksis russkix čislovyx vyraženij* (Wiener Slawistischer Almanach, special volume, 16). Vienna: Institut für Slawistik der Universität Wien.

Mel'čuk, I. A. & É. Bakiza 1987. Les Classes nominales en kirundi. *Bulletin de la Societé de linguistique de Paris* 82: 283–341.

Mills, A. E. 1986. *The Acquisition of Gender: A Study of English and German*. Berlin: Springer.

Miranda, R. V. 1975. Indo-European gender: a study in semantic and syntactic change. *Journal of Indo-European Studies* 3: 199–215.

Mitchell, B. 1985. *Old English Syntax*, I: *Concord, The Parts of Speech, and the Sentence*. Oxford: Clarendon.

Moravcsik, E. A. 1974. Object–verb agreement. *Working Papers on Language Universals* 15: 25–140.

1978. Agreement. In J. H. Greenberg, C. A. Ferguson & E. A. Moravcsik (eds.) *Universals of Human Language*, IV: *Syntax*, 331–74. Stanford: Stanford University Press.

Mučnik, I. P. 1971. *Grammatičeskie kategorii glagola i imeni v sovremennom russkom literaturnom jazyke*. Moscow: Nauka.

Mulford, R. 1985. Comprehension of Icelandic pronoun gender: semantic versus formal factors. *Journal of Child Language* 12: 443–53.

Murkelinskij, G. B. 1967. Lakskij jazyk. In E. A. Bokarev & K. V. Lomtatidze (eds.) *Jazyki narodov SSSR*, IV: *Iberijsko-kavkazskie jazyki*, 488–507. Moscow: Nauka.

Naden, A. J. 1982. Class pronoun desuetude revisited. *Journal of West African Languages* 12: 34–42.

Napoli, D. J. 1975. A global agreement phenomenon. *Linguistic Inquiry* 6: 413–35.

Nerlove, S. & A. K. Romney 1967. Sibling terminology and cross-sex behavior. *American Anthropologist* 69, 2: 179–87.

Newman, P. 1979. Explaining Hausa feminines. *Studies in African Linguistics* 10, 2: 197–226.

Nilsson, K. 1979. Concerning number and gender in a non-congruent construction. *Studia Linguistica* 33: 79–88.

Ojeda, A. E. 1984. A note on the Spanish neuter. *Linguistic Inquiry* 15: 171–3.

1989. Markedness and individuation: the case of the Spanish neuter. Unpublished manuscript, University of California, Davis.

Oomen, A. 1981. Gender and plurality in Rendille. *Afroasiatic Linguistics* 8, 1: 35–75.

Orr, G. J. 1987. Aspects of the second language acquisition of Chichewa noun class morphology. PhD dissertation, University of California, Los Angeles. (Distributed by University Microfilms International, Ann Arbor, reference 8713873.)

Oxotina, N. V. 1985. *Soglasovatel'nye klassy v vostočnyx i južnyx jazykax bantu: Kommunikativnyj status i grammatičeskaja struktura*. Moscow: Nauka.

Palmer, F. 1971. *Grammar*. Harmondsworth: Penguin.

Panov, M. V. (ed.) 1968. *Morfologia i sintaksis sovremennogo russkogo literaturnogo jazyka (Russkij jazyk i sovetskoe obščestvo: Sociologo-lingvističeskoe issledovanie: III)*. Moscow: Nauka.

Parker, E. M. & R. J. Hayward 1985. *An Afar–English–French Dictionary (with Grammatical Notes in English)*. London: School of Oriental and African Studies, University of London.

Parsons, F. W. 1960. An introduction to gender in Hausa. *African Language Studies* 1: 117–36.

Pasch, H. 1985. Possession and possessive classifiers in 'Dongo-ko. *Afrika und Übersee* 68: 69–85.

1986. *Die Mba-Sprachen: Die Nominalklassensysteme und die genetische Gliederung*

References

einer Gruppe von Ubangi-Sprachen (Sprache und Geschichte in Afrika, 6). Hamburg: Buske.

Payne, J. R. 1980. The decay of ergativity in Pamir languages. *Lingua* 51: 147–86.

1989. Pāmir languages. In R. Schmitt (ed.) *Compendium Linguarum Iranicarum*, 417–44. Wiesbaden: Reichert.

Perkowski, J. L. & E. Vrabie 1986. Covert semantic and morphophonemic categories in the Romanian gender system. *Slavic and East European Journal* 30: 54–67.

Philips, S. U., S. Steele & C. Tanz 1987. *Language, Gender, and Sex in Comparative Perspective* (Studies in the Social and Cultural Foundations of Language, 4). Cambridge: Cambridge University Press.

Pillinger, O. S. 1989. Accent, tone and prosodic structure in Rendille. Unpublished PhD thesis, University of London.

Plank, F. 1986. Das Genus der deutschen Ge-Substantive und Verwandtes. (Beiträge zur Vererbungslehre, 1). *Zeitschrift für Phonetik, Sprachwissenschaft und Kommunikationsforschung* 39: 44–60.

Pollard, C. & I. A. Sag 1988. An information-based theory of agreement. In D. Brentari, G. Larson & L. MacLeod (eds.) *CLS 24, Papers from the 24th Annual Regional Meeting of the Chicago Linguistic Society*, part II: *Parasession on Agreement in Grammatical Theory*, 236–57. Chicago: Chicago Linguistic Society.

Poplack, S. & D. Sankoff 1984. Borrowing: the synchrony of integration. *Linguistics* 22: 99–135.

Poplack, S., A. Pousada & D. Sankoff 1982. Competing influences on gender assignment: variable process, stable outcome. *Lingua* 57: 1–28.

Poplack, S., D. Sankoff & C. Miller 1988. The social correlates and lexical processes of lexical borrowing and assimilation. *Linguistics* 26: 47–104.

Popova, M. I. 1958. Grammatičeskie èlementy jazyka v reči detej preddoškol'nogo vozrasta. *Voprosy psixologii* 4, 3: 106–17. (English version: Grammatical elements of language in the speech of pre-preschool children. In C. A. Ferguson & D. I. Slobin (eds.) 1973 *Studies of Child Language Development*, 269–80. New York: Holt, Rinehart and Winston.)

Priestly, T. M. S. 1983. On 'drift' in Indo-European gender systems. *Journal of Indo-European Studies* 11, 3–4: 339–63.

Pullum, G. K. & A. M. Zwicky 1986. Phonological resolution of syntactic feature conflict. *Language* 62: 751–73.

Pulman, S. G. 1983. *Word Meaning and Belief*. London: Croom Helm.

Quirk, R., S. Greenbaum, G. Leech & J. Svartvik 1985. *A Comprehensive Grammar of the English Language*. London: Longman.

Rabel-Heymann, L. 1977. Gender in Khasi nouns. *Mon-Khmer Studies* 6: 247–72.

Reh, M. 1983. Krongo: a VSO language with postpositions. *Journal of African Languages and Linguistics* 5: 45–55.

Richardson, I. 1967. Linguistic evolution and Bantu noun class systems. *La Classification nominale dans les langues négro-africaines*, 373–90. Paris: Centre national de la recherche scientifique.

Roberts, L. & M. Wolontis 1974. Conjunction and concord in Bantu. In E. Voeltz (ed.) *Third Annual Conference on African Linguistics, 7–8 April 1972* (Indiana University Publications, African Series, 7), 231–42. Bloomington: Indiana University.

Robins, R. H. 1951. *Ancient and Mediaeval Grammatical Theory in Europe; with Particular Reference to Modern Linguistic Doctrines.* London: Bell.

1979. *A Short History of Linguistics.* London: Longman. (Second edition: first edition 1967.)

Roca, I. M. 1989. The organisation of grammatical gender. *Transactions of the Philological Society* 87: 1–32.

Rogers, M. 1987. Learners' difficulties with grammatical gender in German as a foreign language. *Applied Linguistics* 8: 48–74.

Rosch, E. 1978. Principles of categorization. In E. Rosch & B. L. Lloyd (eds.) *Cognition and Categorization*, 27–48. Hillsdale, NJ: Lawrence Erlbaum.

Rosetti, A. 1965. *Linguistica.* The Hague: Mouton.

1983. *Études de linguistique générale.* Bucharest: Univers.

Ross, A. S. C. 1936. Sex and gender in the *Lindisfarne Gospels. Journal of English and Germanic Philology* 35: 321–30.

Ross, J. R. 1973. Nouniness. In O. Fujimura (ed.) *Three Dimensions of Linguistic Theory*, 137–257. Tokyo: TEC.

Rothstein, R. A. 1973. Sex, gender and the October Revolution. In S. R. Anderson & P. Kiparsky (eds.) *A Festschrift for Morris Halle*, 460–6. New York: Holt Rinehart.

1976. Uwagi o rodzaju gramaticznym i cechach semantyczych wyrazóv. *Język polski* 56: 241–53.

1980. Gender and reference in Polish and Russian. In C. V. Chvany & R. D. Brecht (eds.) *Morphosyntax in Slavic*, 79–97. Columbus: Slavica.

Royen, G. 1929. *Die nominalen Klassifikations-Systeme in den Sprachen der Erde: Historisch-kritische Studie, mit besonderer Berücksichtigung des Indogermanischen.* Mödling: Anthropos.

Rumsey, A. 1982. *An Intra-sentence Grammar of Ungarinjin North-Western Australia* (Pacific Linguistics, series B, no. 86). Canberra: Department of Linguistics, Research School of Pacific Studies, Australian National University.

Russell, R. A. 1984. Historical aspects of subject–verb agreement in Arabic. In G. Alvarez, B. Brodie & T. McCoy (eds.) *ESCOL '84: Proceedings of the First Eastern States Conference on Linguistics*, 116–27. Columbus, OH: Ohio State University.

Saadiev, Š. M. 1967. Kryzskij jazyk. In E. A. Bokarev & K. V. Lomtatidze (eds.) *Jazyki narodov SSSR, IV: Iberijsko-kavkazskie jazyki*, 627–42. Moscow: Nauka.

Sadek, C. S., J. M. Kiraithe & H. Villarreal 1975. The acquisition of the concept of grammatical gender in monolingual and bilingual speakers of Spanish. In F. M. Aid, M. C. Resnick & B. Saciuk (eds.) *1975 Colloquium on Hispanic Linguistics*, 131–49. Washington, DC: Georgetown University Press.

Sapir, J. D. 1971. West Atlantic: an inventory of the languages, their noun class systems and consonant alternation. In T. A. Sebeok (ed.) *Current Trends in Linguistics*, VII: *Linguistics in Sub-Saharan Africa*, 45–112. The Hague: Mouton.

Schane, S. A. 1970. Phonological and morphological markedness. In M. Bierwisch & K. E. Heidolph (eds.) *Progress in Linguistics*, 286–94. The Hague: Mouton.

Schaub, W. 1985. *Babungo*. London: Croom Helm.

Schmidt, A. 1985. *Young People's Dyirbal: An Example of Language Death from Australia*. Cambridge: Cambridge University Press.

Schenker, A. M. 1955. Gender categories in Polish. *Language* 31: 402–8.

Schupbach, R. D. 1984. *Lexical Specialization in Russian* (UCLA Slavic Studies, 8). Columbus, OH: Slavica.

Senft, G. 1986. *Kilivila: the Language of the Trobriand Islanders* (Mouton Grammar Library, 3). Berlin: Mouton de Gruyter.

Serzisko, F. 1982. Numerus/Genus-Kongruenz und das Phänomen der Polarität am Beispiel einiger ostkuschitischer Sprachen. In H. Seiler & F. J. Stachowiak (eds.) *Apprehension: Das sprachliche Erfassen von Gegenständen*, II: *Die Techniken und ihr Zusammenhang in Einzelsprachen*, 179–200. Tübingen: Narr.

Shanmugam Pillai, M. 1965. *Spoken Tamil*, I (Publications in Linguistics, 4). Annamalainagar: Annamalai University.

Shevelov, G. Y. 1963. *The Syntax of Modern Literary Ukrainian: The Simple Sentence*. The Hague: Mouton.

Shieber, S. M. 1986. *An Introduction to Unification-based Approaches to Grammar* (CSLI Lecture Notes, 4). Stanford: Center for the Study of Language and Information.

Shields, K. 1979. A theory of gender change. *Glossa* 13: 27–38.

Silverstein, M. 1985. Language and the culture of gender: at the intersection of structure, usage, and ideology. In E. Mertz & R. J. Parmentier (eds.) *Semiotic Mediation: Sociocultural and Psychological Perspectives*, 219–59. Orlando: Academic Press.

Smith, P. M. 1985. *Languages, the Sexes and Society* (Language in Society, 8). Oxford: Blackwell.

Smoczyńska, M. 1985. The acquisition of Polish. In D. I. Slobin (ed.) *The Crosslinguistic Study of Language Acquisition*, 595–686. Hillsdale, NJ: Lawrence Erlbaum.

Sobin, N. J. 1985. Case assignment in Ukrainian morphological passive constructions. *Linguistic Inquiry* 16: 649–62.

Speiser, E. A. 1938. The pitfalls of polarity. *Language* 14: 187–202.

Spence, N. C. W. 1980. The gender of French compounds. *Zeitschrift für romanische Philologie* 96: 68–91.

Spitz, E. 1965. Beitrag zur Genusbestimmung der deutschen Substantive. *Deutsch als Fremdsprache* 2, 4: 35–43.

Stankiewicz, E. 1968. The grammatical genders of the Slavic languages. *International Journal of Slavic Linguistics and Poetics* 11: 27–41.

Steele, S. 1978. Word order variation: a typology study. In J. H. Greenberg, C. A.

Ferguson & E. A. Moravcsik (eds.), *Universals of Human Language*, IV: *Syntax*, 585–623. Stanford: Stanford University Press.

Steinberg, E. & A. F. Caskey 1988. The syntax and semantics of gender (dis)agreement: an autolexical approach. In D. Brentari, G. Larson & L. MacLeod (eds.) *CLS 24: Papers from the 24th Annual Regional Meeting of the Chicago Linguistic Society*, part II: *Parasession on Agreement in Grammatical Theory*, 291–303. Chicago: Chicago Linguistic Society.

Steinmetz, D. 1985. Gender in German and Icelandic: inanimate nouns. In J. T. Faarlund (ed.) *Germanic Linguistics: Papers from a Symposium at the University of Chicago, April 24, 1985*, 10–28. Bloomington: Indiana University Linguistics Club.

1986. Two principles and some rules for gender in German: inanimate nouns. *Word* 37: 189–217.

Stevens, F. 1984. *Strategies for Second-Language Acquisition*. Montreal: Eden Press.

Straus, A. T. & R. Brightman 1982. The implacable raspberry. *Papers in Linguistics* 15: 97–137.

Stroganova, I. P. 1952. Process razvitija imennoj klassifikacii v jazykax bantu. *Učenye zapiski LGU* 128: *serija vostočnovedčeskix nauk* no. 3: 199–211.

Suárez, J. A. 1983. *The Mesoamerican Indian Languages*. Cambridge: Cambridge University Press.

Sullivan, W. J. 1983. Sex, gender, and sexism in English. In J. Casagrande (ed.) *The Linguistic Connection*, 261–301. Lanham, MD: University Press of America.

Superanskaja, A. V. 1965. Rod zaimstvovannyx suščestvitel'nyx v sovremennom russkom jazyke. *Voprosy kul'tury reči* 6: 44–58.

Surridge, M. E. 1982. L'Attribution du genre grammatical aux emprunts anglais en français canadien: le rôle des homologues et des monosyllabes. *Glossa* 16: 28–39.

1984. Le Genre grammatical des emprunts anglais en français: le perspectif diachronique. *Canadian Journal of Linguistics* 29: 58–72.

Suzman, M. S. 1982. Strategies for acquiring Zulu concord. *South African Journal of African Languages* 2: 53–67.

Svartengren, T. H. 1927. The feminine gender for inanimate things in Anglo-American. *American Speech* 3 (1927–8): 83–113.

Švedova, N. Ju. 1980. Podčinitel'nye svjazi slov i slovosočetanija. In N. Ju Svedova (ed.) *Russkaja grammatika*, II: *sintaksis*, 13–82. Moscow: Nauka.

Taraban, R., J. L. McDonald & B. MacWhinney 1989. Category learning in a connectionist model: learning to decline the German definite article. In R. I. Corrigan, F. Eckman & M. Noonan (eds.) *Linguistic Categorization* (Amsterdam studies in the theory and history of linguistic science: series IV: Current issues in linguistic theory: 61), 164–93. Amsterdam: Benjamins.

Tasmowski-De Ryck, L. & S. P. Verluyten 1981. Pragmatically controlled anaphora and linguistic form. *Linguistic Inquiry* 12: 153–4.

1982. Linguistic control of pronouns. *Journal of Semantics* 1: 323–46.

References

Tasmowski, L. & S. P. Verluyten 1985. Control mechanisms of anaphora. *Journal of Semantics* 4: 341–70.

Taylor, C. 1985. *Nkore-Kiga*. London: Croom Helm.

Taylor-Browne, K. 1984. The acquisition of grammatical gender by children in French immersion programmes. Unpublished MA thesis, University of Calgary.

Thomas, G. 1983. A comparison of the morphological adaptation of loanwords ending in a vowel in contemporary Czech, Russian and Serbo-Croatian. *Canadian Slavonic Papers* 25: 180–205.

Thorne, B. & N. Henley (eds.) 1975. *Language and Sex: Difference and Dominance*. Rowley, MA: Newbury House. (Includes a large annotated bibliography.)

Thorne, B., C. Kramarae & N. Henley (eds.) 1983. *Language, Gender and Society*. Rowley, MA: Newbury House. (Includes a large annotated bibliography.)

Tolstaya, N. I. 1981. *The Panjabi Language: A Descriptive Grammar* (Languages of Asia and Africa, 2). London: Routledge and Kegan Paul.

Toporova, I. N. 1987. Korrelacija klassov v jazykax bantu. In N. V. Oxotina (ed.) *Imennye klassy v jazykax Afriki*, 5–82. Moscow: Nauka.

Trávníček, F. 1949. *Mluvnice spisovné češtiny*, II: *Skladba*. Prague: Melantrich.

Trudgill, P. 1974. *Sociolinguistics: An Introduction*. Harmondsworth: Penguin.

Tryon, D. T. 1970. Noun classification and concord in the Daly River languages. *Mankind* 7: 218–22. (Data superseded by Tryon 1974.)

   1974. *Daly Family Languages, Australia* (Pacific Linguistics, C 32). Canberra: Australian National University.

Tucker, A. N. & M. A. Bryan 1966. *Linguistic Analyses: The Non-Bantu Languages of North-Eastern Africa* (With a supplement on the Ethiopic Languages by Wolf Leslau). London: Oxford University Press.

Tucker, A. N. & J. T. ole Mpaayei 1955. *A Maasai Grammar: With Vocabulary*. London: Longmans, Green.

Tucker, G. R., W. E. Lambert & A. A. Rigault 1977. *The French Speaker's Skill with Grammatical Gender: An Example of Rule-Governed Behavior*. The Hague: Mouton.

Vachek, J. 1964. Notes on gender in Modern English. *Sborník prací filosofické fakulty Brněnské University* A 12: 189–94.

Vanek, A. L. 1970. *Aspects of Subject–Verb Agreement*. Edmonton: Department of Slavic Languages, University of Alberta. (Republished 1977 in the series Current Inquiry into Language and Linguistics, 23. Edmonton: Linguistic Research.)

Veksler, B. X. & V. A. Jurik 1978. *Latyšskij jazyk* (*samoučitel'*). Riga: Zvajgzne. (Third edition.)

Venberg, R. 1971. The problem of a female deity in translation. *Bible Translator* 22, 2: 68–70.

Voeltz, E. 1971. Surface constraints and agreement resolution: some evidence from Xhosa. *Studies in African Linguistics* 2: 37–60.

Voorhoeve, J. 1968. Noun classes in Bamileke. *Lingua* 21: 584–93.

   1980. Noun classes in Adere. In L. M. Hyman (ed.) *Noun Classes in the Grassfields*

Bantu Borderland (Southern California Occasional Papers in Linguistics, 8), 57–72. Los Angeles: Department of Linguistics, University of Southern California.

Wald, B. 1975. Animate concord in Northeast Coastal Bantu: its linguistic and social implications as a case of grammatical convergence. *Studies in African Linguistics* 6, 3: 267–314.

1979. The development of the Swahili object marker: a study of the interaction of syntax and discourse. In T. Givón (ed.) *Discourse and Syntax* (Syntax and Semantics, 12), 505–24. New York: Academic Press.

Watkins, M. H. 1937. *A Grammar of Chichewa: A Bantu Language of British Central Africa*. Philadelphia: Linguistic Society of America.

Watters, J. R. 1980. The Ejagam noun class sytem: Ekoid Bantu revisited. In L. M. Hyman (ed.) *Noun Classes in the Grassfields Bantu Borderland* (Southern California Occasional Papers in Linguistics, 8), 99–137. Los Angeles: Department of Linguistics, University of Southern California.

Welmers, W. E. 1973. *African Language Structures*. Berkeley: University of California Press.

Wełna, J. 1976. Gender determiners in American English (a study in the grammar of loanwords). *Studia Anglica Posnaniensia* 7: 95–108.

1978. Complex gender in Old English loanwords. *Acta Philologica* 7: 143–64.

1980. On gender change in linguistic borrowing (Old English). In J. Fisiak (ed.) *Historical Morphology* (Trends in Linguistics, 17), 399–420. The Hague: Mouton.

Wertz, C. A. 1977. The number of genders in Polish. *Canadian Slavonic Papers* 19: 50–63.

Wheeler, B. I. 1898. The origin of grammatical gender. *Journal of English and Germanic Philology* 2: 528–45.

Whiteley, W. H. 1967. Swahili nominal classes and English loan-words: a preliminary survey. *La Classification nominale dans les langues négro-africaines*, 157–74. Paris: Centre national de la recherche scientifique.

Wienold, G. 1967. *Genus und Semantik*. Meisenheim am Glan: Hain.

1970. Double gender and change of gender. In *Actes du Xe Congrès International des Linguistes*, IV, 397–402. Bucharest: Éditions de l'Académie de la Republique Socialiste de Roumanie.

1989. Genus und Semantik im Indoeuropäischen. In J. Martin & R. Zoepffel (eds.) *Aufgaben, Rollen und Räume von Frau und Mann*, 79–156. Freiberg: Alber.

Wiese, B. 1983. Anaphora by pronouns. *Linguistics* 21: 373–417.

Wilson, W. A. A. 1961. *An Outline of the Temne Language*. London: School of Oriental and African Languages.

1962. Temne, Landuma and the Baga languages. *Sierra Leone Language Review* 1: 27–38.

1971. Class pronoun desuetude in the Mõõre-Dagbani subgroup of Gur. *Journal of West African Languages* 8: 79–83.

Windisch, R. 1973. *Genusprobleme im Romänischen: Das Neutrum im Rumänischen* (Tübinger Beiträge zur Linguistik, 31). Tübingen: Narr.

References

Winston, F. D. D. 1962. The nominal class system of Lokə. *African Language Studies* 3: 49–70.

Wissemann, H. 1966. Zur Frage des Genuswechsels bei Lehnwörtern im Russischen. *Zeitschrift für Slavische Philologie* 33: 305–13.

Worsley, P. M. 1953–4. Noun classification in Australian and Bantu: formal or semantic? *Oceania* 24: 275–88.

Wurzel, W. U. 1986. Die wiederholte Klassifikation von Substantiven: Zur Entstehung von Deklinationsklassen. *Zeitschrift für Phonetik, Sprachwissenschaft und Kommunikationsforschung* 39: 76–96.

Xajdakov, S. M. *see* Khaidakov, S. M.

Xanmagomedov, B. G.-K. 1967. Tabasaranskij jazyk. In E. A. Bokarev & K. V. Lomtatidze (eds.) *Jazyki narodov SSSR, IV: Iberijsko-kavkazskie jazyki*, 545–61. Moscow: Nauka.

Yokoyama, O. T. 1986. Lexical frequency and its implications: the case of contemporary edited Russian. *Slavic and East European Journal* 30, 2: 147–66.

Yu, E. O. 1988. Agreement in left dislocation of coordinate structures. In D. Brentari, G. Larson & L. MacLeod (eds.) *CLS 24: Papers from the 24th Annual Regional Meeting of the Chicago Linguistic Society*, part II: *Parasession on Agreement in Grammatical Theory*, 322–36. Chicago: Chicago Linguistic Society.

Zaliznjak, A. A. 1964. K voprosu o grammatičeskix kategorijax roda i oduševlennosti v sovremennom russkom jazyke. *Voprosy jazykoznanija* no. 4: 25–40.

Zaręba, A. 1984–5. Osobliwa zmiana rodzaju naturalnego w dialektach polskich. *Zbornik Matice srpske za filologiju i lingvistiku* 17–18: 243–7.

Zawawi, S. M. 1979. *Loan Words and their Effect on the Classification of the Swahili Nominals*. Leiden: Brill.

Zaxarova, A. V. 1958. Usvoenie doskol′nikami padežnyx form. *Doklady Akademii pedagogičeskix nauk RSFSR* 2, 3: 81–4. (English version, A. V. Zakharova, Acquisition of forms of grammatical case by preschool children. In C. A. Ferguson & D. I. Slobin (eds.) 1973 *Studies of Child Language Development*, 281–4. New York: Holt, Rinehart & Winston.)

Zemskaja, E. A. (ed.) 1973. *Russkaja razgovornaja reč′*. Moscow: Nauka.

Zieniukowa, J. 1979. Składnia zgody w zdaniach z podmiotem szeregowym we współczesnej polszczyźnie. *Slavia Occidentalis*. 36: 117–29.

Žirkov, L. I. 1955. *Lakskij jazyk: fonetika i morfologija*. Moscow: Akademija nauk SSSR.

Zubin, D. A. & K. M. Köpcke 1981. Gender: a less than arbitrary grammatical category. In R. A. Hendrick, C. A. Masek & M. F. Miller (eds.) *Papers from the Seventeenth Regional Meeting, Chicago Linguistic Society*, 439–49. Chicago: Chicago Linguistic Society.

1984. Affect classification in the German gender system. *Lingua* 63: 41–96.

1986. Gender and folk taxonomy: the indexal relation between grammatical and lexical categorization. In C. G. Craig (ed.) *Noun Classes and Categorization: Proceedings of a Symposium on Categorization and Noun Classification, Eugene,*

Oregon, October 1983 (Typological Studies in Language, 7), 139–80. Amsterdam: Benjamins.

Žurinskij, A. N. 1987. Sootnošenie sistem imennyx klassov iskonnyx i zaimstvovannyx slov v jazykax bantu. In N. V. Oxotina (ed.) *Imennye klassy v jazykax Afriki*, 179–203. Moscow: Nauka. (See also the appendix, a list of borrowings into Zulu, 216–40.)

Zwicky, A. M. 1977. Hierarchies of person. In W. A. Beach, S. A. Fox & S. Philosoph (eds.) *Papers from the Thirteenth Regional Meeting, Chicago Linguistic Society*, 714–33. Chicago: Chicago Linguistic Society.

1987. Phonologically conditioned agreement and purely morphological features. Report SRC-87-06 of the Syntax Research Center, Cowell College, University of California, Santa Cruz.

Zwicky, A. M. & G. K. Pullum 1983. Phonology in syntax: the Somali optional agreement rule. *Natural Language and Linguistic Theory* 1: 385–402.

AUTHOR INDEX

A few references are to writers from whom examples are taken; in these cases, no initials are included (thus Andrić and Voltaire, but Anderson, S. R.).

Aksenov, A. T., 8
Allan, E. J., 11
Alpher, B., 132, 220
Anderson, S. C., 119, 247
Anderson, S. R., 12
Andrić, 232, 266, 282, 283, 299, 300, 301
Andronov, M., 8, 10
Applegate, J. R., 129
Arden, A. H., 8, 10, 270
Aristotle, 308
Arndt, W., 84
Arnott, R., 31, 193
Asher, R. E., 71, 269, 270
Austin, P., 11

Bakiza, E., 31, 111
Bani, E., 11, 113
Barkin, F., 75
Barlow, M., 112, 119, 242
Baron, D., 223
Baron, N. S., 101–2
Batliner, A., 221, 228, 229
Bauernöppel, J., 262
Beardsmore, H. B., 74
Bechert, J., 247
Becker, A. L., 136
Beit-Hallahmi, B., 93
Beito, O. T., 102
Bell, C. R. V., 196
Bendix, E. H., 221
Bennis, H., 113–14, 141
Berman, R. A., 83, 217
Bhattacharya, S., 10, 31, 168
Bidot, E., 57
Bielefeld, B., 262
Bing, J. M., 54
Black, M. B., see Black-Rogers, M. B.
Black-Rogers, M. B., 21–3
Bleek, W. H. I., 44, 309
Bloomfield, L., 7, 20, 21, 22, 57, 168, 206

Bodine, A., 220, 221
Boel, E., 228
Bokamba, E. G., 48, 265, 275
Bokarev, E. A., 26, 170
Bosch, P., 244, 245–6
Braine, M. D. S., 82, 89
Brauner, S., 276
Bresnan, J., 139, 160
Breva-Charamonte, M., 308
Brightman, R., 22–3, 71, 259
Brosman, P. W., 309
Brown, G., 243
Brown, P., 220
Bruce, L., 32
Brugmann, K., 309
Bryan, M. A., 15, 49, 184
Burquest, D. A., 131
Burrow, T., 10, 168
Burton, M., 96
Byarushengo, E. R., 73
Bybee, J. L., 111
Bynon, T., 75

Cameron, D., 220
Capell, A., 29
Carstensen, B., 84
Caskey, A. F., 278
Castellino, G. R., 32
Cercvadze, I. I., 131, 198
Černyšev, V. A., 280
Chafe, W. L., 192, 220, 313
Chalkley, M. A., 82
Champagnol, R., 89
Channon, R., 213
Chastaing, M., 89
Chiat, S., 85
Childs, T., 98, 313
Clark, E. V., 83
Clarke, M., 93
Claudi, U., 14, 15, 139, 194, 223, 312, 313, 320

Clements, J., 224
Coate, H. H. J., 29
Coates, J., 220
Comrie, B., 24, 99
Connell, B., 119
Cooper, R., 12
Cooper, R. L., 222
Corbett, G. G., 36, 42, 84, 135, 143, 167, 168,
    195, 209, 210–11, 216, 228, 231, 233,
    234, 236, 237, 238, 241, 248, 251, 256,
    267–8, 276, 281, 285–6, 296, 301
Cornish, F., 228, 238, 241, 244
Cosmas, N., 147
Craig, C., 137, 311
Craik, B., 22
Crawford, M., 221
Creider, C. A., 49

Darnell, R., 22
De Houwer, A., 83
De Wolf, P., 160, 172
Dekeyser, X., 102, 242
Delisle, G. L., 265, 303, 304, 305
Demuth, K., 87, 143
Denny, J. P., 49
Dešeriev, Ju. D., 135, 171, 322
Desrochers, A., 74, 91
Desrochers, S., 91
Deutsch, W., 89
Dietze, J., 99
Dimmendaal, G. J., 314
Dirr, A., 310
Dixon, R. M. W., 13, 15–17, 71, 106, 136, 137,
    141, 223
Dorian, N., 18
Doroszewski, W., 285
Dowty, D., 244
Drabbe, P., 116
Drossard, W., 158
Dunnigan, T., 304
Dul′zon, A. P., 131
Duranti, A., 111, 139
Dyła, S., 287

Efimov, V. A., 102
Einarsson, S., 283
Emeneau, M. B., 10, 168
England, J., 230, 267
English, L., 221
Eriksson, O., 216
Ermakova, M. I., 192
Ervin, S. M., 93

Faarlund, J. T., 216
Faraclas, N., 87, 143
Faris, J. C., 73
Farkas, D., 213
Fasske, H., 81, 192

Ferguson, C. A., 322
Findreng, Å., 267, 290
Fisher, R. L., 98
Fisiak, J., 76
Flydal, L., 316
Fodor, I., 146, 309
Foley, W. A., 32, 55, 56, 111, 116, 143, 176,
    177, 264, 322
Forchheimer, P., 129
Francis, W. N., 221
Fried, R., 93
Fritsch, H., 262
Froitzheim, C., 220
Fulkerson, D. C., 221

Gagua, R., 171
Gazdar, G., 129
Gimpelevič, V., 76
Givón, T., 49, 108, 112, 137–8, 139, 141, 142,
    156, 247, 261, 273, 275, 310, 313
Gladkij, A., 147, 161, 165
Goddard, I., 22, 65, 259, 303
Gotteri, N., 222
Gouffe, C., 76
Gould, L. J., 278
Graddol, D., 220
Graham, A., 221
De la Grasserie, R., 30, 309.
Graudina, L. K., 40
Graur, A., 150
Greenbaum, S., 161
Greenberg, J. H., 22–23, 54, 90, 111, 131,
    132, 139, 146, 156, 160, 190, 198, 291,
    310, 311, 313
Gregersen, E. A., 46, 47, 48
Gregor, B., 76
Grevisse, M., 134, 183, 226, 227, 279
Grimm, J., 309
Gruita, G., 288
Gudkov, V., 301
Guiora, A. Z., 93
Gumperz, J. J., 104
Guthrie, M., 45
Gvozdev, A. N., 83

Haas, M. R., 131
Haegeman, L., 113–14, 141
Haiman, J., 159, 215
Hall, R. A., 150
Hallowell, A. I., 20, 21, 23
Harris, A. C., 146
Harris, M., 247
Haugen, E., 75, 102
Hawkinson, A. K., 278
Hayward, R. J., 30, 51, 52, 74, 92, 195, 206,
    210, 211
Head, B. F., 323

Heath, J., 29, 317, 321, 322
Heine, B., 2, 79, 143, 146, 155, 156, 160, 173, 174–5, 312, 313
Hellan, L., 216
Henley, N., 220
Henzl, V. M., 84
Herbert, R. K., 49, 220, 222, 229
Hermant, 226
Hetzron, R., 197
Hewitt, B. G., 24, 108, 113
Hinnebusch, J., 73
Hockett, C. F., 1, 4, 21
Holisky, D. A., 171
Holmer, N. M., 220
Hooper, J. B., 83
Horton, A. E., 275
Humboldt, K. W. von, 309
Huntley, D., 98, 168, 237
Hurford, J. R., 135
Hyman, L. M., 31, 45, 111, 115, 139, 173, 182, 209, 278

Ibrahim, M. H., 309
Ickovič, V. A., 40, 43
Ilola, E., 38
Innes, G., 200, 323
Irvine, J. T., 78, 191
Ivić, M., 173

Jacobson, P., 244
Jakobson, R., 92, 93, 150
Janko-Trinickaja, N. A., 232, 320
Jaworska, E., 234
Jenewari, C. E. W., 12
Jesperson, O., 204
Jones, C., 102
Jonsson, S., 283
Joseph, B. O., 22
Jurik, V. A., 280

Kadagidze, N., 171
Kadagidze, O., 171
Kadima, M., 45, 202, 255
Kanerva, J. M., 160
Karmiloff-Smith, A., 87–8, 90, 245
Katlinskaja, L. P., 40
Kaye, J. D., 54, 74
Keenan, E. L., 105, 129, 141
Kempson, R. M., 244
Khaidakov, S. M., 24–25, 26, 113, 158, 181, 198, 316
Kibrik, A. E., 6, 27, 75, 106, 108, 114, 119, 154, 158, 170, 181, 207, 208, 217, 223, 271
Kiraithe, J. M., 88
Kirk, L., 96
Kitajgorodskaja, M. V., 231

Klajn, I., 205
Klein, E., 129
Klenin, E., 99
Kodzasov, S. V., 6, 27, 75, 106, 114, 119
Köhler, C., 29
Köpcke, K.-M., 50, 84–5, 92, 94, 321
Kopeliovič, A. B., 183, 241
Koval', A. I., 191, 206, 244, 321
Kramarae, C., 220
Krejnovič, E. A., 19–20, 135
Kripka, M., 228
Krishnamurti, B., 153
Kubko, G. V., 191
Kučera, H., 221
Kühner, R., 267, 287
Kuiper, A., 130
Kulak, J., 284
Kunene, E. C. L., 87
Kutik, E. J., 73

Łaciak, W., 284
Lakoff, G., 18
Lambert, W. E., 57, 58, 59–61, 90–1
Lapointe, S. G., 112
Laskowski, R., 168
Leakey, L. S. B., 32, 96
Leech, G., 161
Leeding, V. J., 29, 30
Lehmann, C., 105, 108, 112, 142
Lehmann, W. P., 309
Lenček, R., 263, 266, 280, 281, 294, 298
Leroy, J., 201
Levy, Y., 83
Losoff, A., 93
Luckov, A. D., 73
Luxt, L. I., 65, 150
Lyons, J., 65, 243, 244

McConnell-Ginet, S., 220, 221, 222
McCracken, M. D., 93
McDonald, J. L., 86
McKay, G. R., 132
Mackay, D. G., 221
MacWhinney, B., 86
Madieva, G. I., 190
Magnan, S. S., 88
Magomedbekova, Z. M., 109, 156, 190
Magometov, A. A., 119
Malkiel, Y., 77
Mallinson, G., 150, 288, 289
Malone, J. L., 181
Maratsos, M. P., 82
Marchese, L., 53, 54, 55, 87, 143, 200, 210, 251
Marcoux, D. R., 181
Marcus, S., 147, 150
Markovič, S. B., 239, 240

Martyna, W., 221
Martysiuk, M., 78
Mathiot, M., 12
Mchombo, S. A., 107, 139, 239
Meillet, A., 309
Meinhof, C., 44, 195, 309, 310
Mel'čuk, I. A., 8, 31, 57, 111, 237
Miller, C., 70, 75
Mills, A. E., 50, 83, 84, 85–6, 92, 94–6, 241, 321
Miranda, R. V., 100, 139, 231
Mitchell, B., 102
Moravcsik, E. A., 112, 138
Moto, F., 209
Mpaayei, J. T. ole, 313
Mtenje, A. D., 209, 248, 276
Mučnik, I. P., 78, 80
Mulford, R., 84
Murkelinskij, G. B., 24
Mustajoki, A., 38
Mutaka, N., 209

Naden, A. J., 259
Napoli, D. J., 113
Nerlove, S., 131
Newman, P., 53, 103
Nilsson, K., 216
Nykiel-Herbert, B., 220, 222, 229

Ochs, E., 139
Ojeda, A. E., 214, 215
Olovjannikova, I. P., 6, 27, 75, 106, 114, 119
Oomen, A., 102, 197
Orr, G. J., 87
Oxotina, N. V., 45

Paivio, A., 91
Palmer, F., 169
Panov, M. V., 184, 231, 251–2
Parker, E. M., 51
Parsons, F. W., 190
Pasch, H., 137, 184, 186, 187
Pavanantham, A., 71
Payne, J. R., 102, 117, 142, 221
Perkowski, J. L., 65
Philips, S. U., 220
Pickett, V., 130
Pillinger, O. S., 103
Plank, F., 50
Pollard, C., 244
Poplack, S., 70, 75, 77
Popova, M. I., 83, 84
Popović, 302
Pousada, A., 75
Priestly, T. M. S., 143, 150, 205, 216, 317, 318
Protagoras, 308
Pullum, G. K., 129, 197, 275
Pulman, S. G., 244

Quirk, R., 161

Rabel-Heymann, L., 50, 207
Rao, M., 10, 153, 270–1
Reh, M., 143, 190, 312
Revzin, I. I., 147
Richardson, I., 73, 90
Rigault, A. A., 57, 58, 59–61, 90–1
Roberts, L., 275
Roberts, M., 12
Robins, R. H., 308
Roca, I. M., 290
Rogers, M., 86
Romney, A. K., 131
Rosch, E., 244
Rosetti, A., 150
Ross, A. S. C., 102
Ross, J. R., 218
Rothstein, R. A., 234, 258
Royen, G., 131, 247, 309
Rumsey, A., 207
Russell, R. A., 125, 139

Saadiev, S., 135
Sadek, C., 88
Sag, I. A., 129, 244
Samedov, D. S., 6, 27, 75, 106, 114
Sanctius, 308
Sankoff, D., 70, 75, 77
Sapir, J. O., 104
Sarma, P. S., 154
Schane, S. A., 290–2
Schaub, W., 202
Schenker, A. M., 147
Schmidt, A., 16, 17
Schupbach, R. D., 78
Schwartz, L., 304
Senft, G., 140
Serzisko, F., 196, 197
Shanmugam Pillai, S., 203
Shevelov, G. V., 215
Shieber, S. M., 129
Shields, K., 77
Silverstein, M., 220
Simons, B., 220
Smith, P. M., 220
Smoczyńska, M., 83
Sobin, N. J., 215
Speiser, E. A., 195
Spence, N. C. W., 61
Spitz, E., 93
Stankiewicz, E., 168
Steele, S., 105, 220
Stegmann, C., 267, 287
Steinberg, E., 278
Steinmetz, D., 85
Stevens, F., 88

Still, J., 93
Straus, A. T., 22–3, 71, 259
Stroganova, I. P., 49
Suárez, J. A., 31
Sullivan, W. J., 220
Superanskaja, A. V., 78, 93
Surridge, M. E., 76, 82
Suzman, M. S., 138
Svartengren, T. H., 12
Svartvik, J., 161
Švedova, N. Ju., 239
Swann, J., 220

Tanz, C., 220
Taraban, R. M., 86
Tasmowski, L., *see* Tasmowski-De Ryck, L.
Tasmowski-De Ryck, L., 228, 243–4
Taylor, C., 73
Taylor-Browne, K., 88
Tharaud, 227
Thomas, G., 80
Thorne, B., 220
Tolstaya, N. I., 280
Toporova, I. N., 45
Torrend, J., 310
Trávníček, F., 262
Trudgill, P., 131
Tryon, D. T., 140
Tucker, A. N., 15, 49, 184, 313
Tucker, G. R., 57, 58, 59–61, 90–1

Vachek, J., 12
Van Valin, R. D., 322
Vanek, A. L., 22, 228
Veksler, B. X., 280
Venberg, R., 97
Verluyten, S. P., 228, 243–4
Villarreal, H., 88
Voeltz, E., 275
Voltaire, 227
Voorhoeve, J., 160, 172
Vossen, R., 312
Vrabie, E., 65

Wald, B., 44, 47, 139, 252, 253, 254, 255, 257
Watkins, M., 46
Watters, J. R., 160
Welmers, W. E., 44, 49, 107, 108, 110, 117, 160, 229
Wełna, J., 75, 80
Wertz, C. A., 99
Wheeler, B. I., 309
Whiteley, W. H., 72, 73
Wienold, G., 150, 182, 309
Wiese, B., 112, 245
Wijnen, F., 89
Wilson, R., 104
Wilson, W. A. A., 229, 256, 259
Windisch, R., 150, 289
Winston, F. D. D., 209
Wissemann, R., 72, 77
Wolontis, M., 275
Worsley, P. M., 29
Wurzel, W. U., 318

Xajdakov, S. M *see* Khaidakov, S. M.
Xanmagomedov, B. G.-K., 135

Yoder, C., 93
Yokoyama, O. T., 221
Yu, E. O., 264
Yule, G., 243

Zaliznjak, A. A., 147, 149, 161, 165, 175, 184, 188
Zaręba, A., 100–1, 256
Zawawi, S. M., 44, 73, 252, 255
Zaxarova, A. V., 83
Żelezkiewicz, I., 284
Zemskaja, E. A., 217
Zieniukowa, J., 285–6
Žirkov, L. I., 24
Zubin, D. A., 50, 84, 85, 92, 94, 321
Zubko, G. V., 191
Žurinskij, A. N., 73
Zwicky, A. M., 54, 197, 263, 275

LANGUAGE INDEX

Where necessary, information on language affiliation and background details are given at the first substantial discussion of a language in the text. Language names are standardized here and in the text; in the bibliography they are given as in the original. Terms for groups and families of languages are given here in italic.

Abkhaz, 108, 113
Adamawa-Ubangian, 14
Afar, *see* Qafar
Afro-Asiatic, 2, 51, 52, 129, 131, 207
Akhvakh, 9
Alamblak, 32
Algonquian, 2, 6, 20–4, 64–5, 206, 207, 258, 303, 318
Ami, 140, 311
Amo, 119, 247
Anatolian, 309
Andi, 26, 131, 198–200, 203, 313
    Rikvani dialect, 26, 30, 199
Angas, 131
Anindilyakwa, 29, 30
Arabic, 93, 125, 129, 322
Arawakan, 220
Archi, 26, 27–9, 31, 32, 67, 68, 75, 106, 108, 114–15, 116, 127–8, 158, 170, 181, 207, 208, 223, 271–3, 278, 294, 306, 323
Assamese, 318
Australian, 29, 136, 207, 220, 312, 322
Avar, 170, 190
Avar-Andi-Dido, 9
Awing, 201–2, 316

Babanki, 115, 182
Babungo, 202
Bafut, 201
Baga Koba, 256
Baga Maduri, 256
Baga Sitemu, 256
Bagangu, 201
Bagval, 9
Bambui, 201
Bantu, 31, 32, 43–6, 48–9, 65, 72–3, 87, 88, 90, 96, 98, 99, 103, 107, 109, 110–11, 115, 119, 138–9, 146, 156, 159, 182, 188, 202, 208, 209, 248, 252, 255, 257, 258, 273–4, 275–6, 278, 294, 298, 306, 310, 313, 314
Bantu, Grassfields, 115, 173, 182, 201–2
Bats, *see* Tsova-Tush
Baule, 74
Bayso, 195, 196, 210–11
Beludzhi, 318
Bemba, *see* Chibemba
Bengali, 318
Bezhti, 26
Bondei, 254, 255, 258
Bowili, 79
Burmese, 136

Caucasian, 24, 116, 132
Caucasian, North-Central, 135, 171, 198
Caucasian, North-East, 9, 11, 25, 26, 27, 30, 109, 119, 131, 135, 146, 154, 156, 170, 190, 198, 207–8, 271, 315
Caucasian, North-West, 108
Chadic, 52, 103, 131
Chamalal, 109, 190–1, 315–16, 317
Chechen, 135, 198
Cheyenne, Northern, 22, 23–4, 71
Chibemba, 156, 275, 294
Chichewa, 31, 47, 87, 107, 134, 139, 159–60, 208–9, 211, 212, 239, 243, 248–50, 253, 276–7, 278, 283
Chinyanja, 107
Chippewa, *see* Ojibwa
Chonyi, 254
Cree, 22, 23, 259
Cross, Lower, 119
Cross River, 143, 209, 259
Cushitic, 32, 49, 51, 52, 102, 195–7, 210–11, 218
Czech, 84, 100, 228, 262

Language index

Dagaari, 259
Dagbani, 259
Dagestanian, see Caucasian, North-East
Daly, 30, 139–41, 311, 312
Dama, 220
Danish, 102, 247
Dargva, 25
Defaka, 12, 169
Dido, 26, 190
Diuxi Mixtec, *see* Mixtec
Diyari, 11, 13, 30
Dizi, 11, 13, 30, 31
Dongo, 137, 185
Dravidian, 2, 8, 10, 13, 30, 32, 146, 152, 155,
　168, 202–3, 269, 270, 271, 272, 293, 306
Dutch, 83, 85, 89, 102, 228
Dyirbal, 15–19, 24, 29, 30, 31, 32, 71, 77, 98,
　101, 106, 116, 141, 223, 305, 311, 319
Dzamba, 276

English, 3, 12, 17, 18, 23, 31, 63, 73, 74, 75,
　76, 77, 80, 82–3, 84, 85, 86, 93, 94–6,
　101–2, 131, 136, 138, 146, 147, 161, 169,
　170, 180–1, 183, 213, 217, 218, 221, 222,
　223, 236, 240, 242, 247, 259, 261, 310, 320
Ewe, 79

Finnish, 94
Flemish, 74, 113–14, 141
Forrest River, 29
Fox, 259
French, 1, 3, 7, 10, 23, 50, 57–62, 63, 74, 75,
　76, 80, 82, 83, 85, 87–8, 89, 90, 106, 117,
　134, 138, 139, 143, 149–50, 152–3, 155,
　157, 158, 169, 172, 182, 183, 226–7, 228,
　230, 235, 236, 237, 243, 245, 247, 251,
　256, 257, 258, 279–80, 285, 290–2, 296,
　297, 306, 315, 316
Fula, 31, 191–2, 206–7, 244, 321

Gaelic, 18
Gbobo, *see* Krahn
German, 7–8, 49–50, 51, 62, 66, 76, 77, 78–9,
　80–1, 84–6, 88, 92, 93, 94–6, 99, 124,
　135, 151, 155, 158, 183, 190, 227–8, 235,
　236, 237, 240, 241, 245, 246, 251, 257,
　258, 264, 267–8, 290, 320–1
Germanic, 102, 124, 247
Goajiro, 220
Godie, 53–5, 62, 74, 143, 200, 210, 211, 212,
　251, 313
Godoberi, 9
Gola, 313
Grebo, 200, 313, 323
Greek, 147
Gunzib, 170
Gur, 259, 264

Halkomelem, 11, 31, 64
Hausa, 52–3, 76, 103, 190
Haya, 73
Hebrew, 83, 93, 129, 141, 217, 280
Hindi, 280
Hittite, 309
Hungarian, 2

Icelandic, 75, 84, 283, 292, 298, 306
Indic, 100, 318
Indo-European, 2, 23, 24, 35, 39, 46, 65, 68,
　77, 80, 82, 98, 100, 102, 104, 110, 115,
　119, 123, 126, 133, 137, 143, 146, 152,
　204, 205, 207, 219, 227, 229, 245, 259,
　309, 316, 318
Ingush, 135, 198
Iranian, 102, 116, 318
Iraqw, 49
Iroquoian, 220, 313
Italian, 67, 93, 113, 139

Jacaltec, 311–12

Kala Lagaw Ya, 11, 113
Kami, 254
Kannada, 10, 103–4, 139
Karata, 9, 146, 156
Ket, 19–20, 65, 131, 135
Khasi, 50, 206
Khinalug, 26, 119–23, 132, 135, 142, 154,
　197–8, 207, 208, 312
Khoisan, 2, 29, 220
Khvarsh, 170
Kikuria, 278
Kikuyu, 32, 73, 96–7, 315
Kilivila, 140
Kimbundu (Mbaka dialect), 253
Kinande, 209
Kirundi, 31, 111
Kisi, 313
Klao, 143
Koalib-Moro, 73
Koasati, 131
Kolami, 10, 13, 168–9, 170, 203, 316, 317
Konkani, 26, 100, 230, 235, 237, 257, 258, 314
Kordofanian, 73, 190
Kott, 19
Koyra, 30
Krahn (Gbobo dialect), 54
Krongo, 190
Kru, 53, 54, 143, 200, 210, 251, 259
Kryz, 26, 135

Lak, 24–6, 99, 113, 114, 154, 156, 157, 158,
　170, 181, 207–8
Lama, 264
Landuma, 229, 256

Latin, 1, 7, 37, 45, 75, 80, 133, 139, 151, 152, 203, 254, 267, 287–8, 290, 297, 298, 306
Latvian, 83, 280, 311
Lelemi, 79, 160, 173–5, 315
Lezgian, 27, 119, 123
Likila, 276
Likpe, 79
Lingala, 276
Loko, 209
Lower Sorbian, *see* Sorbian, Lower
Luganda, 108, 264, 273–5, 276, 278
Luguru, 255
Lunda, 98, 314
Luvale, 98, 275

Ma, 185, 318
Maasai, 220, 313–14
Makonde (Mawia dialect), 255
Mampruli, 259
Mankon, 201–2
Marathi, 103–4
Marind, 116, 117, 142
Mayan, 220
Mba, 137, 185–8, 247
Mbaka, 253
Menominee, 22, 206
Meso-American, 311
Mirityabin, 140
Mixtec, 130, 131
Mon-Khmer, 50, 206
Munda, 31
Mundari, 31
Mundum I, 201
Muskogean, 131

Naiki, 168
Nakh, see Caucasian, North-Central
Naudem, 259
Ndjebbana, 132
Ndunga, 185
Nepali, 318
Ngandi, 29
Ngangikurrunggurr, 30, 140
Ngemba, 201, 316
Niger-Congo, 12, 14, 73, 79, 104, 119, 143, 229, 247
Niger-Kordofanian, 2, 14, 43, 73, 137, 143, 146, 184, 190, 207, 259
Nilo-Saharan, 2, 313
Nilotic, 220, 312, 313
Nkore-Kiga, 73
Nkwen, 201
Noni, 173
Norwegian, 75, 216, 316
Nuba, Southeastern, 73
Nunggubuyu, 29, 317, 321, 322

Nyangbo, 79, 82, 101
Nzakara, 15

Oceanic, 140
Ojibwa, 20–2, 23, 42, 64–5, 265, 303–5, 306, 319
Old Church Slavonic (Old Bulgarian), 237
Ollari, 10, 168
Omotic, 11, 30, 206
Ongamo, 312
Oriya, 318
Ossete, 318
Oto-Manguean, 31, 130

Panjabi, 280
Papuan, 55, 111, 176
Parji, 10, 168
Persian, 135, 311, 318
Peve, 97
Pinyin, 201
Polish, 76, 83–4, 99, 100, 220, 223, 229, 230, 233–4, 235, 236, 237, 240, 245, 255, 256, 284–7, 290, 291, 296, 297, 299, 306, 314, 322, 323
Portuguese, 83, 215

Qafar, 51–2, 53, 62, 63, 64, 66, 74, 87, 92, 102, 117, 118, 195, 210–11, 247, 307

Rendille, 52, 102–3, 197
Rikvani, *see* Andi: Rikvani dialect
Ring, 115, 182
Romance, 139, 150, 215, 247, 315, 316
Romansh (Surselvan dialect), 159, 215
Roshani, 116, 142
Rumanian, 65, 67, 145, 150–2, 154, 156, 159, 171, 213–14, 288–90, 297, 306
Russian, 3, 4, 34–43, 45, 46, 49, 50, 51, 62, 64, 65, 67–8, 72, 75, 78, 80, 82, 83–4, 93, 97, 98, 99, 106, 109–10, 111–12, 115, 117, 118, 119, 126, 128, 132–4, 148, 149, 165–8, 170, 175, 177–80, 182, 183–4, 204, 205, 212, 216, 217, 219, 221, 225, 230, 231–2, 235, 237, 238, 240–1, 245, 251–2, 254, 258, 267–8, 300, 314, 316, 320, 323
Rutul, 26

Salish, 13
Sambaa, 253
Santrokofi, 79, 82, 101
Sarikoli, 318
Semitic, 74, 309
Seneca, 192, 220
Sepik Hill, 32
Sepik Lower, 55
Serbo-Croat, 126–7, 157, 161–5, 168, 172–3, 197, 205, 212, 219, 222, 232–3, 235, 236,

237, 239, 240, 251–2, 266, 267–8, 282–3,
  297, 298, 299–303, 306
Sesotho, 87
Shilha, 129–30
Shona, 108, 278
Sino-Tibetan, 136
Siswati, 87
Slavonic, 2, 34, 80, 98–9, 126, 157, 163, 168,
  187, 192, 215, 216, 262, 263, 284, 285,
  296, 299, 313, 317
Slovak, 100
Slovene, 157, 190, 192, 216, 261, 263, 266,
  280–2, 287, 290, 291, 294–5, 296, 297,
  298, 299–300, 301, 302, 306, 317
Somali, 196
Sorbian, Lower, 80
Sorbian, Upper, 80–1, 192–4, 233
Spanish, 57, 58, 67, 75, 76, 88, 129, 214–15,
  230, 235, 237, 267–8, 280, 290, 315
Surselvan, *see* Romansh
Swahili, 43–4, 46–9, 50, 62, 65, 72–3, 98, 107,
  109, 110, 115, 117, 118, 119, 138–9, 185,
  252–3, 254, 255, 256, 257, 265, 276, 310
Swedish, 124, 216, 247

Tabasaran, 24, 135
Tamil, 2, 3, 8–10, 12, 13, 63, 64, 71, 87, 146,
  151, 155, 169, 202–3, 269–70, 271, 278,
  287, 293, 306, 307, 317
Telugu, 2, 10, 32, 71, 153–4, 156, 202–3, 247,
  270–1, 278, 294, 306, 316
Temne, 256, 265
Tepo, 54
Tlapanec, 31
Togo Remnant, 79, 173
Torricelli, 55

Tsakhur, 26
Tsova-Tush, 24, 135, 171–2, 179, 198, 322
Tswana, 275
Turkana, 314
Twi, 79
Tzeltal, 220

Ubangian, 14, 137, 184
Ukrainian, 215–16
Ungarinjin, 29, 207
Upper Sorbian, *see* Sorbian, Upper
Uralic, 2
Urdu, 103–4
Uskade, 119

Vata, 54, 74

West Atlantic, 104, 190–1, 229, 313
Wobe, 143
Wolaitta, 30
Wolof, 104, 190–1

Xhosa, 275
!Xũ, 29–30

Yazgulyam, 102
Yeniseyan, 19
Yidiny, 136
Yimas, 55–7, 64, 111, 115, 143, 176–7,
  179–80, 264, 322

Zande, 14–15, 18, 139, 170, 185, 194, 223,
  312
Zayse, 206
Zigua, 253
Zulu, 73, 139, 275

SUBJECT INDEX

Pages where terms are discussed are indicated in **bold**.

abstracts, 25, 28, 30, 31, 50, 61, 64, 94, 206, 211, 223, 230, 257, 258, 268, 290, 297, 302

accent, 51–2, 62, 64, 74, 102–3, 118

acronyms, 40, 41

adpositions, 113, 142

agreement, 4–6, 7, 12, 14, 19, 28, 31, 33, 37, 43–4, 45, 46, 54, 66, 69, 83, 84, 87, 88, 90, 92, 101, **105**–44 *passim*, 146, 148, 153, 154, 159–60, 161, 162, 166, 169, 175, 187, 189, 190, 217, 236, 238, 244–5, 251, 265, 266, 267, 278, 283, 301, 304, 306, 307, 313, 320
  gaining and losing, 123, 135, 137–42, 201–2, 215, 296, 310–16
  semantic, **225**–7, 229–41, 243, 245, 246, 248–51, 253–4, 256, 260, 268, 308
  syntactic, **226**–7, 229–31, 233–6, 238–40, 243, 245, 248, 252–4, 256, 268, 308
  see also neutral agreement

agreement class, 145, 146, **147**–50, 156–88 *passim*, 189, 192–3, 198, 316

agreement controller, 108, 128–9, 147, 159, 176, 189, 204–5, 240, 242, 243, 245, 249, 261, 267–8, 293, 294, 306
  see also controller gender

Agreement Hierarchy, 214, 225, **226**–42 *passim*, 247, 248, 250, 252, 254, 256, 259–60, 268, 308, 320

agreement target, **5**, 44, 117, 118, 119, 128–9, 137, 139, 141, 142–3, 147, 148, 149, 153, 157, 161, 164, 168, 169, 170, 177, 183, 189, 196, 197, 204–5, 213, 225, 227, 230, 239–40, 242, 243, 245, 246–7, 249, 251, 252, 254, 256, 259–60, 261, 265–8, 274, 275, 314, 315, 317
  see also target gender

alliterative concord, *see* concord, alliterative

ambigeneric, **151**

anaphora, 5, 112, 138–9, 169, 222, 241–4, 246, 248, 259, 288, 311, 312, 322

animacy, 3, 5, 11, 14–32 *passim*, 40–3, 46–9, 64–5, 79, 80, 81, 85–6, 96, 98, 99, 101, 117, 119, 134–5, 140, 163–5, 167–8, 169, 175, 176, 178, 185–8, 192, 193, 199, 206, 208, 211, 223, 236, 252–9, 265, 267–8, 271–2, 275–6, 279, 285–90, 294, 302, 303–5, 309, 311, 314, 317

articles, 11, 85, 87, 106, 139, 149, 150, 197, 215, 221, 247, 310, 313

assignment, 3, 5, **7**–8, 9, 17, 18, 21, 22, 24, 25, 27, 29, 30, 31, 33, 47, 57, 58, 62, 66, 70–1, 74, 75, 78, 81, 82, 91, 92, 93, 97, 101, 103, 104, 146, 164, 169, 173, 175, 181, 182, 199, 207, 226, 248, 270, 273, 292, 293, 298, 304, 306, 315, 317, 318, 319
  conflict of criteria, 38, 52, 63–4, 66, 69, 87–8, 89, 99, 184, 225, 256, 308, 319
  in diachrony, 17–18, 26, 49, 67, 70, 77, 94, 97–104, 182, 248, 251, 252, 255–9, 314, 317
  formal, 3, 32, **33**, 35, 51, 62, 63, 68, 71, 77, 84, 86, 87, 101, 105, 245, 256, 306, 307, 308, 321, 323
  morphological, 3, **33**–51, 57, 58, 61, 64, 65, 68, 72–4, 75, 79, 80, 83, 84, 85, 87, 90, 101, 102, 103, 187, 226, 229, 256, 309, 315, 319
  overlapping of criteria, 28, 34, 38, 49, 52, 53, 58, 61, 63–5, 68, 70, 85, 101, 307, 319
  phonological, 3, **33**, 35, 51–62, 68, 74, 75, 76–7, 84, 86, 87, 88, 90, 92, 98, 102, 103, 104, 226, 259, 319
  semantic, **8**–32, 33, 34, 38, 40, 47, 56, 58, 63–5, 79, 82, 85, 86–8, 101–4, 246, 253, 257, 308, 313, 318; predominantly semantic, **13**–29, 64, 71, 75, 273, 306, 308, 319, 323; strict semantic, **8**–13, 18, 63, 71, 271, 306
  see also borrowings; mythology

associative morpheme/particle, 107–8, 109,
195, 210
augmentative, 30, 31, 44, 47, 89, 192

basic-level terms, 244, 245, 321
'boat nouns', 180–1, 183, 236
borrowings, 4, 7, 16, 23, 49, 67, 70–82, 84,
101, 171, 173, 183, 308, 314–15, 317, 320

case, 35, 109, 112, 115, 119, 132–3, 143, 146,
148, 150, 161, 163, 164, 165, 169, 189,
192, 204, 238, 322
change of gender, *see* assignment: in
diachrony
child language, 4, 15, 39–40, 70, 82–9, 104,
138, 320
classifiers, 5, 105, 136–7, 140–1, 311, 312
clitics, 111, 114, 141, 210, 312
combined gender systems, 184–8
common gender
as opposed to neuter, 102, **124**, 217, 247,
309
type of double gender, **67**, 181, 182
complementizers, 113–14, 141
concept association, **16–17**, 18, 29, 71, 77, 81,
88
concord, 105
alliterative 54, 115, **117**–19
see also agreement
connectionist networks, 86
consistent agreement pattern, 157, 176–**9**,
180–1, 183, 184, 186–7, 225, 254, 308
controller gender, 45–6, 145, 150, **151**–4, 156,
158–60, 161, 168, 188, 189, 190, 200,
202, 207, 208, 210, 211, 213, 218, 257,
261, 277, 297, 316
see also minor controller gender
convergent systems, **155**–6, 157, 158, 190,
192, 201, 203, 264
covert gender, **62**–3, 117
crossed systems, **156**–7, 158, 171, 173, 190,
192, 193, 199, 201, 203, 288, 316

declensional type, 3, 34, 35, 36–9, 40, 41, 42,
45, 46, 49, 50, 72, 76, 80, 83, 98, 133,
148, 164, 182, 183, 258, 301
default agreement form, 125, **205**, 214
defective nouns, 149, 175, 188
definiteness, 54, 124–5, 139, 196
see also articles
demonstratives, 20, 31, 106, 119, 122, 132,
141, 159, 173, 206, 212, 213, 215, 229,
241, 247, 310–11, 312, 313, 314
dependent target gender, **164**–5, 167, 193
derivational morphology, 34, 49–50, 58, 64,
84, 103, 146, 219, 317, 318
diachrony, 198–203, 248–59, 299–306, 310–18

see also agreement: gaining and losing;
assignment: in diachrony; gaining of
gender(s); loss of gender(s)
dialects, 21, 22, 25, 26, 41, 48, 54, 81, 98,
100–1, 102, 113, 138, 153, 159, 191, 192,
198, 199–200, 201, 203, 215, 216, 256–7,
314, 315, 317, 322
diminutive, 11, 13, 21, 30, 31, 32, 42, 44,
47–8, 50, 64, 66, 89, 99, 192, 228, 248,
257, 258, 313, 314
double gender, 67, **181**, 183, 188, 225
dual, 31, 55, 57, 157, 177, 189, 192–3, 261,
263, 266, 280, 281–2, 293, 295, 296, 299

epicene, **67**–8
ergativity, 15, 106, 114, 121, 142
evasive forms, **221**–3
experiments, *see* psycholinguistic experiments

formal assignment, *see* assignment: formal

gaining of gender(s), 198–9, 200–1, 203,
310–14
see also agreement: gaining and losing
gender resolution, *see* resolution rule: gender
Generalized Phrase Structure Grammar, 129
generic pronouns, *see* personal pronouns:
generic use

hybrid nouns, 5, 12, 38, 39, 58, 66, 69, 88, 99,
183–4, 188, 225–60 *passim*, 308, 314, 318,
319, 320
hypocoristics, **37**, 83, 100, 256

indeclinable nouns, 40–1, 72, 76, 81
inflectional morphology, 49–50, 84, 99, 300
see also declensional type; morphological
class
inquorate genders, 10, 160, **170**–5, 179, 185,
188, 200, 271, 316, 319
insects, 15, 19, 25, 26, 27, 28, 30, 31, 32, 42,
199

language death, 18
Last Member Principle, 50, 94
liquids, 25, 28–9, 30, 31, 53, 259
loanwords, *see* borrowings
locative genders, 47, 156, 159–**60**, 276, 313–14
loss of gender(s), 17, 26, 78, 200, 201–3, 215,
259, 315–18

markedness, 18, 77, 78, 206, 210, 219, 223,
290–2
masculine personal, 193, 222, 233–6, 284–6,
290, 291, 296
minor controller gender, **160**
minor target gender, **159**–60

morphological assignment, *see* assignment:
    morphological
morphological class, 46, **49**, 50, 72, 73, 79,
    117, 133–4, 185, 229–30, 248, 252, 254,
    318
motion nouns, 44, **67**, 272
multiple gender, 67, **181**–3, 188, 225, 271
mythology, 10, 16–17, 20, 32, 93, 136, 259,
    305

natural gender, 9
neutral agreement, 37, **159**, 203–18, 276, 291,
    317
non-lexical gender, **159**, 313
noun classes, 5, 10, 15, 24, 44, 55, 106, 109,
    116, 137, **146**, 156, 310
number, 31, 44, 55, 83, 89, 114, 120–3, 126,
    127, 129, 132–3, 143, 148, 154–8, 159,
    176, 189–203, 204, 209, 212, 237, 255,
    290, 292–3, 295, 297–9
    see also dual; resolution rule: number
numerals, 43, 106–7, 113, 115, 118, 134–5,
    136, 143, 154, 168, 169, 170, 185

origin of gender, 6, 308–12
    see also gaining of gender(s)
orthography, 6, 36, 57, 58, 134
overdifferentiated targets, **168**–70, 173, 175,
    177, 188, 314, 316, 319
overt gender, 28, 44, **62**–3, 117–18, 139, 310,
    312, 313, 315, 318

parallel systems, **155**, 157, 192, 193, 199, 201,
    203
participles, 109–10, 123, 126, 127, 159, 162
person, 123, 126–32, 143, 272
    see also resolution rule: person
personal pronouns, 12, 14, 34, 53–4, 83, 85–6,
    87, 95, 97, 99, 100, 101, 102, 105, 111,
    112, 115, 118, 124, 127–32, 138, 143,
    153, 168–70, 178, 180, 183, 185, 194,
    203, 210, 212, 214, 225–50 *passim*, 256,
    259, 260, 263, 268, 288, 298, 310, 311,
    321
    generic use, 12, 221–2
    see also pronominal gender systems
personification, 86, 93, 95, 96, 98, 257, 317
phonological assignment, *see* assignment:
    phonological
pluralia tantum, 46, **175**
polarity, 195–**6**, 197
politeness, *see* respect
possessives, 107, 108–9, 140–2, 197, 231, 237,
    252, 254

pronominal gender systems, 5, 12, 96, **169**–70,
    180, 310
psycholinguistic experiments, 4, 70, 85, 86,
    87–8, 89–92, 104, 221

relative pronouns, 34, 111–12, 118, 165, 169,
    178, 180, 183, 213, 226, 227, 228, 230,
    232–7, 242, 249, 259, 268
residual meaning, 4, 70, 92–3, 97, 104
resolution rule, 128, **261**, 265–71, 280, 294,
    297, 306
    gender, 9, 69, 261, 264–306 *passim*, 308,
    319, 320
    number, 263–4, 266–70, 275, 277, 278,
    281–3, 292, 293, 295
    person, 262–3, 264, 268, 269, 272, 292, 293
respect, 26, 153, 250, 322

second-language acquisition, 1, 8, 86, 88
semantic analogy, **75**–7, 81
semantic assignment, *see* assignment:
    semantic
semantic residue, **13**, 14, 15, 18, 19, 21, 25,
    26, 32, 34–5, 38, 48, 63, 92, 93, 104, 116,
    119, 164, 208, 271
sex-differentiables, 19, 34, 38, 40, 41, 43, 51,
    52, 57, **68**, 72, 76, 206, 227, 292, 309
sexism, 3, 220–23, 323
singularia tantum, 46, 171, **175**
subgender, 2, 34, 42–3, 98–9, 133, 134, 157,
    161, **163**–8, 178, 180, 187, 188, 189, 193,
    313, 317
syncretism, 5, **120**, 122, 123, 133–4, 158,
    164–5, 167, 180, 188, 189, 190, 192,
    193–8, 208, 211, 212, 218

target gender, 45–7, 145, 150, **151**–60, 167,
    173, 179, 189–94, 202, 219, 261, 270,
    277, 283, 293–4, 297, 298
    see also dependent target gender; minor
    target gender; neutral agreement;
    overdifferentiated target
tense, 122, 125–6
titles, 226–7, 230, 235, 236, 237, 251, 257, 258
tone, 51, 52, 53, 74
transliteration, 6, 8, 35
'Trojan horses', **98**–9, 101, 103, 251, 257,
    314, 318

unification, 129
universals, 111, 131, 156, 198

word-order, 31, 99, 125, 322
world view, 18, 21, 24, 32, 303, 305, 318